INTELLIGENT VIDEO
ANALYTICS

INTELLIGENT VIDEO ANALYTICS

Surveillance, Safety, and Operational Efficiency

Dr. Adhiguna Mahendra
Dr. Sisdarmanto Adinandra
Dr. Hasbi Nur Prasetyo Wisudawan

MERCURY LEARNING AND INFORMATION
Boston, Massachusetts

MERCURY LEARNING AND INFORMATION
121 High Street, 3rd Floor
Boston, MA 02110
info@merclearning.com

A. Mahendra. *Intelligent Video Analytics: Surveillance, Safety, and Operational Efficiency.*
ISBN: 978-1-5015-2342-7

Library of Congress Control Number: 2025946592
242526321   This book is printed on acid-free paper in the United States of America.

To my beloved wife Anissa, whose unwavering support, patience, and strength
have carried me through every challenge.

And to my three sons — **Farrel**, **Rafale**, and **Xavier** —
Your curiosity, imagination, and boundless energy are the true
inspiration behind this work.

You remind me every day why we build intelligent systems: to make
the world a safer, smarter, and more compassionate place for the
future you will shape.

With all my love and gratitude.

— Adhiguna Mahendra

To the readers,

I hope this book enhances your knowledge of intelligent video analytics
and trigger new possibilities in the future

To my sons Arkan and Akhtar who always teach me something
new and to my other half Luluk, this book is for you

— *Dr. Sisdarmanto Adinandra*

To the love of my life, *Fenty Kusuma*, whose devotion and loyalty
are treasures beyond measure.

And to my precious children, *Shofiyyah, Aisyah, and Ukasyah*,
whose spirit, cheerfulness, and patience remind me of
life's truest blessings.

And to the readers of this book, may these pages not only deepen your
understanding of *intelligence video analytics* but also ignite new ideas,
innovations, and possibilities for the future.

This book is for you.

— *Dr. Hasbi Nur Prasetyo Wisudawan*

CONTENTS

*P*REFACE

Over the past two decades, the convergence of computer vision, artificial intelligence, and real-time surveillance infrastructure has transformed how societies monitor, protect, and optimize their environments. Yet despite the proliferation of academic research and vendor-driven technologies, there remains a significant gap between theory and deployable systems between understanding "what can be done" and engineering "what actually works."

This book was written to fill that gap.

Intelligent Video Analytics is not just another book on CCTV, network surveillance, or computer vision theory. It is the culmination of years of building real-world IVA systems, from those used in smart cities and critical infrastructure to those used in commercial buildings and national security installations. We, the authors, have designed, deployed, and managed IVA ecosystems that operate under real constraints: unpredictable lighting, budget limitations, complex user needs, cybersecurity risks, and regulatory compliance. This book is where we bring all that knowledge together, paired with our strong academic foundation and decades of research, to offer something no other IVA book does: field-tested blueprints that actually work.

At the core of this book lies the Sense–Understand–Action (SUA) framework. This foundational model recognizes that intelligent video systems must do more than "see." They must make sense of what they observe and respond appropriately.

Each chapter of the book reflects this structure:

- Sense: How to design cameras, sensors, networks, and edge devices that reliably capture data in real-world conditions.
- Understand: How to apply computer vision, deep learning, and analytics frameworks to extract meaning from video feeds accurately and at scale.
- Action: How to integrate video intelligence with decision logic, automation protocols, command centers, and standard operating procedures.

Through this structure, readers are guided not only on *what to build*, but *why, how*, and *in what sequence*, moving from theory to deployment, from design to impact.

This book presents original blueprints and operational workflows that have never been published before, reframing video analytics as a system-level design challenge rather than a mere feature checklist or coding tutorial. It introduces powerful models such as the Decision and

Action Workflow (DAW), which brings auditability, escalation logic, and human-in-the-loop design into modern surveillance systems. Most importantly, it teaches readers how to think like real-world practitioners, balancing critical trade-offs between computational resources, accuracy, cost, integration complexity, latency, and human factors to create systems that are intelligent as well as deployable and sustainable.

No other book combines theory, practice, architecture, and policy design into a single, actionable guide for those needing IVA to work, not just in lab demos, but in buildings, cities, ports, campuses, and factories.

The chapters are purposefully organized to reflect the Sense-Understand-Action structure:

- Chapter 1 introduces CCTV fundamentals (Sense).
- Chapter 2 covers Network Design (Sense).
- Chapters 3 to 5 explore Cameras, Image Processing, and Deep Learning (Sense and Understand).
- Chapter 6 delves into Video Management Systems and Content Analysis (Understand).
- Chapter 7 on Edge and Cloud Computing (Understand).
- Chapters 8 through 10—covering Security-Safety-Operational frameworks, End-to-End System Design, and Deployment embody the "Action" layer, while Chapter 11 looks toward the future of the field.

We also reframe foundational concepts such as camera placement, edge computing, anomaly detection, and regulatory compliance through a deployment-centric lens, grounded in actual projects, operational failures, and strategic wins.

Whether you are a surveillance system integrator, an AI or computer vision engineer, a security and safety officer, a smart city planner, a graduate student, or researcher, this book offers a comprehensive, grounded, and insightful guide to building and scaling intelligent video analytics systems that go beyond theory.

Dr. Adhiguna Mahendra
Dr. Sisdarmanto Adinandra
Dr. Hasbi Nur Prasetyo Wisudawan

CHAPTER 1

INTRODUCTION TO CCTV AND ITS DEVICES

CTV systems have come a long way from their analog roots, evolving into intelligent, connected digital platforms used in urban centers, industries, and homes. Today, they are indispensable for enhancing security, ensuring safety, and improving operational visibility.

This chapter introduces the core concepts, components, and applications of CCTV. It covers the evolution of surveillance technology, compares analog and IP systems, and explains different camera types such as fixed, dome, PTZ, and infrared cameras.

We also explore system elements like lenses, recorders, transmission setups, and monitoring devices. Critical operational aspects, including recording strategies, storage planning, data retention policies, compliance, and metadata indexing are highlighted to show how CCTV systems can be efficient and standards-compliant.

By the end of this chapter, readers will have a strong foundation to approach advanced topics like system design, analytics, deployment, and operations.

WHAT IS CCTV?

Closed Circuit Television (CCTV) is a surveillance technology used to monitor and record activities in environments such as public spaces, businesses, and residential areas. Unlike broadcast television, which transmits signals openly to the public, CCTV transmits video signals to a specific, limited set of monitors. This ensures that the footage is only accessible to authorized personnel, enhancing security and privacy.

Historical Background of CCTV

The concept of CCTV can be traced back to the 1940s. The first documented use of CCTV technology was in Germany in 1942, where it was used to monitor rocket launches. This early system, designed by engineer Walter Bruch, laid the foundation for future developments in surveillance technology.

In the 1960s, CCTV began to be used in commercial and public sectors. Banks, retail stores, and government buildings started to implement CCTV systems to enhance security. The technology continued to evolve, and by the 1970s, it was being used for traffic monitoring and crime prevention.

The 1980s saw significant advancements in CCTV technology, including the introduction of time-lapse recording and multiplexing. These innovations allowed for more efficient use of tape storage and the ability to monitor multiple camera feeds simultaneously. The 1990s brought about the transition from analog to digital systems, leading to improved image quality and storage capabilities.

Modern CCTV Systems

Modern CCTV systems are highly sophisticated, incorporating advanced technologies such as high-definition (HD) cameras, network connectivity, and video analytics. These systems are designed to provide comprehensive surveillance solutions for a wide range of applications.

Digital vs. Analog CCTV Systems

Analog CCTV systems use traditional analog cameras and recorders. The video signals are transmitted over coaxial cables to a digital video recorder (DVR), which digitizes the footage for storage and playback. While analog systems are cost effective and straightforward to install, they have limitations in terms of image quality and scalability.

Digital CCTV systems, also known as IP (Internet Protocol) systems, use digital cameras that capture and transmit video over a network. These systems offer superior image quality, higher resolution, and greater flexibility in terms of installation and expansion. Network video recorders (NVRs) are used to manage and store the digital footage, providing features such as remote access and advanced video analytics.

Applications of CCTV

CCTV systems are used in a variety of applications, each with its specific requirements and objectives. Here are some of the most common uses of CCTV:

1. **Public Safety**

   CCTV is widely used by law enforcement agencies and local governments to monitor public spaces and enhance safety. Cameras are installed in areas such as city centers, parks, and transportation hubs to deter criminal activity and provide evidence for investigations. The presence of CCTV cameras can help reduce crime rates and improve public confidence in safety measures.

FIGURE 1.1 CCTV for public monitoring.

2. **Traffic Management**

CCTV plays a crucial role in traffic management, helping to monitor and control the flow of vehicles on roads and highways. Traffic cameras are used to observe traffic conditions, detect incidents, and enforce traffic laws. By analyzing the footage, traffic authorities can make informed decisions to alleviate congestion and improve road safety.

FIGURE 1.2 CCTV for traffic monitoring.

3. **Retail Security**

Retail businesses use CCTV to prevent theft, monitor employee behavior, and enhance customer safety. Cameras are strategically placed to cover areas such as entrances, cash registers, and high-value merchandise displays. The footage can be reviewed to identify shoplifting incidents, fraudulent activities, and compliance with store policies.

FIGURE 1.3 CCTV for store monitoring.

4.   **Industrial Surveillance**

In industrial settings, CCTV is used to monitor production processes, ensure worker safety, and protect assets. Cameras are installed in areas such as manufacturing floors, warehouses, and loading docks to provide real-time monitoring and recording. This helps in identifying operational issues, preventing accidents, and safeguarding valuable equipment.

FIGURE 1.4 CCTV for manufacturing floor monitoring.

5.   **Residential Security**

Homeowners use CCTV systems to enhance the security of their properties. Residential CCTV systems typically include cameras installed at entry points, driveways, and other vulnerable areas. These systems provide peace of mind by allowing homeowners to monitor their property remotely and receive alerts for any suspicious activity.

FIGURE 1.5 CCTV for residential monitoring.

Components of a CCTV System

A standard CCTV system comprises several key components, each playing a vital role in capturing, transmitting, and storing video footage. The main components include the following:

1. Cameras

Cameras are the primary devices used to capture video footage. They come in various types, including analog, digital, dome, bullet, PTZ, and infrared cameras, each suited for different surveillance needs.

Infrared CCTV

Dome CCTV

PTZ CCTV

Analog CCTV

Bullet CCTV

FIGURE 1.6 Various types of CCTV.

2. Monitors

Monitors display the video footage captured by the cameras. They can be standard LCD or LED monitors, touchscreen monitors, or video walls for large-scale monitoring.

FIGURE 1.7 Wall display showing video footage.

3. Recording Devices

Recording devices store the video footage for future playback and analysis. This includes DVRs for analog systems and NVRs for digital systems. Cloud-based storage solutions are also becoming increasingly popular.

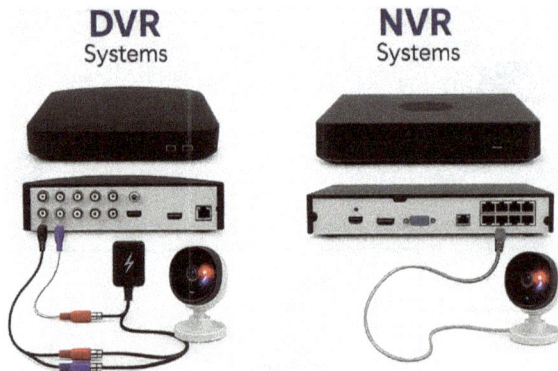

FIGURE 1.8 NVR and DVR system.

4. Transmission Systems

Transmission systems include the cables and network equipment used to transmit video signals from the cameras to the recording devices and monitors. This can involve coaxial cables for analog systems and Ethernet cables for digital systems, as well as wireless transmission technologies.

5. Power Supply Units (PSUs)

PSUs provide the necessary power to the cameras and other components. Power over Ethernet (PoE) is a common solution that allows both power and data to be transmitted over a single Ethernet cable.

FIGURE 1.9 Power supply unit.

Advantages of CCTV Systems

CCTV systems offer numerous benefits, making them an essential tool for security and surveillance:

1. Deterrence of crime: The presence of cameras can deter potential criminals from engaging in illegal activities.
2. Evidence collection: Recorded footage provides valuable evidence for investigations and legal proceedings.
3. Remote monitoring: Modern CCTV systems allow for remote access, enabling users to monitor their property from anywhere with an internet connection.
4. Real-time surveillance: CCTV systems provide real-time monitoring, allowing for immediate response to incidents.
5. Operational efficiency: In industrial and commercial settings, CCTV helps in monitoring processes, ensuring compliance, and improving operational efficiency.

Types of CCTV Cameras

CCTV cameras come in various types, each designed to serve specific surveillance needs. The selection of the appropriate camera type depends on factors such as the surveillance environment, required image quality, and specific security objectives. Below are the primary types of CCTV cameras.

Analog Cameras

Analog cameras are the traditional type of CCTV cameras that have been in use for several decades. They transmit video signals in analog format to a Digital Video Recorder (DVR), where the footage is digitized and stored. Analog cameras are generally less expensive than their digital counterparts and are straightforward to install. However, they offer lower resolution and limited scalability compared to digital cameras.

There are several advantages of analog cameras. They are cost effective, widely available, compatible with existing coaxial cable infrastructure, and easy to install and maintain. However, they typically have lower image resolution and limited features, and are less scalable for large-scale applications.

Digital Cameras (IP Cameras)

Digital cameras, also known as IP (Internet Protocol) cameras, capture and transmit video in digital format over an IP network. These cameras provide higher resolution images and greater flexibility in terms of installation and scalability. IP cameras can be easily integrated into existing network infrastructure and support advanced features such as video analytics and remote access.

Digital cameras have some advantages. They have high resolution images (up to 4K options), are scalable for scalable network integration, and can be easily used for video analytics. However, compared to analog cameras, IP cameras are expensive and require more complex infrastructures and higher bandwidth for operation.

Dome Cameras

Dome cameras are named after their dome-shaped housing, which makes them discreet and less intrusive. They are typically used for indoor surveillance in locations such as offices, retail stores, and hotels. Dome cameras can be equipped with either fixed or varifocal lenses and are available in both analog and digital versions. These cameras can blend in with the interior decor and are vandal-resistant (useful for high-risk areas). However, they offer limited view adjustments due to their structural properties and require regular cleaning.

Bullet Cameras

Bullet cameras have a distinct cylindrical shape and are often used for outdoor surveillance. They are designed to capture images over long distances and are typically installed in fixed positions. Bullet cameras are known for their durability and are often equipped with weatherproof and vandal-resistant housings. They are durable and can be used outdoors, have long-range visibility, and are easy to install. However, they have limited view adjustments.

PTZ Cameras

Pan-Tilt-Zoom (PTZ) cameras offer the ability to remotely control the camera's viewing angle and zoom level. These cameras are ideal for monitoring large areas, such as parking lots or stadiums, where operators need to focus on specific events or activities. PTZ cameras can be programmed to follow pre-set patterns or respond to specific triggers such as motion detection.

While PTZ cameras are programmable for events-based surveillance, they are more expensive than fixed cameras and have a complex installation.

Infrared/Night Vision Cameras

Infrared cameras are equipped with infrared LEDs that enable them to capture images in low-light or no-light conditions. These cameras are essential for nighttime surveillance and are commonly used in outdoor environments. Infrared cameras can provide clear images even in complete darkness, making them invaluable for 24/7 security monitoring. Night vision cameras can be used in low light situations but have a limited range.

Wireless Cameras

Wireless cameras transmit video and audio signals over a wireless network, eliminating the need for extensive cabling. These cameras are ideal for flexible installations where running cables is impractical. Wireless cameras can be either battery-powered or connected to a power source. Wireless cameras are easy to install and have flexible surveillance setups (non-permanent setups), although they have a high dependency on their battery life.

Hidden/Covert Cameras

Hidden or covert cameras are designed to be discreet and blend into their surroundings. These cameras are used for surveillance without alerting the subjects being monitored. They can be disguised as everyday objects such as smoke detectors, clocks, or electrical outlets. These cameras are optimal of cover surveillance or situation where cameras must be hide. However, compared to other types covert cameras have limited functionalities and may violate privacy.

FIGURE 1.10 Hidden camera disguised as a digital clock.

CCTV LENSES

The lens is a critical component of a CCTV camera, as it determines the quality and clarity of the captured image. Different types of lenses are used to achieve various surveillance objectives. The primary types of CCTV lenses include fixed lenses, varifocal lenses, zoom lenses, and pinhole lenses. Below are the typical lenses types used in CCTV.

Fixed Lenses

Fixed lenses have a set focal length, meaning they cannot be adjusted to change the field of view or magnification. They are commonly used in applications where the surveillance area is well-defined and does not require frequent adjustments. Fixed lenses are generally more affordable and simpler to install than other types of lenses. Fixed lenses are cheap and easy to find, and suitable for almost all applications. However, their fixed focal length limits their flexibility, thus requiring many cameras to cover a certain amount of area. Fixed lenses are typically used in environments such as small retail stores, offices, and residential properties, where the surveillance area is relatively static and does not require zoom or field of view adjustments.

FIGURE 1.11 A fixed lens.

Varifocal Lenses

Varifocal lenses offer adjustable focal lengths, allowing operators to manually change the field of view and zoom level. This flexibility makes varifocal lenses ideal for situations where the surveillance requirements may change over time. Varifocal lenses provide a range of focal lengths, typically indicated in millimeters, e.g., 2.8-12 mm. Because of their adjustability, varifocal lenses are can cover a large area and be used in environments that need zoom in-out functionality.

Varifocal lenses are commonly used in commercial settings, parking lots, and large indoor spaces where the ability to adjust the field of view and zoom is necessary to capture detailed images of specific areas or objects.

FIGURE 1.12 A varifocal lens.

Zoom Lenses

Zoom lenses allow for continuous adjustment of the focal length, enabling the seamless transition between wide-angle and close-up views. These lenses are often used in PTZ (Pan-Tilt-Zoom) cameras, where remote control over the zoom function is required. Zoom lenses are more complex and expensive than fixed or varifocal lenses but offer superior versatility. Zoom lenses are ideal for monitoring large areas with varying distances and in high security environments such as airports, stadiums, and critical infrastructure, where operators need the ability to zoom in on specific events or activities from a distance.

FIGURE 1.13 A zoom lens.

Pinhole Lenses

Pinhole lenses (Figure 1.14) are extremely small lenses designed for covert surveillance. They can be concealed within objects or installed in small spaces to capture discreet video footage. Pinhole lenses are used in situations where it is essential to monitor activities without being detected. Pinhole lenses are ideal for covert surveillance by law enforcement, or in sensitive corporate environments where discreet monitoring is necessary.

FIGURE 1.14 Pinhole lenses.

Fisheye Lenses

Fisheye lenses provide an ultra-wide-angle view, capturing a 180-degree or even 360-degree field of view. These lenses are used for panoramic surveillance, allowing a single camera to cover a large area without blind spots. Fisheye lenses (Figure 1.15) are used in large indoor areas, such as warehouses, shopping malls, and open office spaces, where comprehensive coverage with minimal blind spots is required.

FIGURE 1.15 A fisheye lens.

CCTV RECORDING DEVICES

Recording devices are essential components of CCTV systems, and they are responsible for storing the video footage captured by the cameras. There are several types of recording devices, each with its advantages and limitations.

Digital Video Recorders (DVRs)

DVRs are used with analog cameras to convert analog video signals into digital format and store them on hard drives. DVRs typically come with multiple input channels, allowing them to record from several cameras simultaneously. They offer features such as motion detection, scheduled recording, and remote access. DVRs are cost effective solution for analog cameras although their functionality cannot be easily expanded to other camera system.

DVRs are commonly used in small to medium-sized installations, such as retail stores, offices, and residential properties, where the existing infrastructure supports analog cameras.

FIGURE 1.16 A DVR unit.

Network Video Recorders (NVRs)

NVRs are designed for use with IP cameras and record video directly from the network. They offer higher scalability and flexibility compared to DVRs, as they can easily integrate with other networked devices. NVRs support higher resolution recordings and provide advanced features like real-time video analytics and cloud storage. NVRs work well with IP cameras, although the bandwidth must be high enough to accommodate the data transmissions.

NVRs are ideal for large installations, such as corporate campuses, industrial facilities, and smart cities, where high resolution, scalable, and flexible surveillance solutions are required.

FIGURE 1.17 An NVR unit.

Hybrid Video Recorders (HVRs)

HVRs are versatile recording devices that support both analog and IP cameras. They are ideal for transitioning from an existing analog system to a digital one, allowing for gradual upgrades. HVRs combine the functionalities of DVRs and NVRs, providing a unified platform for managing different types of cameras. HVRs can be used for analog and digital cameras, but require careful configuration for optimized performance. HVRs are suitable for organizations looking to upgrade their existing analog systems gradually while incorporating new IP cameras, providing a cost effective and flexible solution.

FIGURE 1.18 An HVR unit.

Cloud-Based Storage

Cloud-based storage solutions are becoming increasingly popular for CCTV systems, offering off-site storage and easy scalability. Video footage is transmitted over the Internet and stored in remote data centers. Cloud storage provides enhanced data security and allows for remote access and management of video recordings from anywhere with an internet connection. Cloud storage is easily expanded and remotely operated. Operational cost and security are two issues that need to be handled well. Cloud-based storage is ideal for large-scale and distributed surveillance systems, such as smart cities, multinational corporations, and remote monitoring applications, where scalability and remote access are critical.

Edge Storage

Edge storage involves storing video footage directly on the camera or on local storage devices close to the camera. This approach reduces the reliance on centralized recording devices and network bandwidth, providing a decentralized storage solution. Edge storage is useful for redundancy but the devices are limited in size and there is the risk of data loss when devices are broken. Edge storage is suitable for environments with a limited network infrastructure or where decentralized storage is preferred for security and redundancy, such as remote sites, transportation systems, and critical infrastructure.

FIGURE 1.19 An edge storage unit.

CCTV Recording Principles

An effective CCTV system is not only defined by its cameras, but also by how it records and retains footage. Choosing the right recording method depends on operational needs, resource availability, and risk profiles. This section explains the main recording principles used in modern CCTV deployments.

Continuous vs. Scheduled Recording

Continuous recording captures video 24/7 and is often used in high security areas such as casinos, critical infrastructure, and control rooms. Its primary advantage is the comprehensive archive it creates, leaving no event undocumented. However, it demands significant storage and bandwidth.

Scheduled recording is programmed based on time intervals (e.g., office hours and non-peak hours) and is useful when surveillance is only needed during specific periods. This method saves storage and power but risks missing unexpected events outside scheduled windows.

Event-Triggered Recording

Instead of recording constantly, many systems rely on triggers to start recording:

- Motion detection initiates recording when movement is detected in the camera's field of view.
- Analytics-driven: Advanced video analytics detect specific patterns like loitering, line-crossing, or crowd density, initiating recording when these rules are triggered.
- External sensor triggers: Systems integrated with sensors (e.g., door contacts and PIR detectors) begin recording when triggered by external events.

Event-based recording optimizes storage and simplifies video review but must be configured precisely to minimize false positives or missed detections.

Frame Rate Considerations

The frame rate (measured in frames per second, fps) determines how smoothly motion is captured. Common standards include

- 5–10 fps: sufficient for static areas or where motion is infrequent (e.g., storage rooms)
- 15–20 fps: standard for general surveillance such as retail stores and offices
- 25–30 fps: required for high-motion environments like intersections or casino tables

Lowering frame rates conserves storage, but extremely low rates may miss fast movements or result in choppy footage.

Resolution Selection Guidelines

Resolution directly affects image clarity and storage needs:

- Low resolution (D1, 720p): suitable for general monitoring with limited detail
- Medium resolution (1080p): common for indoor and outdoor environments where facial or license plate recognition is desired
- High resolution (4K and above): useful in wide-area surveillance or forensic-quality needs, but increases storage and processing requirements

The successful use of cameras requires a balance of clarity and storage efficiency, and so organizations often use high resolution for entrances and transaction points, and lower resolution for general coverage.

Storage Medium Selection

CCTV footage can be stored on different media:

- Local storage (NVRs/DVRs, edge SD cards): offers fast access and control but has limited scalability
- Network Attached Storage (NAS): centralizes video data and supports larger capacities for medium-to-large installations
- Cloud storage: enables remote access, redundancy, and scalable retention. However, it is bandwidth-intensive and may raise regulatory concerns for sensitive environments.

Hybrid strategies (e.g., recording high-priority footage locally while backing up to cloud) offer flexibility and resilience.

Common Recording Strategies by Application

- Retail: often uses event-triggered recording to conserve storage while maintaining coverage of customer interactions and PoS activities
- Industrial facilities: use scheduled or continuous recording during operational hours; event-based recording for after-hours intrusion detection
- Public safety (e.g., city surveillance): typically employs continuous recording with high resolution streams in critical zones, sometimes supplemented by analytics for automated alerts

CCTV Storage Calculations and Strategies

Accurately calculating CCTV storage requirements is essential to ensure that recorded footage meets operational, regulatory, and forensic needs without incurring unnecessary costs. This section outlines how to estimate storage needs and design an effective storage strategy.

Storage Calculation Formula

The following formula provides a baseline for calculating required storage:

$$Storage\,Required\ (GB) = \frac{\text{Bit rate}(\text{Mbps}) \times 3600 \times 24 \times \text{ Retention Days}}{8 \times 1024}$$

$$Storage\ Required\ (GB) = \frac{\text{Bitrate in Mbps} \times \text{Seconds per Hour} \times \text{Hours per Day} \times \text{Retention Days}}{\text{Bits per Byte} \times \text{Megabytes per Gigabyte}}$$

where

- Bit rate (Mbps) is the per-camera video bit rate
- 3600 is the number of seconds per hour
- 24 is the number of hours per day
- 8 converts bits to bytes
- 1024 converts MB to GB

Example Calculation

Let's calculate the storage required for a single camera recording at 2 Mbps, 24 hours a day, for 30 days:

$$Storage\ Required\,(GB) = \frac{2 \times 3600 \times 24 \times 30}{8 \times 1024} = \frac{5,184,000}{8192} = 633.79\,GB \text{ (per Camera)}$$

For 20 cameras: 20 x 633.79 = 12,675 GB = 12.7 TB
Factors Influencing Storage Requirements

- Frame Rate: Higher frame rates (e.g., 25–30 fps) generate more data. Reducing fps can significantly reduce storage needs.
- Resolution: 4K footage requires much higher storage than 1080p or 720p. Matching resolution to use case is crucial.
- Compression Codecs: H.265 (HEVC) provides better compression than H.264, often saving 30–50% storage without sacrificing quality.
- Scene Complexity: Cameras facing dynamic environments (e.g., crowds and traffic) produce more data than those monitoring static areas.
- Recording Mode: Continuous recording consumes more storage than event-based or scheduled recording.

Typical Storage Strategies

- Short-term local storage: NVR/DVRs or NAS devices for storing recent footage (e.g., 7–30 days) on-site. Offers fast access and control, ideal for incident investigation.
- Long-term archival storage: offloading older footage to cost-efficient storage (e.g., LTO tape, cold cloud storage) for compliance or forensic evidence.
- Hybrid strategies: combining local storage for recent data and cloud storage for long-term or multi-site access. This balances responsiveness with redundancy and scalability.

DATA RETENTION POLICIES AND REGULATIONS

Data retention is a critical consideration in CCTV system design and operation. It directly affects storage sizing, compliance, and risk management. This section outlines typical retention requirements across industries, explores relevant global regulations, and discusses practical strategies to align retention policies with legal and operational needs.

Typical Retention Periods by Sector

- Retail: 15 to 30 days. Sufficient to resolve theft or customer service disputes.
- Transportation: 30 to 90 days. Critical for incident review, accident investigation, and compliance with transportation authority requirements.
- Public safety and law enforcement: 30 to 180 days. Depends on local laws and the nature of surveillance (e.g., high-crime areas or critical infrastructure).
- Residential and small offices: 7 to 14 days. Shorter retention is usually adequate and balances cost with usability.

Global Regulatory Examples

- GDPR (Europe) requires organizations to justify the length of video retention. Footage must not be kept longer than necessary for its original purpose. It also mandates secure storage, access control, and, in some cases, data subject rights to access or delete footage.
- U.S. guidelines vary by state, but generally emphasize consent, signage, and securing footage. For example, HIPAA mandates strict retention and access protocols for video in healthcare settings.
- The Asia-Pacific (e.g., Singapore and Australia) typically require clear signage, data access policies, and limited retention (e.g., Australia recommends 30-day retention unless justified otherwise).

Implications for Storage Strategy and Cost

Longer retention increases storage costs exponentially, especially for high resolution or high-frame-rate video. A 90-day retention policy might require three times the capacity of a 30-day system. This makes it essential to

- use efficient codecs (e.g., H.265)
- consider tiered storage solutions
- optimize resolution and frame rates based on criticality of the footage

Compliance Mechanisms: Automatic Deletion and Archiving

To meet retention requirements and manage storage efficiently, most CCTV systems implement automated

- deletion policies that automatically erase footage after the configured period (e.g., 30 days), unless marked as evidence
- archiving routines that transfer important footage to long-term storage (e.g., cloud, tape backup) for regulatory or legal preservation

These mechanisms ensure systems remain compliant while avoiding manual intervention and excessive storage expansion.

Metadata Indexing and Retrieval

Metadata plays a crucial role in enhancing the usability and intelligence of CCTV systems. Without metadata, operators are often left to manually review hours of footage to locate relevant incidents. Metadata adds structured context to video content, allowing systems to retrieve, analyze, and correlate footage far more efficiently.

Importance of Metadata in CCTV

Metadata typically includes

- timestamps: time and date of each frame or event
- camera IDs and locations: identifiers and spatial context (e.g., Entrance A and Lobby 2)
- event tags: labels such as "motion detected," "person entered," "vehicle parked," or "intrusion alert"
- object and behavior annotations: AI-detected entities like faces, license plates, object types, or crowd levels

This information enables fast navigation, filtering, and retrieval of relevant footage based on time, location, or event type.

Typical Metadata Structure and Usage

A well-designed metadata structure may follow a hierarchical or key-value format and can be stored in

- embedded video files (e.g., through ONVIF-compliant formats)
- separate databases indexed by video segment
- JSON/XML schemas used in AI-enhanced analytics pipelines

Usage examples include

- querying all video segments where a person entered through Gate 3 between 2:00–2:15 PM
- searching for frames where a red vehicle appeared within a specific zone
- filtering clips associated with detected anomalies, such as abandoned objects or unusual motion

Best Practices for Tagging and Indexing

- Standardized naming conventions: Use consistent formats for camera IDs, location tags, and event types.
- Automated metadata generation: Integrate AI-based video analytics to automate tagging and reduce human error.
- Synchronization: Ensure time stamp metadata aligns precisely with video frame timing, especially in multi-camera or federated systems.

- Retention policies: Metadata should follow the same data life cycle policies as video content, especially in legal or regulated environments.
- Audit trails: Maintain logs of metadata usage for forensic integrity and regulatory compliance.

Standard Retrieval Tools and Techniques

Most modern Video Management Systems (VMSs) support advanced metadata indexing and retrieval. Common tools and capabilities include

- timeline search: interactive scrub bars with visual indicators for motion or tagged events
- smart search/motion search: identify activity within user-defined regions
- faceted filters: enable search by time, event, camera, or object class (e.g., people, vehicles)
- metadata API access: for integration with third-party applications or command center dashboards
- AI/ML integration: natural language queries (e.g., "show all clips of a person wearing red near entrance after 6 PM") are increasingly supported by AI-powered VMS (discussed in Chapter 6)

By leveraging metadata effectively, CCTV operators can transform raw video into searchable, actionable intelligence. This not only improves response time but also enhances the value of stored footage for compliance, analytics, and investigations.

CCTV MONITORS

Monitors are the display devices used to view the video footage captured by CCTV cameras. They are a crucial part of the surveillance system, providing real-time monitoring and playback capabilities. Below are some common CCTV monitors.

CRT Monitors

Cathode Ray Tube (CRT) monitors were the standard display devices for early CCTV systems. They are bulky and consume more power but offer reliable performance. CRT monitors have largely been replaced by more advanced display technologies. CRT monitors are durable and long lasting; they are also cheap. However, they are heavy and have a low resolution. CRT monitors are rarely used in modern CCTV systems due to their size, weight, and lower image quality. However, they may still be found in legacy systems or environments where durability is a priority.

LCD Monitors

Liquid Crystal Display (LCD) monitors are the most commonly used display devices in modern CCTV systems. They are lightweight, energy-efficient, and provide high resolution images. LCD monitors come in various sizes and can be easily integrated into existing surveillance setups. LCD monitors have a high resolution image quality and are lightweight. However, they have limited angle viewing and are at risk for potential pixel damage over time. LCD monitors are suitable for a wide range of surveillance applications, including control rooms, retail stores, and office environments, where high resolution and energy-efficient displays are required.

FIGURE 1.20 An LCD screen.

LED Monitors

Light Emitting Diode (LED) monitors are a type of LCD monitor that uses LED backlighting. They offer better color accuracy, contrast, and energy efficiency compared to traditional LCD monitors. LED monitors are preferred for their superior image quality and longer lifespan. LED monitors are ideal for environments where image quality and energy efficiency are paramount, such as high security control rooms, retail surveillance, and professional monitoring centers.

Touchscreen Monitors

Touchscreen monitors provide an interactive interface for managing CCTV systems. They allow operators to control PTZ cameras, navigate through recorded footage, and configure system settings with ease. Touchscreen monitors enhance the usability of CCTV systems, making them more intuitive and user-friendly. With touch features, users can easily control and navigate through the system, making them ideal for complex surveillance systems.

Video Walls

Video walls consist of multiple monitors arranged together to form a large display surface. They are used in high security environments, such as command centers and control rooms, where comprehensive monitoring of multiple camera feeds is required. Video walls provide a seamless viewing experience and allow operators to monitor large areas simultaneously. Video walls are suitable for large-scale surveillance operations, such as citywide monitoring, critical infrastructure protection, and high security facilities, where extensive and detailed monitoring is essential.

SUMMARY

CCCTV has evolved significantly since its inception, transforming from simple analog systems to complex digital networks capable of advanced surveillance and data analysis. Understanding the fundamental components and types of CCTV systems is crucial for anyone looking to implement or enhance a security setup.

CCTV technology is not just about capturing video footage; it encompasses a range of devices and components that work together to provide comprehensive surveillance solutions. From the various types of cameras, each designed to meet specific surveillance needs, to the intricate lenses that determine image quality and clarity, every element plays a vital role in the effectiveness of a CCTV system. Recording devices, whether traditional DVRs or modern cloud-based solutions, ensure that captured footage is stored securely and can be accessed when needed. Monitors, from basic LCD screens to advanced video walls, enable real-time viewing and detailed analysis of surveillance feeds.

The knowledge gained from this chapter provides a solid foundation for understanding the core aspects of CCTV systems. This foundation is essential for exploring more advanced topics, such as network topologies, components, and security measures, which will be covered in the subsequent chapters.

CHAPTER 2

NETWORK DESIGN FOR SURVEILLANCE SYSTEMS

C hapter 1 provides a background on the history, types, and technologies used in CCTV from the analog era to current digital era. Modern CCTV systems depend heavily on robust and well-planned network infrastructure. A reliable network ensures seamless video streaming, real-time analytics, efficient storage, and minimal downtime. This chapter explores the elements of CCTV networking, including IP addressing, topology, cabling, switch and router configuration, and transmission technologies. We also introduce advanced network and storage considerations vital for scalable and regulation-compliant deployments.

CCTV NETWORK TOPOLOGIES

Network topology refers to the arrangement of different elements (such as links and nodes) in a computer network. The design and layout of CCTV networks significantly impact their efficiency, scalability, and reliability. The most common topologies used in CCTV networks are star, ring, bus, and mesh, each with its own advantages and disadvantages. Understanding these topologies is essential for designing a robust and effective CCTV system.

Star Topology

In a star topology, all cameras are connected to a central hub or switch. This setup is straightforward and easy to manage, as each camera has a direct path to the central hub. Star topology makes it simple to install and configure the system, robust to individual camera failure, and easy to maintain. However, the entire network depends on the central hub. If the hub fails, the whole network is affected. This topology is commonly used in small to medium-sized installations, such as offices, retail stores, and residential properties.

FIGURE 2.1 Star topology.

Ring Topology

In ring topology, each camera is connected to two other cameras, forming a circular data path. Data travels in one direction until it reaches its destination. In ring topology, each camera has equal access to the network, thus reducing the chance of data collisions.

The main drawback is that if one camera fails, it can disrupt the entire network unless a dual-ring or redundant ring is implemented. Ring topology is less common in modern CCTV networks but can still be found in some legacy systems. It is often used in environments where predictable data flow and equal access are prioritized.

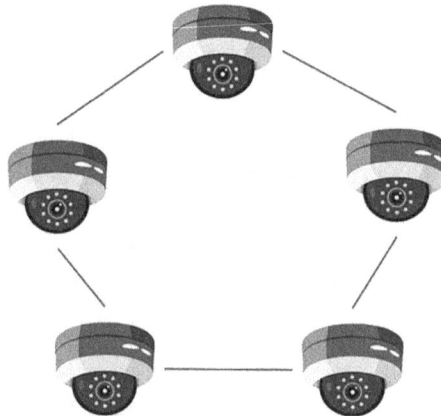

FIGURE 2.2 Ring topology.

Bus Topology

In bus topology, all cameras share a single communication line or backbone. This setup is simple and cost-effective for small networks. Bus topology requires less cabling compared to other topologies. A single backbone cables connects all cameras, making it easy to expand by adding new cameras to the backbone. However, bus topology is prone to collisions and can be difficult to troubleshoot. A failure in the backbone can disrupt the entire network. This topology is less favorable in modern CCTV systems due to its limitations but can be suitable for small, temporary setups or low-budget installations.

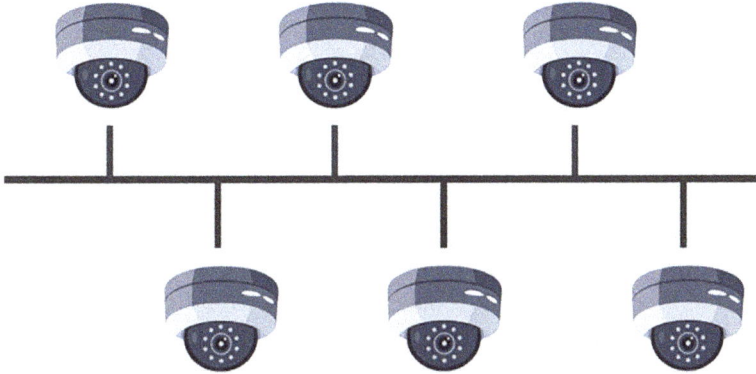

FIGURE 2.3 Bus topology.

Mesh Topology

In mesh topology, each camera is connected to every other camera, creating multiple paths for data to travel. This provides high redundancy and reliability. Mesh topology is well known for its redundancy and scalability. However, it is complex to install and expensive, due to the extensive cabling required. Mesh topology is ideal for critical surveillance environments where high availability and fault tolerance are essential, such as military bases, large industrial facilities, and high-security areas.

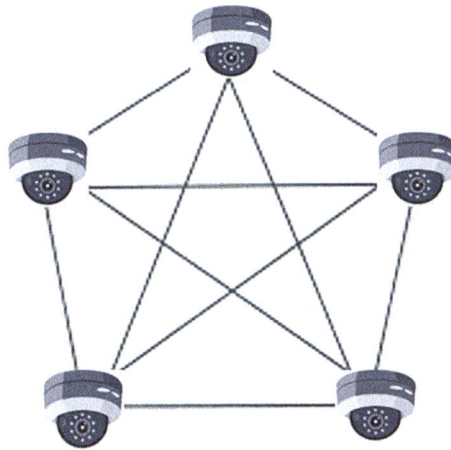

FIGURE 2.4 Mesh topology.

Hybrid Topology

Hybrid topology combines elements of two or more different topologies to take advantage of the strengths of each while mitigating their weaknesses. For example, a hybrid topology might use a star configuration within a building but connect multiple buildings using a bus or ring topology. A hybrid topology can be tailored to specific needs and flexible scalability. However, it can be a challenge to ensure all of the devices are compatible and work seamlessly together.

Selecting the appropriate topology for a CCTV network depends on various factors, including the size of the installation, budget, required scalability, and specific surveillance objectives.

Here are some considerations:

- Size of the network: Smaller networks may benefit from the simplicity and cost-effectiveness of star or bus topologies, while larger networks might require the redundancy and scalability of mesh or hybrid topologies.
- Budget: Cost constraints can influence the choice of topology. Bus topology might be chosen for its cost-efficiency, whereas a more expensive mesh topology could be justified by its high reliability.
- Scalability requirements: Future expansion plans should be considered. Mesh and hybrid topologies offer better scalability compared to bus topology.
- Criticality of surveillance: For critical surveillance environments where downtime is unacceptable, mesh topology provides the highest level of redundancy and reliability.

Here are examples of the how considerations are used in practice:

1. Star topology in a retail store:

   A small retail store might use a star topology, with each camera connected to a central DVR or NVR located in the manager's office. This setup is cost effective and provides easy access to recorded footage.

2. Ring topology in a parking garage:

   A multi-level parking garage might employ a ring topology to ensure continuous monitoring of all levels. Each camera connects to two others, forming a ring that provides redundancy and equal access.

3. Bus topology in a temporary event:

   For a temporary event, such as a music festival, a bus topology can be used to connect multiple cameras along the perimeter. This setup is quick to install and cost effective for short-term use.

4. Mesh topology in a high-security facility:

   A high-security facility, such as a data center, might use a mesh topology to ensure maximum reliability. Each camera connects to multiple other cameras, providing multiple paths for data transmission and minimizing the risk of downtime.

5. Hybrid topology in a corporate campus:

   A corporate campus with multiple buildings can use a hybrid topology, combining star topology within each building and a bus or ring topology to connect the buildings. This approach optimizes performance and scalability across the entire campus.

CCTV NETWORK COMPONENTS

A CCTV network consists of various components that work together to capture, transmit, and store video footage. Understanding these components is crucial for designing and maintaining an effective CCTV system. The primary components of a CCTV network include cameras, recording devices, transmission systems, monitors, and power supply units, as well as video management systems. Cameras, recording devices, and monitors are explained in detail in Chapter 1. Next, we discuss transmission systems and power supply units.

Transmission Systems

Transmission systems include the cables and network equipment used to transmit video signals from the cameras to the recording devices and monitors. Popular transmission systems are

1. Coaxial cables: Commonly used in analog CCTV systems, coaxial cables transmit video signals from cameras to DVRs. They are durable and provide reliable signal transmission over short to medium distances.

FIGURE 2.5 Coaxial cable.

2. Ethernet cables: Used in IP-based CCTV systems, Ethernet cables transmit digital video signals over a network. They support higher data transfer rates and longer transmission distances.

FIGURE 2.6 Ethernet cable.

3. Fiber optic cables: Provide high-speed data transmission over long distances with minimal signal loss. They are ideal for large-scale installations and environments with high electromagnetic interference.

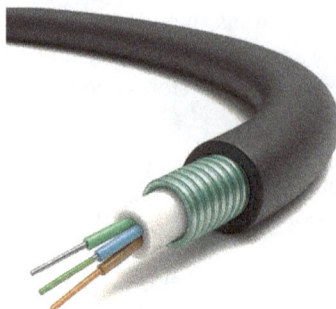

FIGURE 2.7 Fiber optic cable.

4. Wireless transmission: Uses radio frequency (RF) signals to transmit video data. Wireless systems offer flexibility and ease of installation but may be subject to interference and signal degradation over long distances.

5. Power over Ethernet (PoE): A technology that allows both power and data to be transmitted over a single Ethernet cable. PoE simplifies installation and reduces the need for separate power supplies for each camera.

FIGURE 2.8 Power over Ethernet.

Switches and Routers

Switches and routers are essential for managing data traffic within the CCTV network:

1. Switches: Connect cameras and other network devices, allowing data to be transmitted between them. Managed switches offer advanced features like VLANs, QoS, and port mirroring, enhancing network performance, and security.

FIGURE 2.9 Switch.

2. Routers: Manage data flow between different network segments and provide access to external networks, such as the Internet. Routers ensure efficient data routing and can incorporate firewall and VPN functionalities for enhanced security.

FIGURE 2.10 Router.

Power Supply Units (PSUs)

CCTV cameras and other network components require a stable power supply. PSUs provide the necessary power to these devices. Typical PSU types used in CCTV network are as follows:

1. Standard power supplies provide power to individual cameras and devices. Each camera requires a separate power connection, which can be cumbersome in large installations.

2. Power over Ethernet (PoE) technology allows power to be delivered over the same Ethernet cable used for data transmission. PoE simplifies installation, reduces cabling requirements, and ensures a stable power supply to cameras and other network devices.

Video Management Software (VMS)

VMS is essential for managing and analyzing video footage captured by CCTV cameras. It provides a user-friendly interface for monitoring, recording, and retrieving video data. VMS must be able to do the following:

1. Live monitoring allows for the real-time viewing of camera feeds, enabling operators to respond quickly to incidents.

2. Recording and playback facilitate the recording of video footage for future playback and analysis. VMS can store video on local or cloud-based storage solutions.

3. Video analytics incorporate advanced algorithms to analyze video footage for specific events, such as motion detection, facial recognition, and object tracking.

4. Remote access enables users to access video feeds and manage the CCTV system from remote locations using Web-based interfaces or mobile applications.

Genetec, Milestone, and Avigilon are three prominent companies selling VMS on the market, each offering a robust set of features designed to cater to various security and surveillance needs.

Genetec Security Center provides a unified platform that integrates live monitoring, recording, and playback with sophisticated video analytics capabilities. It supports a wide range of cameras and allows for scalable deployments, making it ideal for large-scale operations. Genetec also emphasizes cybersecurity and privacy protection, offering encryption and other security features to safeguard video data. Additionally, its VMS's remote access capabilities allow operators to monitor and manage their video feeds from virtually anywhere, providing flexibility and enhanced situational awareness.

FIGURE 2.11 Typical VMS (Video Management System).

Milestone XProtect and Avigilon Control Center (ACC) are also highly regarded products. Milestone XProtect is known for its modular approach, allowing users to customize their VMS setup according to specific requirements. It offers comprehensive features such as multi-server support, alarm management, and video analytics, which include motion detection and object classification. XProtect's intuitive interface and extensive third-party integrations provide users with a versatile solution that can scale from small installations to complex, multi-site environments.

FIGURE 2.12 VMS with object classification.

Avigilon ACC stands out for its advanced video analytics capabilities, which use artificial intelligence to provide real-time event detection, facial recognition, and license plate recognition. Avigilon's system is designed to be user-friendly, with features like remote access and centralized management that simplify system operation and maintenance.

FIGURE 2.13 VMS with license plate recognition.

Both Milestone and Avigilon offer extensive support for live monitoring, recording, playback, and remote access, allowing for their use in various security applications, from commercial buildings to critical infrastructure.

Auxiliary Components

Auxiliary components can add more functionalities and performance to CCTV systems. Some of important additional components are as follows:

1. Encoders and decoders convert analog video signals to digital format and vice versa, enabling integration of analog cameras into digital systems.
2. Network Interface Cards (NICs) allow devices to connect to the network, facilitating data transmission between cameras, recording devices, and monitors.
3. UPSs (Uninterruptible Power Supplies) provide backup power to ensure continuous operation of CCTV systems during power outages, protecting against data loss and system downtime.
4. Environmental enclosures protect cameras and other components from harsh environmental conditions, such as extreme temperatures, moisture, and dust. Enclosures are essential for outdoor and industrial installations.

Integration and Compatibility

Ensuring the compatibility of various components is crucial for the seamless operation of a CCTV network. Here are some considerations:

1. Protocol compatibility: Ensure that cameras, recording devices, and other network components support common protocols such as ONVIF (Open Network Video Interface Forum) for interoperability.

2. Network bandwidth: Consider the network's bandwidth capacity to handle the data load from multiple high-resolution cameras. Use managed switches and quality of service (QoS) settings to prioritize video traffic.

3. Storage requirements: Calculate the required storage capacity based on the number of cameras, resolution, frame rate, and retention period. Choose appropriate storage solutions, such as NVRs, NAS (Network Attached Storage), or cloud storage.

4. Scalability: Design the network with future expansion in mind. Choose components that can easily be upgraded or expanded to accommodate additional cameras and increased data traffic.

CCTV NETWORK SECURITY

Ensuring the security of CCTV networks is paramount to protect sensitive video footage and prevent unauthorized access. Several measures can be implemented to enhance network security, ranging from physical security practices to advanced cybersecurity protocols. This section covers important aspects of CCTV network security, including network segmentation, encryption, access control, firewalls, intrusion detection and prevention systems (IDPS), regular software updates, and physical security.

Network Segmentation

Network segmentation involves dividing the CCTV network into smaller segments or subnets. This limits the spread of malware and enhances security by isolating critical devices. Each segment can have its own security policies and access controls, making it more difficult for attackers to gain access to the entire network. Here are typical network segmentation techniques:

1. VLANs (Virtual Local Area Networks) can be used to segment the network logically, grouping devices based on function, location, or security level. This helps contain potential security breaches within a specific segment.

2. Subnets: Creating subnets for different parts of the CCTV network ensures that traffic is isolated and managed separately, enhancing security and performance.

3. Segmentation benefits include improved security, reduced network congestion, enhanced performance, and easier management of network resources.

Encryption

Encryption protects data transmitted over the network by converting it into a secure code that can only be deciphered with a key. Implementing encryption protocols ensures that video footage and other data remain confidential and secure. Popular encryption techniques are as follows:

1. Data encryption: Encrypting video streams and control data prevents unauthorized access and eavesdropping. Common encryption standards include AES (Advanced Encryption Standard) and SSL/TLS (Secure Sockets Layer/Transport Layer Security).

2. Encryption in transit: Ensuring that data is encrypted while being transmitted over the network helps protect against interception and tampering.

3. Encryption at rest: Encrypting stored data on DVRs, NVRs, and cloud storage solutions protects against data breaches and unauthorized access to recorded footage.

Access Control

Access control mechanisms restrict who can access the CCTV network and its components. This includes user authentication, authorization, and accounting (AAA) protocols. Implementing strong access control measures helps prevent unauthorized access and ensures that only authorized personnel can manage and view the CCTV system. Practical access control techniques are as follows:

1. User authentication involves verifying the identity of users before granting access to the network. This can include usernames, passwords, biometrics, or multi-factor authentication (MFA).

2. Authorization involves defining user roles and permissions to control what actions users can perform within the network. Role-based access control (RBAC) is commonly used to assign permissions based on job responsibilities.

3. Accounting involves keeping logs of user activities to monitor and audit access to the network. This helps detect and investigate unauthorized or suspicious activities.

Firewalls

Firewalls act as a barrier between the CCTV network and external networks. They monitor and control incoming and outgoing traffic based on predefined security rules. Firewalls help protect the network from external threats and unauthorized access. Typical firewall implementation in networks are as follows:

1. Network firewalls: Deployed at the network perimeter to filter traffic entering and leaving the network. They can block malicious traffic and prevent unauthorized access.

2. Application firewalls: Provide an additional layer of security by inspecting and filtering traffic at the application level. They can protect against specific application-layer attacks.

3. Firewall policies: Configuring firewall rules and policies to allow legitimate traffic while blocking potentially harmful traffic. Regularly updating and reviewing firewall rules is essential to maintain security.

Firewalls can be implemented as either hardware or software solutions, each offering different advantages and catering to various needs.

Hardware firewalls are physical devices placed between the network and the gateway, designed to filter traffic entering and leaving a network. These devices provide robust security and are ideal for protecting larger networks, such as those in enterprise environments.

Hardware firewalls often offer features such as deep packet inspection, intrusion detection and prevention systems (IDS/IPS), and Virtual Private Network (VPN) support.

They are typically easier to manage in terms of performance because they offload the security processing from the host system.

Sample products in this category include Cisco ASA series, which provides high-performance security appliances with advanced threat defense capabilities, and Fortinet FortiGate devices (Figure 2.15), known for their integrated security features and high throughput.

FIGURE 2.14 Generic firewall hardware.

Software firewalls are installed on individual computers or servers and provide security for that specific device.

FIGURE 2.15 Typical firewall software.

These firewalls are ideal for smaller networks or individual users who need a flexible, customizable solution that can be easily updated or configured.

Software firewalls typically offer features such as application-level filtering, user authentication, and Web filtering. Popular software firewalls include Windows Defender Firewall, which is integrated into the Windows operating system and provides a basic level of protection against common threats, and ZoneAlarm, which offers advanced features like application control, identity protection, and intrusion prevention.

While software firewalls are often easier to install and configure, they can consume system resources, potentially impacting performance if not managed properly.

Intrusion Detection and Prevention Systems (IDPS)

IDPS monitor network traffic for suspicious activity and potential threats. They can detect and respond to intrusions in real-time, helping to prevent unauthorized access and mitigate security risks. Practical IDPS implementation involves the following:

1. Intrusion Detection Systems (IDSs) monitor network traffic for signs of suspicious activity or policy violations. They can alert administrators to potential threats but do not take direct action to block them.

2. Intrusion Prevention Systems (IPSs) are similar to IDSs, but with the capability to automatically block or mitigate detected threats. IPSs can actively prevent attacks by dropping malicious packets and blocking traffic from suspicious sources.

3. IDPS Implementations involve deploying IDPS at critical points within the network to monitor traffic and detect anomalies. Regularly updating IDPS signatures and rules to protect against new and evolving threats.

In the field of CCTV cybersecurity, integrating Intrusion Detection Systems (IDS) and Intrusion Prevention Systems (IPS) with Network Video Recorders (NVR) is crucial for protecting video surveillance networks. Three popular commercial IDS/IPS products that complement NVR systems include Cisco Firepower, Palo Alto Networks Next-Generation Firewall (NGFW), and Check Point IPS. Cisco Firepower delivers advanced threat detection and prevention capabilities, allowing for seamless integration with NVRs to monitor network traffic and identify potential risks.

FIGURE 2.16 Generic IPS hardware.

IDS/IPS hardware, such as Palo Alto's NGFW, provides a comprehensive approach to security, combining IDS/IPS features to detect and stop threats in real time, ensuring video data stored on NVRs remains secure (Figure 2.17).

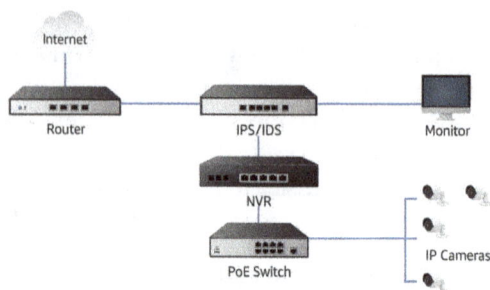

FIGURE 2.17 Secure CCTV Network Architecture with IPS/IDS Integration.

IPS software, such as Check Point, uses machine learning and threat intelligence to block known and unknown attacks (Figure 2.18), offering continuous protection and enhanced detection when used alongside NVR systems. These types of products offer robust solutions to safeguard CCTV networks by detecting, preventing, and mitigating cyber threats.

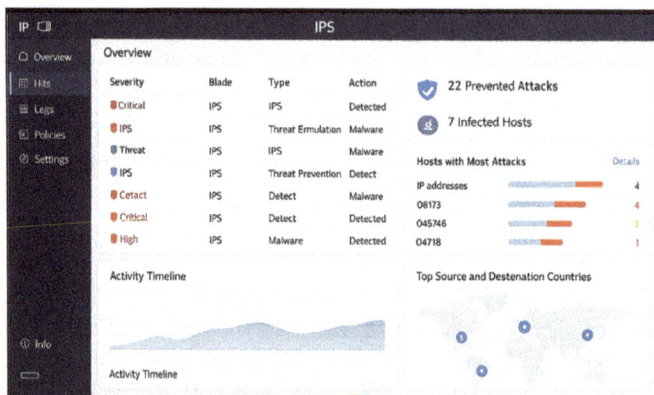

FIGURE 2.18 Typical IPS software.

Regular Software Updates and Patches

Keeping software and firmware up to date is essential for maintaining network security. Regular updates and patches fix vulnerabilities and enhance the overall security of the CCTV system. Updates must be done to the following:

1. Firmware: Update camera firmware, NVR/DVR software, and network device firmware to fix security vulnerabilities and improve performance.
2. Software patches: Apply patches to the operating system, VMS, and other software components to address security flaws and enhance functionality.

Physical Security

Physical security measures protect the hardware components of the CCTV network. This includes securing server rooms, locking network cabinets, and installing surveillance cameras to monitor sensitive areas. Practical physical security checks are as follows:

1. Server room security: Restrict access to server rooms and data centers to authorized personnel only. Implement physical barriers, access control systems, and surveillance cameras to monitor access (Figure 2.19).

FIGURE 2.19 Server room.

2. Equipment enclosures: Use lockable enclosures for network switches, routers, and recording devices to prevent tampering and unauthorized access.
3. Environmental controls: Protect equipment from environmental hazards such as temperature fluctuations, humidity, and dust. Implementing climate control systems and monitoring for environmental conditions.

Implementing a Comprehensive Security Strategy: Tips and Tricks

A comprehensive security strategy for a CCTV network involves a multi-layered approach that includes both physical and cybersecurity measures. Here are the steps to implement an effective security strategy:

1. Risk Assessment: Conduct a thorough risk assessment to identify potential threats and vulnerabilities. Understand the specific security needs of the CCTV network and prioritizing measures based on risk levels.
2. Security Policies: Develop and enforce security policies and procedures. Establish guidelines for user access, data handling, incident response, and regular security audits.
3. Training and Awareness: Educate staff and users on security best practices and the importance of adhering to security policies. Regular training and awareness programs help prevent security breaches due to human error.
4. Monitoring and Response: Continuously monitor the CCTV network for security incidents and respond promptly to any detected threats. Implement incident response plans to address security breaches and minimize their impact.
5. Regular Audits and Assessments: Conduct regular security audits and assessments to evaluate the effectiveness of security measures. Identify areas for improvement and make the necessary adjustments to enhance security.

Designing for Bandwidth Efficiency and Compression in CCTV Systems

As modern CCTV systems grow in scale and complexity, ensuring bandwidth efficiency and effective compression becomes essential for performance and cost optimization. This section provides a detailed look at how to estimate bandwidth requirements and implement compression strategies that reduce network congestion and storage overhead. Mastering these topics is critical for building high-performance, scalable surveillance networks that align with technical and financial constraints.

Bandwidth Calculation for CCTV Networks

In any IP-based CCTV system, network bandwidth is one of the most critical design parameters. An under-provisioned network can lead to video loss, delay in real-time viewing, or degradation in resolution and frame rates. Calculating bandwidth accurately ensures consistent video quality and reliable system performance.

Bandwidth Calculation Formula:

$$Total\,Bandwidth\,(MBps) = Bit\,Rate\,of\,Camera\,(Mbps) \times Number\,of\,Cameras$$

Factors to Consider

- The bit rate per camera depends on resolution, frame rate, compression codec, and scene complexity.
- Headroom: Always include an additional 20–30% headroom to account for peak usage and future scalability.
- Multicast vs. Unicast: For live viewing by multiple clients, multicast reduces total bandwidth usage.
- Sub-streaming: Many cameras support dual or triple streaming, allowing lower-bit-rate feeds for mobile access or live display.

Example: A system has 40 cameras, each streaming at 3 Mbps:

$$3\,Mbps \times 40 = 120\,Mbps\,(baseline)$$

Adding 25% headroom, we obtain

$$120 + (0.25 \times 120) = 150\,Mbps\,total\,bandwidth\,required$$

Use Case

A regional airport plans to deploy 48 cameras in terminals and parking lots. With 2.5 Mbps per stream and 25% headroom, network planners size each backbone segment to handle 150 Mbps, ensuring smooth video transmission even during peak hours and live viewing from the command center.

VIDEO COMPRESSION STANDARDS AND BITRATE OPTIMIZATION

Compression technology plays a central role in managing storage and bandwidth usage in surveillance systems. Raw video streams are enormous, and without compression, even a modest camera network would be unmanageable.

Common Standards

- H.264 (AVC): Widely supported; provides good quality at moderate compression.
- H.265 (HEVC): Reduces bit rate by up to 50% compared to H.264 for the same visual quality, ideal for 4K or storage-constrained deployments.
- MJPEG: High-quality frame-by-frame encoding, but very bandwidth- and storage-heavy; rarely used for continuous recording.

Bitrate Control Strategies

- Constant Bit Rate (CBR): Predictable, fixed bitrate regardless of scene activity. Easier to calculate storage but may waste bandwidth in static scenes.
- Variable Bit Rate (VBR): Adapts to scene complexity; a lower bit rate during inactivity, and a higher one when movement occurs. More efficient but variable load.
- Smart Codec (Dynamic Encoding): Found in many modern IP cameras; region-of-interest encoding, background suppression, and motion-adaptive bit rates.

Savings: A 1080p camera using H.264 at 15 fps might require 3 Mbps; with H.265, the same feed could require only 1.5–2 Mbps.

Example: A logistics warehouse with 60 full-HD cameras switches from H.264 to H.265 and activates smart encoding features. Bandwidth usage drops by 45%, allowing IT to defer a planned switch upgrade and reallocate savings toward analytics infrastructure.

CCTV NETWORK ARCHITECTURE AND BEST PRACTICES

To support scalable and resilient deployments, CCTV networks must go beyond basic connectivity and be intentionally architected with performance, redundancy, and manageability in mind. This section outlines important architectural patterns and best practices that underpin professional-grade video surveillance and analytics deployments.

Layered Network Design

A common best practice is to follow a hierarchical model with three tiers:

- Function: Cameras performing different roles—such as perimeter monitoring, indoor surveillance, or license plate recognition—often have distinct traffic profiles and access needs. Grouping by function allows specialized configurations such as higher priority for perimeter feeds and analytics triggers for LPR.
- Area: Physical zones such as parking lots, building lobbies, restricted offices, or executive floors can be isolated into VLANs for better traffic management and zone-specific monitoring policies. This is particularly useful for managing different privacy levels and alert rules.

- Resolution or Analytics Priority: Cameras streaming at higher resolutions (e.g., 4K) or supporting advanced analytics (e.g., face recognition and behavioral detection) should be grouped separately from standard surveillance feeds. This allows for dedicated bandwidth provisioning and performance tuning to accommodate high-throughput demands without impacting lower-priority feeds.

This model improves scalability, fault isolation, and ease of troubleshooting.

Redundancy and High Availability

To reduce single points of failure, CCTV networks must be built with redundancy at both the network and device level. This ensures the continuous operation in case of a hardware failure, maintenance, or unexpected downtime.

- Dual uplinks between switches with STP or LACP: Connecting switches using dual network paths improves resilience. The Spanning Tree Protocol (STP) helps prevent network loops by automatically blocking redundant paths until needed, while the Link Aggregation Control Protocol (LACP) combines multiple physical links into a single logical one for greater throughput and fault tolerance.

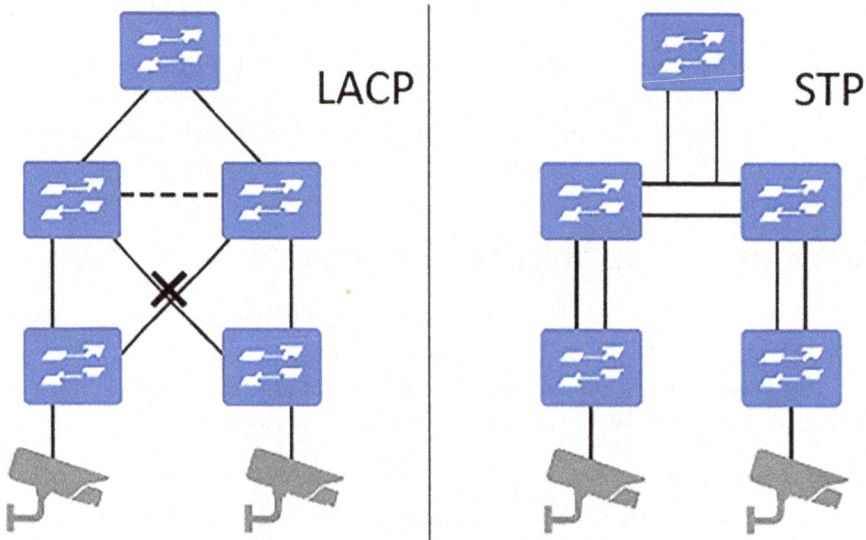

FIGURE 2.20 The LACP and STP topologies.

Figure 2.20 shows that in the STP topology (left side), the network includes multiple switches connected redundantly. One of the links is placed into a blocking state (represented by a dashed line with an "X") to prevent broadcast loops. This blocked link is not used during normal operation. If one of the active links fails, the blocked link becomes active to maintain connectivity. This ensures loop prevention but leads to underutilized capacity in stable conditions.

In contrast, the LACP topology (right side) connects the same devices but bundles multiple links into a single logical channel using the Link Aggregation Control Protocol. All the bundled links are simultaneously active, allowing aggregated bandwidth, load balancing, and immediate redundancy if one or more links fail. This setup maximizes both reliability and throughput under normal operation.

In both diagrams, blue boxes represent network switches, forming the backbone of the CCTV system. The gray icons represent CCTV cameras connected to the access switches. This visual contrast highlights how different redundancy strategies impact bandwidth usage, system performance, and fault tolerance in CCTV infrastructure.

- Deploy N+1 core switches and failover recording servers: The "N+1" model means having one additional device available to take over if any primary device fails. For instance, if a core switch fails, the backup takes over without disrupting service. Similarly, failover recording servers can automatically continue recording if the primary NVR or server goes offline.
- Connect servers with dual NICs and leverage port bonding or teaming: Using two Network Interface Cards (NICs) per server, bonded or teamed for load balancing and redundancy, ensures that server-to-network communication continues even if one link or port fails. Port teaming also boosts throughput by combining multiple links into a single aggregated pipeline.

These measures, when implemented together, create a fault-tolerant surveillance architecture that minimizes downtime, protects critical video data, and supports high-availability command center operations. Redundant paths ensure continuous operation during hardware failures or maintenance windows.

Traffic Prioritization and QoS

Implementing Quality of Service (QoS) is an important strategy to ensure that CCTV traffic receives the necessary priority over less critical network activities, especially in converged networks where surveillance and general IT traffic share the same infrastructure.

CCTV streams—especially high-resolution or real-time feeds—demand consistent, low-latency delivery. QoS mechanisms enable network administrators to assign higher priority to this type of traffic, ensuring that bandwidth is always available for surveillance even during periods of network congestion.

Key QoS practices include the following:

- Using DSCP (Differentiated Services Code Point) tags: These are embedded into IP packet headers to classify and prioritize video packets over other types of traffic such as email, file sharing, or Web browsing.
- Applying VLAN-based QoS policies: By grouping cameras into VLANs based on criticality or function, specific bandwidth guarantees and priority rules can be assigned per VLAN. This makes it easier to enforce differentiated service levels across departments, locations, or surveillance zones.
- Reserving uplink bandwidth: Critical camera groups—such as those monitoring entrances, cash-handling zones, or public intersections—should have dedicated uplink capacity from the access switches to the core to avoid contention and ensure uninterrupted recording.

Example: In a university campus network, QoS policies are configured to guarantee that surveillance video from dormitories and parking structures always receives transmission priority over student Wi-Fi or administrative traffic. This ensures compliance with security requirements while still supporting academic and administrative operations. Effective QoS design protects the integrity of video surveillance streams, minimizes frame drops, and supports real-time decision-making in command center operations.

Network Time Synchronization (NTP)

Network Time Protocol (NTP) is a networking standard designed to synchronize clocks of devices over packet-switched, variable-latency data networks. It enables computers, servers, IP cameras, switches, and other devices to maintain accurate time, which is crucial for applications where time-sensitive operations and forensic integrity are essential.

Accurate time synchronization across all networked CCTV components is critical for ensuring forensic reliability, coherent video playback, and the integrity of analytics-based event correlation. Even slight time discrepancies between cameras, recording servers, and network switches can lead to confusion during incident review and compromise evidentiary value.

- All devices should synchronize to a reliable NTP server: Configure cameras, switches, VMS servers, and storage devices to regularly query an authoritative Network Time Protocol (NTP) server. This maintains clock accuracy across the network. This maintains clock accuracy across the network.
- Avoid time drift between edge and core systems: Edge devices such as IP cameras must remain in lockstep with core systems to ensure consistent video frame timestamps, especially when recordings are aggregated or analyzed across locations.
- Ensure uniform timestamps in logs and footage: Aligning system clocks prevents misalignment of logs, alarms, and recorded footage. This is particularly vital when using video analytics engines, facial recognition systems, or integrating evidence with third-party sources (e.g., police dispatch logs).

Example: In a financial district's control center, investigators reviewing footage of a coordinated theft discover that one set of cameras was 90 seconds out of sync with others, causing confusion about the actual event timeline. After implementing NTP synchronization, all recordings now maintain reliable, consistent timestamps, drastically improving post-event reconstruction and real-time alert accuracy.

Multicast and Sub-streaming Optimization

Multicast and sub-streaming are powerful techniques that allow surveillance systems to scale efficiently while minimizing bandwidth and resource usage.

- Use multicast for real-time video distribution: In traditional unicast streaming, every viewing client creates a separate data stream from the camera or server, consuming additional bandwidth. Multicast allows a single video stream to be transmitted across the network and shared by multiple clients simultaneously. This is especially useful in command centers or large campuses where several operators may monitor the same feed. To use multicast effectively, switches must support IGMP snooping to manage group memberships and prevent unnecessary traffic flooding.

- Enable sub-streaming from cameras: Many modern IP cameras support dual or triple streaming, generating both high-resolution primary streams and lower-resolution substreams. The high-quality stream is used for recording and analytics, while the low-bit rate sub-stream can be sent to mobile apps, operator consoles, or Web interfaces to reduce processing and network load. This approach ensures responsiveness in live views while maintaining detailed archives for forensic review.

Example: In a citywide traffic monitoring center, sub-streams are used for 24/7 real-time viewing at operator stations, while the high-resolution main streams are archived centrally. Multicast is enabled for large video walls and backup control rooms, ensuring scalable, efficient live video distribution without overwhelming the core switches.

Use Case: Smart City Surveillance

A smart city command center integrates 400+ cameras across traffic, public spaces, and buildings. VLANs are used for each district. Core switches are deployed with full mesh uplinks to recording servers. All components sync to a citywide NTP system. Sub-streaming reduces network stress for real-time monitoring while maintaining 4K archives for investigations.

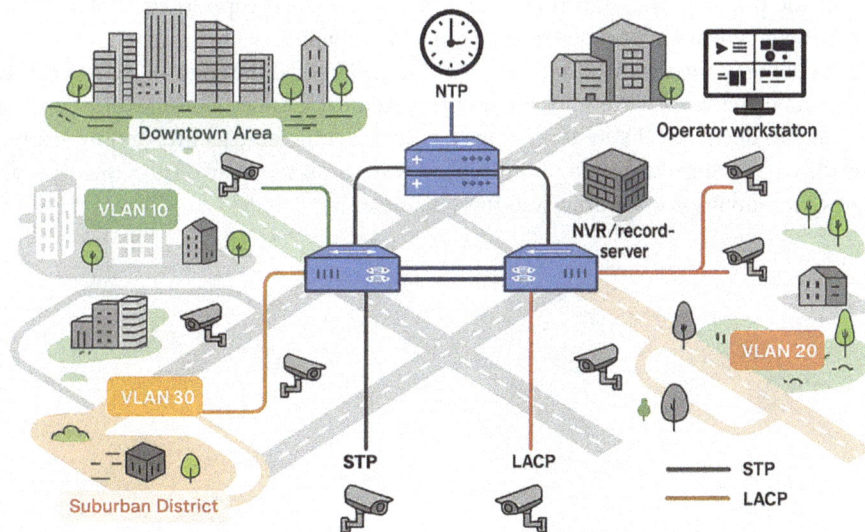

FIGURE 2.21 Smart city CCTV network topology.

These best practices ensure that the network foundation is robust enough to support future growth, intelligent analytics, and integrated command center workflows. Best practices form the foundation of scalable, efficient, and high-performing CCTV deployments. When bandwidth and compression are optimized, organizations not only ensure quality video but also reduce costs and improve overall system robustness. When bandwidth and compression are optimized, organizations not only ensure quality video but also reduce costs and improve overall system robustness.

SUMMARY

In this chapter, we discussed a comprehensive overview of the critical aspects involved in designing and managing a modern CCTV network. It begins with foundational concepts such as network topologies and transmission systems, and progressively advances toward sophisticated design strategies for bandwidth efficiency, compression, segmentation, redundancy, and high availability.

We explored different topology types, including star, ring, mesh, and hybrid models, each offering varying degrees of scalability, fault tolerance, and deployment complexity. Choosing the right topology directly impacts system performance, cost, and resilience. From access-layer PoE switches powering IP cameras to core-layer switches aggregating traffic to NVRs or cloud storage, the interplay between physical devices and logical structure is paramount. Proper planning of bandwidth, VLAN grouping, redundancy, and time synchronization ensures operational integrity and optimized performance.

Emphasis was also placed on network segmentation, encryption, QoS enforcement, and failover strategies. Together with access controls, firewalls, intrusion prevention systems, and physical safeguards, these measures build a secure and resilient video infrastructure. We also detailed advanced techniques such as multicast streaming, sub-streaming optimization, DSCP-based traffic prioritization, and NTP time sync, all of which support scalable command center operations and ensure adherence to regulatory compliance.

This chapter serves as a bridge between the theoretical design and real-world deployment of surveillance networks. It equips engineers, planners, and decision-makers with the tools and knowledge to design CCTV systems that are scalable, efficient, secure, and future-ready. When bandwidth and compression are optimized, organizations not only ensure quality video but also reduce costs and improve overall system robustness.

CHAPTER 3

CAMERA TYPES AND PRINCIPLES

Effective video surveillance begins with choosing the right camera. This chapter introduces core concepts in imaging, sensor types, and lens. As analytics become more advanced, selecting and deploying the appropriate camera is essential to ensure data accuracy and operational efficiency. This chapter also covers technologies like analog, IP, and mono and stereo vision systems. As intelligent video analytics become more sophisticated, selecting and deploying the right camera for the right use case is essential. Whether optimizing for face recognition, people counting, or long-range tracking, the physical and optical characteristics of a camera determine the reliability and accuracy of the data it captures.

LIGHT

Light is a critical factor in determining the quality of an image. This section explores the different types of light and their unique characteristics and how each type impacts image quality. Understanding these factors is essential for users and professionals to achieve the desired visual effects. We also discuss the concept of illuminance, which measures the amount of light that falls on a given surface, influencing exposure settings and overall image clarity.

Furthermore, the discussion on color temperature highlights how different light sources emit varying hues, affecting the overall color balance of images. This knowledge enables users to adjust their cameras' white balance settings to achieve accurate color reproduction. Finally, we cover how cameras can effectively operate in low-light conditions by utilizing near-infrared light. This light, which lies just beyond the visible spectrum, can be used to capture unique images with distinct tonal qualities, particularly in situations where visible light is limited.

Type of Light

Understanding the types of light present in a scene or captured by a camera is crucial for optimizing image quality. Below are the primary types of light that can emerge in a scene based on their origin and interactions with the objects.

1. Natural light is sunlight, which varies throughout the day and can be affected by weather conditions. It can be characterized by its intensity, color, and direction. Natural light can be limited in certain situations, such as during sunrise, sunset, or in shaded areas, affecting the camera's low-light performance.

2. Artificial light originates from man-made sources, including incandescent bulbs, fluorescent lights, LEDs (Light Emitting Diodes), tungsten light, flash, softbox, HMI (Hydrargyrum Medium-Arc Iodide) light, and portable on-camera light. Each type emits distinct qualities of light that affect the image. This type of light includes a colored light. While artificial light offers control and flexibility, it also comes with several drawbacks that can affect the quality of images and overall shooting experience such as unnatural appearance, harsh shadow, and limited coverage.

3. Ambient light refers to the overall light present in a scene, typically a combination of both natural and artificial sources. This type of light overcomes the weaknesses of lighting when used individually.

The following are types of light based on their interaction with objects:

1. Directional light is characterized by the light source from a specific angle, creating pronounced shadows and highlights. Frontal light, sidelight, and backlight are forms of directional light that impact image quality in distinct ways.

2. Diffused light occurs when light is scattered or softened, typically through clouds, mist, or diffusion materials. This type of light is ideal for achieving smooth skin tones and minimizing distractions in the background, leading to a more polished final image.

3. Reflected light is light that bounces off surfaces before illuminating a subject, often adding dimension and richness to an image. The quality of reflected light can vary depending on the surfaces it bounces off, which can alter its color and intensity.

To determine the direction of light in a scene, you can use a few simple techniques:

1. Observing shadows: Shadows provide a clear indication of where the light is coming from. The length, direction, and sharpness of the shadows tell you the position and type of light: Short shadows indicate light coming from directly above. Longer shadows suggest a lower angle, such as side or backlighting. Soft or diffused shadows signal light that has been scattered or diffused.

2. Using your hand or an object: Hold your hand or an object in front of the subject and rotate it to observe how the light and shadows shift on its surface. By watching these changes, you can easily detect the direction of the main light source.

3. Looking for highlights: Pay close attention to where the brightest highlights appear on the subject, as the area with the most light is typically facing the light source directly. The stronger the highlight, the more direct the light source.

4. Move around the subject: Walk around the subject or scene to observe how the light affects it from different angles. On one side, the light might create strong shadows (side lighting), while from another angle, it may evenly illuminate the subject (frontal lighting).

Illuminance

Illuminance refers to the amount of light that falls onto a surface, typically measured in lux (lx). It quantifies how brightly an area is lit, directly affecting how well a camera can capture details in different lighting conditions. High illuminance levels are needed for clear, detailed images in well-lit environments, while low illuminance can cause dim or grainy images, especially in low-light scenarios.

Typical lux levels for capturing good images vary based on lighting conditions. In bright sunlight, lux can range from 10,000 to 100,000 lux, while overcast days provide around 1,000 to 5,000. Indoor lighting typically falls between 200 to 500 lux, and evening or twilight conditions drop to 50 to 200 lux, suitable for atmospheric shots. Understanding illuminance is crucial when selecting or adjusting lighting to ensure optimal image quality in various applications. The illuminance of the object can be measured using a tool called *lux meter*. Knowing the illuminance level required is important for choosing the right camera-specific type (Table 3.1).

TABLE 3.1 Typical Minimum Illuminance (Lux) Requirements and Recommended Lux Levels. (Source: *https://wavelength-oe.com/optical-calculators/field-of-view/*)

Camera Type	Minimum Lux Level	Lux Level for Good Image
Digital Cameras (DSLRs and Mirrorless)	1 to 5 lux	100 to 500 lux
Smartphone Cameras	5 to 10 lux	100 to 300 lux
Low-Light Surveillance Cameras	0.01 to 0.5 lux	1 to 10 lux
Night Vision Cameras	Near 0 lux	N/A
Cinematography Cameras	1 lux	200 to 1000 lux
Point-and-Shoot Cameras	10 to 20 lux	100 to 300 lux
Action Cameras	10 to 30 lux	100 to 400 lux
Webcams	10 to 20 lux	50 to 150 lux

Lux-level requirements are determined by the dimensions of the area and the activities conducted within it. To calculate the illuminance in lux for a specific room area, you can use the following formula.

$$Illuminance\ (lux) = \frac{Luminous\,Flux\ (Lumens)}{Area\ (Square\,meters)}$$

where

- illuminance (lux): The amount of light per unit area
- luminous flux (lumens): The total amount of visible light emitted by a light source
- area (square meters): The area being illuminated

Here is an example of the calculation.

Given

- luminous flux (lumens): 800 lumens (for a standard LED bulb)
- room area: 20 square meters (e.g., a small room)

Solution:

$$Illuminance\,(lux) = \frac{800\,lumens}{20\,m^2} = 40\,lux$$

This calculation indicates that the room will be illuminated with an average of 40 lux when the LED bulb is used, which may be sufficient for activities like reading or working, depending on the specific requirements for that activity.

Color Temperature

Color temperature is the characteristic of visible light emitted by a light source, measured in Kelvin (K). It describes the color appearance of the light and ranges from warm (yellowish) to cool (bluish) tones. Light sources with lower Kelvin values (below 3,500 K) are considered warm and produce a soft, yellow-red glow similar to candlelight or incandescent bulbs; they are often used to create cozy and relaxing atmospheres.

The middle range of color temperature, around 4,000 K, is considered neutral white, balancing both warm and cool qualities, making it suitable for general lighting. Color temperatures are shown in Figure 3.1.

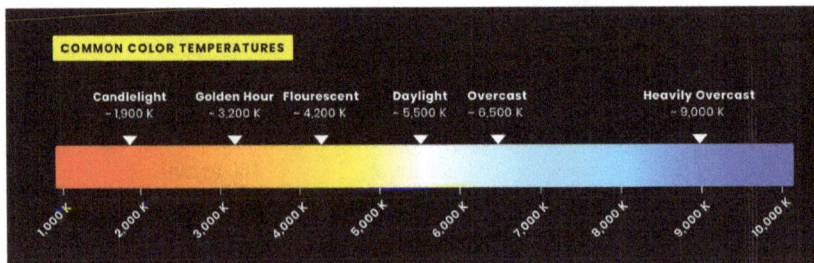

FIGURE 3.1 The color temperature chart in Kelvin
(Source: *https://www.studiobinder.com/blog/what-is-color-temperature-definition/*).

In video surveillance, color temperature plays a critical role in ensuring clear and accurate visual recordings, especially in varying lighting conditions. Surveillance cameras often operate in environments where lighting can fluctuate, such as outdoor settings or areas with both natural and artificial light sources. Using appropriate color temperature settings enhances image clarity and detail. For example, cool white light (above 5,000 K) is commonly used in surveillance systems for its ability to closely mimic daylight, offering sharp, high-contrast visuals that help in identifying objects or individuals, especially during the day. Conversely, a warmer color temperature may be preferred for nighttime or low-light environments to reduce glare and balance the scene, ensuring better visual performance of the camera's infrared capabilities. Thus, selecting the right color temperature ensures surveillance footage remains clear and usable across diverse lighting conditions.

IR Illuminators

An infrared (IR) illuminator is a device that emits infrared light, which is useful in low-light or nighttime environments. IR illuminators are commonly used in applications like security surveillance, wildlife observation, and night vision systems. In video surveillance, IR illuminators are frequently paired with night-vision cameras to enhance image clarity in total darkness. An image comparison between the human eye, day/night-vision, and a camera with IR is shown in Figure 3.2.

FIGURE 3.2 How the human eye, day/night camera, and a night camera with IR view the same scene (Source: *https://irilluminators.wordpress.com/2013/11/22/how-night-vision-works-with-ir-lights/*).

Infrared (IR) illuminators vary in wavelength and LED type, each suited to different applications and camera types. Here are some common IR wavelengths and LED types used in IR illuminators:

1. **Far-red 730 nm wavelength:** At 730 nm, the light is less likely to disrupt or alert subjects, allowing for covert operations. It also helps reduce glare on reflective surfaces, making it easier for cameras to capture detailed images, especially in scenarios like identifying individuals inside vehicles or monitoring nocturnal animal behavior. Additionally, this wavelength can be used alongside visible lighting, blending seamlessly without affecting the natural appearance of the scene. Modern windshields are engineered to block specific light wavelengths, primarily to shield occupants from UV rays and reduce cabin heat by filtering out some infrared light.

2. **850 nm wavelength:** This is one of the most commonly used IR wavelengths for surveillance and night vision cameras. At 850 nm, the IR light produces a faint red glow visible to the human eye but still remains relatively discreet. It is ideal for general surveillance and is highly compatible with most IR-sensitive cameras.

3. **940 nm wavelength:** Illuminators in the 940 nm range emit IR light that is completely invisible to the human eye, making it useful for covert operations, such as in military applications or wildlife observation, where stealth is crucial. However, cameras may require higher sensitivity to capture clear images at this wavelength, especially in low-light conditions.

4. **Hybrid:** A hybrid illuminator combines both infrared (IR) and white light LEDs, offering flexible illumination options to suit varying surveillance needs. This dual-function illuminator can switch between IR and visible light modes, allowing operators to choose the best lighting based on time of day, visibility requirements, or environmental conditions.

Figure 3.3 shows the IR vision comparison using different wavelengths. The figure shows that the 730 nm light clearly produces the sharpest images for identifying individuals inside the vehicle compared to the other wavelengths tested.

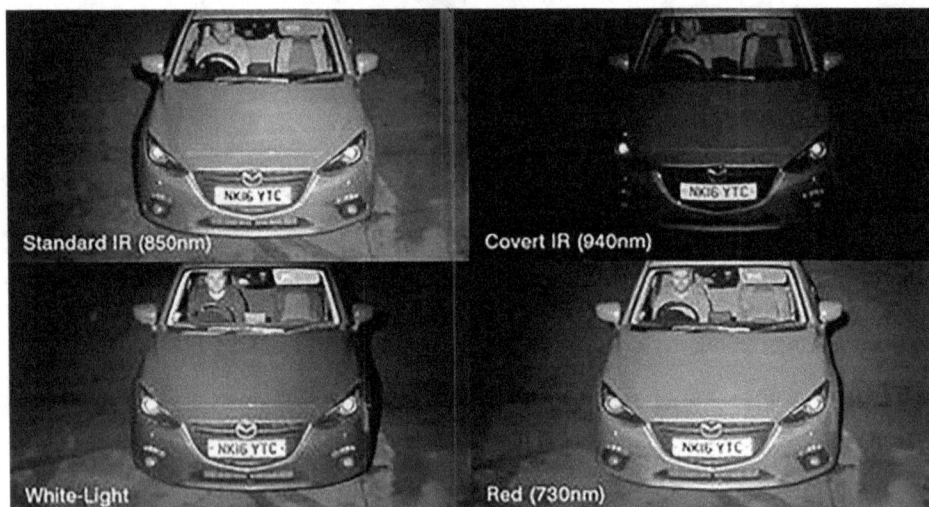

FIGURE 3.3 Comparison of images using different light types
(Source: *https://www.securityworldmarket.com/na/News/Themes/comparing-light-types-for-perimeter-surveillance-systems*).

5. LED types:

- Through-hole LEDs: These traditional LEDs are often used in smaller, low-power IR illuminators and are effective for short-range applications.
- Surface-Mounted Device (SMD) LEDs: These compact LEDs allow for high-density designs, making them suitable for powerful IR illuminators with a longer range.
- High-power LEDs: Often used in high-performance IR illuminators, high-power LEDs can produce strong IR beams that reach long distances, ideal for large outdoor surveillance areas.
- Laser diode LEDs: Laser-based IR LEDs offer a focused IR beam that can reach extended distances with high precision. They are typically used in advanced security systems where long-range, high-contrast IR illumination is required.

IR illuminators come with various beam angles, allowing users to tailor the IR coverage to specific needs. Here are common angles for IR illuminators and their typical applications:

1. Narrow angle (5–20°): Narrow beam IR illuminators focus light on a specific, distant target, often reaching up to several hundred meters. These are ideal for long-range surveillance, such as monitoring entry points or narrow outdoor spaces where distance is more critical than width.

2. Medium angle (30–60°): Medium-angle illuminators provide a balance between range and coverage area. They are typically used for general-purpose surveillance of medium-sized spaces, like parking lots or building perimeters, where moderate area illumination is required.

3. Wide angle (80–120°): Wide-angle IR illuminators disperse light over a larger area, covering shorter distances with a broader spread. These illuminators are well-suited for monitoring large, close-range areas, such as warehouses, yards, or building interiors, where wide coverage is more important than range.

4. Ultra-wide angle (120° and above): Ultra-wide beam IR illuminators are designed for very short-range applications, providing full coverage in close, confined spaces. They are commonly used in small rooms or spaces where even illumination across the entire area is necessary, such as in small indoor surveillance setups.

Choosing the right angle depends on the specific surveillance needs, balancing the trade-offs between coverage width and effective range. In video analytics, selecting the appropriate IR illuminator beam angle is crucial for ensuring optimal object detection, facial recognition, and movement tracking in low-light or no-light environments. For long-range surveillance, where narrow-angle IR illuminators (5–20°) are used, video analytics algorithms should be optimized for long-distance object recognition and motion tracking. In these scenarios, high-resolution cameras with enhanced zoom capabilities can work in tandem with AI-powered analytics, such as behavioral pattern analysis and anomaly detection, to identify suspicious activities over extended distances. Additionally, thermal imaging combined with IR illumination can further enhance target identification when visible light conditions are extremely poor.

For wide and ultra-wide IR coverage (80° and above), advanced AI-driven analytics must be implemented to handle distortion effects and uneven illumination across large areas. In crowd surveillance applications, real-time people counting, behavior monitoring, and density estimation rely on consistent IR illumination to avoid false positives due to fluctuating light conditions. To ensure accurate detection, image processing techniques such as adaptive histogram equalization and noise reduction filters should be applied to maintain clarity and contrast. Additionally, integrating multi-camera stitching with wide-angle IR setups can enhance situational awareness, creating seamless panoramic views for better scene understanding in large public spaces, warehouses, and industrial facilities.

OPTICS AND LENS

In video surveillance, optics and lenses are critical in determining image quality, coverage area, and the ability to capture details at various distances. The primary components to consider include the focal length, lens type, aperture, and optical coating, all of which influence the camera's field of view (FOV), depth of field, and performance under different lighting conditions. The typical structure of a lens is shown in Figure 3.4.

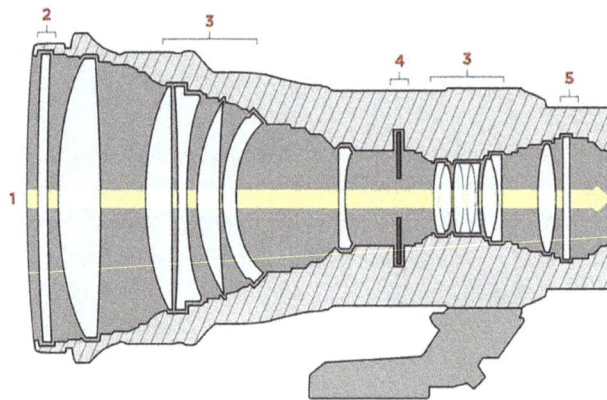

FIGURE 3.4 The typical structure of a lens
(Source: *https://www.canon-europe.com/pro/infobank/aperture*).

The lens structure in Figure 3.4 is composed of (1) light entering the lens, (2) the front element, (3) various lens groups with different functions, such as image stabilization, focusing, or diffraction correction, (4) aperture blades to control the light input that reaches sensors, and (5) rear element.

Lens Type and Focal Length: Generally, there are three types of lenses: fixed, varifocal, and zoom. In a fixed lens, the focal length is only fixed in one field of view. Unlike a fixed lens, a varifocal lens has a varying range of focal lengths, typically measured in millimeters (mm), that directly affects the camera's FOV and zoom capabilities. Short focal lengths (e.g., 2.8–4 mm) provide a wider FOV and are ideal for covering broad areas such as parking lots or building exteriors. Longer focal lengths (e.g., 12–50 mm) offer narrower FOVs but allow for better zoom, making them suitable for monitoring distant objects in high detail. Varifocal lenses, which allow focal length adjustments, provide flexibility, enabling operators to manually or automatically adjust the FOV based on the surveillance requirements. In video surveillance and analytics, the lens type and focal length play a crucial role in object detection, facial recognition, and behavior analysis, directly impacting the accuracy and effectiveness of AI-driven analytics. Fixed lenses, with their constant focal length and field of view (FoV), are commonly used in static monitoring scenarios such as access control, entrance surveillance, and indoor security, where a consistent view is needed. In contrast, varifocal lenses offer the ability to adjust focal length dynamically, making them ideal for adaptive surveillance applications where changing scene requirements demand flexibility, such as retail stores, bank lobbies, and traffic intersections. AI-powered analytics can leverage this adjustability to enhance automatic tracking, ensuring that objects remain in focus regardless of their distance from the camera.

For long-range monitoring, zoom lenses with longer focal lengths (e.g., 12–50 mm or higher) are essential for critical infrastructure protection, perimeter security, and license plate recognition (LPR). These lenses allow video analytics systems to magnify distant objects while maintaining high-resolution detail, enabling applications like vehicle tracking, facial identification at entry gates, and anomaly detection in restricted areas. However, higher zoom levels can introduce motion blur and stabilization issues, which can be mitigated by AI-based image stabilization and auto-focus algorithms. In smart city surveillance, integrating varifocal and zoom lenses with AI-powered PTZ (Pan-Tilt-Zoom) cameras enhances automated event detection, ensuring that the camera dynamically adjusts its focus based on movement, traffic congestion, or security incidents for more intelligent and responsive surveillance systems.

Type of Aperture: The lens aperture, measured by the f-stop controls the amount of light entering the camera sensor. The aperture diameter and f-number are related as follows:

$$Aperture\ diameter = \frac{focal\ length\ (f)}{f\text{-}number}$$

The f-stop value is written with a slash: for example, f/1.4, f/2.0, and f/16. A larger aperture, like f/1.4, indicates a wider opening compared to a smaller aperture, such as f/16. Figure 3.5 shows the comparison between the f-stop and aperture opening size. From Figure 3.5, we notice that the larger aperture is, the lower the f-number that allows more light in, enhancing the low-light performance and depth of field. This is essential in nighttime surveillance, where brighter images with less noise are needed. Low-dispersion (LD) and aspheric lenses help reduce chromatic aberrations and edge distortions, providing sharper images, particularly under challenging lighting conditions.

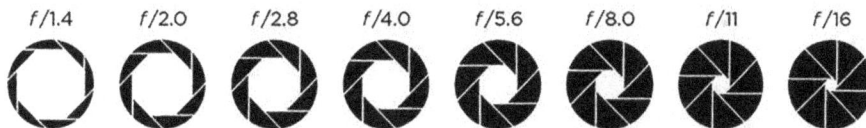

FIGURE 3.5 The f-stop values and their aperture opening size
(Source: *https://www.canon-europe.com/pro/infobank/aperture/*).

In CCTV surveillance and video analytics, the lens aperture (f-stop) is a crucial parameter that directly impacts image quality, low-light performance, and depth of field, all of which are essential for accurate AI-based video analysis. A larger aperture (lower f-number, e.g., f/1.4) allows more light to reach the sensor, significantly improving nighttime surveillance by producing brighter images with reduced noise. This is particularly important for applications such as facial recognition, license plate recognition (LPR), and object detection in low-light environments like parking lots, alleyways, and perimeter security.

From a video analytics perspective, a wide aperture (e.g., f/1.4–f/2.0) provides a shallow depth of field, which can be beneficial for tracking individuals and isolating targets from the background in crowded areas. However, a narrower aperture (e.g., f/8–f/16) increases the depth of field, ensuring that both foreground and background objects remain in focus—ideal for wide-area surveillance and traffic monitoring, where details at different distances need to be analyzed. To further enhance image clarity and reduce distortions, low-dispersion (LD) and aspheric lenses are used to minimize chromatic aberrations, which is particularly valuable in high-resolution video analytics systems that rely on AI-based object classification, behavior analysis, and automated threat detection. Selecting the optimal aperture setting in CCTV cameras is therefore critical to balancing the light sensitivity, clarity, and focus depth for achieving high-performance video surveillance and analytics in various environmental conditions.

Optical Coatings

Optical coatings are applied to improve an optical component's transmission, reflection, or polarization characteristics. For instance, an uncoated glass component typically reflects around 4% of incoming light at each surface. Using an anti-reflective coating can reduce this reflection to below 0.1%, while a highly reflective dielectric coating can boost reflectivity to over 99.99%. Advanced coating technology incorporates anti-glare coatings that are optimized to work across different light wavelengths. These coatings enhance light transmission and minimize reflections and play a critical role in accurately managing color rendition. Coatings and their effects on images are shown in Figure 3.6.

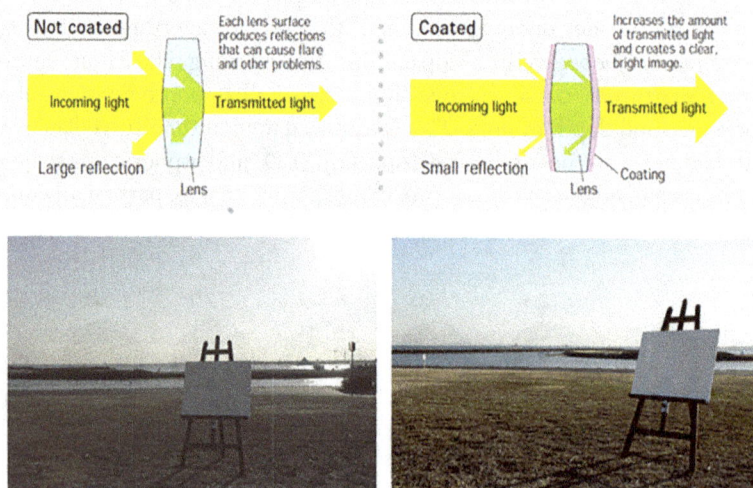

FIGURE 3.6 Coating effects
(Source: *https://av.jpn.support.panasonic.com/support/global/cs/dsc/knowhow/knowhow17.html*).

Weather-resistant coatings protect the lenses in outdoor environments, preventing fogging, water spots, and dust buildup. Hydrophobic coatings resist moisture, ensuring clear visuals in rainy or humid conditions. In CCTV surveillance and video analytics, optical coatings play a vital role in enhancing image quality, improving detection accuracy, and optimizing AI-based analytics. Anti-reflective coatings significantly reduce glare and unwanted reflections, ensuring that surveillance cameras capture clearer images with better contrast, especially in high-glare environments such as glass buildings, highways, and water surfaces. This is crucial for applications like license plate recognition (LPR), facial recognition, and object detection, where excessive reflections can reduce detection accuracy. Additionally, highly reflective dielectric coatings enhance infrared (IR) performance, improving night vision and thermal imaging, which is essential for 24/7 surveillance in low-light conditions. Moreover, advanced coatings that optimize color rendition ensure that AI-powered video analytics systems can more accurately differentiate between objects, detect anomalies, and classify behaviors without distortions caused by chromatic aberration or excessive light loss. By integrating coated optical components, CCTV systems can deliver sharper, more reliable footage, enhancing the effectiveness of intelligent video analytics in security, traffic monitoring, and forensic investigations.

IMAGE SENSORS

An image sensor is a device that captures incoming light and converts it into electrical signals or digital signals that can be processed to form an image. Sensors can be categorized in several types (such as the structure type (CCD or CMOS), color capability (color or monochrome), shutter type (global or rolling shutter)) and their attributes (such as resolution, frame rate, pixel size, and sensor format). A camera's sensor size has a great impact on the size of the camera and lenses, image quality and resolution, angle of view, depth of field, and low-light performance.

CCD and CMOS Sensors

A Charge-Coupled Device (CCD) image sensor is a type of technology used in cameras and imaging devices to capture high-quality images. The CCD has characteristics such as global shutter, high dynamic range, medium range frame rates, and low noise. Unlike CCD, the CMOS sensors technology has become more prevalent due to its lower power consumption and faster processing. The CMOS sensors shown in Figure 3.7 have several functions. First, photoelectric conversion occurs, where incoming photons are converted into electrons. Next, the sensor performs charge accumulation, collecting the generated electrons as a signal charge. This charge is then moved to a detection node in the signal transfer stage. Following this, the sensor conducts signal detection, converting the accumulated charge into an electrical signal (voltage). Finally, in the analog-to-digital conversion stage, the voltage signal is translated into a digital value, enabling further image processing and display.

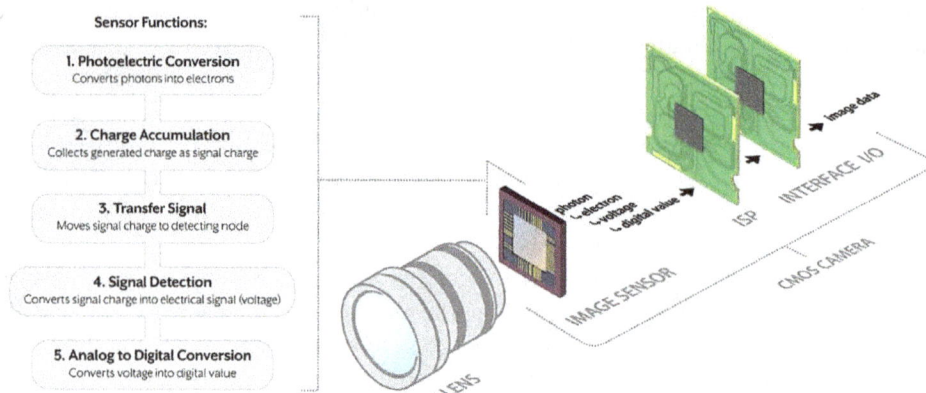

FIGURE 3.7 The CMOS sensor installed in a camera
(Source: *https://thinklucid.com/tech-briefs/understanding-digital-image-sensors/*).

Familiarity with some categories of image sensors is essential for selecting the right sensor for any specific application. For Megapixel and HDTV network cameras, the application must have the required megapixel sensors. A megapixel sensor is an image sensor with a resolution of one million pixels or more, commonly used in digital cameras, video surveillance, smartphones, and other imaging devices such as medical and scientific imaging and machine vision. A pixel is the smallest element of a digital image that can appear on a display device. The megapixel count indicates the number of light-sensitive sites on the sensor. Therefore, a 24-megapixel camera contains 24 million photosites on its sensor. Megapixel sensors provide enhanced image detail, which is essential in fields where high-resolution images are beneficial. However, selecting the right megapixel count should balance the resolution needs with practical limitations, such as light sensitivity, storage, processing power, and application requirements.

Resolution and Depth

Camera *resolution* refers to the number of pixels in each frame, affecting the sharpness and level of detail visible in the footage. Higher resolution allows for clearer identification of faces, objects, and incidents, especially when zooming in or enlarging parts of an image. The resolution of a sensor is also closely related to the CMOS sensor format. *Depth*, or depth perception, involves capturing three-dimensional information about a scene, which can be vital in distinguishing objects at different distances or creating a more accurate spatial representation of the environment. In practice, there are three types of camera resolution: pixel count, system, and angular resolutions.

Pixel Resolution: In imaging, the term *pixel resolution* can refer to different aspects depending on the context. For image sensors, pixel resolution is defined by the total number of light-capturing photodiode wells, which determine the amount of detail that can be captured in a photograph. In displays and projectors, pixel resolution refers to the total number of light-emitting elements, affecting the clarity and sharpness of the displayed image. For digital images themselves, pixel resolution is the total number of pixels that make up the image, determining its detail and quality.

The system resolution: The *system resolution*, or sharpness, is measured as a Spatial Frequency Response (SFR), also known as Modulation Transfer Function (MTF). System sharpness is influenced by factors such as the lens, the sensor (including pixel count and anti-aliasing filters), and the signal processing methods used, particularly sharpening and noise reduction. In real-world conditions, sharpness can also be affected by camera shaking (where a sturdy tripod can help), focus precision, and atmospheric conditions, like thermal effects and airborne particles. The effect of SFR on computer vision is shown in Figure 3.8.

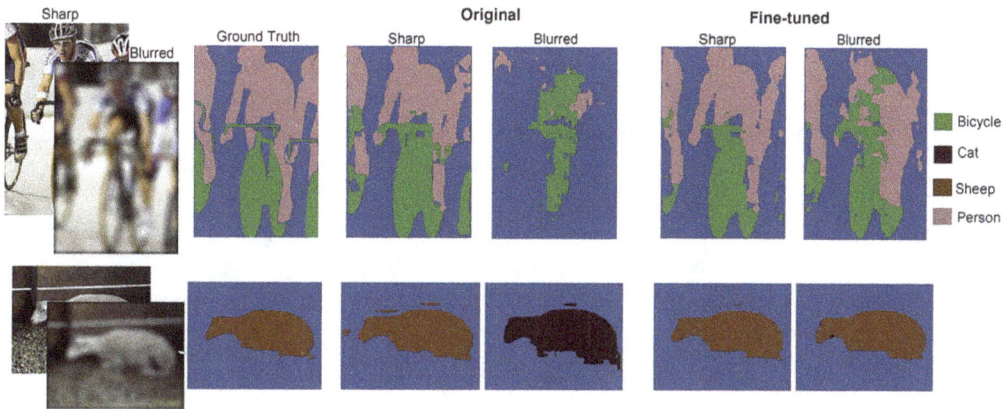

FIGURE 3.8 Semantic segmentation results in sharp and blurred images using the Zoomout network (Source: *https://arxiv.org/pdf/1611.05760*).

The Angular Resolution

The *angular resolution* is the number of pixels per degree of Field of View (FOV), or the number of pixels per unit distance across an object. In visualizing an object, the user must consider the vertical and horizontal FOV, which is illustrated in Figure 3.9.

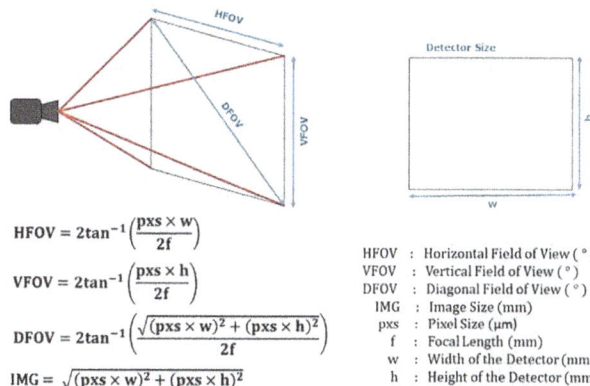

$$HFOV = 2\tan^{-1}\left(\frac{pxs \times w}{2f}\right)$$

$$VFOV = 2\tan^{-1}\left(\frac{pxs \times h}{2f}\right)$$

$$DFOV = 2\tan^{-1}\left(\frac{\sqrt{(pxs \times w)^2 + (pxs \times h)^2}}{2f}\right)$$

$$IMG = \sqrt{(pxs \times w)^2 + (pxs \times h)^2}$$

HFOV : Horizontal Field of View (°)
VFOV : Vertical Field of View (°)
DFOV : Diagonal Field of View (°)
IMG : Image Size (mm)
pxs : Pixel Size (μm)
f : Focal Length (mm)
w : Width of the Detector (mm)
h : Height of the Detector (mm)

FIGURE 3.9 An illustration of the horizontal field of view and vertical field of view and their calculations (Source: *https://wavelength-oe.com/optical-calculators/field-of-view/*).

The angular resolution affects different applications. In video surveillance, high angular resolution is crucial for identifying details like faces or license plates at a distance. Cameras with higher megapixels and long focal lengths are preferred for such applications. High angular resolution is important for detecting fine defects or measuring precise dimensions in computer vision such as industrial inspection or robotic systems.

Four factors influence the field of view of a camera. First, the effective focal length (EFL) of the lens, which is a fundamental optical parameter, should not be confused with mechanical parameters such as the Back Focal Length (BFL) or Flange Focal Distance (FFD). In license plate recognition (LPR), a telephoto lens with a longer Effective Focal Length (EFL) (e.g., 50 mm or more) is used to zoom in on plates from a distance while maintaining high detail. In contrast, wide-angle lenses (shorter EFL) are preferred in city surveillance to cover larger areas efficiently.

For applications like facial recognition at entry points, selecting a lens with an optimal EFL and aperture ensures high-resolution, distortion-free images, improving identification accuracy and reducing false positives.

Second, the image sensor's active area, which is determined by the pixel size and the total number of pixels in the image or video, plays a significant role; cropping the output will alter the FoV. In traffic monitoring, cameras with large-format sensors (e.g., 1-inch or APS-C sensors) provide a wider FoV, enhancing vehicle tracking accuracy. However, cropping or digital zooming can reduce the effective FoV, impacting detection at long distances.

To mitigate this, using high-resolution sensors (e.g., 4K or 8K) enables post-processing zooming without significant loss of detail, making it especially useful for forensic video analysis and long-range surveillance.

Third, the relative illumination of a lens refers to the variation in the light transmitted through the lens depending on the position in the image space. In the camera industry, the term *image circle* is often used to describe the area where the relative illumination is around 50%. In low-light surveillance, cameras with high relative illumination and larger sensors (e.g., full-frame or large-format CMOS) perform significantly better in areas with uneven lighting, such as parking lots at night, ensuring clearer image capture. For facial recognition systems, maintaining consistent relative illumination across the sensor is crucial to prevent bias in AI models, as uneven brightness can degrade recognition accuracy and increase false positives.

Finally, lens distortion, which is a common aberration in wide-angle and fisheye lenses, affects the FoV by compressing the angular resolution, making the lens appear to have a broader field of view than it technically does. In crowd analytics, fisheye cameras are commonly used in public spaces to provide 180° or 360° views, maximizing coverage. However, the extreme lens distortion can warp object shapes, affecting detection accuracy.

To address this, applying distortion correction algorithms (e.g., OpenCV's undistort) during pre-processing ensures objects remain recognizable and proportionally accurate, significantly improving AI-based object detection performance.

Mono and Stereo Camera Systems

Mono and stereo camera systems are two common types of camera configurations used in various applications such as computer vision, robotics, and surveillance. They differ in how they capture images and extract depth or 3D information from a scene. The comparison between mono and stereo camera system is shown in Table 3.2.

TABLE 3.2 Mono and stereo camera system characteristics

Parameter	Mono Camera	Stereo Camera
Number of cameras	1	2
Depth Perception	No direct depth information	Direct depth information through stereo matching
Complexity	Simple system, easy to implement	More complex system with stereo matching and processing
Cost	Lower	Higher (due to additional hardware processing)
Accuracy of Depth	Estimated through software (less accurate)	Accurate depth estimation based on disparity
Environmental Sensitivity	Less affected by environmental conditions	Can be affected by poor lighting or low-texture areas
Application	Surveillance, Barcode Scanning, Object Detection	Robotics, Augmented Reality (AR), Autonomous Vehicles, 3D Mapping
Device example	Nest Cam, Logitech C920, Raspberry Pi Camera Module V2, Arducam Mini Module Camera	Intel RealSense Depth Camera D435, ZED 2 Stereo Camera (by Stereolabs), VicoVR, LiDAR and Camera Fusion (Velodyne LiDAR and Stereo Cameras)

For instance, in video analytics for smart cities, mono cameras are commonly used for license plate recognition (LPR), face recognition, and object detection in traffic monitoring due to their cost-effectiveness and scalability. Stereo cameras are preferred for pedestrian tracking, vehicle distance estimation, and obstacle detection in autonomous driving, where depth accuracy is crucial.

CAMERA DEPLOYMENT PLANNING FOR ANALYTICS

The success of intelligent video analytics systems hinges not only on the capabilities of the analytics engine but also on the thoughtful planning of camera deployment. Improper placement, insufficient pixel density, or incompatible hardware can severely degrade analytic accuracy. This section introduces core principles and best practices for aligning camera deployment with analytic objectives in real-world environments.

Camera Placement and Coverage Planning

Effective placement ensures that cameras capture the necessary details for identification, tracking, or behavioral analysis. The horizontal field of view (FoV) is determined by the lens focal length and sensor size and can be calculated to ensure that each area of interest is adequately covered without gaps or blind spots. An important metric is *pixel density*, measured in pixels per meter (PPM) or pixels per foot (PPF), which influences how well objects or persons can be identified. The following are examples:

- Facial recognition: Requires ~40–50 pixels between the eyes (~400 PPM)
- License plate recognition: 130–160 PPM for accurate OCR
- People detection: As low as 20–40 PPM may suffice
- Vehicle counting: Typically requires 20–50 PPM depending on the detection range and vehicle size
- Queue monitoring: ~40–60 PPM to detect individual positions and spacing reliably
- Object left behind detection: 60–100 PPM to reliably distinguish small stationary objects
- In-store theft (hand gestures or item movement): 100–150 PPM for detailed tracking of hand/object interactions

To estimate whether a camera placement meets the necessary pixel density, use the following formula:

$$PPM = \frac{Image\,Width\,in\,Pixels}{Scene\,Width\,in\,Meters}$$

Example 1: Parking Lot Entrance
A 4 MP camera (2688 x 1520 resolution) is installed to cover a 10-meter-wide parking lot entrance:

$$PPM = \frac{2688}{10} = 268.8 \text{ PPM}$$

This exceeds the pixel density required for license plate recognition (130–160 PPM), making it highly suitable.

Example 2: Warehouse Aisle
The same camera is now used to monitor a 20-meter-wide aisle:

$$PPM = \frac{2688}{20} = 134.4 \text{ PPM}$$

This is still acceptable for license plate or people detection, but falls short for high-quality facial recognition unless the camera is zoomed in or repositioned.

Example 3: Facial Recognition Zone
To ensure reliable face recognition with 50 pixels between the eyes and assuming the average eye distance is 12.5 cm (0.125 m), the required PPM is

$$PPM = \frac{50}{0.125} = 400\,PPM$$

To achieve 400 PPM with a 2,688-pixel width, the scene width must be as follows:

$$Scene\,Width = \frac{2688}{400} = 6.62 \text{ meters}$$

This means the camera should not cover more than 6.72 meters if used for facial recognition at this resolution.

Strategic camera positioning must account for distance, target size, angle, and obstructions. Planning tools such as lens calculators, simulation software, and CAD/BIM integrations are essential for validating coverage plans and ensuring performance aligns with analytic goals. Planning tools such as lens calculators and CAD integrations are essential for validating coverage plans.

Distance vs. Scene Width Consideration

Pixel density is influenced by the camera's distance to the scene because the farther the camera is from the area of interest, the wider the scene appears in the image. A wider scene means fewer pixels are distributed across each meter, reducing detail. To calculate the maximum allowable distance for a given scene width, use the camera's FoV. For example, a camera with a 90° horizontal FoV covering a 6.72-meter-wide scene would be positioned as follows:

$$Distance = \frac{(Scene\,Width\,/\,2)}{\tan(\dfrac{FoV}{2})} = \frac{(6.72\,/\,2)}{\tan(45°)} = 3.36\,\text{meters}$$

Strategic camera positioning must account for distance, target size, angle, and obstructions. As the distance between the camera and the target increases, the scene width naturally widens, reducing the pixel density. This is why a camera placed too far from a subject may not deliver sufficient detail for accurate identification or analytics. Conversely, moving a camera closer or using a narrower lens can concentrate more pixels into the area of interest, increasing detail. Therefore, FoV and camera distance must be carefully planned to match the required pixel density of the intended analytic task. Planning tools such as lens calculators, simulation software, and CAD/BIM integrations are essential for validating coverage plans and ensuring performance aligns with analytic goals.

Camera Selection Matrix Based on a Use Case

Different surveillance and analytic goals require specific camera technologies and configurations to achieve optimal performance. The right choice is not just about resolution—it must also consider the camera's form factor, lens type, placement orientation, and the scene's environmental and lighting conditions.

For example, a dome camera might be excellent for discreet indoor monitoring, but may not deliver the focal length or clarity required for license plate recognition in a fast-moving traffic environment. Conversely, a telephoto box camera might excel in capturing details from afar, but is often less suited for areas requiring wide coverage or aesthetic discretion.

The table below outlines recommended camera types for common analytics-driven surveillance tasks.

TABLE 3.3 Recommended camera types for surveillance tasks

Use Case	Recommended Camera Type	Resolution	Special Notes
Face Recognition	Fixed or Varifocal	4MP+	Frontal angle, ~1.5–2 m height
People Counting	Ceiling-mounted Fisheye	2MP+	Top-down, minimal occlusion

(Continued)

TABLE 3.3 Continued

Use Case	Recommended Camera Type	Resolution	Special Notes
License Plate Recognition	Telephoto (Box/Zoom)	2MP+	Perpendicular to plate, low angle
Perimeter Intrusion	Bullet/IR Camera	4MP+	Long-range IR, weather-proof
Loitering or Object Detection	Fixed Dome/PTZ	4MP+	Consistent FoV for time analysis
Vehicle Counting	Fixed or Zoom Bullet	2MP+	Overhead or side view, sufficient frame rate
Queue Monitoring	Ceiling-mounted Dome	3MP+	Top-down angle to observe spacing and movement
Object Left Behind Detection	Fixed Dome	4MP+	Wide FoV, low occlusion zone
In-store Theft Detection	Indoor Dome/PTZ	4MP+	Over-the-shoulder view, high pixel density zone

Choosing the wrong camera—even with sufficient resolution—can render analytics ineffective due to factors like optical distortion, poor focal depth, wide-angle compression, or improper mounting height. Matching the camera type to both the analytic function and physical environment is critical for successful deployment.

Mounting Height and Angle Considerations

Mounting height and camera angle play a crucial role in capturing high-quality, analyzable footage. If a camera is mounted too high, it may not capture the necessary facial or object detail required for precise identification. Conversely, cameras mounted too low can be easily tampered with or may become obstructed by moving people or equipment. The mounting strategy must balance analytics requirements with physical and operational constraints.

General mounting guidance is as follows:

- Facial recognition: Mount cameras at eye-level to ~2.5 meters. A frontal angle is critical for capturing sufficient facial features. Angles that are too steep will distort proportions and reduce the number of usable pixels on the face.
- People counting: Requires a top-down view at a height greater than 3 meters, ideally positioned directly above entrances or corridors to minimize occlusion and overlapping individuals.
- License Plate Recognition (LPR): Mount between 1.2 and 2.5 meters high, with the camera aligned within a 20° angle relative to the license plate plane to ensure legibility and avoid reflective glare.
- Queue monitoring and object tracking: Position cameras at moderate heights (~2.5–3 meters) to maintain visibility across the target area while minimizing occlusions. Angles should be chosen to allow clear separation of individuals in a line.
- In-store theft detection: Mount at shelf or shoulder height (~2–2.5 meters) with an angle allowing clear visibility of hand-object interactions, especially in high-risk product zones.

Excessive downward tilt can create perspective distortion, making it difficult for analytics engines to extract features such as faces, movement patterns, or object size. Shallow oblique angles reduce the resolution density across the subject. Proper alignment maximizes detail in the region of interest while maintaining situational context. Optimal results often require iterative adjustments in placement and angle, verified through on-site testing and simulation tools.

Environmental Suitability and Protection

Outdoor deployments, tunnels, low-light areas, or marine facilities all require robust environmental considerations to ensure consistent image quality and equipment longevity under harsh or unpredictable conditions. Environmental challenges can directly affect visibility, image clarity, camera operation, and system reliability—impacting the effectiveness of analytics and surveillance. Important environmental protection considerations include the following:

- Ingress Protection (IP66/67): A rating of IP66 or higher ensures protection from heavy rain, dust, or wind-driven particles. IP67 offers additional water submersion protection, ideal for flood-prone zones.
- Impact Resistance (IK10): In public or vandal-prone areas, IK10-rated housings withstand impact from blunt force or intentional damage, helping reduce service disruptions.
- Operating Temperature Range: Cameras deployed in arctic or desert climates must function reliably at temperature extremes (e.g., −40°C to +60°C). Using built-in heaters, blowers, or climate-controlled housings may be required.
- Infrared (IR) Capability: IR cameras are essential for night-time and tunnel environments. Ensure the IR range matches the monitored area and that overexposure (IR washout) is avoided through proper distance calibration or smart IR features.
- Anti-fog and Anti-condensation Coatings: Coastal or humid environments demand lenses with protective coatings or sealed enclosures to prevent image degradation caused by fogging or moisture buildup.
- Vibration Resistance: In roadside, bridge, or rail environments, use vibration-resistant mounts and optically stabilized lenses to maintain image sharpness.

In highway environments, LPR cameras must resist constant vibration from passing vehicles, provide consistent and synchronized IR illumination for high-speed license plate capture, and maintain optical focus at long distances. Choosing improperly rated general-purpose dome cameras for this use often leads to poor image sharpness, higher false negative rates in OCR analytics, and premature equipment failure due to environmental exposure.

SUMMARY

In CCTV surveillance and video analytics, understanding the fundamentals of camera technology is critical for optimizing security monitoring, object detection, and AI-driven analytics. The insights from this chapter provide a foundation for selecting the right camera type, lens system, and sensor technology based on specific surveillance needs. For example, high-resolution digital cameras with low-light sensors and advanced optical coatings significantly enhance facial recognition accuracy and forensic video analysis, while thermal and IR-enabled cameras improve nighttime and perimeter security.

With advancements in imaging technology, modern AI-powered surveillance systems leverage computational photography, real-time edge processing, and intelligent analytics to provide automated threat detection, anomaly recognition, and behavior analysis. The evolution of deep learning algorithms combined with high-efficiency image sensors allows for more accurate and scalable video analytics, enabling applications such as crowd monitoring, traffic analysis, and access control. As surveillance systems continue to integrate machine learning and IoT connectivity, selecting the appropriate camera configurations becomes even more crucial to ensure effective monitoring, reduced false alarms, and enhanced situational awareness in smart cities, industrial security, and critical infrastructure protection.

CHAPTER 4

IMAGE PROCESSING PRINCIPLES FOR VIDEO ANALYTICS

M odern intelligent video analytics relies on more than just algorithms. It depends on high-quality, analyzable video frames. This chapter considers classical image processing concepts through the lens of real-world CCTV and AI-driven surveillance applications. It provides the foundational imaging knowledge required to understand how light, sensor design, resolution, and compression all influence analytic outcomes. Computer vision builds directly upon image processing to enable machines to interpret, reason, and act upon visual input. Within the context of Intelligent Video Analytics (IVA), computer vision serves as the decision-making layer that transforms enhanced and structured image data into actionable insights, whether that means identifying an intruder, recognizing a face, or counting individuals in a queue.

IMAGE PROCESSING BASICS

Image processing has emerged as a critical field in computer science and engineering, focusing on the manipulation, analysis, and understanding of visual data. It involves a range of techniques designed to enhance, compress, transform, detect, and segment images for better analysis and interpretation.

This chapter repositions classical image processing concepts through the lens of real-world CCTV and AI-driven surveillance applications. It provides the foundational imaging knowledge required to understand how light, sensor design, resolution, and compression all influence analytic outcomes.

Unlike traditional image processing textbooks, which emphasize fields like medical imaging or remote sensing, this chapter is built around applied use cases for facial recognition, license plate reading, object tracking, and event detection in smart cities, retail, and transportation. Whether you are configuring a low-light outdoor camera or optimizing frame rates for queue monitoring, the insights here help bridge the gap between theoretical imaging principles and real-time system deployment.

In the context of intelligent video analytics (IVA), these techniques are tailored to optimize video input from surveillance systems. Image enhancement improves visibility in challenging conditions such as fog, nighttime, or low-light tunnels. Compression strategies reduce bandwidth without compromising analytic reliability. Transformation methods, like wavelets and Fourier analysis, help extract frequency-based features useful for anomaly detection and motion analysis. Detection and segmentation techniques allow systems to identify faces, vehicles, loiterers, or unattended objects in dynamic scenes.

These image processing foundations also underpin broader tasks in computer vision, such as object recognition, scene understanding, and visual tracking, where IVA systems transform raw visual data into actionable insights for safety, security, and situational awareness in smart cities, retail, transportation, and critical infrastructure. The goal is to provide practical, field-ready guidance that aligns directly with design considerations in modern video surveillance systems.

While image processing prepares the raw data (e.g., via denoising, contrast adjustment, or segmentation), computer vision extracts semantic meaning. This includes tasks such as the following:

- Object detection and classification: identifying entities like persons, vehicles, bags, or animals using models such as YOLO, SSD, and EfficientDet
- Pose estimation: inferring human posture or body orientation, relevant in crowd behavior analytics or fall detection in elderly care
- Facial recognition and attribute analysis: extracting facial embeddings for identity verification, sentiment analysis, or demographic classification
- Action and event recognition: recognizing behaviors like running, loitering, or fighting, crucial for real-time situational awareness
- Re-identification (Re-ID): matching individuals across non-overlapping camera views in public transit or shopping malls

To perform these functions, modern IVA systems rely heavily on deep learning and real-time inference powered by GPU/TPU accelerators. Computer vision frameworks like OpenCV, PyTorch, and TensorFlow are foundational tools for developing these applications. High-level APIs like Detectron2, MMDetection, and cloud services (e.g., AWS Rekognition and Google Cloud Vision) accelerate deployment without requiring deep algorithmic development from scratch.

Example IVA Stack:

1. Image input: captured via IP camera in RGB format
2. Preprocessing: resized, denoised, normalized
3. Inference layer: object detector locates and classifies individuals
4. Tracking layer: assigns unique IDs for cross-frame continuity
5. Event engine: raises alarm if a person enters a restricted zone or remains idle for too long

Example: In a retail setting, a computer vision pipeline identifies repeat customers using face recognition, measures time spent in aisles using pose estimation and tracking, and flags potential theft scenarios via suspicious movement patterns (Figure 4.1).

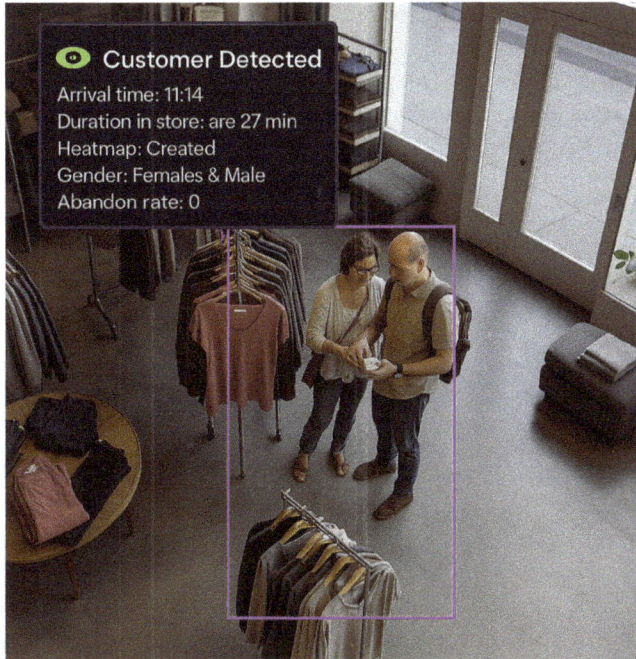

FIGURE 4.1 Video analytics for retail.

By bridging enhanced imagery and AI inference, computer vision operationalizes image processing, turning pixels into knowledge that empowers surveillance systems to not just watch, but understand and respond. Modern intelligent video analytics relies on more than just algorithms—it depends on high-quality, analyzable video frames.

Image Analysis for Intelligent Surveillance

Image analysis is a multidisciplinary domain that empowers modern surveillance systems to extract, interpret, and act upon meaningful visual data from video streams. It combines elements of signal processing, computer vision, machine learning, and artificial intelligence to deliver intelligent, context-aware decision-making. While image analysis traditionally found applications in fields like healthcare and industrial inspection, its relevance in surveillance has accelerated, driven by the explosion of camera deployments, real-time analytics demands, and public safety priorities.

In the context of Intelligent Video Analytics (IVA), image analysis encompasses a set of structured operations, typically executed in real-time or near real-time (Figure 4.2):

- *Preprocessing* includes filtering (e.g., Gaussian and median), histogram equalization, and normalization to reduce lighting variation and noise. These steps standardize the input image for consistent downstream analysis.
- *Feature extraction* detects edges, corners, and keypoints that characterize objects in the scene. For instance, the Histogram of Oriented Gradients (HOG) or Scale-Invariant Feature Transform (SIFT) are used to localize humans or vehicles.

- *Segmentation* isolates the foreground from the background or partitions the image into regions of interest using background subtraction, motion segmentation, or deep learning models like U-Net, SAM, or DeepLab.
- Object detection and classification: Deep learning-based algorithms such as YOLO, SSD, or Faster R-CNN identify and classify specific targets—humans, vehicles, bags, or even specific behaviors.
- Object tracking: This maintains identity of objects over time and across frames or cameras. Multi-object tracking (MOT) algorithms like Deep SORT or ByteTrack allow robust tracking in crowded scenes.

FIGURE 4.2 Object segmentation (left) and object tracking (right).

These techniques form the analytical backbone of IVA systems and support important applications such as the following:

- Smart forensic search (filtering video by color, gender, or activity)
- Real-time intrusion alerts in restricted zones
- Loitering detection in public areas
- Left-object detection in airports or bus terminals
- Crowd density and flow monitoring

For example, in a metro station, real-time IVA continuously segments and tracks individuals across multiple entry and platform cameras. It detects prolonged loitering in isolated zones and identifies known shoplifters through facial recognition embeddings linked to a backend database.

Image analysis is not only vital in fixed surveillance systems but also serves as a foundation for dynamics surveillance systems like intelligent transportation applications, particularly autonomous vehicle systems. In an end-to-end approach, sensor data from onboard cameras and LiDAR devices captures continuous visual and spatial information from the vehicle's surroundings. This data is fed into deep learning models, primarily convolutional neural networks (CNNs) and recurrent neural networks (RNNs) that have been trained to interpret road features, object proximity, and motion patterns. These models autonomously determine actions such as steering, speed adjustment, lane centering, and braking based on learned patterns from massive anno-tated driving datasets. Cameras capture road curvature, traffic signals, and lane markings, while LiDAR adds precise depth estimation and obstacle detection capabilities. The synergy of these inputs enables autonomous systems to respond in real-time with accurate control commands.

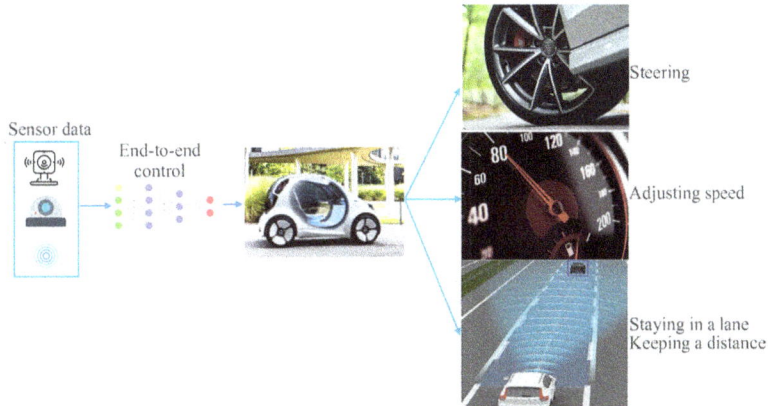

FIGURE 4.3 Sensor data includes images used for controlling the car in the end-to-end autonomous vehicle that uses deep learning (Source: *https://arxiv.org/html/2112.11561v5*).

Figure 4.3 illustrates how image analysis and deep learning play a critical role in autono-mous vehicle systems through an end-to-end approach. Sensor data, such as from cameras and LiDAR, captures visual and spatial information about the vehicle's surroundings. This data is then processed using deep learning models, particularly neural networks, which learn the direct relationship between sensor inputs (e.g., road images or nearby vehicles) and control actions (such as steering, adjusting speed, and maintaining distance). The model autonomously deter-mines actions like vehicle direction, appropriate speed, and staying in the correct lane by identi-fying patterns in the sensor data learned during training.

Digital Imaging System in Surveillance

In intelligent surveillance systems, the move from analog to digital imaging enables sophisti-cated real-time analysis, robust storage, and seamless transmission of video data. Digital imaging systems are critical to the functioning of IVA platforms, as they ensure that visual data is cap-tured in a format that supports advanced processing operations.

A digital imaging system integrates hardware and software to capture, process, store, and ana-lyze images in digital form for various applications. As illustrated in Figure 4.4, hardware compo-nents include image acquisition devices such as cameras, medical scanners (e.g., X-ray, MRI, and ultrasound), and microscopes, which capture analog signals. These signals are converted into a digital format using image sensors (CCD or CMOS) and Analog-to-Digital Converters (ADC). Processing units like GPUs enable real-time image processing, while storage devices and high-fidelity monitors handle data storage and visualization. On the software side, image processing tools perform operations like filtering, noise reduction, and compression (e.g., JPEG, PNG) to enhance image quality and reduce file size.

Reality world	Image acquisition	Converter	Software	Storage/ Display
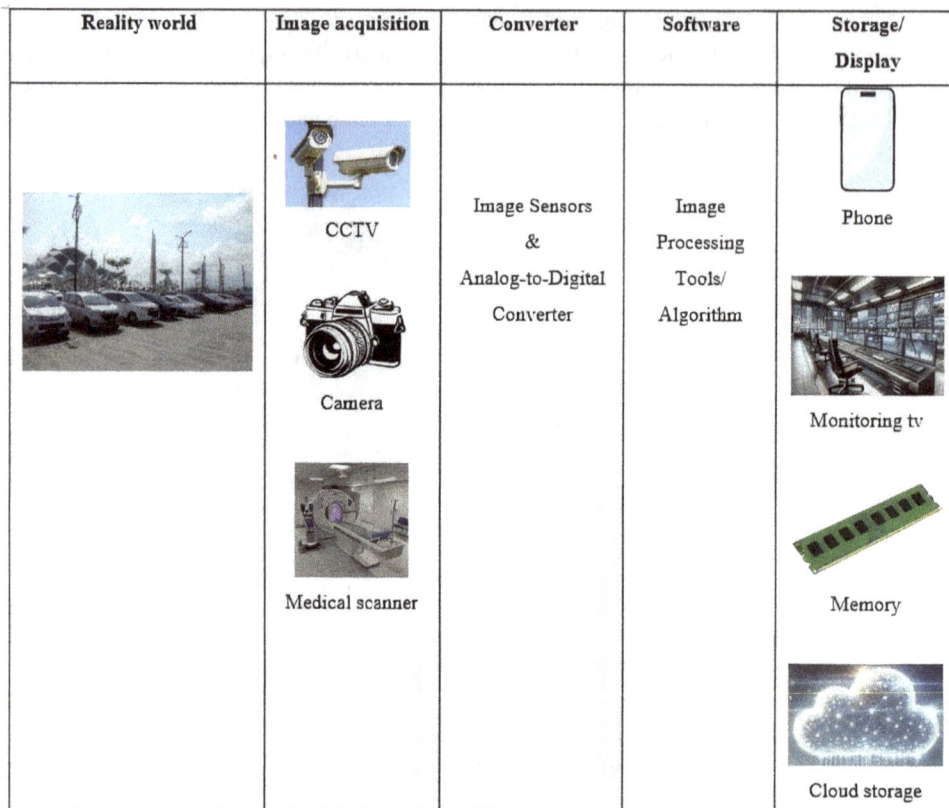	CCTV Camera Medical scanner	Image Sensors & Analog-to-Digital Converter	Image Processing Tools/ Algorithm	Phone Monitoring tv Memory Cloud storage

FIGURE 4.4 Digital image processing system.

The process of transforming an analog image to a digital image comprises three main steps: scanning, sampling, and quantization.

1. *Scanning* refers to the process of systematically capturing the analog image or scene using a device such as a scanner, camera, or sensor. This step converts the continuous analog signal, such as light intensity or reflections, into an electrical signal that can be measured.

2. *Sampling* follows scanning and involves dividing the continuous image into a grid of discrete points or pixels. Each pixel corresponds to a small portion of the original image, capturing spatial details such as brightness, color, and other features at specific locations. The resolution of the image depends on the pixel density, referred to as the sampling rate, with higher rates providing greater image detail. The sampling rate, or the number of samples taken per unit area, determines the resolution of the digital image; higher sampling rates capture more detail, providing finer spatial representation. For example, a 1920×1080 image, commonly used in high-definition displays, contains 2,073,600 pixels, offering a high level of detail suitable for sharp visuals and fine textures. In contrast, a 640×480 image, often used in older standard-definition formats, has only 307,200 pixels, resulting in significantly less detailed and blocky, pixelated appearance when magnified or viewed on larger screens.

The sampling rate for digitizing an analog image is determined by the resolution of the desired digital image, which is typically represented by the number of pixels in the horizontal and vertical dimensions of the grid. The formula for the sampling rate can be expressed as

$$Sampling\,Rate\left(\frac{pixels}{unit\,area}\right) = \frac{Number\,of\,pixels\,(horizontal)}{Width\,of\,the\,image} \times \frac{Number\,of\,pixels\,(vertical)}{Height\,of\,the\,image}$$

Parameters:

- Number of pixels (horizontal): the number of pixels along the width of the digital image
- Number of pixels (vertical): the number of pixels along the height of the digital image
- Width of the image: the physical width of the analog image (in units such as inches, centimeters, or millimeters)
- Height of the image: the physical height of the analog image (in the same units as the width)

Example: If you have an analog image measuring 4 cm x 3 cm that you want to sample at resolution of 1024 x 768, the sampling rate can be calculated as

$$Horizontal\,Sampling\,Rate = \frac{1024}{4\,cm} = 256\ pixels/cm$$

$$Vertical\,Sampling\,Rate = \frac{768}{3\,cm} = 256\ pixels/cm$$

Hence, the overall sampling rate is $256 \times 256 = 65536$ pixels/cm^2. Note that the Nyquist Sampling Theorem must be satisfied to avoid aliasing, ensuring the sampling rate. i.e., at least twice the highest frequency present in the analog image.

3. *Quantization* assigns each sampled point a discrete intensity value from a finite set of levels. This step is essential because digital images, unlike analog ones, can only represent a limited number of intensity or color levels per pixel. By converting the infinite range of possible values into a finite set, quantization simplifies storage and processing. This process maps the continuous range of analog intensity values into a digital representation, where the number of levels depends on the bit depth (e.g., an 8-bit grayscale image has 256 levels). For color images, quantization partitions the color space into distinct intervals within the RGB channels. The mapping process is determined by three main steps, i.e., step size, mapping, and reconstruction.

- Step Size (ΔI): Determine the range of each quantization level. A smaller step size provides finer quantization, preserving more details but requiring more storage space.
- Mapping: The analog intensity value $I(i, j)$ is scaled relative to the step size and mapped to the nearest quantization level using the floor function.
- Reconstruction: The quantized value is reconstructed by multiplying the quantization index by the step size and adding back the minimum intensity.

Mathematically, the quantized intensity value can be computed with the following formula:

$$Q(i,j) = \left\lfloor \frac{I(i,j) - I_{min}}{\Delta I} \right\rfloor \cdot \Delta I + I_{min}$$

where

- $Q(i,j)$: quantized intensity value for the pixel at position (i,j)
- $I(i,j)$: original intensity value of the analog signal at pixel(i,j)
- I_{min}: minimum intensity value in the analog signal
- ΔI: step size or interval between quantization levels, calculated as

$$\Delta I = \frac{I_{max} - I_{min}}{L}$$

where L is the number of quantization levels (e.g., $L = 256$ for an 8-bit image)
- $\lfloor \cdot \rfloor$: floor function, which rounds down to the nearest integer

Note that quantization introduces the *quantization error*, defined as the difference between the original and quantized values. It can be computed as

$$Quantization\, Error = I(i,j) - Q(i,j)$$

Example: For a grayscale image, suppose the analog intensity values range from $I_{min} = 0$ to $I_{max} = 255$, and we want 8 quantization levels ($L = 8$). Here is the solution:

1. Step 1: Calculate ΔI.

$$\Delta I = \frac{255 - 0}{8} = 31.875$$

2. Step 2: Compute the quantized value $Q(i,j)$ for an analog intensity value $I(i,j) = 100$.

$$Q(i,j) = \left\lfloor \frac{100 - 0}{31.875} \right\rfloor \cdot 31.875 + 0$$

$Q(i,j) = \lfloor 3.14 \rfloor \cdot 31.875 = 3 \cdot 31.875 = 95.625 \approx 96$. Hence, the quantized intensity value is 96.

Example: For an RGB image, quantization is applied independently to each of the three color channels: red (R), green (G), and blue (B). Assume the analog intensity range for each channel is $I_{min} = 0$ to $I_{max} = 255$. We want to quantize the image to 4 levels per channel $(L = 4)$. Here is the solution:

1. Step 1: Calculate the step size (ΔI).
   For each channel (R, G, B),

$$\Delta I = \frac{I_{max} - I_{min}}{L} = \frac{255 - 0}{4} = 63.75$$

2. Step 2: Quantize the pixel values.

For an analog pixel value of
- red channel: R=200
- green channel: G=150
- blue channel: B=50

We apply the quantization formula:

$$Q(i,j) = \left\lfloor \frac{I(i,j) - I_{min}}{\Delta I} \right\rfloor \cdot \Delta I + I_{min}$$

Red Channel $(R = 200)$:

$$Q_R = \left\lfloor \frac{200 - 0}{63.75} \right\rfloor \cdot 63.75 = \lfloor 3.14 \rfloor \cdot 63.75 = 3 \cdot 63.75 = 191.25 \approx 191$$

Green Channel $(G = 150)$:

$$Q_G = \left\lfloor \frac{150 - 0}{63.75} \right\rfloor \cdot 63.75 = \lfloor 2.35 \rfloor \cdot 63.75 = 2 \cdot 63.75 = 127.5 \approx 128$$

Blue Channel $(B = 50)$:

$$Q_B = \left\lfloor \frac{50 - 0}{63.75} \right\rfloor \cdot 63.75 = \lfloor 0.78 \rfloor \cdot 63.75 = 0 \cdot 63.75 = 0$$

3. Step 3: Combine the quantized values.

The quantized RGB pixel becomes

$$Q(i,j) = (Q_R, Q_G, Q_B) = (191, 128, 0)$$

Example Application: In a smart traffic monitoring setup, a 5 MP IP camera with global shutter captures high-speed vehicles at a toll gate. The digital imaging pipeline ensures each frame is crisp, uniformly sampled, and delivered in real time to a backend analytics engine performing license plate recognition.

Surveillance-Specific Considerations:

- integration with VMS (Video Management Systems) and ONVIF standards for multi-vendor interoperability
- optimization of digital signal flow to support sub-streaming for live viewing and full-stream archival for investigation
- onboard preprocessing for motion detection, noise suppression, and privacy masking

These systems offer superior robustness compared to analog, including greater resilience to degradation, enhanced compatibility across platforms, and full support for AI-based analysis. In large-scale deployments, such as citywide CCTV grids, digital imaging forms the core infrastructure that feeds intelligent decision-making engines.

Image Representation

Image representation is fundamental in image processing, and it involves determining how visual information is structured for analysis and processing. In the context of IVA, the choice of image representation impacts everything from compression efficiency to object detection accuracy.

There are three different kinds of images: analog or continuous, digital, and multichannel. Analog images are continuous representations of light intensity or color in a scene. Examples include photographs on film, images displayed on CRT screens, and aerial image. These images can be represented as a continuous function $f(x,y)$, where x and y are spatial coordinates, and $f(x,y)$ gives the intensity value at any point in the image. In contrast, digital images are discrete approximations represented by a grid of pixels, where each pixel stores intensity or color values. Digital images, i.e., monochrome images, have a defined resolution (width × height) and bit depth, with grayscale images typically using 8 bits per pixel and color images using 24 bits (8 bits for each RGB channel).

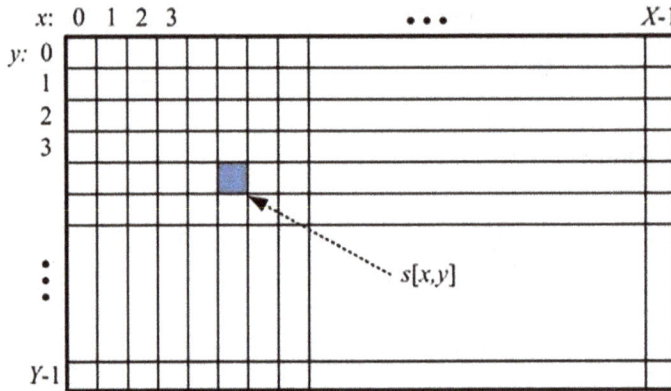

FIGURE 4.5 Two-dimensional X × Y matrix.

To construct a digital image from an analog image, the continuous function $f(x,y)$ is sampled and quantized to form a grid of discrete points called pixels as depicted in Figure 4.5. Each pixel corresponds to a specific location $s[x,y]$ within the grid, where x and y are spatial coordinates representing the horizontal and vertical positions, respectively. The total spatial dimension of the digital image is defined by $X \times Y$, where X is the number of pixels along the width, and Y is the number of pixels along the height. At each pixel $s[x,y]$, the intensity or color value is obtained by sampling the corresponding point in the analog image. The resolution of the digital image, determined by $X \times Y$, directly influences the level of detail captured; higher resolutions provide finer spatial detail. This discrete representation enables precise encoding of visual information, making the image suitable for storage, processing, and analysis using digital systems.

Multichannel images extend digital representation by including multiple layers of information for each pixel. The most common example is an RGB image, composed of three channels (red, green, and blue) that combine to form full-color visuals. Beyond RGB, hyperspectral images capture hundreds of channels, each representing a specific wavelength, and are widely used in remote sensing, agriculture, and environmental monitoring. Multimodal medical images, combining data from modalities like MRI and CT, also exemplify multichannel representation, enabling comprehensive analysis for tasks like tumor detection. While multichannel images provide richer information and support complex tasks, they demand greater storage and computational resources. These representations have revolutionized various fields by offering detailed and multidimensional insights into visual data.

Digital surveillance systems rely on several types of image representations, each optimized for different analytic tasks:

- Binary images: These are the simplest representations, where each pixel is either 0 or 1. Binary images are commonly used in motion masks, intrusion zone detection, and background subtraction logic. They allow quick processing but are unsuitable for detailed analytics.
- Grayscale images: Each pixel holds intensity values between 0 and 255. Grayscale feeds are frequently used for infrared (IR) and night vision footage, as well as for analytics tasks such as motion detection, object counting, and shadow detection in low-light scenes.
- Color (RGB) images: Each pixel comprises three 8-bit channels (Red, Green, Blue). RGB images are the default input for most AI models in surveillance—including face recognition, clothing-based search, and license plate detection—due to their richness in contextual cues.
- Multiband or multichannel images: These extend the representation to include more than three bands (e.g., IR, UV, thermal, and hyperspectral). Though uncommon in traditional CCTV, they are increasingly relevant in perimeter security and critical infrastructure monitoring.

Digital images are constructed from analog sources through three fundamental steps:

1. Scanning converts the optical image from a lens into an electronic signal via image sensors (typically CMOS).
2. Sampling divides the image into a grid of discrete pixels. The number of pixels (e.g., 1920×1080 for Full HD) determines the image resolution, which directly affects analytic granularity.
3. Quantization assigns a fixed numerical value to each pixel based on its light intensity or color. Most systems use 8 bits per channel (256 levels) for balance between quality and bandwidth.

Real-World Considerations:

- Surveillance systems often stream sub-sampled versions (e.g., 480p or 720p) for live view, while preserving full-resolution 1080p or 4K streams for forensic search and analytics.
- IVA platforms may internally convert RGB streams to alternative formats like YUV or HSV to enhance detection under variable lighting.
- Bit depth and color space affect how well AI can separate foreground from background and detect fine-grained features such as facial landmarks.

Example Application: In a city surveillance command center, grayscale substreams are used for real-time motion analytics to save bandwidth, while full-color high-resolution streams are retained for identity verification and face matching. Thermal overlays (an additional band) help detect unauthorized presence in low-light industrial zones. Effective image representation ensures that visual data is both processable and analytically useful, serving as the foundation for every downstream IVA task from segmentation and detection to prediction and alerting.

Scenes with high contrast (e.g., indoor-outdoor transitions and entryways) require WDR (Wide Dynamic Range) technology to preserve both shadow and highlight details. Scenes with high contrast (e.g., indoor-outdoor transitions and entryways) require WDR technology to preserve both shadow and highlight details.

1. True WDR uses multiple exposures in one frame to extend dynamic range.
2. Digital WDR applies gamma correction or histogram stretching to boost image contrast post-capture.

Example Application: For buildings with glass doors, WDR enables analytics to identify subjects entering from sunlight without silhouetting.

IMAGE ENHANCEMENT

Image enhancement refers to a collection of techniques used to improve the visual quality and analytic readiness of surveillance footage. Unlike traditional photography, where aesthetic appeal may be the focus, image enhancement in intelligent video analytics (IVA) aims to optimize video feeds for machine-based interpretation. Enhancements are designed to ensure that features relevant to object detection, facial recognition, or behavioral analysis remain clear and consistent under a wide range of conditions.

Several challenges commonly affect surveillance image quality:

1. Noise: Introduced through low-light capture, sensor quality, or transmission compression, noise can obscure fine details, reduce edge clarity, and lead to false detections.
2. Improper brightness levels: Underexposed or overexposed video can hide subjects or key features, undermining face or license plate recognition accuracy.
3. Blurriness: Resulting from poor focus or compression artifacts, blur reduces feature sharpness required for re-identification or detection models.
4. Lens defects and motion blur: Chromatic aberrations or fast object motion during low shutter speeds introduce distortion, particularly detrimental for vehicle analytics.
5. Geometric distortion: Fisheye or wide-angle lenses can warp the spatial layout of scenes, complicating person tracking or object localization.

To address these issues, image enhancement techniques fall into two main categories:

- Spatial domain techniques operate directly on pixels using filters and intensity mapping.
  - Contrast stretching expands dynamic range, especially useful in foggy or dim indoor scenes.
  - Gamma correction adjusts brightness using power-law transformation.
  - Smoothing (blurring) reduces random noise using Gaussian or median filters.
  - Sharpening enhances edges using Laplacian, Sobel, or unsharp masking, which is important for motion analytics and shape detection.

- Frequency domain techniques modify an image's frequency components to emphasize or suppress features.
    - Fourier transform separates high and low-frequency features for targeted enhancement.
    - High-pass filtering highlights fine details such as vehicle license text or facial landmarks.
    - Wavelet transform decomposes images at multiple scales, ideal for balancing enhancement across textured and smooth regions.

These methods are foundational for IVA systems that must operate in adverse environments while maintaining high detection accuracy. From optimizing visibility in nighttime traffic footage to clarifying distorted frames during motion events, image enhancement plays a vital role in preparing footage for downstream AI modules.

Imaging Challenges in Low-Light Conditions

These challenges were introduced in Chapter 3, where we discussed camera hardware specifications and field deployment considerations. Here, we revisit these challenges from an image processing perspective, focusing on enhancement strategies to restore visual clarity in low-light scenes and improve the performance of AI analytics engines.

Key Processing-Oriented Challenges:

- Low contrast between subjects and background
- Excessive noise affecting motion detection and facial clarity
- Motion blur during low shutter-speed recording
- Color shifts or grayscale fallback under poor lighting

Processing-Based Mitigation Approaches:

- Apply histogram equalization or adaptive contrast enhancement.
- Use spatial denoising filters (median, Gaussian) or temporal denoising in VMS.
- Combine motion deblurring algorithms with object stabilization pipelines.
- Integrate IR-enhanced streams with contrast boosting for grayscale scenes.

For a full treatment of sensor-level considerations (e.g., IR illumination and wide dynamic range), refer back to Chapter 3.

Example Application: In a tunnel monitoring scenario, image enhancement pipelines help restore license plate clarity using contrast stretching and noise filtering, even when captured with mid-range CMOS sensors in low ambient light.

IMAGE COMPRESSION

While hardware-level decisions on resolution, frame rate, and exposure were discussed in Chapter 3, this section explores how image enhancement and compression algorithms downstream preserve analytic fidelity even under suboptimal conditions.

Image compression and signal optimization are at the heart of scalable video analytics infrastructure. While the resolution, frame rate, and bandwidth settings originate from camera configuration, it is the downstream image processing and compression techniques that ensure footage remains analytically usable despite aggressive resource constraints.

Compression reduces video file size while aiming to maintain visual quality for both human interpretation and machine analytics. The process removes three key types of redundancy:

• Spatial redundancy: pixels with similar values in close proximity
• Psycho-visual redundancy: visual information that is imperceptible to the human eye
• Coding redundancy: inefficient data representation, often using more bits than needed

Compression algorithms fall into two primary categories:

• Lossless compression preserves the original pixel values entirely. Used in regulated industries, forensics, or when image fidelity is paramount. Formats: PNG, TIFF, and GIF.
• Lossy compression removes less critical image data to achieve higher compression ratios. Ideal for live streaming, real-time analytics, and storage efficiency. Formats: JPEG, H.264, H.265, WebP, and HEIF.

Table 4.1 provides an overview of common image compression file formats, their compression types, applications, and key features.

TABLE 4.1 The common image compression file formats and their application

File Format and Extension	Compression Type	Application	Feature
JPEG (.jpg, .jpeg)	Lossy	Photography, Web images, and digital cameras	High compression ratio, suitable for natural images; may introduce artifacts at high compression
JPEG2000 (.jp2, .j2k)	Lossy or Lossless	Medical imaging, digital cinema, and satellite imagery	Wavelet-based compression; supports both lossy and lossless compression; better for detailed images
PNG (.png)	Lossless	Web graphics, logos, and images requiring transparency	Preserves image quality; supports transparency; larger file size than JPEG
GIF (.gif)	Lossless	Animated graphics, simple images with limited colors	Limited to 256 colors; supports animation
TIFF (.tiff, .tif)	Lossy or Lossless	Professional photography, publishing, and medical imaging	High-quality image preservation; supports multiple layers and transparency
HEIF/HEIC (.heif, .heic)	Lossy or Lossless	Smartphone photography (used in iOS devices), modern web applications	High compression efficiency; better quality than JPEG at the same file size
WEBP (.webp)	Lossy or Lossless	Web images and modern web applications	Designed for web use; better compression than JPEG and PNG

(Continued)

TABLE 4.1 Continued

File Format and Extension	Compression Type	Application	Feature
EPS (.eps)	Lossy or Lossless	Printing and publishing	Supports vector and raster data; scalable without quality loss
BMP (.bmp)	Uncompressed or Lossless	Basic image storage, graphics editing	Large file size, simple structure, no compression by default, but can support lossless compression

The image compression process consists of two primary stages. The first stage involves converting a raw image into a compressed format, reducing its file size while retaining essential details. This step is known as *encoding*, and the software responsible for this function is called an *encoder*. The second stage reconstructs the compressed image back into an uncompressed format, ensuring it remains visually recognizable. This step is referred to as *decoding*, and the software performing this task is known as a *decoder*. A system that integrates both an encoder and a decoder is called a *codec*, a term derived from "coding" and "decoding."

The detail about codec is described below.

1. Encoding Process (Compression Stage):

    The encoder is responsible for compressing the image by reducing redundancy and optimizing data representation. The encoding process follows these main steps:

    • Transformation: The image is converted from the spatial domain to a different domain, such as the frequency domain using the Discrete Cosine Transform (DCT) or Wavelet Transform. This step helps separate important image components from redundant information.
    • Quantization: The transformed image coefficients are mapped to a finite set of discrete values, reducing precision and further eliminating insignificant details (especially in lossy compression). This step significantly contributes to reducing file size.
    • Entropy Encoding: The quantized data is further compressed using entropy coding techniques such as Huffman coding or Arithmetic coding, which replace frequently occurring data with shorter binary codes to optimize storage efficiency.

    At the end of the encoding process, a compressed bitstream is generated, which represents the image in a more compact format (e.g., JPEG, PNG, or WebP).

2. Decoding Process (Decompression Stage):

    The decoder reconstructs the image from the compressed bitstream. This process reverses the encoding steps and restores the image as closely as possible to its original form. The steps include the following:

    • Entropy Decoding: The compressed bitstream is decoded back into quantized values using the same entropy decoding methods applied during encoding.
    • Dequantization: The quantized values are converted back to their approximate original form, though with some loss of precision in the case of lossy compression.

3. Inverse Transformation: The dequantized data is transformed back into the spatial domain using an inverse transform (e.g., Inverse Discrete Cosine Transform (IDCT) or Inverse Wavelet Transform), reconstructing the image's pixel representation.

The output of the decoder is a reconstructed image. If lossless compression was used, the image is identical to the original. If lossy compression was used, some data is permanently lost, but the image remains visually similar to the original.

Smart codecs (e.g., H.265 and AV1) further support several intelligent encoding techniques designed to optimize storage without compromising analytic accuracy:

- ROI Encoding (Region of Interest): Smart codecs can allocate a higher bit rate and lower compression to specific regions within the frame—such as moving persons, license plates, or facial zones—while aggressively compressing static background areas. This is especially useful in IVA settings where only certain parts of a frame contain critical intelligence. For example, in a traffic surveillance camera, the codec can retain full clarity on license plates and reduce the bit rate on the surrounding road surface.
- Scene-Adaptive Bitrate Control: This feature adjusts compression dynamically based on scene complexity. Low-motion scenes (e.g., empty hallways) are encoded with higher compression, while high-motion or complex scenes (e.g., crowds or vehicle intersections) are preserved with lower compression and higher fidelity. This ensures optimal use of storage and transmission bandwidth without manual intervention.
- Sub-Streaming: Many smart video systems generate multiple resolution streams from the same source. A lower resolution stream (e.g., 480p or 720p) is used for real-time operator viewing on low-bandwidth links, while a higher resolution stream (e.g., 1080p or 4K) is archived for forensic search, object re-identification, or advanced analytics. This dual-streaming approach enables efficient monitoring without sacrificing evidentiary quality.

IVA systems also rely on advanced post-compression enhancement to maintain analytic reliability, especially when working with compressed or degraded video inputs:

- Super-Resolution: When input video is streamed at low resolution due to bandwidth limitations or camera constraints, AI-based super-resolution algorithms reconstruct finer details from the limited input. This technique boosts the visibility of facial features, license plates, or small objects—enabling reliable recognition from suboptimal footage.
- Frame Interpolation: For scenes recorded at low frame rates (e.g., 10 fps to save bandwidth), frame interpolation techniques can estimate and insert intermediate frames. This smooths motion, supports better tracking, and reduces the likelihood of dropped detections caused by rapid movement or object occlusion.
- Artifact Suppression: Aggressive compression often introduces artifacts such as macroblocking, mosquito noise, and ringing edges. Image processing filters, especially AI-trained models, can selectively reduce these distortions while preserving important visual features like edges, shapes, and texture. This significantly improves the accuracy of downstream analytics such as facial embedding, motion detection, and shape-based alerts.

By intelligently combining compression with enhancement and prioritization, modern video systems achieve a balance of fidelity, efficiency, and analytic reliability.

IMAGE TRANSFORMATION FOR INTELLIGENT VIDEO ANALYTICS

In intelligent video analytics (IVA), *image transformation* refers to a set of techniques used to modify the geometry, intensity, or structural layout of images to enable better alignment, correction, and interpretation. Unlike enhancement or compression, which focus on improving perceptual quality or storage efficiency, transformation is concerned with spatial and structural manipulation. These operations are especially critical when working across multiple cameras, viewpoints, or time frames, where image alignment and perspective correction are necessary to achieve reliable detection and tracking.

Image transformations are fundamental in IVA applications such as the following:

1. *Multi-camera tracking* across overlapping or non-overlapping fields of view that ensures consistent identification of the same person or vehicle across different camera views (Figure 4.6) is crucial for large-scale surveillance in places like airports, malls, or smart cities. In overlapping views, the object identity is handed off using shared visual zones, aided by homography, re-identification (Re-ID), and spatiotemporal matching. In non-overlapping views, deep learning-based Re-ID models match appearances across time and space using contextual cues. This enables seamless monitoring, blind spot reduction, and advanced analytics like route reconstruction and anomaly detection.

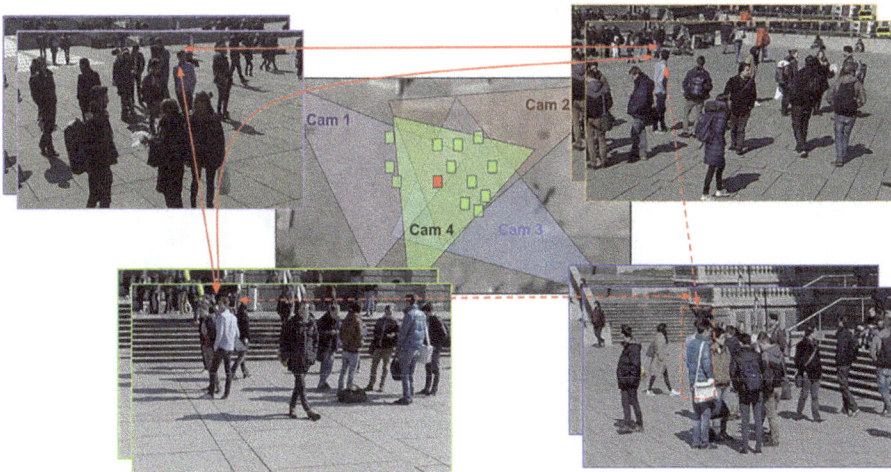

FIGURE 4.6 Multi-camera tracking (Source: *https://www.researchgate.net/publication/363908522_LMGP_Lifted_Multicut_Meets_Geometry_Projections_for_Multi-Camera_Multi-Object_Tracking*).

2. *Bird's Eye View reconstruction* for crowd flow or vehicle movement mapping transforms angled camera footage into a top-down perspective, enabling a clearer spatial analysis of people or vehicle movements. By applying geometric transformations and camera calibration, IVA systems project detected objects onto a ground plane, making it easier to track flow patterns, monitor density, and generate heatmaps. BEV is essential for crowd analytics, queue monitoring, and traffic behavior mapping in complex environments like intersections (Figure 4.7), transit hubs, or retail spaces.

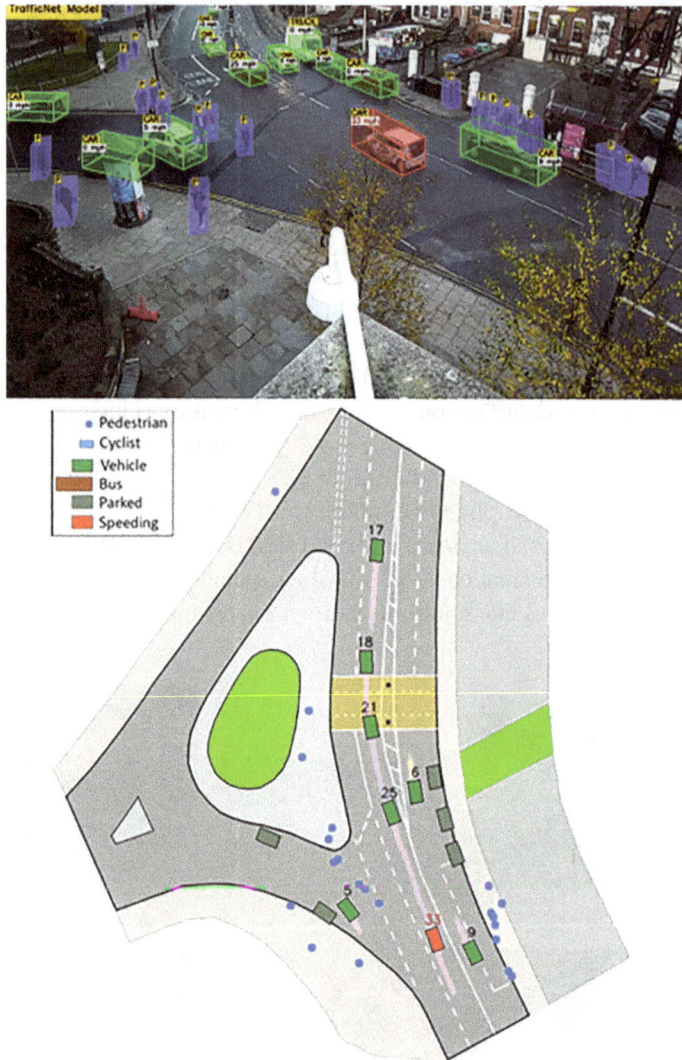

FIGURE 4.7 Bird-Eye View (Source: *https://arxiv.org/pdf/2109.09165*).

3. *Camera calibration and rectification* is for correcting lens distortion such as barrel or fish-eye effects; it is performed by estimating intrinsic parameters like focal length, optical center, and distortion coefficients. This process ensures that straight lines in the real world remain straight in the image, improving spatial accuracy for analytics. Rectification is essential for reliable object detection, distance estimation, and multi-camera alignment in IVA systems (Figure 4.8).

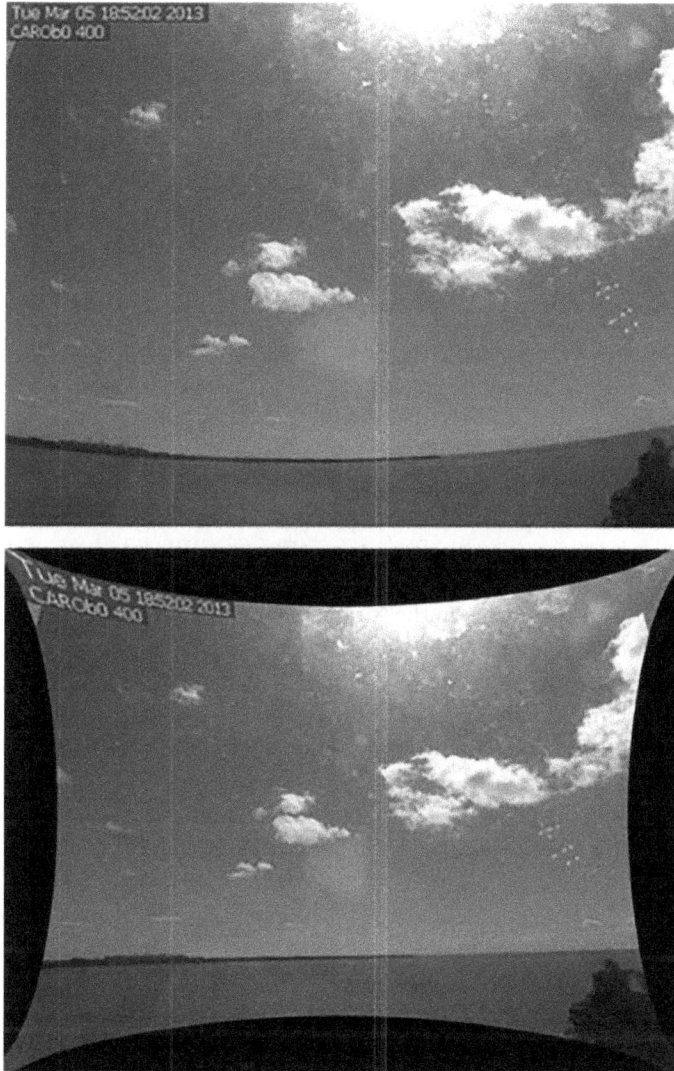

FIGURE 4.8 Camera rectification (Source: *https://www.researchgate.net/publication/288997861_Stereophotogrammetry_of_Oceanic_Clouds*).

4. *Perspective warping* transforms images captured from angled or skewed viewpoints into a normalized, top-down or frontal view using projective geometry. This technique enables consistent object size, shape, and orientation—critical for accurate detection, counting, and heatmap generation in IVA, especially in scenarios with oblique camera angles like hallways, lobbies, or entrances (Figure 4-9).

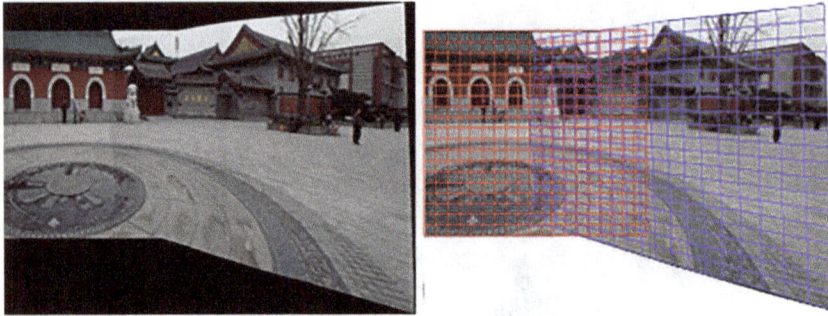

FIGURE 4-9 Perspective warping (Source: https://arxiv.org/pdf/1605.05019).

Transformations can be classified into the following categories:

1. Geometric Transformations

These modify the spatial relationship of pixels in an image without changing the content itself. Common geometric transformations (Figure 4.10) include the following:

- *Translation* shifts an image in the X or Y direction. Used in motion stabilization or when aligning frames from jittery cameras.
- *Rotation* rotates the entire image by a specified angle. Useful in overhead surveillance to normalize orientation.
- *Scaling* resizes an image up or down. Often applied in zoom functions or when unifying resolution between camera feeds.
- *Shearing* skews the image by shifting rows or columns relative to each other. Rare in surveillance but applicable in forensic image matching.

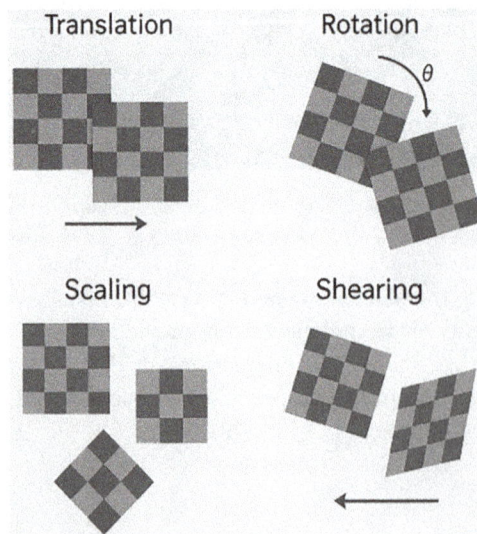

FIGURE 4.10 Geometric transformation.

2. Affine and Projective Transformations
    • Affine transformations preserve straight lines and parallelism. Widely used in IVA for aligning video frames or reprojecting scenes in multi-camera layouts (Figure 4.11).
    • Projective (perspective) transformations enable full viewpoint normalization by correcting perspective distortion, which is essential when analyzing slanted or oblique views (e.g., entrances and stairways).

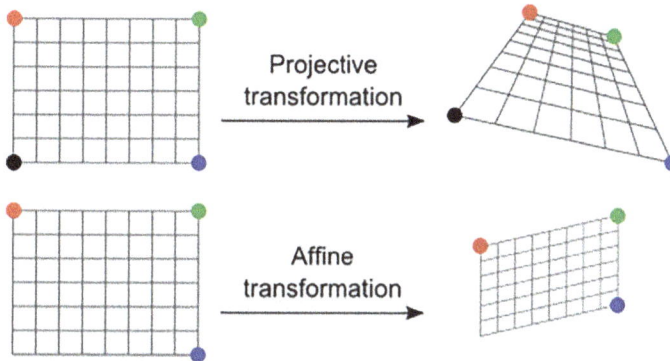

FIGURE 4.11 Affine and projective transformation.

Use Case: In a mall, security uses projective transformation to convert oblique camera angles into top-down maps, making it easier to perform real-time people counting and heatmap generation.

3. Intensity Transformations

    These change the pixel brightness values rather than their positions:
    • Histogram equalization enhances contrast by spreading out intensity distribution. Critical in indoor environments with poor lighting.
    • Log and power-law adjustments tailor brightness for dark or overly bright scenes.

4. Frequency and Wavelet Transformations
    • Fourier transform converts spatial pixel data into frequency components. Helps in filtering repetitive noise or enhancing edge content.
    • Wavelet transform decomposes images at multiple resolutions, suitable for scalable feature extraction in tasks like face detection or vehicle recognition under low resolution.

5. **Morphological Transformations**

    These are applied to binary or segmented images to refine object boundaries:
    • Dilation and erosion adjust shape size by adding or removing pixels from object borders. Useful for noise cleaning and contour smoothing.
    • Opening and closing are compound operations that improve blob detection and foreground object integrity.

Example Application: In a smart intersection, traffic cameras feed multiple perspectives into an IVA engine. Affine transformations align feeds from different angles, followed by image stitching to create a composite top-down map. This unified frame is used for real-time vehicle tracking and trajectory prediction.

Ultimately, image transformation in video analytics enables spatial normalization and consistency across time and sensors. When deployed correctly, it strengthens AI reliability in complex environments with varied camera positions, field distortions, and lighting asymmetries.

Compression (especially under a low bit rate) can introduce artifacts such as blocking, blurring, or ghosting, all of which negatively impact AI model accuracy.

- Impact on detection: Facial recognition and object tracking are especially sensitive to edge degradation and noise.
- Mitigation: Use smart encoding profiles (ROI encoding) to avoid excessive compression in critical zones.

IMAGE DETECTION

Image detection is a core capability in Intelligent Video Analytics (IVA) that enables surveillance systems to identify and localize specific entities, such as people, vehicles, bags, or license plates, within video frames. Unlike traditional image classification that labels an entire frame, detection focuses on extracting spatial coordinates (bounding boxes) for each object of interest, allowing for downstream tasks like tracking, counting, behavior recognition, and rule violation alerts.

In modern surveillance environments, object detection is used in real-time for applications such as the following:

- Intrusion detection: identifying unauthorized entry into restricted areas
- Facial recognition: localizing and analyzing faces for identity verification or watchlist matching
- Traffic monitoring: detecting vehicles for flow analysis, speed estimation, or violation capture
- Left object detection: identifying unattended items in public spaces

Detection systems in IVA typically rely on deep learning-based models due to their accuracy, speed, and robustness across varying lighting, viewpoints, and occlusions. Some of the most commonly used deep learning models include the following:

- YOLO (You Only Look Once): This is a real-time object detector that processes entire frames in a single pass; widely used in edge deployments.
- SSD (Single Shot Detector): This balances detection speed and accuracy by predicting bounding boxes from feature maps at multiple scales.
- Faster R-CNN: This is more accurate but a computationally heavier model using region proposal networks for refined detection; ideal for forensic or high-end analytics.

Each model outputs a set of bounding boxes, class labels, and confidence scores per frame. These outputs feed into further processing pipelines such as the following:

- Object tracking: maintain object identity across frames
- Event triggering: raise alerts when detections match predefined conditions
- Heatmaps and behavior maps: accumulate object presence data over time for spatial analysis

These techniques enhance the robustness and accuracy of image detection, making it suitable for high-performance applications such as self-driving cars and facial recognition systems. Figure 4.12 illustrates the process of CNN-based object detection, specifically following the Region-based Convolutional Neural Network (R-CNN) approach. It consists of four main steps:

1. Input image: The process begins with an input image that contains objects of interest, such as a person riding a horse. The primary objective is to detect and classify the objects present in the image accurately. This involves analyzing different regions of the image to determine whether they contain specific objects.

2. Extract region proposals (~2k): Rather than examining the entire image at once, the algorithm first generates approximately 2,000 region proposals using a technique such as Selective Search. These proposed regions serve as potential locations where objects might be present within the image. Each region is enclosed within a bounding box (highlighted in yellow), which helps focus the analysis on specific areas of interest. By narrowing down the search space, this approach improves efficiency and accuracy in detecting and classifying objects.

3. Compute CNN features: Once the regions of interest are extracted, each region is resized (warped) to a fixed dimension to ensure consistency in processing. These resized regions are then fed into a Convolutional Neural Network (CNN), which analyzes them to extract essential features such as edges, textures, and patterns.

4. Classify regions: The extracted features are fed into a classifier, such as a Support Vector Machine (SVM) or a softmax layer, to determine the presence of specific objects. The classifier assigns labels to each region (e.g., "car," "cat," or "dog") and determines whether an object is present. In this example, the classifier correctly identifies a "person" in one of the regions while rejecting other categories.

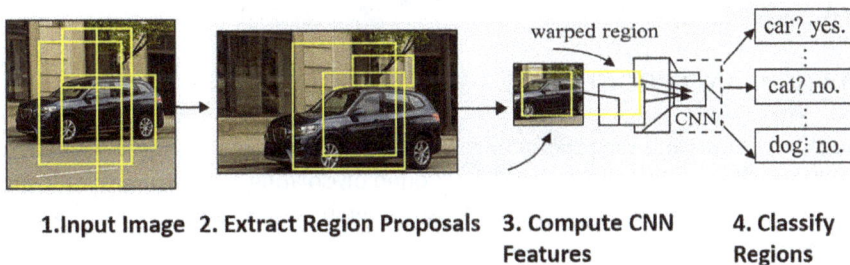

1.Input Image 2. Extract Region Proposals 3. Compute CNN Features 4. Classify Regions

FIGURE 4.12 Object detection system using R-CNN (Source: *https://arxiv.org/pdf/1311.2524*).

Mathematically, image detection often involves filtering operations, feature extraction, and classification functions. For example, edge detection can be represented using the gradient magnitude of an image:

$$G(x,y) = \sqrt{(I_x)^2 + (I_y)^2}$$

where I_x and I_y are the derivatives of the image intensity $I(x,y)$ along the x and y directions. Another common approach is convolution in CNN-based detection, expressed as

$$f(x,y) = \sum_i \sum_j I(i,j).K(x-i,y-j)$$

where $I(i,j)$. represents the input image, and $K(x-i,y-j)$ is the convolution kernel that detects specific features. The illustration of image detection using a CNN-based detection model can be described below.

- Input image: The process starts with an input image containing multiple objects.
- Feature extraction (convolutional layers): A convolutional neural network (CNN) extracts features such as edges, textures, and object parts.
- Region proposal: The model generates regions of interest (RoIs) that likely contain objects.
- Classification and localization: Fully connected layers classify objects and refine their bounding box coordinates.
- Output (detected objects): The final output consists of bounding boxes around detected objects with their class labels.

Deep learning-based methods utilize bounding box regression to locate objects, typically represented as

$$L_{box} = \sum_i (x_i - \hat{x}_i)^2 + (y_i - \hat{y}_i)^2 + (\omega_i - \hat{\omega}_i)^2 + (h_i - \hat{h}_i)^2$$

where $(x_i, y_i, \omega_i, h_i)$ are the predicted bounding box parameters, and $(\hat{x}_i, \hat{y}_i, \hat{\omega}_i, \hat{h}_i)$ are the ground truth values. These mathematical models help optimize detection accuracy by minimizing errors and improving feature localization.

SEGMENTATION AND PROCESSING

Image segmentation is the process of partitioning an image into multiple meaningful regions, often distinguishing objects from their background or isolating specific areas for analysis. In the context of Intelligent Video Analytics (IVA), segmentation plays a foundational role in enabling precise localization, identification, and contextual understanding of visual scenes. Whether it is isolating a human silhouette in a crowded intersection or separating parked vehicles from road markings, segmentation sets the stage for higher-level AI tasks such as classification, tracking, and behavior recognition.

Deep Learning-Based Segmentation Techniques

Traditional threshold-based and region-growing methods have been largely superseded by deep learning models due to their superior accuracy and robustness. Important architectures in modern IVA deployments include the following:

- Fully Convolutional Network (FCN): the first deep learning architecture designed for pixel-wise segmentation

- U-Net: popular in both medical imaging and surveillance for its encoder-decoder structure and ability to work with small datasets
- DeepLabV3+: incorporates atrous convolutions and spatial pyramid pooling to capture context at multiple scales—ideal for outdoor scenes and dense environments
- Vision Transformers (ViTs) and Segment Anything Model (SAM): leverage attention mechanisms for flexible, prompt-based segmentation across categories and environments

Applications in Video Analytics

- People masking and pose analysis segment individual persons for tracking, pose estimation, and privacy masking.
- Vehicle segmentation separates vehicles from roadways, enabling better license plate reading and trajectory analysis.
- Crowd and queue detection tracks grouped individuals, determines queue lengths, and triggers alerts when density thresholds are crossed.
- Intrusion detection and boundary crossing defines scene regions such as perimeters, ensuring that only segmented foreground objects crossing into these zones trigger alerts.

Post-Processing and Refinement

Following the initial segmentation, post-processing methods enhance the output for better operational use:

- Conditional Random Fields (CRFs) improve boundary sharpness and remove noise.
- Graph cuts and morphological operators are used to clean edges and enforce object integrity.
- Feature embeddings involve deep features from the segmentation mask that can be used to classify object type, behavior, or match across cameras.

Advanced Models and Learning Strategies

- Self-supervised and semi-supervised segmentation reduce labeling burden by leveraging large unlabeled datasets.
- Swin transformers and Mask2Former offer state-of-the-art performance by combining convolutional and transformer approaches with multi-scale awareness.
- GAN-based segmentation: Generative Adversarial Networks can produce refined masks by learning the distribution of real versus predicted segmentations. A generator creates masks, and a discriminator critiques them improving mask quality iteratively.

Example Application: In a shopping mall, IVA systems use SAM or U-Net to segment each customer walking through the entrance. These segmented masks feed into a re-identification pipeline that tracks the same individual across multiple non-overlapping cameras while avoiding distractions like mannequins or reflections (Figure 4.13). Simultaneously, segmentation allows the system to detect objects left behind near seating zones by comparing foreground object maps across time.

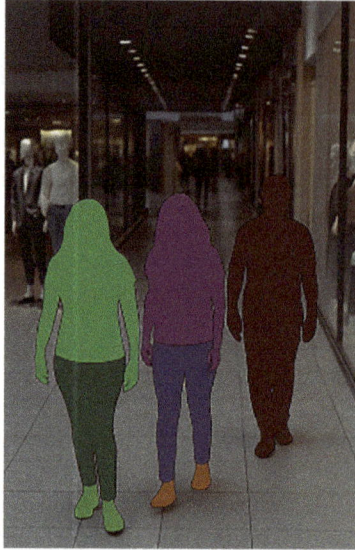

FIGURE 4.13 Image segmentation application.

Segmentation is thus not just a preprocessing step, but a critical enabler for intelligent video systems ensuring that AI agents interpret the world with spatial precision and contextual clarity.

SUMMARY

We have outlined the core principles and practical techniques of image processing as they apply to Intelligent Video Analytics. We contextualized these concepts within real-time surveillance systems, highlighting how each technique, from enhancement to segmentation, contributes directly to operational decision-making.

We began by examining image representation, including how spatial resolution, color depth, and image structure affect analytic reliability. We continued into enhancement techniques such as noise reduction, contrast adjustment, and histogram equalization critical for ensuring image clarity under varying environmental conditions. We also explored geometric and projective transformations used to align multi-camera feeds, correct perspective distortion, and normalize views for trajectory mapping and behavioral understanding. Compression and optimization strategies were discussed not only from a storage perspective but with attention to how codec design and bitrate control influence detection accuracy and analytic robustness. More advanced topics, such as object detection and semantic segmentation, were presented as essential capabilities for intelligent surveillance, crowd analytics, and anomaly detection.

We concluded by emphasizing that modern IVA relies on a symbiotic relationship between hardware-level imaging and AI-driven interpretation. Techniques such as GAN-based refinement, attention-driven segmentation, and real-time enhancement are not merely supportive—they are essential components of scalable, trustworthy, and intelligent visual systems.

As surveillance moves toward autonomous decision-making, the integration of image processing with deep learning models is the foundation on which future smart cities and security systems will be built.

CHAPTER 5

DEEP LEARNING AND COMPUTER VISION FUNDAMENTALS

In Chapters 1 through 4, we laid the foundation for understanding CCTV systems, network infrastructure, and basic image processing pipelines, the hardware and signal-level layers that form the backbone of any modern surveillance system. However, in real-world Intelligent Video Analytics (IVA), infrastructure alone is not enough. What transforms raw video into actionable insights is the application of deep learning and computer vision. This chapter is an important transition, from capturing and transmitting visual data, to interpreting and understanding it using AI-powered models. Here, we discuss the essential deep learning components that power intelligent detection systems: Convolutional Neural Networks (CNNs) for spatial feature extraction, activation functions, pooling strategies, and fully connected layers. We explore how these models identify patterns such as humans, vehicles, and behaviors directly from raw footage.

The chapter also introduces advanced architectures like Recurrent Neural Networks (RNNs) and LSTMs, which are capable of modeling sequences across time, critical for understanding behavior, motion, and anomalies in video. We place special emphasis on transfer learning, a practical strategy that allows IVA developers to build accurate models without massive datasets. Real-world examples such as helmet detection on construction sites and PPE compliance in industrial zones demonstrate how pre-trained models can be repurposed with minimal data.

By the end of this chapter, you will have a clear, IVA-specific understanding of how deep learning enables systems to detect, classify, and respond to what cameras see, completing the journey from hardware to high-level visual intelligence.

DEEP LEARNING BASIC

Deep learning is the foundational engine powering modern Intelligent Video Analytics (IVA) systems. *Deep learning* is a specialized subset of machine learning that trains multi-layered artificial neural networks to learn complex visual patterns and semantic features directly from video data. This eliminates the need for handcrafted features and rules, which were traditionally used in early surveillance systems. In the context of IVA, deep learning enables a wide range of automated visual understanding tasks such as person detection, vehicle tracking, facial recognition, suspicious behavior detection, crowd analytics, and license plate recognition. These tasks rely on the ability of deep networks, particularly Convolutional Neural Networks (CNNs) and Transformer-based Vision Models, to extract spatial and temporal features from video streams.

Unlike traditional video surveillance that relies on motion sensors or static thresholds, deep learning models continuously learn and adapt from video frames, identifying context-aware patterns such as loitering, fall detection, or unauthorized entry with high accuracy.

Deep learning models deployed in IVA systems are typically optimized for real-time inference, often integrated into edge devices, NVRs, or central command servers, depending on latency, bandwidth, and cost constraints. The combination of hierarchical learning and end-to-end training pipelines allows these systems to adapt across diverse environments, retail, airports, highways, stadiums, and smart cities, delivering intelligent and proactive surveillance (Figure 5.1).

FIGURE 5.1 Computer vision surveillance system (Source: *Nodeflux*).

The Neuron and Perceptron

To understand the mechanics of deep learning in video analytics, we must start with its inspiration: the biological neuron. In the human brain, neurons receive and transmit signals through dendrites and axons, enabling complex cognitive functions like perception and decision-making. This biological structure inspired the development of artificial neurons, the basic building block of deep learning models. The *perceptron*, introduced in the 1950s, was the first mathematical model of a neuron capable of learning from data. It receives multiple input signals, multiplies them by learned weights, sums them, and applies an activation function to decide the output, typically a binary decision. In video analytics, this simple structure evolves into deep stacks of artificial neurons, where each layer extracts progressively abstract features from video frames. The early layers might detect edges or textures, while deeper layers capture complex semantics such as faces, moving objects, violent gestures, or abandoned luggage.

The significance of the perceptron is not in its simplicity but in how it laid the groundwork for modern deep learning architectures, such as

- convolutional layers, which scan video frames to identify visual patterns like objects, people, or scenes
- recurrent layers or temporal modules, which learn time-based patterns such as motion, trajectory, or anomalous behavior
- attention mechanisms, which dynamically focus on key regions in a frame or across frames, improving recognition under occlusion or crowd scenarios

While the biological neuron operates via electrical signals, the artificial neuron operates on vectorized pixel values, enabling machines to interpret and act on visual data, a cornerstone capability of any intelligent video system (Figure 5.2).

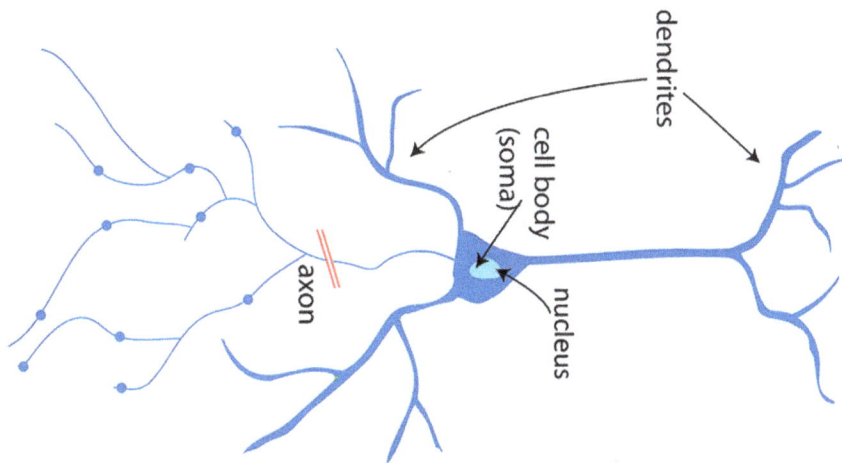

FIGURE 5.2 A biological neuron (Source: *https://qbi.uq.edu.au/brain/brain-anatomy/what-neuron*).

The perceptron is the simplest form of an artificial neuron, designed to mimic the signal processing behavior of biological neurons. While rudimentary on its own, it forms the computational core of more complex architectures that power IVA systems today. In the context of IVA, perceptrons serve as the first mathematical abstraction capable of learning from pixel-based inputs, such as video frames, to make binary decisions, for instance, whether or not a human is present in a scene (Figure 5.3).

A perceptron receives multiple input values, such as pixel intensities, motion vectors, or bounding box features, each of which is multiplied by a learned weight. These are summed together with a bias term, and the result is passed through an activation function to produce a decision output:

$$y = f\left(\sum_{i=1}^{n} \omega_i x_i + b\right)$$

Figure 5.2 represents a single-layer perceptron model, which follows the mathematical formulation.

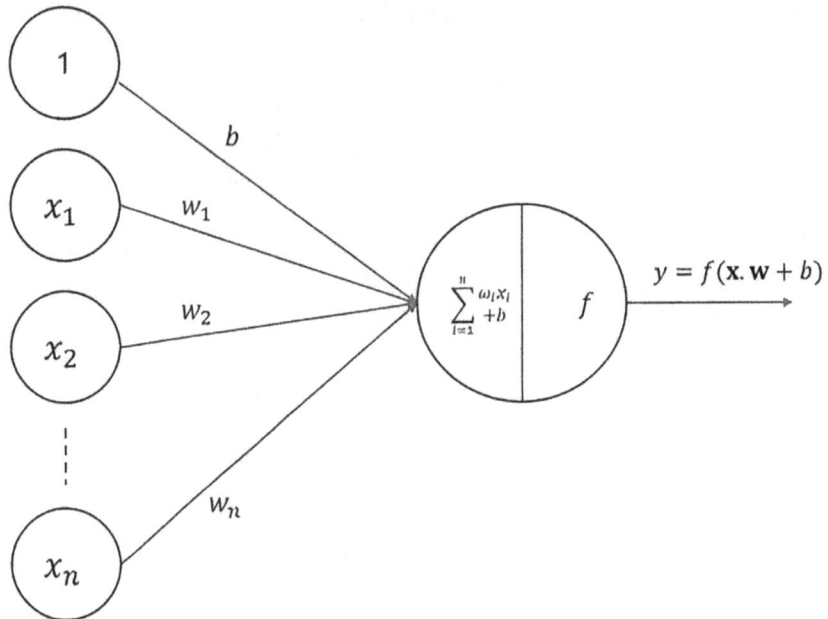

FIGURE 5.3 The perceptron.

The figure illustrates how a perceptron processes multiple inputs and applies an activation function to generate an output. The final output is given by $y = f(\mathbf{x}.\mathbf{w} + b)$ or $y = f(\mathbf{w}^T\mathbf{x} + b)$. It shows the vectorized computation of the perceptron, where all inputs and weights are processed in a dot product operation, followed by an activation function.

The perceptron forms the fundamental building block of more advanced neural networks. However, to accurately perform classification tasks, it must learn to adjust its weights and bias based on training data. This learning process is governed by the perceptron learning algorithm, which iteratively updates the model parameters to improve classification accuracy. The *perceptron learning algorithm* is a supervised learning method that enables the perceptron to update its parameters iteratively to find the best decision boundary for separating different classes. The perceptron learning process can be described as follows.

Step 1: Initialize weights and bias.

• Initialize weight vector **w** and bias b with small random values or zeros.
• Choose a learning rate η (typically a small positive value, e.g., 0.01).

Step 2: For each training example, compute the output.
For each training sample (x, y):

• Compute the weighted sum:

$$z = \mathbf{w}^T\mathbf{x} + b$$

- Apply the activation function f(z):

$$\hat{y} = f(z)$$

- where $\hat{y}$ is the predicted output.

Step 3: Update the weights and bias based on error.

If the prediction $\hat{y}$ does not match the true label y, update the weights and bias using the following update rule:

$$\mathbf{w} \leftarrow \mathbf{w} + \eta(y - \hat{y})\mathbf{x}$$
$$b \leftarrow b + \eta(y - \hat{y})$$

Where

- $\eta \rightarrow$ Learning rate. Its function is to controls how much weights are updated per iteration.
- $(y - \hat{y}) \rightarrow$ Error term, where: If the prediction is correct, no update is needed. If incorrect, the weight and bias are adjusted to reduce future errors.

Step 4: Repeat until convergence is reached.

- Repeat Steps 2 and 3 for all training samples.
- Continue iterating until all samples are correctly classified or a maximum number of iterations is reached.

The perceptron learning algorithm works well when data is linearly separable, for example, when detecting objects with distinct appearances or lighting. However, in real-world video analytics, data is rarely that simple. Overlapping objects, occlusions, varying camera angles, and lighting changes often create non-linear patterns.

In such cases, a single-layer perceptron fails to converge, it cannot find a decision boundary. To overcome this, modern IVA systems rely on the following:

- Multilayer perceptrons (MLPs) have hidden layers and non-linear activations (e.g., ReLU, Sigmoid), enabling the network to learn complex features such as abnormal behavior in a crowd or vehicle types in traffic.
- Kernel methods (like in Support Vector Machines) map inputs into higher-dimensional spaces, though less commonly used today in deep learning pipelines due to scalability.

These advancements allow models to handle complex, noisy, and non-linearly separable video data, a critical requirement for robust video surveillance and intelligent decision-making in smart environments.

Neural Network

Neural networks began with the perceptron in 1958, but its inability to solve non-linear problems (like XOR) limited early progress. The breakthrough came with Feedforward Neural Networks (FNN), where information flows layer by layer, from input to output, enabling the learning of complex patterns.

In IVA, this architecture allows systems to detect motion, identify faces, and classify objects by stacking layers that learn increasingly abstract features, from edges to full object categories.

The revival in the 1980s through multilayer perceptrons (MLPs) and backpropagation enabled deeper learning (Figure 5.4). Later, Convolutional Neural Networks (CNN) and transformers brought major advances in analyzing spatial and temporal patterns in video, making real-time intelligent surveillance a practical reality (Figure 5.5).

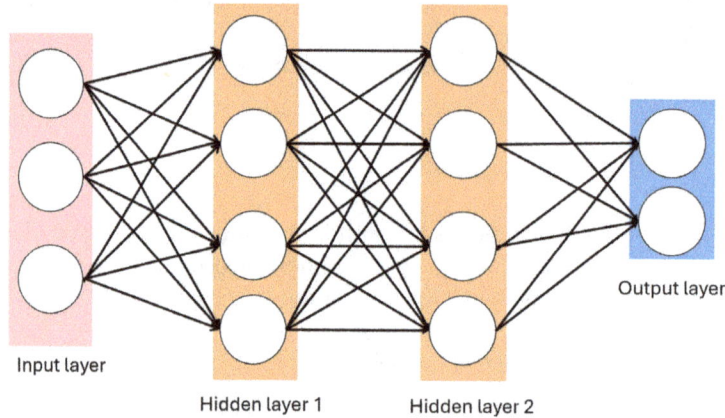

FIGURE 5.4 Four layer feedforward neural network.

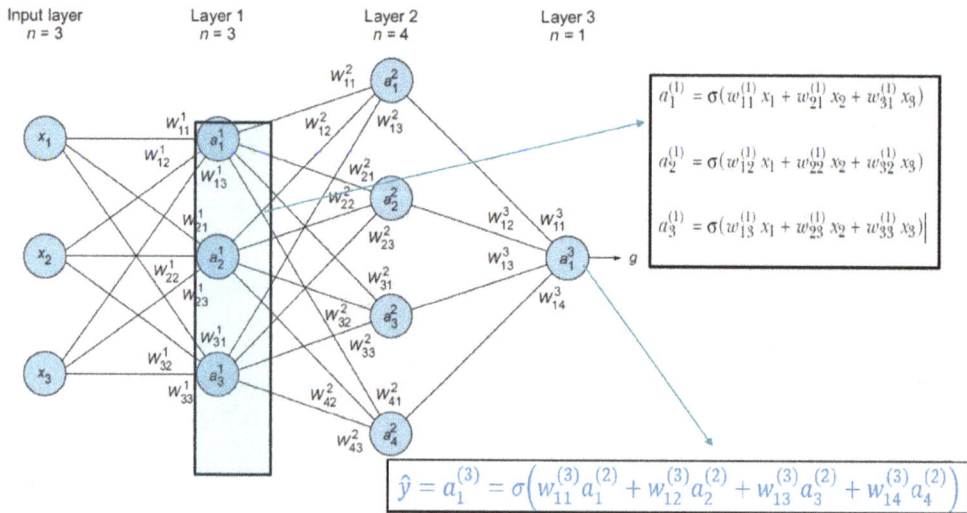

$$a_1^{(1)} = \sigma\left(w_{11}^{(1)} x_1 + w_{21}^{(1)} x_2 + w_{31}^{(1)} x_3\right)$$

$$a_2^{(1)} = \sigma\left(w_{12}^{(1)} x_1 + w_{22}^{(1)} x_2 + w_{32}^{(1)} x_3\right)$$

$$a_3^{(1)} = \sigma\left(w_{13}^{(1)} x_1 + w_{23}^{(1)} x_2 + w_{33}^{(1)} x_3\right)$$

$$\hat{y} = a_1^{(3)} = \sigma\left(w_{11}^{(3)} a_1^{(2)} + w_{12}^{(3)} a_2^{(2)} + w_{13}^{(3)} a_3^{(2)} + w_{14}^{(3)} a_4^{(2)}\right)$$

FIGURE 5.5 Fully connected feedforward neural network with inputs x_1, x_2, x_3 and output y.

Figure 5.4 represents a fully connected feedforward neural network (FNN) with three layers: an input layer, two hidden layers, and an output layer. The network follows a forward propagation process, where input features are transformed through multiple layers using weighted connections and activation functions. The network structure can be described as follows.

1. **Input Layer** ($n = 3$):

   The network takes three input features: x_1, x_2, and x_3.

   Each input node is connected to all neurons in Layer 1 through weights w_{ij}^1.

2. **Hidden Layer 1** ($n = 3$):

   This layer has three neurons a_1^1, a_2^1, and a_3^1.

   Each neuron computes a weighted sum of the inputs and applies an activation function σ, such as a Sigmoid, ReLU, or Softmax function.

3. **Hidden Layer 2** ($n = 4$):

   It contains four neurons a_1^2, a_2^2, a_3^2, and a_4^2.

   Each neuron receives inputs from the previous hidden layer with associated weights, w_{ij}^2.

4. **Output Layer** ($n = 1$):

   A single output neuron is computed as: $\hat{y} = \sigma\left(w_{11}^3 a_1^2 + w_{12}^3 a_2^2 + w_{13}^3 a_3^2 + w_{14}^3 a_4^2\right)$

   The final activation function σ is applied (e.g., Sigmoid for binary classification, Softmax for multi-class classification, or no activation for regression tasks). The output can also be represented in terms of input vector and weight matrix as follows.

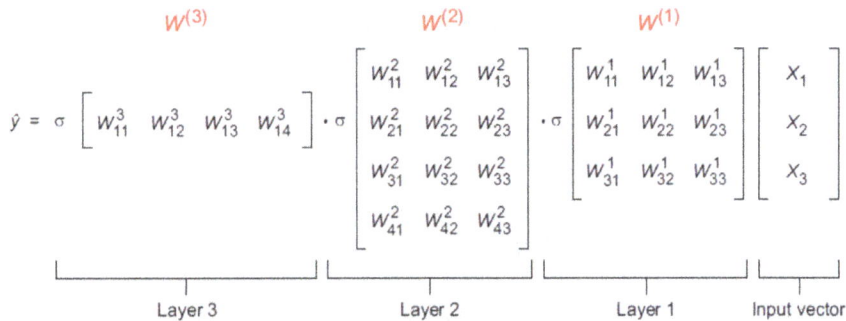

FIGURE 5.6 Input vector and weight matrix.

Activation Function

Activation functions introduce non-linearity into neural networks, allowing them to learn complex patterns from video data, essential in tasks like object detection, crowd analysis, and action recognition. Without activation functions, a neural network would behave like a linear model, unable to handle the diverse, non-linear scenarios found in real-world surveillance footage. These functions determine if a neuron "activates" based on its inputs, enabling the network to recognize subtle behaviors, track movement, or differentiate between overlapping objects. Let's discuss the different types of activation functions.

- **Sigmoid**

  Mathematical Function:

$$f(x) = \frac{1}{1+e^{-x}}$$

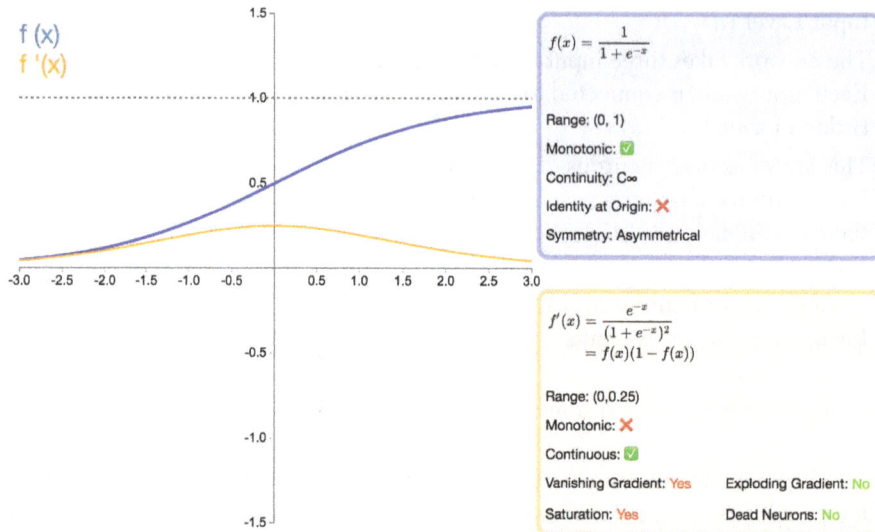

f (x)
f '(x)

$$f(x) = \frac{1}{1+e^{-x}}$$

Range: (0, 1)

Monotonic: ✅

Continuity: C_∞

Identity at Origin: ✗

Symmetry: Asymmetrical

$$f'(x) = \frac{e^{-x}}{(1+e^{-x})^2}$$
$$= f(x)(1 - f(x))$$

Range: (0,0.25)

Monotonic: ✗

Continuous: ✅

Vanishing Gradient: Yes   Exploding Gradient: No

Saturation: Yes   Dead Neurons: No

FIGURE 5.7 Sigmoid activation function (Source: Huawei AI For Junior Developers teaching materials).

The sigmoid function maps inputs to a range between 0 and 1, making it suitable for binary classification tasks often found in IVA, such as detecting the presence vs. absence of motion or a person vs. non-person.

Key Characteristics:

- smooth and differentiable, supporting gradient-based learning
- ideal for simple classification tasks or as the final layer in binary detectors

Advantages:

- stable gradients in shallow networks
- naturally suited for probabilistic outputs (e.g., "Is this person wearing a helmet?")

Limitations:

- Vanishing gradient in deeper layers slows learning.
- Not zero-centered, which can hinder optimization.
- May saturate on extreme inputs, reducing learning efficiency.
- While rarely used in deep layers of IVA models, sigmoid remains useful in output layers for binary detection tasks.

- **Hyperbolic Tangent (Tanh)**
  Mathematical Function:

$$f(x) = \frac{e^x - e^{-x}}{e^x + e^{-x}}$$

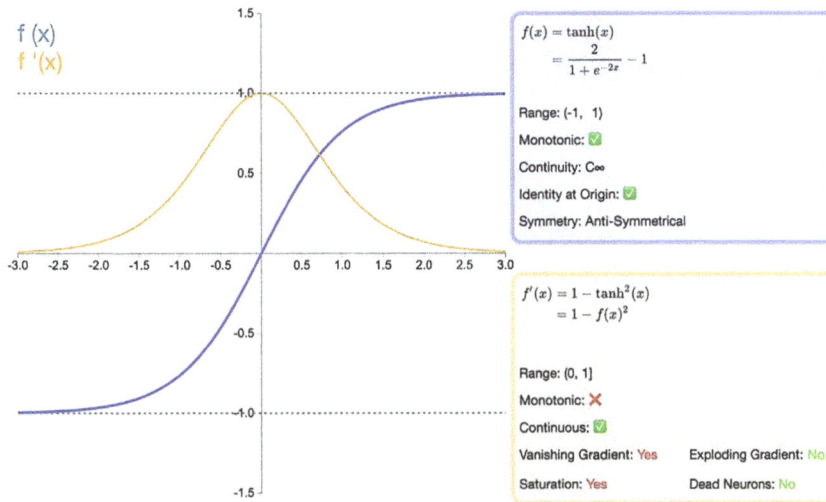

$$f(x) = \tanh(x)$$
$$= \frac{2}{1 + e^{-2x}} - 1$$

Range: (-1, 1)

Monotonic: ✅

Continuity: C_∞

Identity at Origin: ✅

Symmetry: Anti-Symmetrical

$$f'(x) = 1 - \tanh^2(x)$$
$$= 1 - f(x)^2$$

Range: (0, 1]

Monotonic: ❌

Continuous: ✅

Vanishing Gradient: Yes   Exploding Gradient: No

Saturation: Yes   Dead Neurons: No

FIGURE 5.8 Tanh activation function (Source: Huawei AI For Junior Developers teaching materials).

The tanh function maps inputs between −1 and 1, offering zero-centered outputs, which help stabilize training in deep video analytics models.

Key Characteristics:

- often used in recurrent models for motion prediction or temporal behavior analysis in IVA
- produces both positive and negative activations, improving gradient flow

Advantages:

- zero-centered, enabling more balanced weight updates
- helps avoid exploding gradients, unlike some unbounded activations
- rarely produces dead neurons, useful in sequential data like video frames

Limitations:

- Suffers from the vanishing gradient in deep networks.
- Saturates at extreme values, reducing learning efficiency.
- In IVA, tanh may be used where temporal consistency matters, like trajectory prediction or activity classification in RNN-based pipelines.

- **Rectified Linear Unit (ReLU)**
  Mathematical Function:

$$y = \begin{cases} x, & \text{if } x \geq 0 \\ 0, & \text{if } x < 0 \end{cases}$$

This means that
- If x is positive, the function outputs x (i.e., it remains unchanged).
- If x is negative or zero, the function outputs 0.

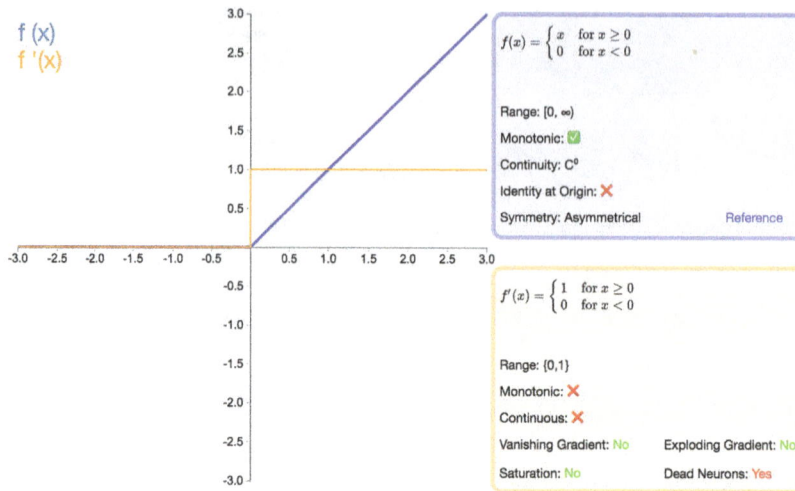

f (x)
f '(x)

$$f(x) = \begin{cases} x & \text{for } x \geq 0 \\ 0 & \text{for } x < 0 \end{cases}$$

Range: [0, ∞)

Monotonic: ✅

Continuity: C⁰

Identity at Origin: ✗

Symmetry: Asymmetrical   Reference

$$f'(x) = \begin{cases} 1 & \text{for } x \geq 0 \\ 0 & \text{for } x < 0 \end{cases}$$

Range: {0,1}

Monotonic: ✗

Continuous: ✗

Vanishing Gradient: No   Exploding Gradient: No

Saturation: No   Dead Neurons: Yes

FIGURE 5.9 ReLU activation function.

ReLU (Rectified Linear Unit) is the most commonly used activation in modern Intelligent Video Analytics, enabling models to learn complex visual patterns, efficiently and at scale.

Characteristics:

- introduces non-linearity by outputting zero for negative inputs and linear for positives
- powers most CNN-based IVA systems, from object detection to facial recognition

Advantages:

- fast training and convergence, ideal for real-time analytics
- computationally efficient, uses simple comparison instead of exponentiation
- avoids vanishing gradients, allowing deep networks to learn effectively
- less prone to exploding gradients compared to exponential activations

Limitations:

- Not differentiable at zero, but this rarely impacts performance.
- Dying ReLU problem: some neurons may stop activating if they receive only negative inputs.

To mitigate this, IVA models often use ReLU variants like

- Leaky ReLU: allows small negative outputs
- PReLU / ELU / SELU: adaptively handle negative inputs to prevent inactive neurons

These variants improve model robustness, especially in complex scenarios like low-light surveillance or occluded object detection.

- **Softmax**

  The Softmax function is used in the output layer of neural networks for multi-class classification, ideal for IVA tasks like object type recognition (e.g., car, bike, person, or animal).

  It transforms raw outputs (logits) into a probability distribution, where each class is assigned a confidence score, and all scores sum to 1.

  This enables the system to make interpretable decisions, such as "85% confidence this is a pedestrian."

  Softmax is essential in IVA when distinguishing among multiple object categories or activity types in a scene.

Mathematical Function:

$$f(z_i) = \frac{e^{z_i}}{\sum_{j=1}^{n} e^{z_i}}$$

Some important properties of the softmax formula are as follows:

- z_i is the element of output vector **z**, i.e., $\mathbf{z} = (z_1, z_2, \ldots, z_n)$. Each of the n components represents the likelihood that the given input data corresponds to one of the n possible categories.
- Every value $f(z_i)$ is in the $[0,1]$ range. The total sum of values **z** is equal to 1.
- $\sum_{j=1}^{n} e^{z_i}$ normalizes the values so that the outputs represent a valid probability distribution.
- Argmax for the final prediction: The model typically selects the class with the highest Softmax probability as the final predicted category.

Example of Softmax in the output layer:
Suppose a neural network predicts three class scores as follows:

$$z = [2.0, 1.0, 0.1]$$

We apply Softmax to obtain

$$f(2.0) = \frac{e^{2.0}}{e^{2.0} + e^{1.0} + e^{0.1}} \approx 0.659$$

$$f(1.0) = \frac{e^{1.0}}{e^{2.0} + e^{1.0} + e^{0.1}} \approx 0.242$$

$$f(0.1) = \frac{e^{0.1}}{e^{2.0} + e^{1.0} + e^{0.1}} \approx 0.099$$

The final output probabilities are

$$[0.659, 0.242, 0.099]$$

Since Class 1 has the highest probability (65.9%), the model predicts Class 1 as the most likely outcome.

Regularization

In Intelligent Video Analytics, overfitting is a serious challenge, especially when training models with limited surveillance footage or in environments with noisy labels. Regularization techniques help models generalize better by discouraging them from memorizing irrelevant details or anomalies in the training set. There are two kinds of regularization:

- L1 (Lasso) adds a penalty to the absolute values of weights, encouraging sparsity. This can help focus on key features, like helmet edges or uniform patterns, while ignoring background noise.
- L2 (Ridge) penalizes the squared values of weights, making the model more stable and less sensitive to outliers often found in surveillance video (e.g., glare, reflections).

These are especially useful in transfer learning scenarios (e.g., adapting a pre-trained model to detect PPE compliance or restricted zone violations) where overfitting is likely due to small labeled datasets.

1. **Data Augmentation**

   Deep learning models for Intelligent Video Analytics often require large, diverse datasets to generalize well in real-world conditions. When annotated video data is limited, data augmentation becomes a practical way to prevent overfitting and improve model robustness. Common techniques are as follows:
   - Image augmentation: In IVA, this includes rotation, scaling, flipping, brightness adjustment, cropping, and noise injection applied to video frames, helping models generalize across camera angles, lighting changes, and occlusions. Care must be taken to preserve label consistency (e.g., not flipping license plates or faces unnaturally).

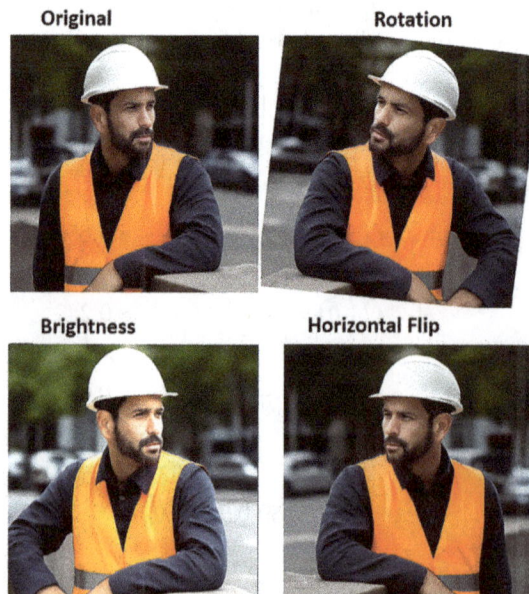

FIGURE 5.10 Image augmentation.

• Synthetic data generation: When surveillance data is scarce (e.g., for rare events like fights or intrusions), Generative Adversarial Networks (GANs) can be used to create realistic training examples, such as simulated night-time scenes or low-light conditions.

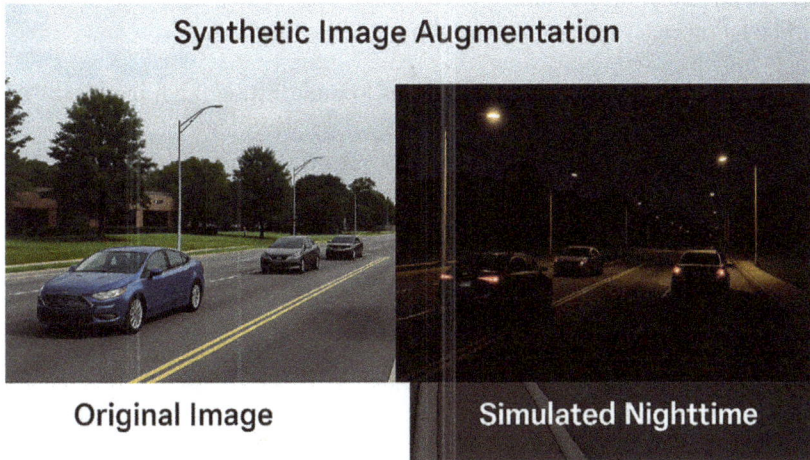

FIGURE 5.11 Synthetic Data Generation.

These augmentation strategies are essential for training robust IVA models, especially in environments where privacy, security, or edge deployment constraints limit data collection.

2. **Dropout**

   Dropout is a regularization technique used to prevent overfitting in deep learning models, especially when training on limited surveillance data. During each training step, a random portion of neurons (e.g., 20%) is temporarily deactivated, preventing the model from relying too heavily on specific features (Figure 5.12).

   This encourages the network to learn more general and robust patterns, which is critical in IVA tasks where lighting, angles, and occlusions vary significantly between camera feeds.

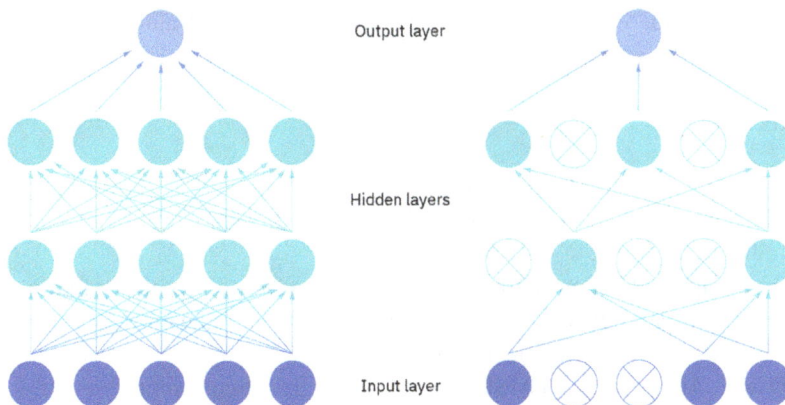

FIGURE 5.12 The dropout during training in input, hidden, and the output layer.

3. **Early Stopping**

    Early stopping helps prevent overfitting by monitoring the model's validation loss during training. In IVA tasks, like person detection or PPE compliance, models can easily overfit when trained too long on limited or repetitive surveillance data.

    The following are shown in typical training curves:

    • On the left side, stopping too early leads to underfitting (high bias)—the model has not learned enough.
    • On the right side, training too long causes overfitting (high variance)—the model starts memorizing background noise or camera-specific artifacts.

Early stopping halts training at the point where validation loss is lowest, often controlled with a patience parameter to wait a few more epochs in case improvements resume. This ensures better generalization to unseen video streams.

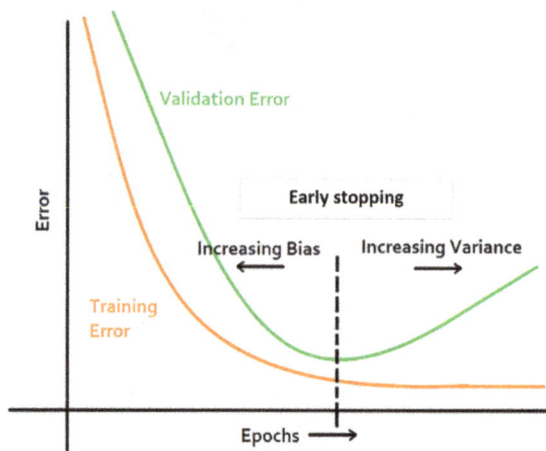

FIGURE 5.13 Early stopping for a particular number of epochs during training.

Optimizer

In Intelligent Video Analytics, optimizers are essential for training deep neural networks efficiently, adjusting weights to minimize prediction errors on tasks like object detection and action recognition.

Key Techniques:

• Mini-Batch Gradient Descent (MBGD): Commonly used in IVA, it balances speed and stability by updating weights on small batches of video frames—ideal for large-scale surveillance datasets.
• Adam (Adaptive Moment Estimation): This is the "go-to" optimizer in most IVA systems, combining the strengths of momentum and adaptive learning rates, ensuring fast and stable convergence even on noisy or complex video data.
• SGD with Momentum / RMSProp: This is useful when tuning fine-grained tracking or frame-by-frame object recognition, offering good control over convergence behavior.

In practice, Adam is the most widely adopted due to its robustness and minimal parameter tuning, making it well-suited for deep IVA pipelines deployed in real-world environments.

COMPUTER VISION CONCEPTS: CONVOLUTIONAL NEURAL NETWORKS

Computer vision enables machines to interpret and analyze images and video, making it the core of IVA. It powers important tasks like object detection, tracking, face recognition, and scene segmentation in real-time surveillance systems. The backbone of modern computer vision is the Convolutional Neural Network (CNN), a deep learning architecture specialized in extracting spatial features from video frames. Unlike fully connected networks, CNNs use convolutional layers to detect visual patterns, such as edges, shapes, and textures, critical for identifying people, vehicles, and behaviors in surveillance footage. CNNs are optimized for scalability, efficiency, and accuracy, making them the "go-to" model for IVA across smart cities, transportation hubs, and industrial sites.

Convolutional Networks

CNNs are optimized neural networks designed to process high-dimensional visual data like video frames. Unlike fully connected networks, CNNs use local receptive fields and weight sharing to efficiently extract spatial patterns, which is crucial for IVA tasks like object detection, crowd counting, and facial recognition.

Key distinctions:

- CNNs reduce parameters by connecting neurons only to small regions of the input (e.g., parts of an image), avoiding the computational overload of fully connected layers.
- They process input as 3D volumes (height × width × depth), allowing them to build hierarchical features—from edges and shapes to faces or moving vehicles.

By combining convolutional, pooling, and fully connected layers, CNNs generate compact representations that feed into classification or detection heads (Figure 5.14), making them ideal for real-time, scalable video analytics in smart environments.

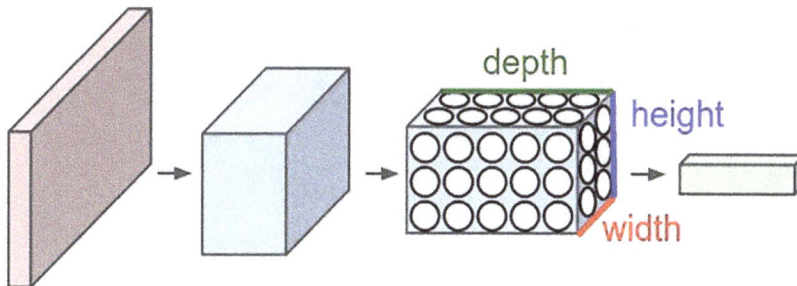

FIGURE 5.14 The visualization of a Convolutional Neural Network (CNN) processing an input image in three dimensions: width, height, and depth (Source: *https://cs231n.github.io/convolutional-networks/*).

CNNs process input frames as 3D volumes, width × height × depth, where depth often corresponds to color channels (e.g., RGB).

Each convolutional layer applies filters to detect spatial patterns like edges, textures, and object parts, transforming the input into progressively more abstract feature maps. This allows the network to recognize complex visual cues in surveillance footage, such as faces, vehicles, or unusual movements.

To manage computational load and focus on essential features, CNNs use pooling layers (Figure 5.15):

- Max pooling selects the highest value in a region, preserving strong signals.
- Average pooling summarizes regions with their mean value.

These operations reduce spatial size while retaining critical information, enabling CNNs to efficiently process high-resolution video streams for real-time IVA tasks.

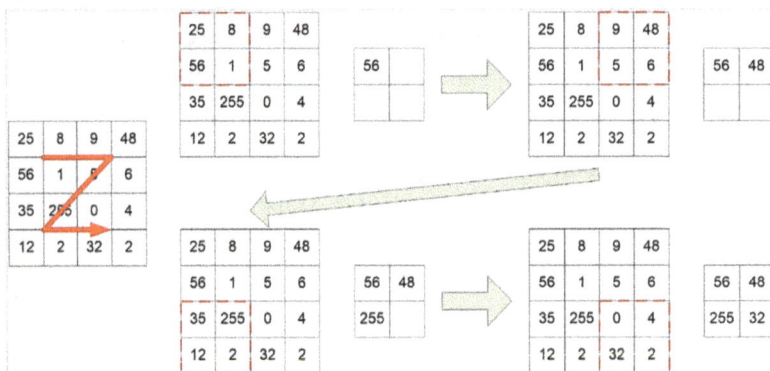

FIGURE 5.15 Max pooling operation with size of 2x2 (Source: Huawei *AI For Junior Developers* teaching materials).

The fully connected layer at the end of a CNN aggregates learned features to make final predictions, such as object type, activity category, or person ID.

- For binary tasks (e.g., intruder vs. no intruder), a Sigmoid activation is used to output probabilities between 0 and 1.
- For multiclass tasks (e.g., vehicle type detection: car, bus, truck), a Softmax layer outputs class probabilities that sum to 1.

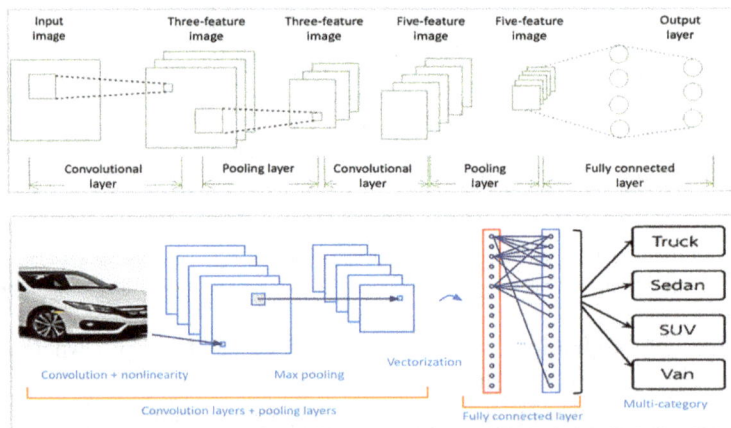

FIGURE 5.16 Example of CNN architecture for multicategory image classification (Source: Huawei *AI For Junior Developers* teaching materials).

This structure enables IVA systems to classify and interpret visual content in real time, based on deep, learned representations of video frames. Table 5.1 shows an example CNN layer.

TABLE 5.1 The example dimensions of a CNN layer with a 5x5 kernel and 2x2 pooling size.

Layer	Example Dimension (Height × Width × Depth)
Input Layer	128 × 128 × 3
Convolution Layer 1	124 × 124 × 32
Pooling Layer 1	62 × 62 × 32
Convolution Layer 1	58 × 58 × 64
Pooling Layer 2	29 × 29 × 64
Fully Connected Layer	1024
Output Layer	4

Fully Connected Networks for Regression

While CNNs are commonly used for classification, they are also effective for regression tasks in IVA, where the goal is to predict continuous values rather than categories.

Common IVA Regression Use Cases:

• Crowd density estimation in city squares, events, or transport hubs
• Vehicle speed or count prediction from traffic camera footage
• Footfall estimation in retail or smart building analytics
• Suspicious behavior scoring or anomaly likelihood prediction

How It Works:

1. Input: video frames (and optionally, sensor metadata)
2. Convolutional and pooling layers: Extract spatial features from scenes, such as object density, spatial flow, and size patterns.
3. Flattening and integration: Combine visual features with metadata (e.g., time of day, location).
4. Fully connected layers: Learn complex mappings between scene features and real-world quantities (e.g., number of people).
5. Output layer: A single neuron with linear activation outputs a continuous value, such as estimated crowd count.

Improving Generalization:
To avoid overfitting and improve accuracy, use the

• Dropout and weight regularization (L1/L2)
• Batch normalization for stable training
• Data augmentation (e.g., blur, scale, light changes) to simulate real-world conditions
• Early stopping based on validation loss trends

CNN for Image Classification

CNNs are highly effective for visual classification tasks in IVA. They extract both low-level features (e.g., motion edges and textures) and high-level semantics (e.g., faces, vehicles, and behaviors) from video frames through layered processing, making them ideal for tasks like object detection, intrusion recognition, or safety compliance monitoring.

While toy datasets (small, simplified dataset used to quickly test or demonstrate an algorithm or concept, often lacking the complexity of real-world data) like CIFAR-10 are useful for learning CNN principles, production-level IVA systems require more realistic datasets. Some commonly used ones include the following:

- VisDrone is a drone-based video dataset for vehicle and pedestrian detection, tracking, and crowd analysis.
- Cityscapes has street-level video frames for semantic segmentation and urban scene understanding, which is useful for smart transportation applications.
- UCF Crime is a surveillance dataset containing anomalous activities (e.g., robbery, assault, and vandalism), and is used for behavior classification and crime detection.
- AI City Challenge is focused on vehicle re-identification, traffic flow analysis, and anomaly detection in smart city environments.
- AVA Dataset (Atomic Visual Actions) is designed for spatiotemporal action recognition from surveillance videos, capturing fine-grained human behaviors.

These datasets offer high-resolution, real-world surveillance footage, and multi-label annotations, providing ideal training material for CNN-based IVA models.

Here is the CNN structure in IVA:

- Convolutional layers capture localized visual features such as helmets, number plates, or abnormal body posture.
- Pooling layers reduce feature map dimensions, improving generalization and speed.
- Fully connected layers aggregate spatial features for final decisions like "loitering detected," "person with weapon," or "vehicle wrong direction."

To ensure robustness, data should be split into the following:

- a training set for learning feature representations
- a validation set for tuning hyperparameters and preventing overfitting
- a test set for evaluating model performance on unseen scenarios

Input image

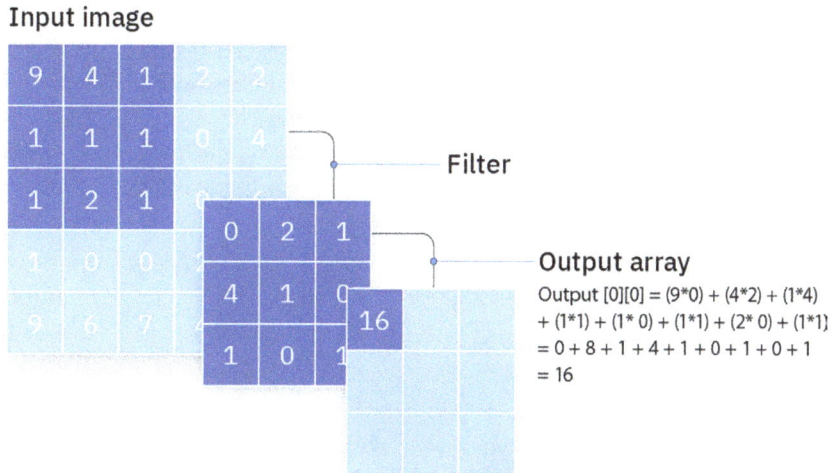

Filter

Output array

Output [0][0] = (9*0) + (4*2) + (1*4)
+ (1*1) + (1* 0) + (1*1) + (2* 0) + (1*1)
= 0 + 8 + 1 + 4 + 1 + 0 + 1 + 0 + 1
= 16

FIGURE 5.17 The convolutional operation using a 3x3 filter kernel on a 5x5 image.

Convolutional operations apply filters to input frames, capturing important spatial patterns like edges, shapes, or motion cues, essential for tasks such as object detection or facial recognition in video analytics (Figure 5.19). Pooling layers (e.g., max pooling) reduce spatial dimensions while retaining critical features, making models more efficient and robust to position and scale changes. For example, a 2×2 max pooling reduces a 224×224×64 input to 112×112×64, preserving depth while simplifying computation (Figure 5.18). These operations help IVA systems process high-resolution video streams in real time without losing essential context.

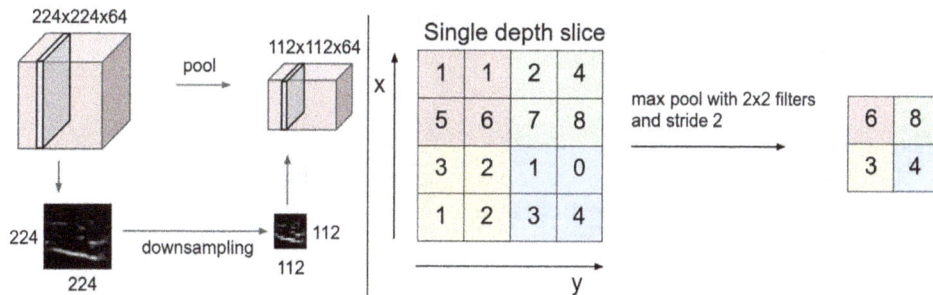

FIGURE 5.18 The max pooling operation, where a 2x2 pooling filter with a stride of 2 is applied to a feature map (Source: *https://cs231n.github.io/convolutional-networks/#conv*).

Fully Connected Layers

After convolution and pooling, CNNs flatten the extracted features into a 1D vector and pass them through fully connected layers to perform final classification (Figure 5.19), such as identifying a vehicle type, person identity, or detected behavior.

Each neuron in these layers connects to all neurons in the next, enabling deep feature learning. The final output layer assigns probability scores to each class, helping IVA systems make confident, interpretable decisions in real time.

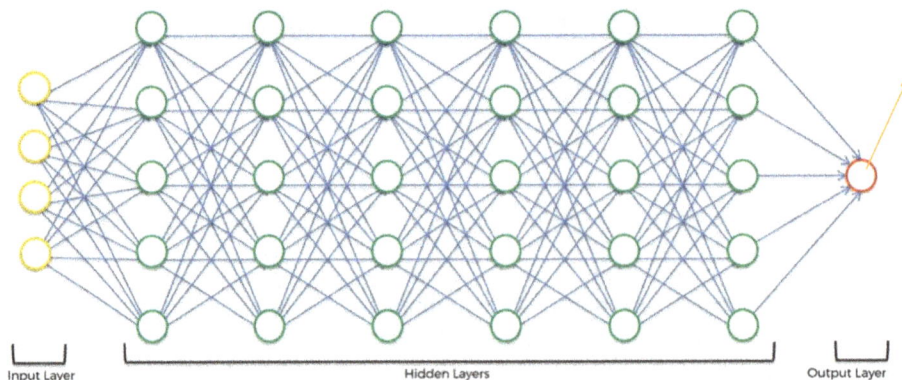

FIGURE 5.19 The structure of a fully connected layer.

Key Components of Fully Connected Layers

- Neurons: Each neuron connects to all previous outputs and computes a weighted sum.
- Weights and biases are learnable parameters that shape the model's predictions.
- Activation functions add non-linearity (e.g., ReLU and Softmax) to capture complex patterns in surveillance data.

The Output Layer

In IVA classification tasks (e.g., person with helmet or vehicle type), a Softmax layer converts the output into probabilities, selecting the most likely class for the final prediction.

Types of CNN and Pretrained Models

While standard NNs excel at spatial analysis, advanced architectures like Recurrent Neural Networks (RNNs) extend IVA capabilities to temporal sequence modelling, critical for understanding motion patterns, behavior over time, or activity prediction in surveillance footage.

1. Recurrent Neural Networks (RNNs): RNNs are designed to process sequential data by maintaining context across video frames, enabling the model to recognize evolving patterns, such as loitering, vehicle movement trajectories, or abnormal behavior progression (Figure 5.20).

By introducing recurrent connections, RNNs can retain information over time, making them suitable for frame-by-frame analysis and short-term video memory, which traditional CNNs alone cannot achieve.

Figure 5.16 illustrates the basic structure of an RNN unit at a single time step:

- X_t represents the input at time step t. It is part of a sequential input and is fed into the network at each step.
- S_t is the memory unit (hidden state) at time t, responsible for caching previous information. It is updated using both the current input X_t and the hidden state from the previous time step S_{t-1}. The hidden state is computed as follows:

$$S_t = \sigma\left(UX_t + WS_{t-1}\right)$$

and can be extended to a longer sequence as

$$S_t = \sigma(UX_t + W\left(\sigma\left(UX_{t-1} + W\left(\sigma\left(UX_{t-2} + W(...)\right)\right)\right)\right))$$

Here, U and W are weight matrices that determine how much influence the current input and previous state have on the new hidden state. The ó is an activation function, such as Tanh, ensures non-linearity and helps regulate the values.

- O_t is the output of the hidden layer at time t, obtained by applying a transformation to the hidden state:

$$O_t = \sigma\left(VS_t\right)$$

The weight matrix V controls how the hidden state maps to the output. After passing through multiple hidden layers, O_t contributes to the final output sequence at time t, which may be used for tasks such as classification, prediction, or sequence generation.

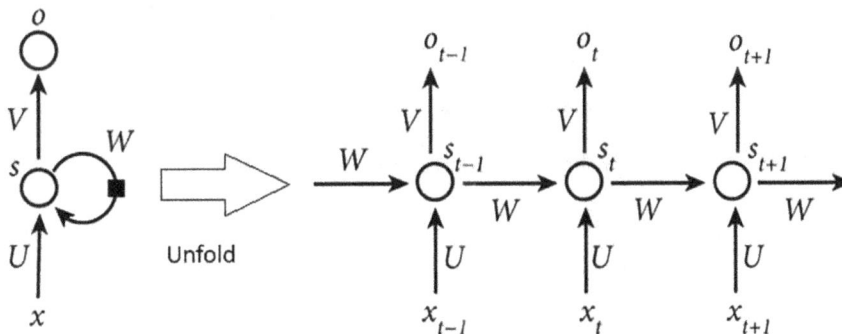

FIGURE 5.20 The RNN architecture.

In video analytics, RNNs can track short-term visual sequences, such as a person entering a restricted area. However, they often struggle with long-term dependencies—for instance, recognizing if someone loitered for several minutes or returned after a long absence. This limitation arises from vanishing gradients, which cause earlier information to fade over time.

To solve this, Long Short-Term Memory (LSTM) networks were introduced. LSTMs use specialized memory gates to retain critical information over longer time spans, making them well-suited for IVA tasks involving extended activity recognition, delayed anomalies, or sequence-based threat detection.

2. Long Short-Term Memory (LSTM) Networks: LSTM networks are an advanced form of RNNs designed to handle long-term dependencies in sequential data solving the vanishing gradient problem found in standard RNNs. In IVA, LSTMs are especially useful for tasks like the following:

- long-duration activity recognition (e.g., loitering, escalation of violence)
- video frame prediction for anticipating motion or behavior
- event pattern tracking over extended time spans

LSTMs use gating mechanisms (such as forget, input, and output gates) to control what information is retained or discarded, enabling models to remember relevant visual context across long sequences.

The LSTM network is shown in Figure 5.21. The figure consists of three LSTM cells representing three consecutive time steps: $t-1, t,$ and $t+1.$

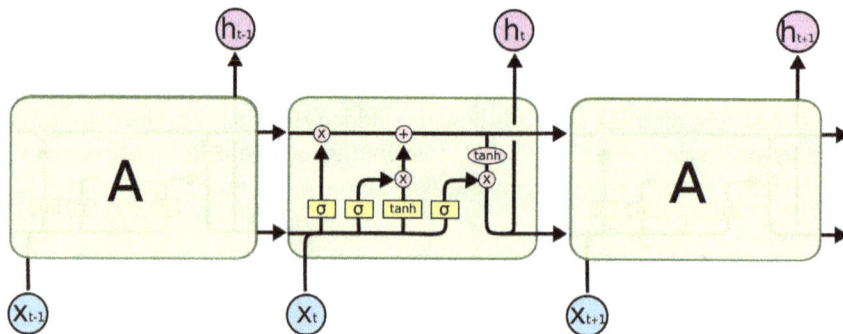

FIGURE 5.21 The LSTM Architecture (Source: *https://colah.github.io/posts/2015-08-Understanding-LSTMs/*).

An LSTM unit consists of the following components:

- The forget gate determines which information from the previous cell state should be discarded. The forget gate can be written as

$$f_t = \sigma\left(W_f\left[h_{t-1}, x_t\right] + b_f\right)$$

- The input gate decides which new information should be stored in the cell state. The input gate can be written as

$$i_t = \sigma\left(W_i\left[h_{t-1}, x_t\right] + b_i\right)$$

- The cell state stores long-term dependencies and updates based on the input and forget gates. The two cell state, candidate cell state $(\tilde{C}_t)$, updated cell state (C_t), and hidden state update (h_t) are written as follows:

$$\tilde{C}_t = \tanh\left(W_C\left[h_{t-1}, x_t\right] + b_C\right)$$

$$C_t = f_t * C_{t-1} + i_t * \tilde{C}_t$$

$$h_t = o_t * \tanh\left(C_t\right)$$

- The output gate controls the output of the memory cell based on the current state. The output gate is written as follows:

$$o_t = \sigma\left(W_o\left[h_{t-1}, x_t\right] + b_o\right)$$

Vision Transformers (ViT): An Emerging Alternative to CNNs

While CNNs have long been the backbone of computer vision in IVA, Vision Transformers (ViTs) are emerging as a powerful alternative, especially when capturing global spatial relationships is critical. Unlike CNNs, which process images using local receptive fields, ViTs split images into fixed-size patches (e.g., 16×16), flatten them into vectors, and feed them into a transformer architecture (Figure 5.22). This model uses self-attention to learn long-range dependencies between patches, enabling deeper understanding of scene-level context.

In surveillance applications, ViTs can be valuable for the following:

- multi-object tracking across wide fields of view
- scene understanding in crowded areas
- PPE compliance detection with complex contextual cues
- multi-camera fusion, where attention across views is needed

For example, a ViT model could not only detect a person wearing a helmet but also reason whether they are entering a restricted zone, based on global scene understanding.

Limitations and Considerations

- ViTs typically require large-scale datasets to perform well.
- In IVA scenarios with limited labeled data, hybrid models (e.g., CNN-ViT combinations) or transfer learning from ViTs pretrained on large video datasets (e.g., VideoMAE or DINOv2) are more practical.

While still maturing in real-time edge deployments, ViTs are an important step toward context-aware IVA systems that go beyond local object recognition to full-scene reasoning.

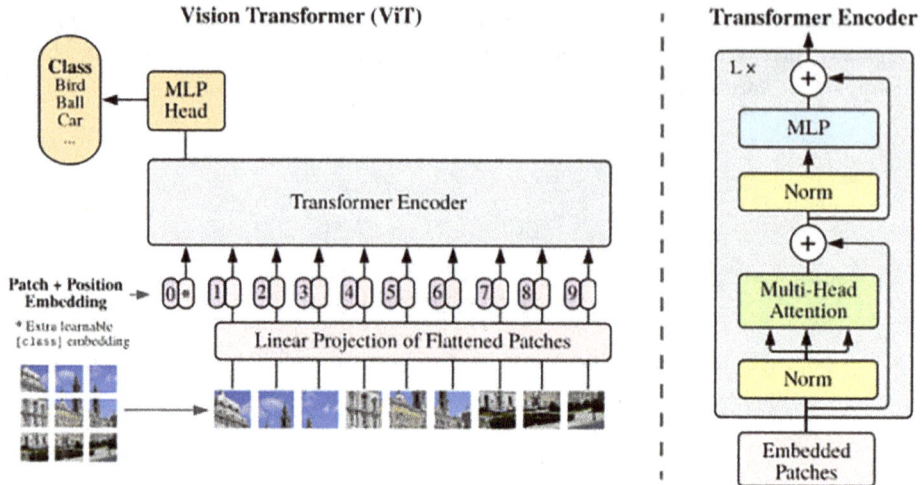

FIGURE 5.22 Vision transformer (Source: *https://arxiv.org/abs/2010.11929*).

Introduction to Transfer Learning

Training deep CNNs from scratch is data- and compute-intensive, which is often impractical in real-world IVA where annotated video is limited. *Transfer learning* solves this problem by using pre-trained CNNs (e.g., on ImageNet), reducing training time and data requirements. Here is how it works in IVA:

1. Get a pretrained network: A neural network model that has already been trained on a large dataset (e.g., ImageNet) is selected. This pretrained model contains useful feature representations learned from the original task.

2. Modify the network: The pretrained model is adapted for the new task by modifying its architecture, such as replacing the final classification layers to match the number of output classes in the target dataset.

3. Prepare a new dataset: The new dataset is collected and preprocessed, including data augmentation, normalization, and splitting into training and validation sets.

4. Retrain the network: The modified network is trained using the new dataset, depending on the transfer learning approach such as feature extraction and fine-tuning.

5. Predict new data: The trained model is evaluated using validation data, and predictions are generated for new, unseen inputs.

Transfer learning is especially effective for IVA use cases with small labeled datasets, enabling fast, high-accuracy deployment with minimal training (Figure 5.23).

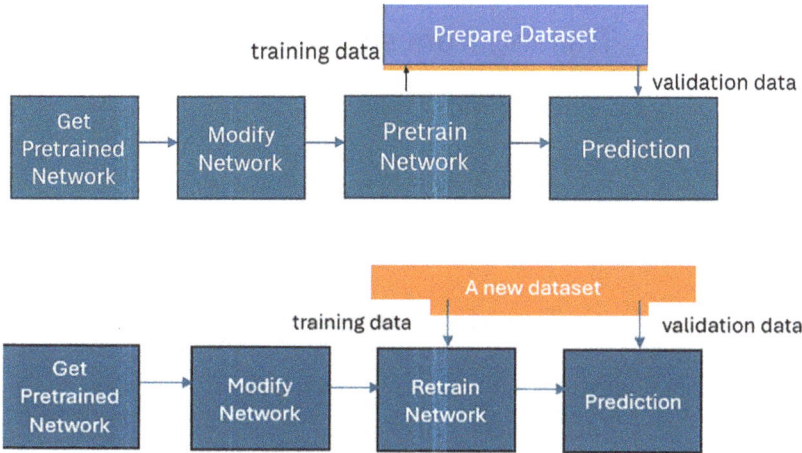

FIGURE 5.23 Transfer learning steps.

In real-world IVA, collecting and labeling large-scale datasets (e.g., for behavior detection or PPE compliance) is often impractical. Transfer learning addresses this problem by using pre-trained CNNs, accelerating development while preserving model performance. Two common strategies are (Figure 5.24):

1. Feature extraction uses a pre-trained model as a fixed feature extractor. The convolutional layers remain frozen, and only the final classification layers are trained on new data. This is ideal for small datasets, helping avoid overfitting while still benefiting from robust visual features like edges and shapes. A model like ResNet50, pre-trained on ImageNet, can be used as a fixed feature extractor. The early layers capture generic visual patterns—edges, textures, shapes—which are relevant even in surveillance contexts. You freeze the backbone and train only the final layers to distinguish between "person with helmet" vs. "person without helmet." This approach is effective when working with limited labeled footage from newly deployed CCTV systems.

2. Fine-Tuning: Unfreezes part or all of the pre-trained model and re-trains it on the new dataset, allowing the network to adapt to domain-specific patterns (e.g., surveillance angles and environmental variations). Fine-tuning works best when the new dataset is larger or slightly different from the source. When domain-specific visual cues (e.g., camera angles, lighting, and uniforms) differ from the source dataset (e.g., ImageNet or MS COCO), fine-tuning is critical. You start with a pre-trained backbone like EfficientNet or ResNet101, unfreeze mid-to-deep layers, and fine-tune using annotated video frames from the deployment site. This allows the network to learn local visual priors such as occlusions, shadows, or camera-specific color cast.

Training from scratch

Pre-trained model

Learned features

Person without helmet ✓

Person with helmet ✗

Transfer learning

Pre-trained model

Pre-trained model

New task

Person without helmet ✗

Person with helmet ✓

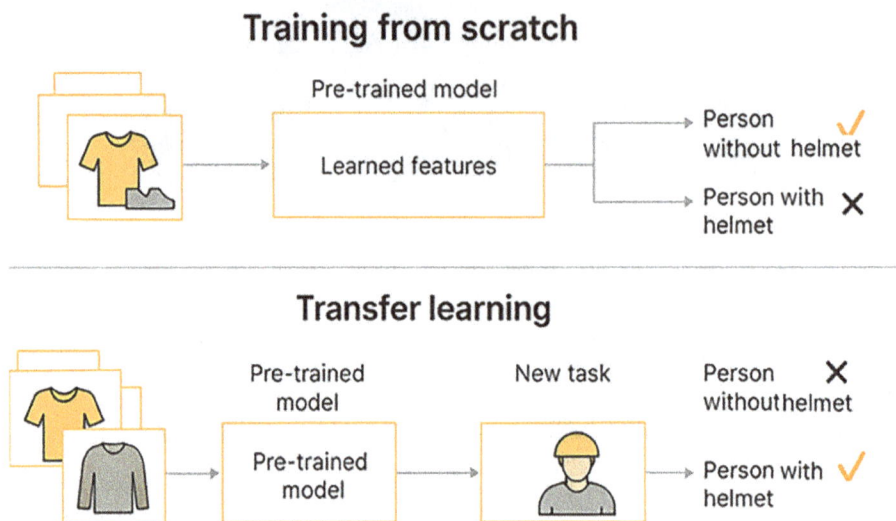

FIGURE 5.24 Transfer learning vs. training from scratch.

Challenges in Transfer Learning

- Negative transfer: If the source and target domains are too different, performance may decline. For example, using a model trained on retail CCTV (indoor lighting or stationary angles) might harm performance when transferred to outdoor construction sites with mobile PTZ cameras.
- Transfer bound: There is a limit to how well pre-trained features generalize. Choosing which layers to freeze or update is critical. For example, in rare-event detection (e.g., fights, falls, or theft), the pre-trained features might be too generic. In such cases, partial fine-tuning with domain-specific augmentation (like motion blur or night-time noise) becomes essential.

In practice, effective transfer learning in IVA requires the following:

- careful selection of the pre-trained model (YOLOv8 vs. ResNet vs. MobileNet, depending on the target device)
- custom data augmentation pipelines to simulate real conditions (e.g., fog and crowd density)
- layer-freezing strategies that consider computational limits at the edge while preserving accuracy

Transfer learning remains a cornerstone of deploying scalable, performant IVA systems in environments where data is scarce, hardware is constrained, and accuracy is non-negotiable.

OBJECT DETECTION

CNNs are essential for object detection in IVA, enabling systems to locate and classify targets like people, vehicles, or unattended objects in surveillance footage.

Popular CNN-based detectors include the following:

- YOLO (You Only Look Once): real-time detection
- Faster R-CNN: high accuracy for complex scenes
- SSD (Single Shot Detector): balance of speed and precision

Transfer learning enhances these models by reusing features from pretrained backbones (e.g., ResNet and EfficientNet) trained on large datasets like ImageNet. This reduces data needs and accelerates training, which is ideal for IVA deployments with limited labeled footage. Recently, transformer-based detectors have emerged as powerful alternatives to CNNs, especially for complex, multi-object, and context-rich IVA environments. These models use self-attention mechanisms to understand global relationships across an entire scene, making them highly effective in surveillance scenarios with overlapping objects, varying scales, or dense activity.

Leading transformer-based models include the following:

- DETR (DEtection TRansformer) introduced the concept of object detection as a set prediction problem, removing the need for anchor boxes and enabling end-to-end training.
- RT-DETR (Real-Time DETR) is a faster variant that brings DETR-level accuracy with real-time speed, suitable for live IVA systems.
- RF-DETR (Region-aware Fully Transformer Detector) pushes performance further by integrating region-awareness into the attention mechanism, achieving better localization in crowded or high-density surveillance scenes.
- Grounding DINO fuses vision and language, allowing surveillance systems to detect objects via text prompts, e.g., "person without helmet" or "red truck near exit."
- The Swin Transformer + Cascade Mask R-CNN combines the power of hierarchical vision transformers with strong region-based refinement, ideal for scene-level understanding and segmentation tasks.

These transformer models are particularly relevant for IVA applications that demand contextual reasoning, zero-shot detection, or multi-modal integration. While they are more resource-intensive than traditional CNNs, they are increasingly optimized for deployment on cloud backends or high-performance edge devices.

Introduction to Object Detection

In IVA, object detection identifies and locates specific objects, like people, vehicles, or bags, in video frames. Unlike image classification, it not only labels objects but also draws bounding boxes around them (Figure 5.25).

Each detection typically includes the following:

- class label (e.g., person, car, motorcycle)
- confidence score (e.g., 0.92 means 92% certainty)
- bounding box coordinates in the top-left corner and the bottom-right corner

This structure allows IVA systems to track, count, or trigger alerts based on the object presence and movement in specific zones.

FIGURE 5.25 Object detection for a highway.

Object detection in IVA has progressed from basic methods to advanced real-time models. Below are the important approaches:

1. The Sliding Window (Classic Approach) scans the image with fixed-size windows and uses classifiers to detect objects. Though simple, it is computationally inefficient and rarely used today in IVA.

2. Two-Stage Detection (e.g., Faster R-CNN) generates region proposals first, then classifies and refines bounding boxes. It offers high accuracy, making it suitable for critical surveillance tasks, but it is slower for real-time needs.

3. One-Stage Detection (e.g., YOLO and SSD) predicts object class and location in a single pass, making it ideal for real-time IVA applications like traffic monitoring or intrusion detection. It is slightly less accurate than two-stage models in complex scenes, but significantly faster than them.

4. Transformer-Based Detection (e.g., DETR) uses attention mechanisms to detect objects without region proposals. It is emerging in IVA for multi-object tracking, scene understanding, and integration with multi-modal inputs (such as combining video with audio or text).

Object Detection with YOLO

YOLO (You Only Look Once) revolutionized object detection by treating it as a single-pass regression problem, making it ideal for real-time IVA tasks like intrusion alerts, traffic monitoring, and safety compliance detection.

This is how YOLO works:

1. Image grid: The frame is split into a grid (e.g., 13×13); each cell predicts objects centered within it.
2. Bounding boxes: Each cell predicts box coordinates and confidence scores.
3. Class prediction: It assigns class labels (e.g., a person, car, or truck) to each box.
4. Non-Max Suppression (NMS): This removes overlapping boxes, keeping the most likely one.
5. Final output: This returns the detected objects with the class, confidence, and bounding box info.

YOLO's speed and accuracy make it a top choice for real-time surveillance and smart city applications.

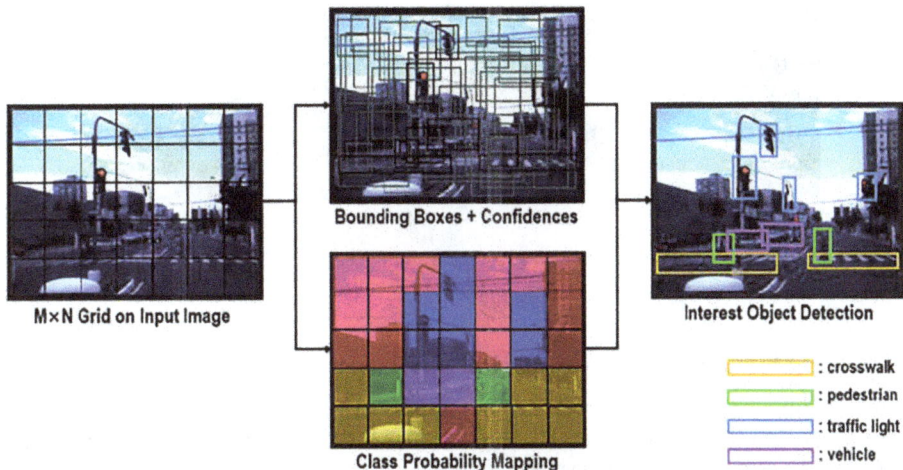

FIGURE 5.26 YOLO detection process for identifying a crosswalk, pedestrian, traffic light, and vehicle.

Object Detection with Faster R-CNN

Faster R-CNN is a two-stage object detector known for its high accuracy, making it suitable for IVA applications that require precise detection, such as identifying weapons, unattended baggage, or face detection in high-risk zones. Its workflow is as follows:

1. Feature Extraction – An input image is passed through a CNN (e.g., ResNet) to get feature maps.
2. Region Proposal Network (RPN) – It learns to suggest object regions dynamically, replacing older hand-crafted methods.
3. ROI Pooling – It standardizes the proposal sizes for classification.
4. Classification and Refinement – Each region is classified, and the bounding boxes are refined.

Compared to YOLO, Faster R-CNN is slower but more accurate, making it ideal for critical analysis tasks where precision matters more than speed.

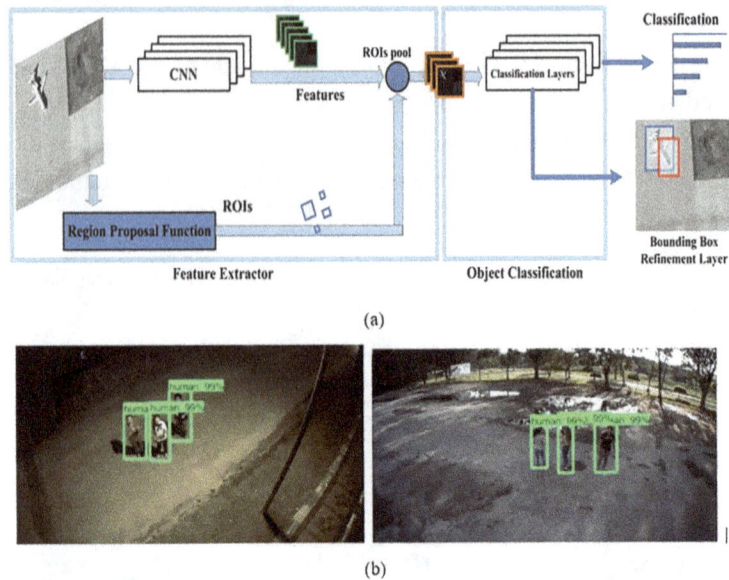

(a)

(b)

FIGURE 5.27 a) Faster R-CNN architecture, b) Application of Faster R-CNN for pedestrian detection from drone images (Source: *https://dl.acm.org/doi/abs/10.1007/s42979-020-00125-y*).

Object Detection for Smart City Application

Object detection is a core technology behind IVA, driving automation in urban security, traffic systems, and public space management. Powered by deep learning models like YOLO, Faster R-CNN, and RF-DETR, it enables real-time monitoring and decision-making, which are critical to building responsive, efficient, and secure smart cities. In surveillance, AI-powered cameras can detect unauthorized access, anomalous behavior, or unattended objects, improving situational awareness for law enforcement and emergency response teams.

At airports and immigration zones, object detection supports facial recognition, baggage scanning, and access control. In traffic management, vehicle detection and counting help optimize signal timing, reduce congestion, and support electronic traffic law enforcement, automating tasks like detecting red light violations or illegal parking. People counting and crowd estimation assist in managing public spaces and ensuring safety during large events. Object detection also supports environmental monitoring, identifying issues like illegal dumping or tracking wildlife near urban areas.

1. Real-time Monitoring of Vital Areas

   By integrating object detection into surveillance systems, cities can enhance crime prevention, public safety, and emergency response efficiency, making urban spaces more secure and resilient.

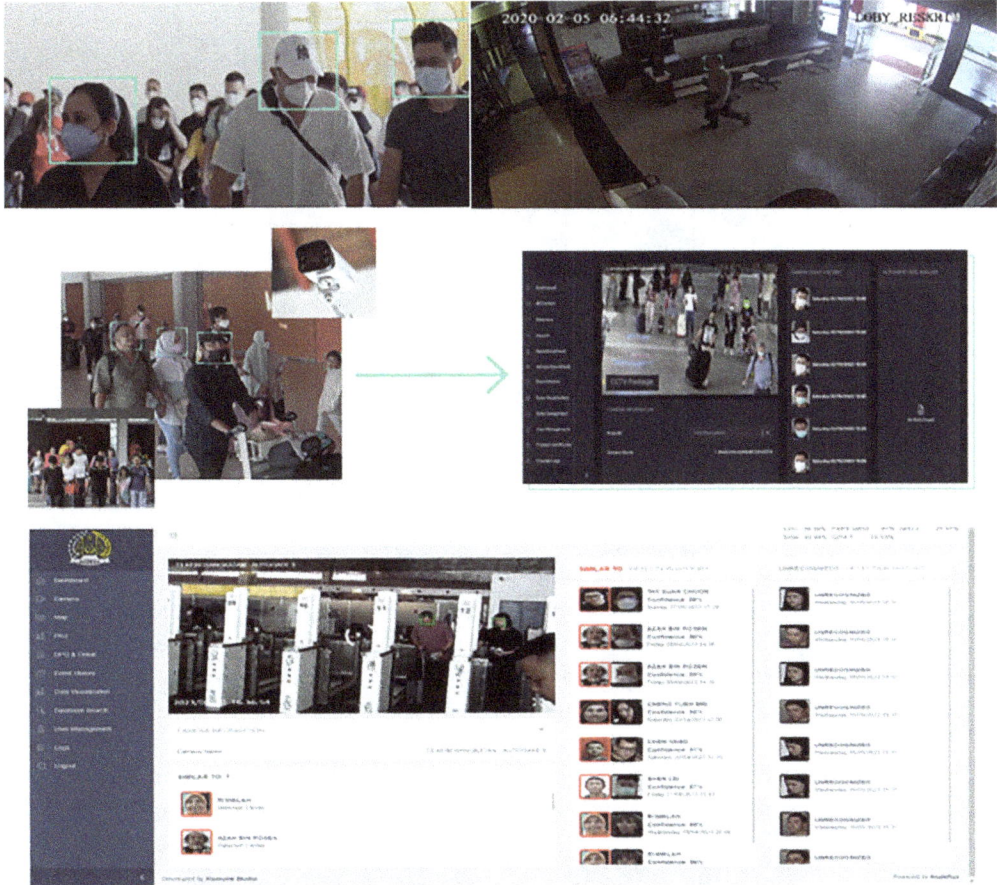

FIGURE 5.28 Real-time people monitoring and identification in a vital area, such as an office, the airport, or immigration counters (Source: *Nodeflux*).

2. Vehicle Detection and Counting

Many object detection algorithms, such as YOLO and Faster R-CNN, are widely used in traffic monitoring systems to identify and count vehicles in real-time, helping to optimize traffic signals, reduce congestion, and enhance road safety. In automated toll collection, AI-powered cameras detect vehicle types and license plates for seamless payment processing. Similarly, parking management systems utilize object detection to monitor available parking spaces, guiding drivers efficiently to free spots. Law enforcement agencies use vehicle detection for speed monitoring, detecting traffic violations, and issuing automated fines through traffic ticketing systems. In addition, smart transportation systems integrate vehicle detection with predictive analytics to enhance public transport efficiency and route optimization. Figure 5.29 illustrates an example of vehicle detection and counting using AI, showing multiple cars detected on a busy urban road, with bounding boxes indicating identified vehicles.

FIGURE 5.29 An example of vehicle detection and counting using object detection implemented on CCTV cameras (Source: *Nodeflux*).

3. People Counting and Crowd Estimation

In public events or area, crowd estimation helps authorities monitor attendee density, ensuring safety measures like controlled entry points and emergency evacuation planning. Similarly, in smart retail, people counting enables businesses to analyze foot traffic patterns, optimize store layouts, and enhance customer experiences. Public transportation hubs, including train stations and airports, use people detection to manage passenger flow and prevent overcrowding. Figure 5.30 shows a real-time people counting system in an urban square and a public area, with bounding boxes highlighting detected individuals.

FIGURE 5.30 Example of people counting and crowd estimation (Source: *Nodeflux*).

4. Environmental Monitoring

   AI-driven object detection systems are widely used in river monitoring to track water pollution, floating debris, and illegal waste disposal, helping authorities take timely action to maintain water quality. Drones and fixed surveillance cameras equipped with deep learning models can detect plastic waste, oil spills, or abnormal water levels, providing essential data for environmental conservation efforts. In air pollution control, object detection helps analyze urban emissions by recognizing industrial smoke and vehicle pollution sources. Figure 5.31 shows an AI-powered river monitoring system, locating floating waste and water contamination through object detection techniques.

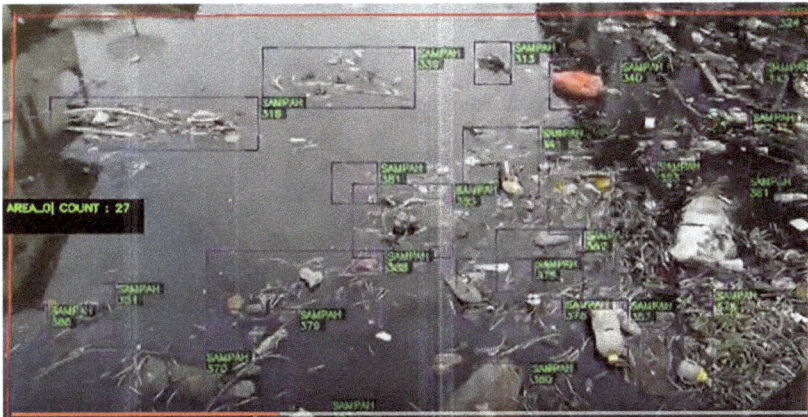

FIGURE 5.31 Waste detection in a river using object detection (Source: *Nodeflux*).

5. Electronic Traffic Law Enforcement

   Electronic Traffic Law Enforcement (ETLE) uses object detection and computer vision to automatically monitor, detect, and penalize traffic violations without human intervention. AI-powered cameras equipped with deep learning models are used to identify vehicles, license plates, and driver behaviors in real-time. ETLE systems are widely deployed for speed limit enforcement, red light violations, lane discipline monitoring, and illegal parking detection. Through Automatic Number Plate Recognition (ANPR), traffic authorities can efficiently issue fines to violators based on captured evidence. Additionally, object detection is used to detect helmet compliance for motorcyclists, seatbelt usage, and mobile phone usage while driving. Smart intersections integrate ETLE systems with traffic management networks to optimize traffic flow and enhance road safety (Figure 5.32). By implementing object detection in traffic law enforcement, cities can achieve fairer, more efficient, and scalable traffic regulation, reducing manual monitoring efforts and improving compliance with road safety laws.

FIGURE 5.32 Car plate recognition applied on ETLE system (Source: *Nodeflux*).

FACE RECOGNITION

Face recognition is a biometric technology that identifies or verifies an individual's identity based on facial features extracted from an image or video. It is widely used in security systems, identity verification, and user authentication in smartphones, banking, and law enforcement. Face recognition is a technology capable of verifying (1 vs 1) or identifying (1 vs N) a person from a digital image or a video frame obtained from a video source. While face recognition determines who a person is by comparing facial features against a database, *face detection* is the preliminary step that simply identifies the presence and location of faces within an image or frame. Face detection does not assign an identity to the detected faces, whereas face recognition matches the detected face to a known identity using deep learning models such as FaceNet, DeepFace, or ArcFace. The comparison of face detection and recognition is shown in Figure 5.33.

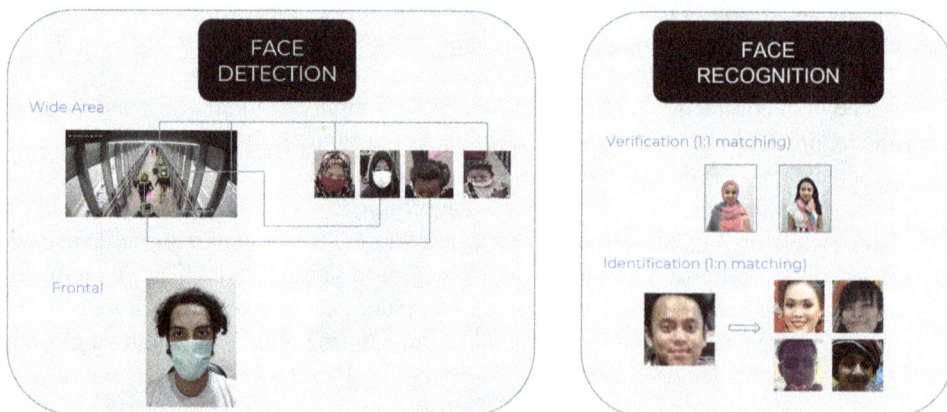

FIGURE 5.33 The face detection and recognition comparison.

The accuracy of a face detection model is commonly evaluated using the Mean Average Precision (mAP), which measures how precisely the model detects faces across different scenarios.

The mAP metric calculates the average precision of correctly predicted faces relative to the total number of faces in an image or video frame. A higher mAP score indicates better detection performance. In addition, the accuracy of model is highly dependent on the quality of the captured images and its ability to differentiate between individuals with similar facial features.

In some cases, the model may produce false positives due to factors such as lighting conditions, facial attributes, head angles, and image resolution. Just like the human eye, face recognition systems may struggle to distinguish individuals with highly similar characteristics, especially under certain angles or poor lighting. This limitation is particularly evident in cases involving identical twins, where facial biometrics alone may not be sufficient for accurate differentiation. To improve reliability, advanced face recognition models incorporate preprocessing techniques, feature enhancement, and diverse training datasets to reduce misclassification and enhance performance in real-world scenarios. The face recognition application is shown in Figure 5.34.

FIGURE 5.34 An example of face recognition (Source: *Nodeflux*).

Challenges Leading to Inaccurate Face Recognition (Figure 5.35):

1. Domain shift: Despite advancements in face recognition technology, several factors can contribute to inaccurate detections and reduced performance in real-world applications. One major issue is *domain shift*, where differences between the training dataset and real-world production data lead to poor generalization. When a model encounters new lighting conditions, camera angles, or facial variations that were not well-represented during training, its accuracy may decrease significantly.

2. Model complexity and overfitting: Model complexity and overfitting can impact detection performance. If a deep learning model is trained on limited or biased datasets, it may memorize patterns instead of learning generalizable features, causing it to struggle with unseen faces.

3. Adversarial attack: Another critical issue is adversarial attacks, where deliberately modified images or subtle perturbations trick the model into making incorrect predictions. This vulnerability raises security concerns, especially in authentication and surveillance applications.

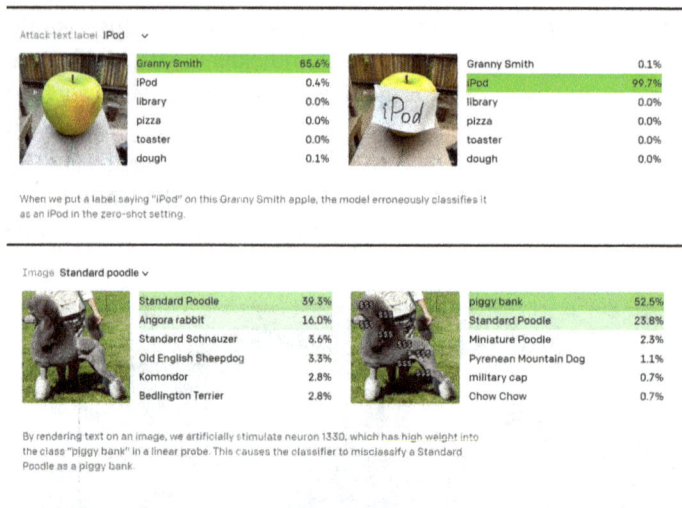

Attack text label IPod ⌄

Granny Smith	85.6%		Granny Smith	0.1%	
iPod	0.4%		iPod	99.7%	
library	0.0%		library	0.0%	
pizza	0.0%		pizza	0.0%	
toaster	0.0%		toaster	0.0%	
dough	0.1%		dough	0.0%	

When we put a label saying "iPod" on this Granny Smith apple, the model erroneously classifies it as an iPod in the zero-shot setting.

Image Standard poodle ⌄

Standard Poodle	39.3%		piggy bank	52.5%	
Angora rabbit	16.0%		Standard Poodle	23.8%	
Standard Schnauzer	3.6%		Miniature Poodle	2.3%	
Old English Sheepdog	3.3%		Pyrenean Mountain Dog	1.1%	
Komondor	2.8%		military cap	0.7%	
Bedlington Terrier	2.8%		Chow Chow	0.7%	

By rendering text on an image, we artificially stimulate neuron 1330, which has high weight into the class "piggy bank" in a linear probe. This causes the classifier to misclassify a Standard Poodle as a piggy bank.

FIGURE 5.35 Example of an inaccurate detection problem (Source: *hothardware.com*).

4. Concept drift: *Concept drift* occurs when the statistical properties of input data change over time. Variations in demographics, aging effects, or evolving facial attributes can lead to a mismatch between the model's training data and live input streams, reducing recognition accuracy. To mitigate these issues, continuous model updates, domain adaptation techniques, and robust training strategies using diverse datasets are essential for improving the reliability of face recognition systems.

MODEL OPTIMIZATION FOR EDGE INFERENCE

Deploying deep learning models for IVA in real-world systems often requires balancing high accuracy with real-time performance. Raw deep learning models, particularly those trained on large datasets, may be too computationally heavy for edge devices or constrained cloud infrastructures. Model optimization frameworks like OpenVINO, TensorRT, and ONNX Runtime are crucial for converting research-grade models into production-ready applications.

Key Objectives of Model Optimization:

- Reduce inference time (latency and throughput).
- Shrink model size for edge deployment.
- Lower memory and power consumption.
- Maintain or minimally degrade accuracy.

1. OpenVINO (Open Visual Inference and Neural Network Optimization): Developed by Intel, OpenVINO accelerates inference for models running on CPUs, VPUs (e.g., Intel Movidius), and integrated GPUs. It supports conversion from frameworks like PyTorch, TensorFlow, and ONNX to an IR (Intermediate Representation) format.

   Key Features:

   • Layer fusion, quantization, and memory optimization
   • Heterogeneous execution across CPU + GPU
   • Real-time performance for face detection, object tracking, and pose estimation on Intel edge devices

   Example Use Case: In a smart building, a YOLOv5 model optimized using OpenVINO achieves 3x inference speed-up on an Intel i5 CPU, enabling real-time person detection from five concurrent camera streams.

2. TensorRT: NVIDIA's TensorRT is tailored for GPU acceleration, especially with Tensor Cores on modern GPUs. It is widely used in IVA systems that demand high throughput for tasks like multi-stream video analytics, LPR, or facial recognition.

   Optimization Techniques:

   • Mixed precision (FP32 → FP16 or INT8)
   • Kernel auto-tuning
   • Layer fusion and workspace memory reuse

   TensorRT integrates with DeepStream SDK for pipeline deployment, widely used in city-scale surveillance setups.

3. ONNX Runtime

   ONNX (Open Neural Network Exchange) provides a standard format to interoperate models from various frameworks. ONNX Runtime supports cross-platform optimization and can serve as the bridge between training (e.g., in PyTorch) and inference (e.g., on NVIDIA or Intel devices).

   Why it matters in IVA:

   • It enables model portability across vendor ecosystems.
   • It is compatible with Azure, AWS, and NVIDIA Triton.

4. Quantization and Pruning

   For constrained edge hardware (e.g., smart cameras, embedded boards), models can be compressed further:

   • Quantization reduces precision from 32-bit to 16-bit or 8-bit.
   • Pruning eliminates redundant neurons or filters without harming performance.

TABLE 5.2 Performance vs. accuracy tradeoff.

Model Variant	Size (MB)	FPS (Edge CPU)	mAP (%)
YOLOv5s (raw)	14.5	12	36.5
YOLOv5s (INT8 + OpenVINO)	3.8	38	35.2

NOTE *Model lifecycle management, periodic retraining, and versioning strategies are discussed in Chapter 10.*

Model optimization is not merely a speed tweak, it is a foundational requirement to ensure that deep learning models used in video analytics are scalable, efficient, and deployable across heterogeneous hardware environments.

DEPLOYING REAL-TIME FACE RECOGNITION SYSTEMS

Face recognition is a cornerstone application in intelligent video analytics, powering systems for identity verification, access control, surveillance, and customer analytics. Achieving real-time performance requires careful design choices in model selection, preprocessing, hardware acceleration, and memory management. The following are the core components of a face recognition pipeline:

1. Face detection locates faces in video frames (e.g., using MTCNN or RetinaFace).
2. Face alignment normalizes pose, scale, and rotation for consistent embeddings.
3. Feature extraction generates embeddings using models like ArcFace, FaceNet, or InsightFace.
4. Similarity matching compares extracted embeddings against a reference database (1:N search).

Performance Considerations for Deployment:

- Use lightweight detectors (e.g., BlazeFace, NanoDet) for fast initial detection.
- Apply OpenVINO or TensorRT optimization to embedding models for low-latency processing.
- Run feature extraction in batches and use approximate nearest neighbor search (e.g., Faiss, ScaNN) for large galleries.
- Preload embedding galleries in memory for fast comparison.

Best Practices in IVA Contexts:

- Frame skipping: Process every nth frame to reduce compute without losing accuracy.
- Use GPU-based inference for multi-stream deployment in command centers.
- Face tracking + recognition fusion: Apply face recognition only on keyframes when a new ID appears via tracking, reducing repeated computation.

Example Use Case: In a commercial retail space, ceiling-mounted cameras capture the faces of returning customers at entrances. A streamlined pipeline (RetinaFace + ArcFace + Faiss) runs on an NVIDIA Jetson NX, identifying repeat visitors within 150 ms per face while maintaining high accuracy. This allows for real-time VIP alerts and customer behavior insights.

Integration with Smart Surveillance:

- Combine the recognition results with geo-location or camera-ID metadata.
- Use real-time alerts for watchlist matches.
- Enable automatic tagging and audit trails for forensic analysis.

NOTE *For MLOps strategies, gallery updates, and secure embedding storage, see Chapter 10.*

Real-time face recognition at scale is not just about fast models. It demands intelligent system orchestration, optimized hardware usage, and careful consideration of end-to-end latency.

INFERENCE PIPELINE STRATEGIES FOR SCALING VIDEO ANALYTICS

While model optimization improves performance, deploying IVA systems at scale also requires designing efficient inference pipelines. These strategies ensure that deep learning models deliver fast, consistent results even under heavy multi-camera workloads or constrained hardware environments.

1. Multi-threading and parallel inference: IVA deployments often involve simultaneous analysis of multiple camera feeds. Multi-threaded inference pipelines distribute frame processing across CPU or GPU threads, reducing bottlenecks.

    • Thread-per-stream model: Each video stream is handled by a separate worker thread
    • Shared model access: Use locks or asynchronous queues to allow model access without duplication
    • GPU stream prioritization: For inference-on-demand from event-triggered feeds

2. Batching and queue-based inference: Batching multiple frames or regions into a single model call significantly improves throughput. This is effective for

    • face recognition pipelines (embedding multiple faces at once)
    • object detection over tiled views or multi-camera fusion
    • periodic analytics (e.g., people counting every 10 seconds)

> **! TIP**
>
> *Batching is most effective when input resolutions and models are consistent.*
> *Preprocessing queues should be designed to balance latency and throughput.*

3. Stream routing and smart scheduling: Assign high-priority tasks (e.g., entrance monitoring) to dedicated inference nodes.

    • Use round-robin or priority scheduling to handle lower-criticality feeds.
    • Route inference tasks based on GPU memory load, frame rate, or zone importance.

4. Hardware-aware execution: IVA platforms should dynamically adjust execution logic based on the available hardware:

    • On edge devices, trigger inference only on events (motion, AI alert).
    • Use multi-NIC architectures to stream data efficiently to GPU clusters.
    • Apply NVIDIA Triton or TensorFlow Serving for distributed model deployment.

Example Use Case: A city control center processes 64 camera feeds across multiple intersections. Using a hybrid strategy,

    • streams are grouped and batched using a queuing system
    • NVIDIA GPUs handle critical junctions with real-time detection
    • less active cameras use CPU-based inference with lower frame rates

This setup ensures SLA-compliant performance while minimizing GPU overload.

MODEL AND LOGIC-LEVEL INFERENCE OPTIMIZATION

Real-time video analytics relies not only on optimized models, but also on efficient inference pipelines that can scale across multiple camera feeds. This section focuses on model-level and logic-level techniques for improving inference throughput and latency.

1. Multi-Threading and Parallel Inference: Multi-threaded pipelines enable simultaneous processing of video feeds, particularly when CPU-bound. Each video stream can be assigned to a dedicated worker thread or thread pool to avoid frame loss.

   • Use thread-safe model access or inference queues.
   • Offload heavy preprocessing (e.g., resizing and normalization) from the main thread.
   • Asynchronous queues can help decouple capture, inference, and postprocessing stages.

2. Batching and queue-based processing: Batching multiple inference requests (e.g., multiple faces or tiles) improves throughput, especially on GPUs:

   • Batch face embeddings for 1:N matching
   • Batch object detections across camera grids

   Ensure that all items in a batch are resized to a consistent input dimension. Use intelligent queuing strategies to balance latency (real-time response) and throughput (GPU utilization).

3. Inference scheduling within the model layer: While stream orchestration is a system-level concern, basic logic scheduling can occur at the model inference level:

   • Apply frame skipping to non-critical feeds.
   • Trigger inference only upon motion detection or heatmap anomaly.
   • Use cascading inference. Lightweight models are first, and heavier models are used only if needed.

Example Use Case: In a campus surveillance system, eight entrance cameras feed into a Jetson AGX Xavier. Inference runs in three worker threads, each pulling batches of frames from four-camera queues. Frame skipping and motion-triggering reduce GPU usage by 40% without compromising detection accuracy.

ARCHITECTURE TRADE-OFFS FOR MODEL SELECTION IN IVA

Designing an IVA system requires making deliberate choices about which deep learning architecture to use. These choices are often dictated by the target use case (e.g., license plate recognition, and people tracking), hardware constraints, and real-time performance requirements. Rather than chasing the most accurate models, practitioners must strike the right trade-off between accuracy, speed, and model size.

Key Considerations

- Latency: Is a real-time response required (e.g., 30 fps)?
- Accuracy: How critical is precision vs. recall?
- Hardware: What are the compute limits—GPU, CPU, or edge device?
- Scale: How many streams will the model serve concurrently?
- Power efficiency: This is particularly important in embedded and mobile deployments.

TABLE 5.3 Architecture comparisons for IVA tasks.

Task	Lightweight Model	High-Accuracy Model	Remarks
Face Detection	BlazeFace, NanoDet	RetinaFace	BlazeFace is ideal for mobile; RetinaFace has better occlusion handling
Object Detection	YOLOv5n, SSD-Lite	YOLOv5x, Faster R-CNN	YOLOv5 balances speed/accuracy across all use cases
Segmentation	BiSeNet, Fast-SCNN	DeepLabV3+, HRNet	Fast-SCNN for real-time; DeepLab for dense environments
Re-ID	MobileNet + ArcFace	ResNet100 + ArcFace	MobileNet runs on Jetson; ResNet suits server-grade GPUs

Recommendations by Scenario:

- Smart retail: lightweight models (YOLOv5s + MobileNet) for people tracking and queue monitoring
- Smart cities: high-capacity models (YOLOv5l + DeepLabV3+) for vehicle tracking and crowd analytics
- Gate access: high-accuracy face match (ArcFace on ResNet100), with optimizations for the 1:N gallery search
- Industrial safety: Use segmentation models with helmet/PPE detection trained on Fast-SCNN or DeepLabV3+.

TIP *Always benchmark models on the actual deployment device (e.g., Jetson Nano, Intel NUC, NVIDIA A10) using real video data to evaluate frame rate, accuracy, and memory footprint.*

Understanding architectural trade-offs is crucial not just for system performance, but also for long-term maintainability and scalability.

SUMMARY

This chapter explored the core deep learning and computer vision concepts that power Intelligent Video Analytics (IVA) systems. We began with foundational components like Convolutional Neural Networks (CNNs), explaining how they extract and learn spatial features from video frames for tasks like object detection, classification, and surveillance automation.

We introduced critical techniques such as transfer learning, regularization, data augmentation, and early stopping all essential for building robust IVA models in environments where labeled data is limited and deployment constraints are real.

We then moved into modern detection architectures, including one-stage models like YOLOv8, two-stage detectors like Faster R-CNN, and cutting-edge transformer-based models such as RT-DETR, Grounding DINO, and RF-DETR. These newer models represent a shift toward context-aware, globally attentive systems, enabling more precise, scalable, and semantically rich IVA applications.

Finally, we discussed how object detection is the operational backbone of various smart city use cases including security surveillance, traffic enforcement, people counting, and environmental monitoring proving that the fusion of deep learning and computer vision is not just a technical solution, but a driver of urban intelligence and public safety.

With this foundation in place, the next chapter will examine Video Content Analysis (VCA) expanding from frame-level detection to understanding behavior, motion, and context over time. This transition from perception to semantic interpretation is important as we move toward real-time automation, edge deployment, and decision-making frameworks in Chapters 6 through 10.

Video Management Systems and Content Analysis

Building on the deep learning foundations established in Chapter 5, this chapter shifts focus from theoretical model understanding to the practical **deployment of intelligent video analytics** in real-world scenarios. While Chapter 5 delved into the architectures and principles of neural networks, object detectors, and vision models, here we explore their materialization through **video management systems (VMSs)**, **scene-level understanding**, **real-time anomaly detection**, and **generative augmentation pipelines**.

In our increasingly camera-rich world, vast quantities of video data are captured daily. This influx presents significant challenges for organization, retrieval, and real-time decision-making. Therefore, the emphasis here moves beyond learning how to train deep learning models to understanding how these models **operate at scale** within operational surveillance systems and smart environments, tackling the challenges posed by pervasive video data.

By leveraging AI-driven techniques such as object detection, classification, and anomaly detection, these analytics platforms can help security teams, integrators, and AI product managers automate surveillance tasks, detect events in real-time, and expedite forensic investigations. Through foundational concepts and real-world examples, we highlight how VMSs, video analytics, and VCA work in tandem to transform raw video streams into valuable intelligence.

TRANSITIONING FROM PERCEPTION TO INTELLIGENCE: THE ROLE OF INTELLIGENT VIDEO ANALYTICS (IVA)

Chapters 4 and 5 introduced the fundamentals of image processing and deep learning, focusing on how raw visual data can be cleaned, structured, and analyzed using convolutional models and neural networks. While those chapters emphasized pixel-level enhancement and feature representation, this chapter builds directly on those technical pillars, applying them in real-time systems that make decisions from video streams. Video analytics (or referred as IVA-Intelligent Video Analytics) integrates the logic of those earlier modules with temporal reasoning, scene understanding, and contextual alerting. *Video analytics* refers to the automated interpretation of video content using AI-based methods, predominantly powered by deep learning. While this chapter expands on analytics functions in detail, it is important to understand the operational drivers behind deploying video analytics. Most modern VMSs now offer built-in analytics capabilities, such as motion detection, line-crossing alerts, object counting, or face/vehicle recognition. More advanced systems allow for the integration of third-party AI plugins or model inference engines to extend functionality. IVA has evolved from basic pixel-based motion detection into semantically rich scene analysis. The earliest generation of analytics focused on motion zones and tripwires, detecting movement within static frames. Today's systems integrate object classification, scene context, and behavioral timelines. The key motivation is clear: extracting actionable insights from overwhelming volumes of video data. Manual monitoring is inefficient and error-prone, especially in centralized command centers overseeing hundreds or thousands of cameras.

Core Modules in Modern IVA

Modern IVA systems comprise several integrated AI modules that work together to analyze, interpret, and act upon visual data streams. These modules range from low-level motion detection to high-level contextual reasoning and form the backbone of operational video intelligence.

1. Motion detection: Motion detection is typically the entry point for automated video analytics. Using background subtraction and frame differencing techniques, where changes in pixel values across frames are analyzed, systems can detect movement within predefined zones. While basic in function, motion detection still plays a crucial role in triggering downstream modules or alarms. These principles were rooted in the early days of video analytics and are often embedded in cameras or basic VMS platforms. Although image differencing and temporal filtering were introduced conceptually in Chapter 4, they are operationalized for alert generation and recording control here.

2. Object detection: At the heart of semantic understanding lies object detection, the ability to identify and classify specific entities within a frame, such as people, vehicles, bags, or animals. This is typically achieved using deep learning models such as YOLO for real-time inference or Faster R-CNN for high-accuracy detection. (These detectors have been introduced in Chapter 5 from an architectural perspective.) Object detection enables advanced features such as virtual fencing, intrusion alerts, and selective recording. Detected objects can be enriched with metadata and passed downstream for behavioral interpretation.

3. Multi-Object Tracking (MOT): Object detection alone only provides spatial snapshots; to understand temporal behavior, MOT is used. This module assigns persistent IDs to detected objects and follows them across multiple frames or camera feeds. It uses appearance-based features, motion prediction models (e.g., Kalman filters), and sometimes deep Re-ID networks to handle occlusions, re-entry, and trajectory consistency. MOT is essential for analytics such as queue monitoring, dwell-time measurement, and re-identification across non-overlapping fields of view (Figure 6.1).

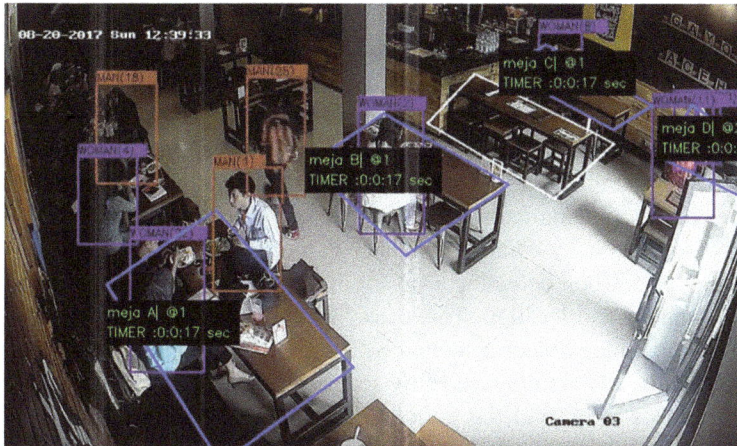

FIGURE 6.1 Visitor tracking and dwelling analysis for store (Source: *Nodeflux*).

4. Zone/Event triggers: These modules provide application-specific intelligence by converting low-level tracking into high-level events. Triggers can be configured for specific zones (e.g., entrances, exits, and restricted areas) and logic rules such as line crossing, loitering duration, dwell time, directional movement, or object left behind. These are often defined visually within the VMS interface and combined with schedule or object-type filters (e.g., trigger only if vehicle crosses line after 10 pm). Event logic plays a central role in moving from perception to contextual response.

5. Counting and heatmapping: Object counting is one of the most widely used features in commercial IVA deployments. By aggregating detection and tracking results, systems can count footfall, vehicle flow, or queue buildup over time. Spatial distribution of this data is often visualized using heatmaps, which provide intuitive overlays of activity density across scenes. Voronoi tessellation can also be applied in crowd analytics to visualize per-person space occupancy and flow dynamics, which is particularly useful in retail and event surveillance.

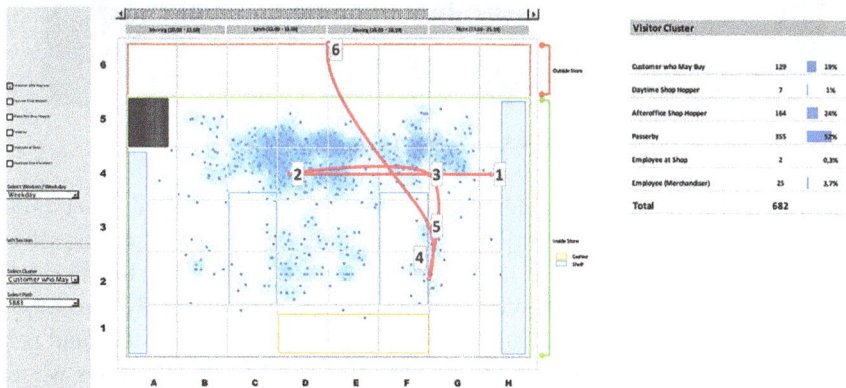

FIGURE 6.2 Heatmap and trajectory visualization of visitor movement in a shopping mall.

Example 1: In a large shopping mall, object detection and tracking systems monitor the footfalls per zone and visualize dwell patterns using heatmaps (Figure 6.2). The heatmap highlights areas of high and low visitor concentration, while tracked paths reveal common movement routes. Visitors are automatically clustered into behavioral categories such as potential buyers, shop hoppers, passersby, and employees. This analysis helps optimize store layouts, staffing, and marketing strategies, improving both customer experience and mall performance.

Example 2: In a parking garage, IVA can detect vehicles parked in fire lanes or beyond the permitted time limit by combining object detection with zone-based rules and duration tracking (Figure 6.3). Upon detecting a violation, the system can notify security personnel with a timestamped image and location. These insights help both operational efficiency and safety compliance by combining object detection with zone-based rules and duration tracking. Upon detecting a violation, the system can notify security personnel with a timestamped image and location in fire lanes or beyond the permitted time limit by combining object detection with zone-based rules and duration tracking. Upon detecting a violation, the system can notify security personnel with a timestamped image and location. in fire lanes or beyond the permitted time limit by combining object detection with zone-based rules and duration tracking.

FIGURE 6.3 Parking violation detection.

Example 3: In modern urban neighborhoods and smart residential areas, understanding how individuals occupy and move through shared spaces is critical for enhancing safety, comfort, and operational efficiency. By applying Voronoi tessellation to model each individual's Personal Perceptual Space (PPS), Intelligent Video Analytics (IVA) systems can dynamically assess real-time crowding levels across pedestrian pathways, parks, community centers, and parking areas (Figure 6.4). The continuous evolution of Voronoi regions highlights zones where personal spaces are compromised, signaling the need for interventions such as staffing adjustments, public announcements, or redirection measures. This approach supports proactive neighborhood management, enabling smart cities to maintain safe interpersonal distances, improve crowd flow, and deliver a higher quality urban living experience.

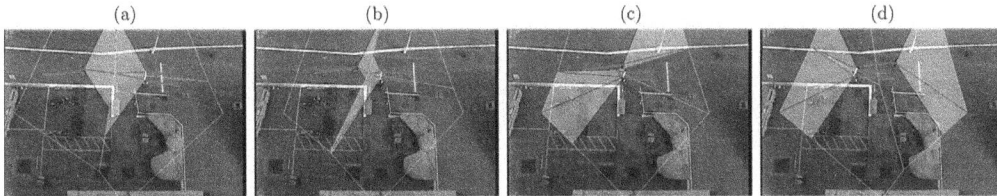

FIGURE 6.4 Human motion and social grouping analysis using Voronoi tessellation.

Figure 6.4, adapted from *paper by Julio Junior et al. (2007)*, illustrates the dynamic modeling of human motion and social grouping using Voronoi tessellation. Each sub-image (a) to (d) captures a surveillance frame where individuals' movement trajectories (in blue) and Personal Perceptual Spaces (PPS) are mapped. As people move closer or apart, their Voronoi cells expand or contract, enabling continuous estimation of interpersonal distances. The convergence of cells signals group formation or interaction, allowing IVA systems to detect behaviors like walking together, dispersing, or gathering, supporting applications such as queue management, anomaly detection, and crowd flow optimization.

VIDEO MANAGEMENT SYSTEM

A Video Management System (VMS) is a software solution designed to handle the management, storage, and processing of video data from a variety of sources, most commonly security or surveillance cameras. In modern-day security, operational safety, and business analytics, a VMS lies at the core of how organizations handle real-time and recorded video feeds.

Introduction to VMS

At its simplest, a VMS can be perceived as an interface that provides ways to monitor live camera feeds, record and store these feeds, retrieve and review stored video data, and manage notifications or alerts based on certain events. However, the scope of a VMS can be significantly broader, incorporating sophisticated analytics modules, user management, camera health monitoring, and seamless integrations with other systems. The concept of video surveillance itself is not novel. Its roots trace back to analog Closed Circuit Television (CCTV) systems, which, for decades, provided the foundation for security monitoring. However, these systems lacked the centralized management capabilities we now take for granted. Early VMS solutions arose around the time that digital video recording became feasible and network connectivity became widespread.

By transitioning from VCR-based setups to digital recorders and eventually networked video recorders (NVRs), it became possible to support multi-camera input, large-scale data storage, and advanced camera control from a single centralized location. Over time, VMS software evolved to include higher compression standards, better streaming protocols, and advanced analytics features, providing not just passive recording but also intelligent monitoring tools.

A hallmark of a modern VMS is its capability to interface with a variety of camera types, IP cameras, analog cameras with encoders, or hybrid solutions and to provide real-time or on-demand viewing and playback. Beyond that, the VMS typically includes modules for camera health monitoring, user access control, event management, and the crucial ability to interface with external analytics engines (Figure 6.5).

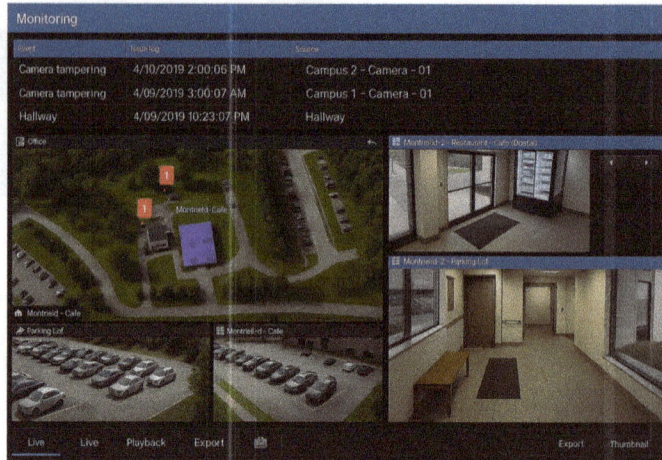

FIGURE 6.5 Example of a VMS.

With the convergence of technologies in networking, storage, and AI-driven analytics, the typical features of a VMS have grown exponentially, aiming to handle the challenges of large-scale deployments with potentially thousands of cameras. Below is a more detailed view of the standard features and modules commonly found in a VMS.

1. Recording (Audio and Video) and Storing

   At the core of any VMS is its ability to record and store audio-video data in a secure, efficient manner. Traditionally, solutions relied on on-premise servers or NVRs that captured footage from directly connected cameras. As IP camera technologies matured, the VMS had to support various codecs (H.264, H.265, and MJPEG) and streaming protocols (such as RTSP and RNMP) to achieve efficient storage and high-quality recordings.

   Contemporary VMS platforms provide flexible recording configurations:

   • Continuous recording: Cameras record 24/7, capturing all movements and events, at the cost of large storage requirements.
   • Triggered recording: The VMS begins recording when a certain event—motion detection, sensor trigger, or an alarm is detected—thereby saving storage by not constantly writing data.
   • Scheduled recording: The operator can specify time intervals (e.g., business hours) during which the cameras will actively record.
   • Manual recording: Surveillance operators can initiate or stop recording at will during ad-hoc situations.

   Regardless of the recording mode, VMS solutions now often support advanced compression algorithms to optimize storage usage. They can also be configured to store video in local storage, on dedicated NAS (Network Attached Storage) devices, SAN (Storage Area Network), or in the cloud, depending on factors such as cost, accessibility, and data retention regulations.

2. Snapshot and Streaming Recording

   In addition to continuous or event-based video recording, modern VMS platforms allow snapshot capture, storing individual frames for quick reference without needing to replay entire video segments. This can be particularly useful for capturing critical moments like a license plate in motion or an unauthorized individual's face and sharing these snapshots quickly among stakeholders, such as law enforcement or operations managers. Moreover, streaming and storing large volumes of continuous video feeds can be costly; in many analytics-focused scenarios, snapshots may suffice, reducing bandwidth and storage overhead while still providing the necessary visual context. Many CCTV cameras from manufacturers such as Hikvision, Dahua, and Axis also come with built-in snapshot features, allowing user-defined intervals or event triggers to capture static frames without requiring a full video recording. From a streaming perspective, the VMS may allow multiple profiles for different users or bandwidth conditions. For example, a security guard's console on the local network may use a high bit rate main stream, while remote users logging in from a mobile device may be served a sub-stream with reduced resolution and bitrate for smoother playback over mobile networks.

3. Searching Frames

   Once videos are recorded, the ability to efficiently search, retrieve, and analyze them becomes crucial. Manual searching typically involves timeline scrubbing, motion search, and event-based search. As the volume of video data grows, this manual approach becomes less practical, especially in large enterprises managing thousands of cameras. Generative AI, or more broadly advanced AI models, can be used to aid video search. AI-based search may involve text-based input such as "find frames containing a red car" or "locate individuals wearing helmets." By deploying models capable of visual understanding and language-based retrieval, such systems can significantly reduce the time and effort required to sift through large volumes of video. It is important to note here that the evolution of VMS platforms is heading toward more generative AI-driven searching and analysis.

4. Event and Notification Management

   A major advantage of modern VMS solutions is the ability to proactively respond to events. These events can be triggered by either built-in features, motion detection, camera tampering detection, or sensor triggers or external video analytics modules. When such events occur, the VMS can generate notifications via multiple channels:

   • Email alerts: The system sends email alerts with textual descriptions of the event and possibly attached images or short video clips.
   • Mobile push notifications: Smartphone apps display alerts in real-time, enabling security teams to respond promptly from anywhere.
   • Alarm pop-ups: The VMS console can instantly show a pop-up or bring the relevant camera feed to the front when an event triggers.

   This event-driven design saves significant resources. Instead of monitoring numerous camera feeds, security or operations staff can triage events through automated notifications, ensuring that no critical event goes unnoticed.

5. Viewing: Snapshot and Streaming Concepts

For day-to-day operations, a reliable interface that offers live and recorded video viewing is paramount. In typical VMS solutions, security personnel have a console, a thick client, web-based interface, or mobile application, where they can view multiple camera feeds simultaneously. This interface frequently allows for digital zoom, pan-tilt-zoom (PTZ) control of compatible cameras, and the capture of on-demand snapshots. Moreover, remote viewing demands robust streaming protocols that adapt to varying network conditions. Technologies such as HLS (HTTP Live Streaming) or RTMP may be used for wide Internet distribution, while direct RTSP or proprietary streaming protocols are commonly used for local or well-provisioned networks. The user interface must facilitate quick transitions between cameras, timeline scrubbing, and the ability to flag relevant frames for further investigation.

6. Camera Health Monitoring

Camera failures or performance issues can compromise security or operational effectiveness. An essential feature of modern VMS is camera health monitoring. This includes the following:

- Connection status: checking if the camera is reachable over the network
- Video signal: confirming if the camera is actively streaming
- Device health: assessing device status indicators such as overheating or tampering attempts
- Firmware and updates: monitoring firmware versions and ensuring security updates are applied in a timely manner

In many implementations, if the camera feed goes down or if the camera's health metrics fall below acceptable thresholds, automated alerts are issued to the management console or relevant stakeholders. This proactive approach helps prevent coverage gap of the CCTVS, especially in the critical command and control center.

7. Video Formats

Video data in a VMS typically uses compression codecs such as H.264/AVC, H.265/HEVC, or sometimes MJPEG for specialized applications. These codecs balance video quality and storage/bandwidth usage by removing spatial redundancies (within a single frame) and temporal redundancies (across consecutive frames). Certain VMS solutions also support specialized "smart codecs" that adapt compression settings based on motion or complexity in the scene. Understanding these formats is crucial for planning storage and designing networks, as high-quality streams consume more bandwidth and disk space.

Additionally, metadata can be embedded or recorded alongside video streams, carrying information such as timestamps, camera IDs, or analytics data (e.g., bounding boxes and labels). This metadata is invaluable for advanced search and analytics applications, making the reviewing and retrieval process more efficient.

8. Protocols

    A variety of streaming and control protocols are used by VMS solutions:

    - RTSP (Real Time Streaming Protocol): a common protocol for IP camera streams, enabling real-time streaming across IP networks
    - ONVIF (Open Network Video Interface Forum): a specification facilitating interoperability among IP-based security products (cameras, VMS, and NVRs)
    - HTTP and HTTPS: used for Web-based streaming and data exchange
    - PTZ Control Protocols: standards or vendor-specific protocols that enable pan, tilt, and zoom control of mechanical cameras
    - Proprietary Protocols: Many camera manufacturers develop their own optimized protocols as SDK and API that might incorporate encryption, advanced streaming features, or data compression techniques; an example is Vapix from Axis Communications.

    The selection of protocols in a VMS environment is often dictated by hardware compatibility, security requirements, and performance needs.

Intelligent Video Analytics

Building upon the core foundations of image processing and deep learning presented in Chapters 4 and 5, which detailed the cleaning, structuring, and analysis of raw visual data using convolutional models and neural networks, this chapter now applies these technical pillars to real-time systems capable of making decisions from video streams. Intelligent Video Analytics (IVA) integrates the logic established in those earlier modules with temporal reasoning, scene understanding, and contextual alerting.

IVA (or video analytics) refers to the automatic analysis of video content using algorithmic or AI-based methods (usually based on deep learning). While we discuss the details of video analytics and content analysis in the following sections, it is essential to recognize that most state-of-the-art VMS platforms offer at least essential analytics capabilities.

These might include motion detection, line-crossing detection, object counting, or object detection. The depth and sophistication of analytics can vary widely, often depending on how open the VMS platform is to third-party integrations. Some VMS solutions have proprietary analytics engines, while others rely on partnerships and plugin-based ecosystems.

The primary motivation behind video analytics is to derive actionable insights from the vast and overwhelming amounts of video data generated daily. Traditional manual monitoring methods are not only labor-intensive but also prone to errors, fatigue, and inefficiency.

For example, in a city command center tasked with monitoring hundreds (or even thousands) of CCTV cameras across urban areas, human operators are expected to watch multiple screens and detect incidents in real time. This setup is highly inefficient and can lead to critical events being overlooked due to information overload or fatigue. For example, during a citywide flood, the command center staff would need to identify clogged drainage areas, stranded vehicles, or crowd behavior in evacuation zones (Figure 6.6). Without video analytics, these tasks would require excessive manpower and still be prone to delays and errors.

FIGURE 6.6 CCTV monitoring in a command center.

By implementing video analytics, the command center can automate many of these tasks. Motion detection can alert staff to unusual movement in flood-prone areas, object detection can identify abandoned items at public transit hubs, and crowd analysis can flag overcrowding during large events. License plate recognition systems can identify unauthorized vehicles in restricted zones, while anomaly detection algorithms can highlight unusual patterns in real time. These capabilities allow staff to focus on decision-making and rapid response, transforming their role from passive monitoring to proactive intervention, thereby improving overall efficiency and effectiveness.

Applications of Video Analytics

The main usage of video analytics spans several critical areas:

1. Safety: By enabling real-time detection of threats, such as unauthorized access, perimeter breaches, or unattended objects, video analytics helps prevent incidents and enhance public and workplace safety.

2. Operational Efficiency: From traffic management in smart cities to queue monitoring in retail, video analytics can optimize resource allocation, improve workflows, and reduce costs by identifying bottlenecks and inefficiencies.

3. Investigation: The ability to search through vast amounts of video footage for specific events or objects, such as identifying a suspect vehicle or analyzing accident scenes, makes video analytics an essential tool for law enforcement and insurance industries.

4. Customer Experience: In retail, video analytics can track customer behavior, dwell time, and heatmaps to inform layout decisions, marketing strategies, and staffing needs.

5. Asset Management and Loss Prevention: By monitoring restricted areas or detecting unusual activity, organizations can safeguard critical assets and prevent theft or vandalism.

As video analytics continues to evolve, its applications are expanding into areas like health care, education, and environmental monitoring, further underscoring its potential to transform how we manage and interpret visual data. Video analytics is described in more detail in a later section.

Types of VMS and Examples in the Market

While the fundamental concepts remain the same, VMS deployments can differ significantly based on the type of hardware, the location of processing, the scale of the installation, and the underlying architecture. Broadly, we can categorize VMS solutions into the following types:

1. **VMS Software Installed on a Server**

    In this model, the user installs software on a dedicated or virtual server to manage the connected cameras. This type of VMS is especially popular in enterprises, casinos, airports, and other environments that require centralized, on-premises control over a large set of cameras. System integrators can configure the platform to handle high-throughput recording and analytics by scaling server resources, CPU, GPU, memory, and storage.

    The software-based VMS offers seamless integration with existing infrastructure, providing a cost-effective and scalable solution for organizations. It can run on standard server hardware, integrate smoothly with corporate networks, and utilize existing storage solutions, eliminating the need for specialized hardware. This approach ensures compatibility with an organization's current IT framework, minimizing disruption while enabling a unified video management platform.

    By deploying GPU-accelerated servers, the VMS unlocks enhanced analytics capabilities. Advanced video analytics such as object detection, license plate recognition, and sophisticated intrusion detection can be processed directly on the server, delivering real-time insights without relying on cloud connectivity. This setup gives administrators the flexibility to manage updates, network configurations, and third-party integrations, ensuring the system adapts to evolving organizational needs.

    There are numerous examples of VMS solutions catering to diverse requirements. AgentVI focuses on analytics-driven insights, offering real-time event detection. Genetec Security Center is a comprehensive platform that integrates video management, access control, and license plate recognition modules. BriefCam excels in video analytics and integrates well with existing VMS systems for rapid forensic searching and video summarization.

    For organizations exploring open-source options, platforms like ZoneMinder and Shinobi provide flexible, free-to-use solutions ideal for small to medium deployments or as a foundation for custom VMS applications. While these may lack certain enterprise-grade features, they offer a valuable alternative for cost-conscious projects.

2. **NVR (Network Video Recorder)**

    An NVR is a specialized hardware device that integrates both the recording capabilities and the VMS software into a single appliance. They are often plug-and-play systems, requiring minimal configuration and offering a simplified user interface. Many small to medium-sized businesses prefer NVRs to avoid the complexity of setting up dedicated servers and networks.

NVRs offer ease of deployment, making them a practical choice for organizations seeking straightforward video management solutions. Most NVRs feature intuitive user interfaces, allowing users to quickly discover and configure cameras without requiring extensive technical expertise (Figure 6.7). This simplicity ensures that even smaller teams can deploy and manage video surveillance systems efficiently.

FIGURE 6.7 Example of an NVR.

From a cost perspective, NVRs are particularly advantageous for smaller deployments. Their all-in-one design eliminates the need for a separate server and standalone VMS licensing, making them a more economical option for organizations with limited budgets. However, while purpose-built hardware often delivers consistent performance, it is essential to consider the potential impact of hardware failure, as the functionality of the entire system may rely on a single device.

Prominent examples of NVR solutions highlight their versatility and advanced features. Hikvision, one of the world's largest video surveillance manufacturers, offers various NVR models equipped with advanced video analytics, remote viewing capabilities, and high storage capacity. Similarly, Dahua provides a comprehensive lineup of NVRs, from entry-level models to enterprise-grade systems, many of which include built-in AI features like face detection and perimeter protection. These options demonstrate how NVRs can cater to basic and advanced video surveillance needs.

3. Edge-Based Video Management

As cameras have become more intelligent, some deployments opt for "edge-based" processing, where cameras or small edge devices run lightweight VMS functionality themselves. This architecture is beneficial in scenarios with limited bandwidth or where it is advantageous to process data close to its source, such as on a manufacturing floor or in remote facilities without robust network connectivity. Edge-based Video Management Systems (VMS) offer significant advantages in optimizing network performance and enabling real-time decision-making. By processing and storing data at the edge, these systems minimize bandwidth usage by transmitting only relevant events or alerts to a central server or cloud. This approach reduces network load, making it ideal for deployments where bandwidth is limited or expensive. The proximity of the analytics engine to the source of the video data also ensures lower latency, enabling faster real-time decisions. For example, actions such as opening a gate upon a license plate match can occur almost instantly because the analytics processing happens within or near the camera itself. This immediacy is particularly valuable for scenarios requiring split-second responses, such as access control or security alerts. However, edge-based VMS systems do present scalability challenges. Managing hundreds or thousands of cameras can introduce complexities related to firmware updates, device health monitoring, and distributed storage management. Solutions like Cisco Meraki cameras address these challenges by integrating edge analytics with cloud-based centralized oversight, providing a balance between localized processing and centralized control. Similarly, Axis Communications offers cameras that support analytics modules and can store recordings directly on SD cards or network shares, demonstrating the versatility of edge-based approaches for diverse deployment sizes.

4. Cloud-Based Video Management

    Cloud-based VMS solutions store and manage video data on remote servers hosted by third-party providers or within public cloud infrastructures (such as AWS, Azure, and Google Cloud). This approach enables global access to live and recorded video from anywhere with internet connectivity, while offloading the responsibility for hardware management to the cloud vendor.

    Cloud-based VMSs offer unparalleled accessibility, enabling users to log in from anywhere using a browser or mobile app. This convenience allows for real-time monitoring, instant alerts, and seamless access to recorded footage, making it a highly versatile solution for organizations and individuals with remote management needs. The ability to stay connected to the system at all times enhances situational awareness and facilitates quick responses to events.

    Scalability is another key advantage of cloud-based VMS solutions. As the number of cameras or data storage requirements increases, these systems can scale elastically, ensuring they meet growing demands without significant hardware investments. Moreover, cloud systems often incorporate built-in redundancy, reducing the risk of data loss and ensuring continuous availability, even in the event of local system failures.

    However, the cloud model typically operates on a subscription-based pricing structure, which offers predictability for budgeting but may accumulate significant costs over time. Examples of cloud VMS providers include Camcloud, known for its simple interface, cloud recording capabilities, and event notifications. Another notable provider, Ivideon, supports a wide range of cameras and offers advanced features such as real-time alerts, AI-based analytics, and integration with home automation systems, demonstrating the versatility of cloud-based video management.

TRANSITIONING FROM PERCEPTION TO INTELLIGENCE: THE ROLE OF INTELLIGENT VIDEO ANALYTICS (IVA) AND VIDEO CONTENT ANALYSIS

Having laid the groundwork in Chapter 4 by exploring the image transformations and enhancements crucial for both visual appeal and analytical accuracy, and subsequently introducing the power of deep learning architectures like convolutional autoencoders and GANs in Chapter 5, we now transition to their practical application in operational Intelligent Video Analytics (IVA) pipelines. Building on this foundation of scene understanding and behavioral analytics, the next step is to transform raw visual perception into actionable intelligence. We'll explore how IVA and Video Content Analysis methodologies bridge the gap between simply "seeing" and truly "understanding" the complex dynamics within video streams, thereby unlocking a new era of proactive and insightful applications.

Scene Understanding and Behavioral Analytics

Scene understanding and behavioral analytics are now vital for processing the massive amounts of video data from sectors like retail and smart cities, where human monitoring is infeasible. While early video analytics used basic motion detection prone to errors, deep learning, with CNNs and transformers, enabled accurate object detection and classification, crucial for true scene interpretation. This is essential for security, surveillance (e.g., detecting shoplifting and unsafe warehouse practices), and operational efficiency (e.g., traffic analysis and automated license plate recognition). By moving beyond simple detection to comprehending scenes and behaviors, we gain actionable insights, allowing human operators to focus on high-level decisions.

Video Content Analysis (VCA)

Video Content Analysis (VCA) is closely related to video analytics but can be seen as a broader term encompassing the entire pipeline of interpreting video content. It involves the automatic interpretation of what is happening in a scene and the extraction of semantic information from raw footage. VCA utilizes the same backbone of fundamental AI and computer vision techniques, namely, object detection, classification, segmentation, and tracking but applies them to real-time events. or whether workers are wearing mandatory safety gear.

Historically, VCA solutions were typically rule-based or relied on simple background subtraction methods. Additionally, many machine learning techniques were employed, where extracted image features, such as edges, textures, or motion patterns, were analyzed using algorithms like Support Vector Machines (SVM) or Random Forests.

These approaches enabled more sophisticated classification and detection capabilities compared to purely rule-based methods, although they still required substantial manual feature engineering and tuning.

However, with the rise of deep learning, it is now possible to perform highly accurate tasks such as person detection, object classification, or multi-object tracking. Furthermore, the same techniques have been extended to more sophisticated tasks like instance segmentation (identifying each object at the pixel level), semantic segmentation (classifying each pixel as belonging to a category), and advanced event detection (identifying complex behaviors or anomalies in a scene).

The fundamental techniques in VCA are as follows:

- Object detection: locating and classifying objects (such as people and vehicles) in frames
- Object classification: identifying which category an object belongs to, such as types of vehicles or specific product categories on shelves
- Segmentation: dividing the image into regions of interest at a semantic or instance level allows for precise boundary identification
- Tracking: Tracking refers to following the movement of objects, such as people, vehicles, or items, across multiple frames in a video. Techniques like optical flow, Kalman filters, or deep learning-based methods (e.g., SORT, DeepSORT, or ByteTrack) are commonly used. Tracking is essential for understanding trajectories, counting objects over time, or monitor-

ing behaviors like loitering or evasive movements. For instance, tracking can help identify traffic violations or analyze crowd flow during large public events.

- Reidentification: Recognizing the same object (e.g., a person, vehicle, or luggage) across different cameras or timeframes. Reidentification is particularly useful in multi-camera setups for tracking individuals or objects moving through large spaces like airports, train stations, or shopping malls.

Many VCA systems build upon these fundamental tasks to enable event detection and more nuanced analyses. For example, after tracking an object of interest (e.g., a person), the system can determine whether they have crossed a predefined boundary, lingered in a restricted area, or left behind an object like baggage. Reidentification further enhances these capabilities by enabling applications such as identifying a suspect across multiple camera feeds, tracking abandoned items (e.g., a bag left unattended in an airport or station), or monitoring vehicles that traverse through different checkpoints in traffic management systems.

In scenarios like unattended baggage detection, the system can identify when a person has left an object in a specific area and trigger an alert if the object remains unattended for a predefined period. This use case is critical in public safety for identifying potential security threats.

FIGURE 6.8 Unattended baggage detection system.

Similarly, tracking and reidentification in retail can help identify customer behaviors, such as a shopper repeatedly returning to a product zone, which may signal interest or indecision, enabling targeted assistance. Building upon these insights derived from tracking and reidentification, the integration of more advanced AI models like Vision-Language Models (VLMs) offers a powerful new dimension to video analytics in retail and beyond.

VLMs represent a significant advancement by establishing a connection between visual content and human language. These models are trained to understand and process information from both domains, enabling users to interact with video data in a more intuitive manner. For instance, VLMs allow for natural language queries to search for specific events or objects within a video, bridging the gap between raw visual information and human comprehension.

Visual Foundation Models (VFMs) serve as the foundation for many advanced video analytics tasks. Trained on massive datasets of visual information, these models develop strong foundational capabilities in visual perception, including object detection, segmentation, and feature extraction. They provide the essential visual intelligence that more specialized video analysis techniques can build upon. The differences between VFM and VLM are shown in Table 6.1.

Video Content Analysis (VCA) directly benefits from these advancements. VFMs offer the sophisticated visual understanding necessary for accurate identification and tracking of objects and actions within a video stream. VLMs enhance the usability and flexibility of VCA systems by enabling natural language-based search and querying, making it easier for users to retrieve specific information. Furthermore, generative AI can complement VCA by creating synthetic data to improve the training of VCA models or by simulating potential future scenarios based on the patterns identified by VCA, leading to more proactive and insightful video analytics solutions.

TABLE 6.1 Differences between VFM and VLM.

Feature	Visual Foundation Models (VFMs)	Vision-Language Models (VLMs)
Core Function	To learn rich, general-purpose visual representations from large image and video datasets	To learn joint representations of visual and textual data, enabling understanding and interaction across both modalities
Primary Input	Images and/or video	Images/video and text (captions, descriptions, and queries)
Primary Output	Visual features, such as image/video embeddings, object detections, and segmentations	Matches between visual content and text, answers to visual questions, and text descriptions of images/video
Key Capability	Strong general visual understanding and feature extraction	Understanding and relating visual content to natural language
Example Models	CLIP (vision encoder part), ResNet, EfficientNet, Swin Transformer, DINO (vision part), and SAM	CLIP (full model), BLIP, ALIGN, Flamingo, ViT-GPT2, and Grounding DINO
Use Cases	• providing robust visual features for object recognition in VCA • segmenting objects in a scene • detecting anomalies based on visual patterns • image retrieval based on visual similarity	• searching video using natural language queries (e.g., "find a person wearing a red hat") • generating textual descriptions of video content • answering questions about the content of an image or video • grounding textual descriptions to specific visual regions
Relation to VCA	Provide the foundational visual perception capabilities that VCA systems rely on for understanding the visual elements within a video	Enhance VCA by enabling more intuitive and flexible interaction through natural language search and understanding of complex textual queries related to video content

Event Detection and Searching

Event detection in VCA refers to the automated process of identifying defined actions or anomalies within a video feed. This could be a simple event such as "detect motion" or a more complex one like "detect a fight or a slip-and-fall in a crowded scene." Rule-based logic can still be used for simpler tasks, but machine learning, especially deep learning, excels at handling more complex or subtle events.

Searching for events involves the post-hoc retrieval of video segments that contain events matching specified criteria. Without VCA, operators would have to manually examine hours or days of footage. With VCA-based indexing, an operator can search for "people wearing red shirts" or "vehicles making sudden stops" and narrow down the relevant clips or frames quickly. This capability is invaluable in forensics and law enforcement, where time is often critical (Figure 6.9).

The integration of VCA, generative AI, VLMs, and VFMs has transformed how video data is analyzed across various sectors, enabling exhaustive use cases in security, health, safety, and environment (HSE), commercial retail, hospitality, and healthcare.

VCA-based indexing allows operators to search for specific events or objects, such as "people wearing red shirts" or "vehicles making sudden stops," to quickly identify relevant footage.

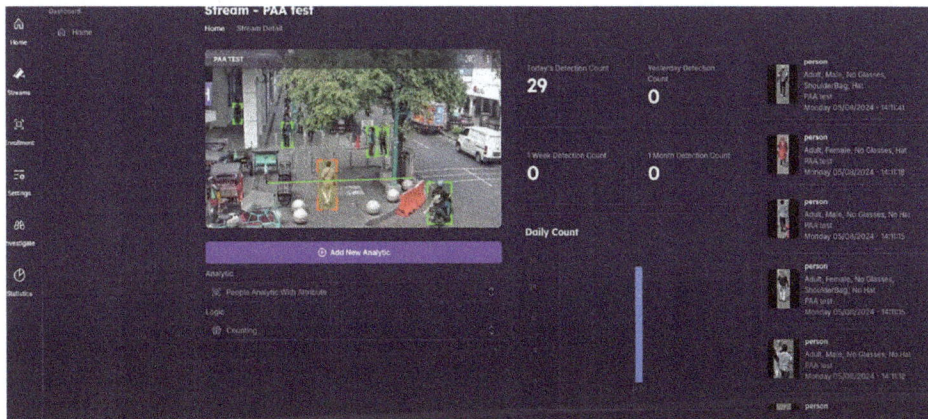

FIGURE 6.9 Capturing all people with a single attribute, such as a hat (Source: *Nodeflux*).

This capability is critical in forensics and law enforcement, where time is often important.

Recent progress in VLMs like CLIP, BLIP, and Grounding DINO allows for searching and analyzing video with natural language. By learning joint image-text embeddings, VLMs enable zero-shot querying of surveillance footage, eliminating the need for predefined categories. Instead of fixed labels like "person," users can search using phrases like "man in a red hoodie carrying a black backpack" or "white SUV parked near a loading dock." VLMs match these natural language queries to relevant visual content, offering flexible, human-like search within VMSs, accelerating tasks like forensics and reducing manual labeling. This bridges the gap between structured metadata and freeform reasoning, transforming video into an interactive knowledge base, as seen in retail searches for "a child left unattended."

Generative AI and VFMs empower systems to synthesize visual information with unprecedented accuracy, opening up advanced applications across multiple industries. In security, these technologies enable intruder detection through robust person and object detection algorithms, identifying unauthorized entries, and triggering alerts. They also support anomaly detection to flag unusual patterns like loitering, unattended baggage, or suspicious crowd behavior, leveraging both rule-based and deep learning approaches.

In commercial retail and hospitality, VCA can monitor customer behavior, optimize service, and ensure safety by tracking incidents like unattended items in stores or identifying overcrowding in a theme park. Queries like "list all individuals carrying umbrellas across camera feeds" or "highlight customers lingering in the electronics section for over 10 minutes" allow businesses to gain actionable insights for improving operations and customer experiences.

In health care, particularly in hospitals and elderly or childcare facilities, these systems enable critical use cases such as monitoring patient movement, detecting falls, or identifying staff response times to emergencies. Advanced capabilities like reidentification allow tracking of individuals across multiple areas, ensuring the safety of vulnerable populations.

Video analytics further enhance HSE applications by identifying potential hazards and ensuring compliance with safety protocols across diverse environments (Figure 6.10). For example, in oil rigs, construction sites, and factories, video analytics can detect whether workers are wearing mandatory safety gear such as helmets, high-visibility vests, gloves, or protective eyewear (such as their personal protective equipment or PPE).

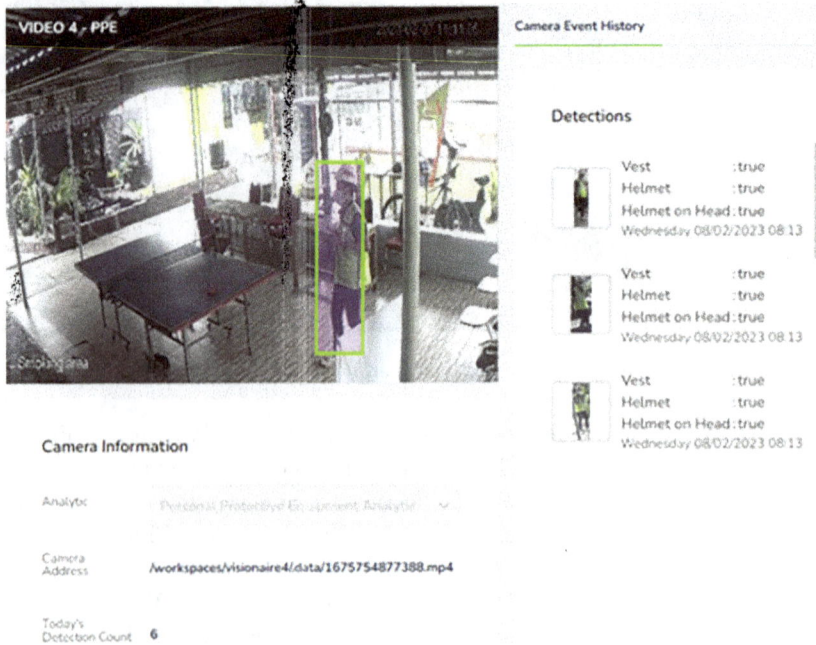

FIGURE 6.10 PPE detection system (Source: *Nodeflux*).

Alerts can be triggered in real-time if non-compliance is detected, helping to enforce safety regulations and prevent accidents. Similarly, analytics systems can monitor dangerous zones to ensure workers do not enter restricted areas without proper authorization or equipment.

Other advanced use cases include detecting slippery floors in manufacturing plants or warehouses, flagging potential fall risks on scaffolding, or identifying heavy machinery operating without nearby personnel wearing required protective gear. In environments like factories or chemical plants, video analytics can also monitor for hazards such as unattended spills, open flames, or leaks. Heat detection and thermal imaging integrated with video analytics can further identify overheating machinery or high-temperature zones that might pose fire risks.

In construction and oil and gas operations, video analytics can anticipate crowd density surges in high-risk areas, ensuring that emergency protocols are followed and evacuation routes remain clear. For instance, systems can detect workers congregating too closely around active heavy machinery, raising alerts to reduce the risk of accidents. Similarly, behavior-based analytics can identify signs of fatigue or unsafe actions, such as improper lifting techniques or workers operating equipment recklessly, allowing supervisors to intervene proactively. These examples demonstrate how video analytics not only enhance hazard detection but also actively promote a culture of safety and compliance in high-risk industries.

In police forensics, generative AI accelerates investigations by enabling precise queries like "track the suspect in the red jacket across all camera feeds" (Figure 6.11) or "find all vehicles with a specific license plate pattern," reconstructing timelines and tracing suspects across multiple locations.

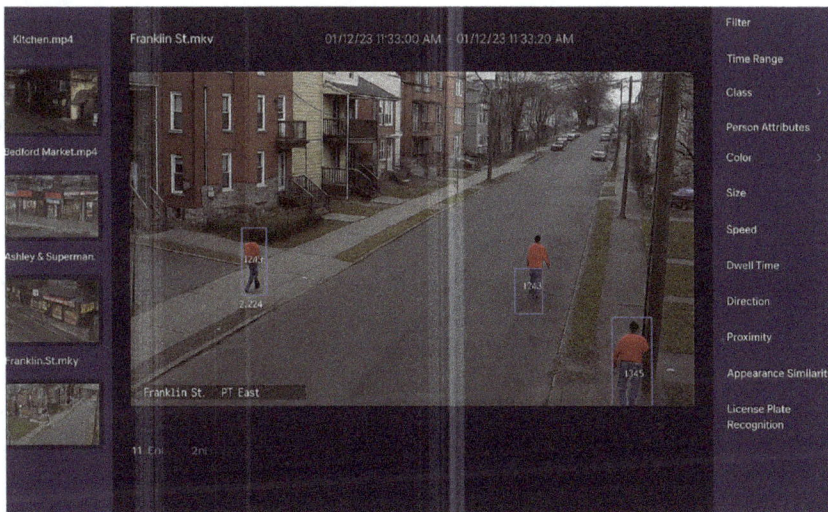

FIGURE 6.11 Searching for a person with a red shirt.

Simulating hypothetical scenarios for risk assessment or predicting future incidents based on patterns further highlights the transformative power of these technologies. Together, these advancements provide robust, multi-domain solutions, enhancing real-time monitoring, proactive intervention, and post-event analysis in ways previously unattainable.

Temporal Behavior Modeling and Timeline Intelligence

While object detection and tracking provide frame-by-frame understanding, truly intelligent surveillance systems must model how behavior evolves over time. This capability, known as *temporal behavior modelling*, allows IVA systems to interpret not just where objects are, but how they behave across sequences. This understanding is essential for high-level situational awareness, anomaly detection, and predictive alerting. At its core, timeline intelligence fuses object identity (from detection/tracking modules), spatial context (zones or regions), and temporal consistency (duration, recurrence, and motion patterns). These combined elements are processed to detect the *behavioral signatures* that signal meaningful or unusual patterns.

Key Use Cases:

- Loitering and Progressive Behavior Detection: Instead of triggering alerts solely on static dwell times, advanced systems recognize *progressive behavior*—such as a person walking in circles near an ATM over several minutes. This involves tracking temporal consistency and path irregularity across multiple zones and timestamps.
- Repetitive Visits and Anomaly Scoring: Identifying individuals or vehicles that return to the same scene within suspicious time intervals (e.g., scouting patterns and potential theft). This use case utilizes appearance-based re-identification over non-contiguous time blocks, matched against spatial zones.
- Trajectory Deviation Monitoring: This involves comparing object paths against typical flow models. For instance, if 95% of visitors walk straight from the entrance to the check-in desk, but a certain individual makes erratic detours or reverses direction frequently, the system raises a trajectory anomaly alert.
- Fall Detection and Human Stability Estimation: For public safety in stations or eldercare facilities, IVA systems monitor upright posture continuity. Sudden acceleration followed by immobility can trigger fall alarms. These rely on keypoint trajectories extracted via pose estimation and temporal smoothing filters (see Chapter 5).

Timeline-Based Event Reconstruction

By associating object IDs, time ranges, and behaviors, the system builds *semantic timelines*—allowing operators to query events like "show all vehicles that entered Zone A and then stayed parked beyond 2 hours in Zone C." This feature is fundamental to forensic search and operational audit trails. The algorithmic techniques used are as follows:

- Recurrent Neural Networks (RNNs) and Long Short-Term Memory (LSTM) networks model long-term dependencies in object trajectories and behavioral timelines.
- Graph-based Spatiotemporal Modeling construct interaction graphs over time to detect coordinated behavior (e.g., group loitering and social distancing violations).
- Optical Flow + Re-ID Integration enhances motion continuity across occlusions or scene transitions.

Example: In a prison cafeteria under surveillance by ceiling-mounted cameras, IVA detects an inmate rapidly approaching another and initiating physical contact. The system analyzes the speed of movement, sudden physical interaction, and body language, immediately classifying it as a "fight initiated." The system logs the precise timestamp, flags the incident as "active inmate altercation," and triggers an urgent alert to the prison guards, including a synchronized video feed of the event and a brief analysis of the initiating actions (Figure 6.12).

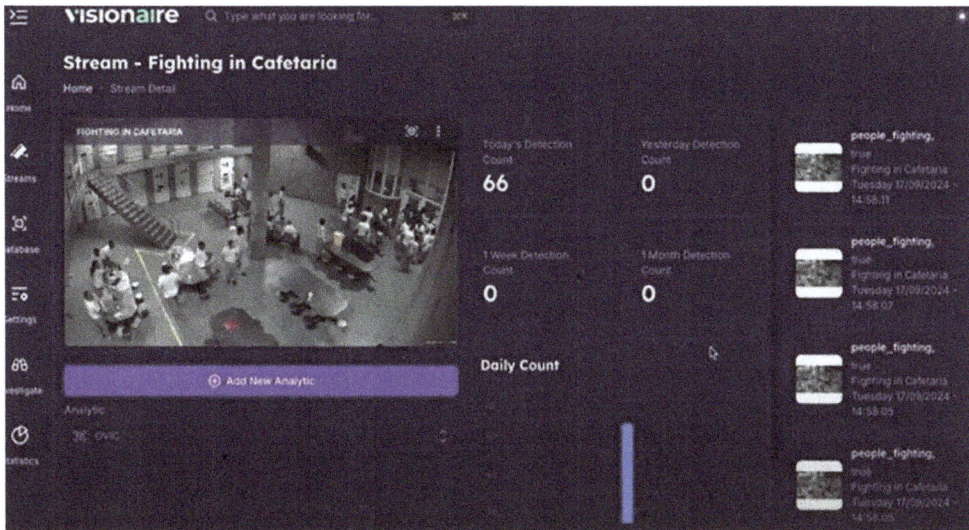

FIGURE 6.12 Capturing an inmate altercation in a prison (Source: *Nodeflux*).

Generative AI in Video Analytics

This section demonstrates how these generative models overcome significant limitations inherent in real-world scenarios, such as incomplete data coverage, challenges in transferring knowledge across different domains, and the infrequency of critical events. While earlier sections of this chapter focused on analyzing visible events, through detection, tracking, and behavioral modelling, generative AI introduces a powerful new dimension: simulating, augmenting, and predicting video content. This capability is especially crucial in scenarios where data is scarce, events are rare, or environments are too complex for traditional training datasets. Generative models do not merely analyze the world, they create plausible versions of it. These creations can then be used to train better detectors, simulate edge cases, or even provide visual explanations. The primary applications of generative AI in video analytics are as follows:

1. Synthetic Data Generation for Training: IVA systems often suffer from data scarcity for rare or dangerous events such as theft, accidents, or violence. Collecting real-world data for these scenarios is impractical or unethical.

    - Generative Adversarial Networks (GANs) and diffusion models are used to simulate realistic surveillance scenes.
    - These scenes may include rare poses (e.g., collapsing bodies), crowd congestion, or specific lighting conditions (e.g., nighttime with glare).
    - Synthetic data is used to augment real datasets, improving model robustness and generalization.

    Example: To train a loitering detection model, a GAN is trained on crowd behavior in open plazas. It generates scenarios where individuals exhibit slow pacing or repetitive paths near sensitive areas like building entrances.

2. Anomaly Detection via Prediction Error: *Anomalies* are deviations from normal patterns. Predictive generative models are trained to "expect" what happens next. When reality diverges sharply from prediction, it signals novelty or risk.

   • Autoencoders and Temporal GANs can reconstruct or predict the next video frame.
   • A high reconstruction error (difference between predicted and actual frame) implies an anomaly (e.g., sudden running in a calm zone or an abandoned object appearing unexpectedly).

   Techniques used are as follows:

   • ConvLSTM autoencoders model spatial and temporal correlations for smooth scene prediction.
   • Conditional GANs predict scene evolution under expected behavior constraints.

   Example: In a subway platform, a model trained on normal commuter flow suddenly registers a person jumping onto the tracks, flagged by the sharp anomaly in movement pattern and pixel structure.

3. Video Synthesis and Enhancement: Generative models can also enhance poor-quality footage, crucial for low-light, foggy, or compressed feeds. This is especially relevant in real-world surveillance settings, where video quality can degrade due to network bandwidth, weather, or sensor aging.

   • Super-resolution networks upscale low-res frames, improving clarity for face or license plate recognitn.
   • Low-light enhancement GANs adjust contrast, suppress noise, and restore color fidelity.
   • Domain translation models (e.g., CycleGANs) can convert daytime scenes to nighttime and vice versa for invariant model performance.

   Example: In a street surveillance system, low-light footage at 2 a.m. is passed through a night-to-day translation model. The enhanced output enables the recognition of a suspect vehicle that would otherwise be a dark blur (Figure 6.13).

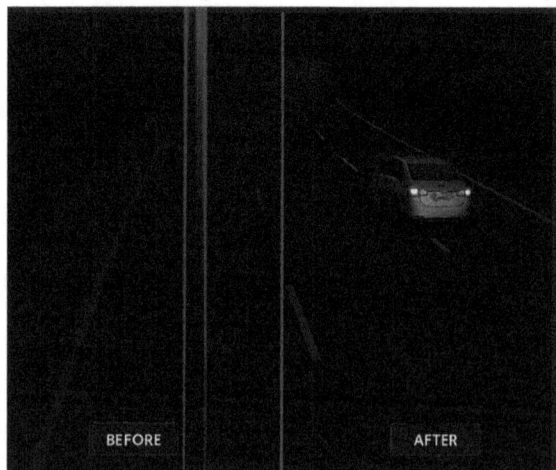

FIGURE 6.13 Enhancing the image quality with GAN.

Emerging Trends: Industry Adoption of Generative AI and Vision-Language Models (VLMs)

The integration of generative AI and Vision-Language Models (VLMs) has begun to reshape the video analytics industry, signaling a shift from rigid object detection toward semantic-level scene understanding. Several pioneering companies are already embedding these sophisticated models into their offerings. For instance, Zensors has created Momenta™, a multimodal transformer architecture that fuses visual and linguistic data to achieve a more profound understanding of video content, as highlighted on their AI Platform.

Similarly, Ambient.ai uses contextual video intelligence powered by AI, and while they do not explicitly mention VLMs, their approach resonates strongly with vision-language methodologies, according to their Web page. Nodeflux has adopted OpenCLIP model to enable contextual video searching and semantic analysis, allowing users to perform queries using natural language (as confirmed through direct communication with their Product Manager in 2025). Furthermore, Spot AI has integrated Meta's SAM2, a segmentation model that facilitates generalized object detection based on both textual prompts and visual inquiries, as detailed on their Labs page.

TABLE 6.2 AI companies using Gen AI or VLM technology.

Company	Generative AI/ VLM Usage	Notable Model or Feature
Zensors	Yes	Momenta™ Multimodal Transformer
Ambient.ai	Likely	Contextual Inference (Implicit VLM use)
Nodeflux	Yes	OpenCLIP for Semantic Search
Spot AI	Yes	SAM2 for Prompt-based Segmentation

The examples discussed highlight a clear trend among leading Intelligent Video Analytics (IVA) providers, indicating they are increasingly adopting multimodal, generative architectures (Table 6.2).

This strategic shift is driven by the need to deliver significant advancements in important areas, including accelerating the speed and efficiency of forensic investigations, enabling more intuitive and natural operator interfaces for enhanced usability, and achieving greater adaptability to meet the evolving and novel demands of modern surveillance scenarios.

SUMMARY

Chapter 6 has illustrated the critical transition from sensing and pixel-level processing into true scene understanding and intelligent interpretation. Building upon the foundational concepts of image processing (Chapter 4) and deep learning (Chapter 5), this chapter demonstrated how modern Video Management Systems (VMSs), Video Content Analysis (VCA), and Intelligent Video Analytics (IVA) work together to discover actionable insights from massive video streams.

We explored how IVA platforms now go far beyond basic motion detection, integrating real-time object tracking, behavioral analysis, semantic searching with Vision-Language Models (VLMs), and dynamic segmentation driven by Foundation Models like SAM2 and OWL-ViT.

We also discussed how generative AI enhances video analytics through synthetic data generation, anomaly prediction, and intelligent video synthesis.

Today's leading IVA systems empower security operations, public safety, smart cities, and enterprise automation, moving the surveillance world from passive recording to proactive intelligence and semantic reasoning. Importantly, we also highlighted how the industry is shifting toward multimodal, generative architectures, making IVA systems more scalable, adaptable, and intuitive.

Building on the foundation of these applications, the next chapter will introduce the technological fundamentals enabling these advanced systems. We will cover the essential concepts of GPUs and CPUs, which power the computational demands of video analytics and AI, and explore the principles of edge computing. Edge computing is particularly critical for real-time analytics, allowing processing to occur closer to the data source, reducing latency, and optimizing bandwidth usage. This chapter will provide a comprehensive understanding of the computing architectures driving the intelligent systems discussed in Chapter 6, setting the stage for their practical deployment and scalability.

Chapter 6 completes the "Understanding" phase in the Sensing–Understanding–Act (SUA) framework of this book. In Chapter 8, we shift focus toward the "Action" phase examining how intelligent analytics trigger operational responses, decision frameworks, alarms, and real-world interventions, turning insights into real-time actions that shape environments and behaviors.

COMPUTING AND EDGE COMPUTING PRINCIPLES

Chapters 1 through 6 established the foundation for Intelligent Video Analytics (IVA), from the deployment of sensing devices (cameras and networks) and the extraction and enhancement of visual data (image processing and computer vision) to the application of deep learning for interpreting scenes and detecting events. Chapter 7 transitions from understanding this information to using it within the IVA framework. This chapter addresses a crucial question: *How can infrastructure transform insights into real-time operational decisions once insights are extracted from video streams?* IVA requires powerful models as well as a carefully engineered computing ecosystem designed for scalability, real-time responsiveness, fault-tolerance, and resource optimization. Without suitable infrastructure, even the most advanced analytics pipelines will struggle to keep up with the scale and velocity of video data. We explore the foundational principles of computing and edge computing in the context of intelligent video analytics systems by examining the roles of Central Processing Units (CPUs) and Graphics Processing Units (GPUs), highlighting their respective strengths in handling sequential tasks and parallelized AI workloads. As video analytics systems increasingly rely on deep learning and real-time inference, the chapter underscores the critical role of GPU acceleration in enabling scalable and responsive applications. We then discuss edge computing as a transformative paradigm that addresses key limitations of cloud-centric architectures, including latency, bandwidth consumption, and data privacy. By processing data closer to the source, such as within smart cameras or local edge nodes, edge computing enables faster decision-making, reduces network dependency, and improves overall system efficiency. In addition to covering hardware and processing architectures, we consider a real-world case study involving an edge-based traffic monitoring system, demonstrating how edge AI can be deployed effectively in urban environments. To support practitioners and system designers, the chapter concludes with a framework for building production-grade video analytics systems, emphasizing four core principles: latency, modularity, resilience, and privacy. These principles are critical for ensuring that analytics solutions function effectively in real-world conditions and are scalable, secure, and maintainable.

The topics in this chapter provide a comprehensive foundation for understanding and implementing the computing infrastructure required for modern, intelligent video analytics in smart cities, industrial automation, healthcare, and beyond.

INTRODUCTION

Computing technologies have significantly transformed various industries, with AI and computer vision driving advancements in video analytics. The ability to process, analyze, and interpret vast amounts of visual data in real time has become crucial for security surveillance, autonomous systems, smart cities, and industrial automation applications. Over the past decade, AI-powered video analytics has become essential in security and surveillance, enabling faster response times and more accurate detection of potential threats. Traditional video surveillance systems relied on manual monitoring, which was not only inefficient but also prone to human error. With advancements and cheap computing technologies, AI can process vast amounts of video data automatically, identifying patterns, recognizing faces, and detecting anomalies with minimum human intervention. However, the growing adoption of video analytics has led to an explosion of data, which poses challenges in storage, processing speed, and real-time decision-making. This necessitates powerful computing architectures that can handle high-speed data processing and inference tasks. CPUs and GPUs play a critical role in addressing these demands, with GPUs being particularly effective in handling complex AI workloads due to their parallel processing capabilities. Moreover, the emergence of edge computing further optimizes video analytics by enabling decentralized processing, reducing latency, and enhancing efficiency (Figure 7.1).

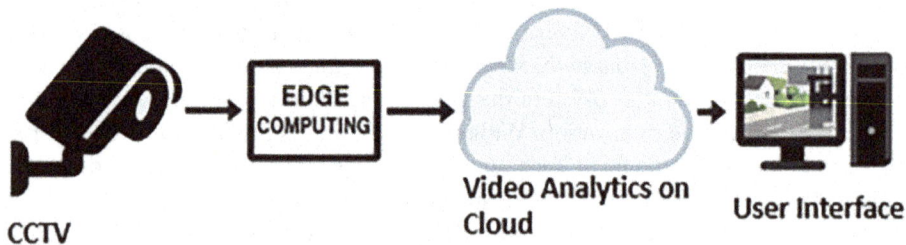

FIGURE 7.1 Edge computing for video analytics.

By examining the interplay between computing and edge computing principles, this chapter provides a comprehensive understanding of how modern computing technologies empower intelligent video analytics systems, ensuring real-time, efficient, and scalable solutions for various industries.

The Role of Computing in Video Analytics

Computing is the backbone of intelligent video analytics, enabling complex image recognition, pattern detection, and anomaly identification in real time. Traditional video processing relied heavily on cloud computing, where large volumes of video data were transmitted to remote data centers for analysis. While cloud computing provides substantial computational power, it also introduces latency, bandwidth constraints, and potential security risks. This led to the rise of edge computing, which brings computation closer to the data source, ensuring faster and more efficient processing of video streams.

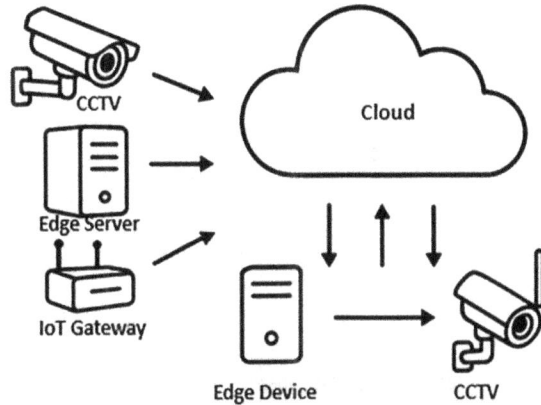

FIGURE 7.2 Hybrid computing.

Cloud computing has traditionally played a significant role in video analytics by offering scalable resources for data storage and processing. High-performance cloud servers allow centralized AI models to analyze video streams from multiple locations, making it possible to derive insights and manage large-scale surveillance systems efficiently. Important advantages of cloud computing in video analytics are scalability, centralized data management, and easy AI model adaptation. However, cloud computing introduces challenges such as high latency, bandwidth limitations, and security threats.

To compensate for the drawbacks of cloud computing, edge computing was introduced. Edge computing addresses the limitations of cloud computing by processing video data closer to its source. In this decentralized approach, AI algorithms are executed on edge devices such as smart cameras, edge servers, and IoT gateways, enabling real-time decision-making without relying heavily on cloud infrastructure. Important advantages of edge computing in video analytics are low latency, smaller bandwidth, lower security threats, and more reliability.

Another approach combines both cloud and edge computing as a hybrid approach (Figure 7.2). In a hybrid setup, edge devices process time-sensitive data locally, while cloud-based servers perform in-depth analysis, model training, and long-term storage.

CPU vs. GPU in Video Analytics

CPUs, or Central Processing Units, have traditionally been the primary computing units in most general-purpose systems. They are designed for sequential task execution, making them ideal for handling a wide range of computational tasks, including logical operations and decision-making. However, CPUs face challenges in processing large-scale video data in real-time AI applications due to their limited parallel processing capability. This situation led to the creation of Graphics Processing Units or GPUs. GPUs, initially developed for rendering high-resolution graphics, have become essential in AI and deep learning applications due to their high parallel processing power (Figure 7.3). Unlike CPUs, which have a few powerful cores optimized for sequential processing, GPUs consist of thousands of smaller cores capable of executing multiple computations simultaneously. This parallelism is particularly beneficial for deep learning-based video analytics, where tasks like object detection, facial recognition, and motion analysis require rapid matrix computations.

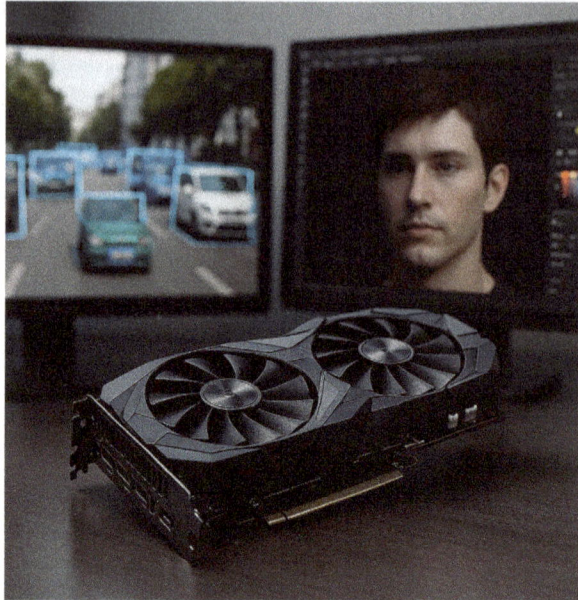

FIGURE 7.3 Typical GPU for computer vision and computer graphics.

COMPUTING BASICS

Video analytics systems rely on two fundamentally different processor architectures, CPUs and GPUs, each optimized for specific types of computational workloads. CPUs are older than GPUs, and CPUs are used in modern-day computers. Thus, CPUs are the first choice for use with video analytics. GPUs are commonly used within the gaming community, where graphical performance is a crucial in order to get the best gaming experience. The competition in developing video graphics performance means GPUs are cheap and powerful computation solutions for video analytics as well as AI.

The CPUs

The Central Processing Unit's (CPU) evolution began with the 1823 discovery of silicon. Key milestones include Tesla's 1903 electrical logic circuits, the 1947 invention of the transistor at Bell Labs (later mass-produced by IBM), and the crucial 1958 creation of the integrated circuit by Noyce and Kilby. The first microprocessor, Intel's 4004, emerged in 1971, followed by significant processors like Intel's 8008, 8086/8088, and Motorola's 68000 in the 1970s. The 1990s saw competition with AMD's AM386, Intel's Pentium, and Cyrix's Cx5x86. The early 2000s brought dual-core processors from AMD and Intel's Core 2 Duo and i5. Since 2010, Intel has expanded its high-performance Core i series.

CPUs consists of three major units: memory or storage unit, control unit and arithmetic logic unit (ALU). The basic architecture of CPUs is shown in Figure 7.4.

Memory Unit

When people discuss the RAM of their computers, laptops, or smartphones, they are referring to the memory or storage unit. This component of the CPU is responsible for storing data, instructions, and both intermediate and final results during processing. It also facilitates data transfer between various CPU components as needed. The memory or storage unit is often called main memory, primary storage, or Random Access Memory (RAM). The size of RAM significantly impacts a system's performance, speed, and processing efficiency.

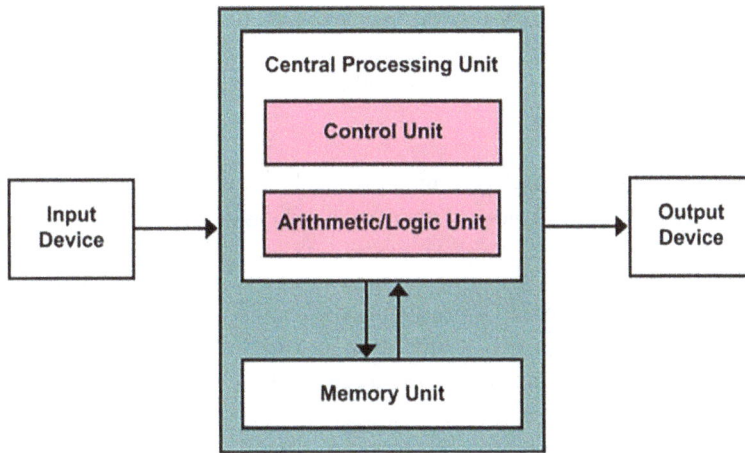

FIGURE 7.4 Basic CPU architecture.

In essence, the primary memory serves the following functions:

1. Storing instructions and data required for processing.
2. Holding intermediate results while a task is being executed.
3. Retaining final results before sending them to the output device for user access.

Since primary memory retains only the data and instructions currently processed by the CPU, it is classified as *volatile memory*. All stored data is lost if the power supply is interrupted, earning it the alternative name temporary memory.

Control Unit (CU)

As the name suggests, the Control Unit (CU) is responsible for overseeing and directing the operations of a computer system without engaging in actual data processing. The CU utilizes electrical signals to fetch instructions stored in RAM, decode them, and direct the computer to execute them accordingly. An important function of the control unit is to ensure the smooth flow of data through the processor. Some of the major functions of the CU are as follows:

1. Supervising and managing data flow within the CPU.
2. Coordinating data exchange between the CPU and external devices.
3. Regulating execution units such as the ALU, data buffers, and registers.

4. Transferring processed data from memory to input and output devices.

5. Overseeing the operation of all other computer units.

It is to be noted that the CU role is purely directive and regulatory.

Arithmetic Logic Unit (ALU)

The Arithmetic Logic Unit (ALU) is a fundamental CPU component that performs both arithmetic and logical operations. Arithmetic operations include addition, subtraction, multiplication, and division, while logical operations involve comparisons, data selection, matching, and merging. Depending on the system, a CPU may contain one or multiple ALUs. The ALU is divided into two main sections, which together enable the CPU to process both numerical calculations and logical decisions:

- The arithmetic section handles all mathematical computations.
- The logic section performs logical operations such as decision-making and comparisons.

Type of CPUs

Since the inception of the CPU, processors developed by Intel and AMD have dominated the market. However, the choice of a processor goes beyond selecting a manufacturer. One of the most important factors to consider is the number of CPU cores, as they significantly impact system performance. A CPU core is a fundamental processing unit that reads and executes instructions (Figure 7.5). Generally, the higher the number of cores, the better the system's performance.

Below are the major types of CPUs, categorized based on the number of cores:

1. A single-core CPU is the earliest and most basic type of processor, featuring only one core. Since it can process only one command at a time, it is not designed for multitasking. In a single-core processor, each process must wait for the previous task to complete before execution. When multiple applications run simultaneously, performance significantly declines as the processor continuously switches between tasks. The clock speed plays a crucial role in determining the efficiency of single-core processors. Measured in gigahertz (GHz), it represents the number of instructions a CPU can execute per second.

2. A dual-core processor consists of two independent processing units within a single integrated circuit (IC). Each core has its own controller and cache, but they work together to improve system performance. Due to the presence of multiple cores, dual-core processors enable better multitasking and operate significantly faster than single-core CPUs.

3. Quad-core processors take the concept further by incorporating four independent cores into a single integrated circuit (IC). These processors significantly enhance multitasking capabilities and outperform dual-core CPUs. Since each core can independently read and execute instructions, quad-core processors can efficiently handle multiple tasks at once. This results in high performance without solely relying on clock speed. However, the benefits of a quad-core processor are most evident in systems that support multiprocessing.

4. Hexa/Octa/Deca/more- core processors consistof six/eight/ten/or more independent cores, offering faster performance than quad-core and dual-core processors.

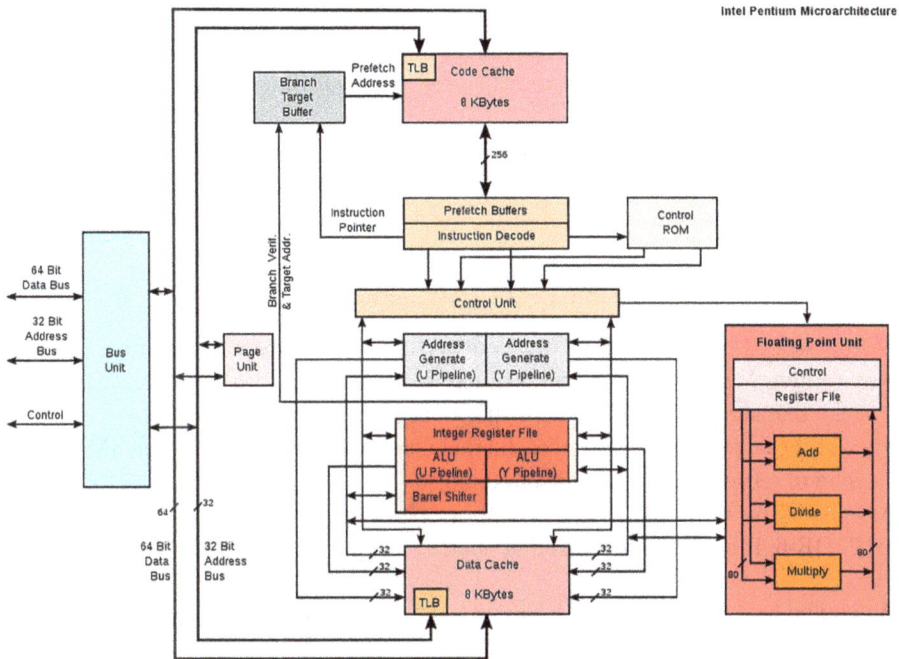

FIGURE 7.5 Standard CPU architecture.

The GPUs

The GPU is a specialized electronic circuit initially designed for accelerating computer graphics. GPUs were found to be a very powerful solution for parallel computing problems for non-graphical applications.

GPUs works rather differently than CPUs. Rather than focusing on the memory latency issues, GPUs ensure they have enough computations to keep all the cores busy.

Initially designed for graphics acceleration, GPUs proved highly effective for parallel computing in broader applications due to their architecture, which prioritizes maximizing core utilization over minimizing memory latency, contrasting with CPUs. The 1980s saw early graphics processors like NEC's μPD7220 and TI's TMS34010. In 1994, Sony used "GPU" for the PlayStation's geometry engine. A turning point was 3dfx Interactive's 1996 Voodoo1, the first dedicated 3D rendering chip, which transformed gaming graphics.

The Rise of Modern GPUs (1999)

NVIDIA redefined the industry by introducing the GeForce 256, the first GPU to integrate all stages of the 3D graphics pipeline into a single chip. This breakthrough significantly enhanced rendering capabilities and laid the foundation for modern graphics technology.

- **2000s:** NVIDIA continued to develop cutting-edge products like the GeForce 8800 GTX, which introduced advanced shading technologies. ATI (later acquired by AMD) introduced powerful dual-GPU solutions such as the Radeon HD 5970, delivering unprecedented performance.

- **2002:** The release of the ATI Radeon 9700 marked a major milestone, becoming the first Direct3D 9.0 accelerator. This enabled more sophisticated pixel and vertex shading operations, giving GPUs greater flexibility and bringing them closer to CPU-like processing capabilities.
- **Since 2002:** More powerful GPUs were developed, mainly from NVIDIA (with its RTX-series) and AMD (with its Radeon series).

GPUs Architecture

Basic GPUs consist of the following:

- Processor clusters (PC): The GPU consists of several clusters of streaming multiprocessors.
- Streaming Multiprocessors (SM): Each SM has multiple processor cores, and a layer-1 cache that allows it to distribute instructions to its cores.
- Layer-2 cache: This is a shared cache that connects SMs together; each SM uses the layer-2 cache to retrieve data from global memory.
- DRAM: This is the GPU's global memory, typically based on a technology like GDDR-5 or GDDR-6. It holds instructions that need to be processed by all the SMs.

A detailed look at NVIDIA's GPU architecture is shown in Figure 7.6.

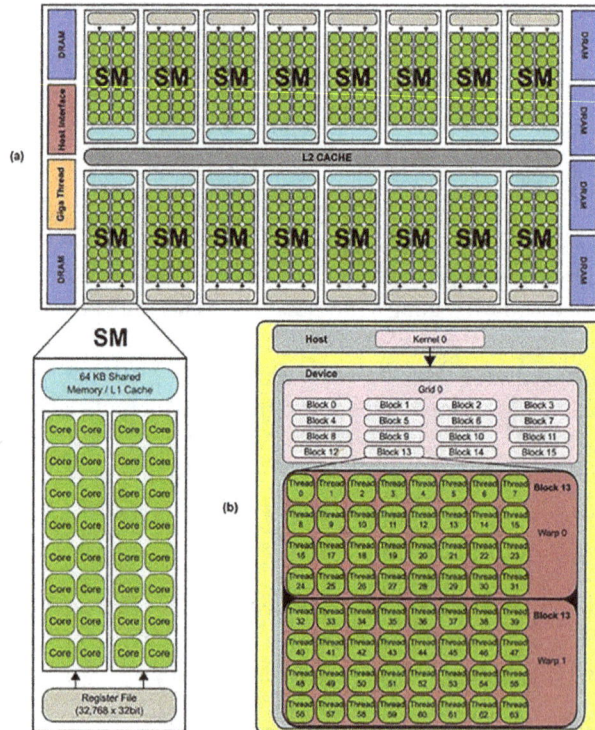

FIGURE 7.6 Basic NVIDIA GPU architecture.

NVIDIA GPUs used the famous Compute Unified Device Architecture (CUDA). CUDA provides an API that lets developers utilize GPU resources without requiring specialized knowledge about GPU hardware. An NVIDIA GPU allocates memory according to a specific CUDA hierarchy. CUDA developers can optimize memory use directly via the API.

The GPU components that developers can control directly from their programs when using CUDA architecture are as follows:

- Registers are memory allocated to individual CUDA cores, managed as "threads" in the CUDA model. Data in registers can be processed faster than in any other level of the architecture. From here on, every component processes data progressively slower.
- Read-only memory is on-chip memory available to SMs.
- L1 Cache is on-chip memory shared between cores, managed within CUDA as "CUDA blocks." The L1 cache is hardware-controlled and thus enables fast data transfer.
- L2 Cache is memory shared between all CUDA blocks across multiple SMs. The cache stores both global and local memory.
- Global memory enables access to the device's DRAM. This is the slowest element to access for a CUDA program.

The Role of CPUs and GPUs for the IVA: A Recipe

The previous sections explained CPUs and GPUs, their architecture, and recent development. When should CPUs or GPUs be used? Users can use the information below to decide whether they should use CPUs or GPUs.

From roles in video analytics pipeline, CPUs are responsible for initial video frame ingestion and preprocessing and running non-parallelizable components such as component management, system orchestrations and lightweight analytics. GPUs are responsible for parallel processing of multiple video streams and computation of intensive operation such as object classification, real-time feature extractions, and neural network interference.

Table 7.1 shows the strengths of CPUs and GPUs in terms of their latency, bandwidth, and power efficiency.

TABLE 7.1 The strengths of CPUs and GPUs.

Metric	CPU Strengths	GPU Strengths
Processing Type	Serial operations	Parallel operations (1000x+ threads)
Latency Tolerance	Low-latency execution	High latency tolerance
Memory Bandwidth	50-100 GB/s	400-1000 GB/s
Power Efficiency	3-5 GFLOPs/Watt	15-30 GFLOPs/Watt

TPU and NPU

Tensor Processing Units (TPUs) and Neural Processing Units (NPUs) represent a significant evolution in hardware acceleration, specifically tailored to the demands of deep learning workloads. These specialized processors excel at the matrix multiplications and tensor operations that form the core of many deep learning algorithms. Google's TPUs are engineered for high-throughput tensor computations, making them particularly well-suited for both the intensive training phases and the rapid inference stages of sophisticated vision models like YOLOv5, DeepSORT, and even complex transformer-based architectures.

Complementing TPUs, Neural Processing Units (NPUs) are increasingly integrated directly into smart edge devices. This trend is evident in AI-powered IP cameras and mobile edge gateways, where NPUs enable the execution of real-time video analytics tasks directly on the device. Applications such as object detection, anomaly detection, and facial recognition can be performed locally, eliminating the need to constantly transmit vast amounts of video data to centralized cloud infrastructure. A practical illustration of this capability is an NPU-equipped smart camera running a lightweight YOLO model on-device. This allows for the immediate detection of events like unauthorized entries, with only critical alerts being sent upstream. This localized processing drastically reduces both bandwidth consumption and latency, leading to more responsive and efficient systems.

Building upon the deep learning models discussed in Chapter 5, TPUs and NPUs provide the necessary hardware foundation for their practical deployment. As noted previously, the CNNs used for object recognition and LSTMs employed for temporal analysis are computationally demanding.

EDGE COMPUTING

In IVA systems, *edge computing* refers to processing video data closer to the source of capture, typically within cameras, local servers, or specialized gateways, rather than sending all data to a centralized core or cloud. By enabling preliminary analytics such as motion detection, object tracking, or anomaly flagging directly at the edge, IVA solutions can reduce network congestion, minimize latency, protect privacy, and achieve real-time responsiveness. This architectural shift is critical for scalable IVA deployments in smart cities, transportation hubs, and critical infrastructure monitoring.

CPU and GPU Difference

CPUs or GPUs have been used intensively in video analytics, which often considered as normal for video analytics. CPUs or GPUs are placed in a specific location where all video data are sent before they are processed into useful and important information. Each has strengths and weaknesses in terms of IVA (Figure 7.7).

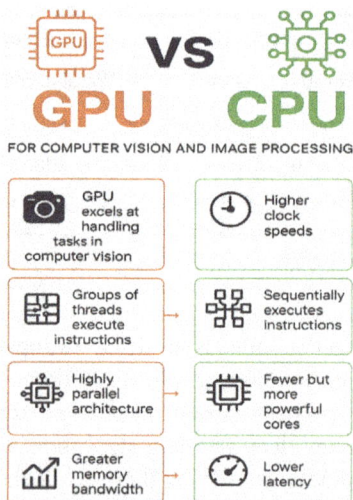

FIGURE 7.7 GPUs vs. CPUs for image processing and video analytics.

Edge computing addresses **bandwidth costs and latency** by processing data closer to its source, rather than sending everything to the cloud. This proximity drastically reduces network traffic and enables near **real-time decision-making**, offering significant advantages over the inherent delays of centralized cloud processing. The development and flexibility of **GPUs** are key to this, as their parallel processing power efficiently handles the demanding AI and machine learning tasks increasingly performed directly at the edge.

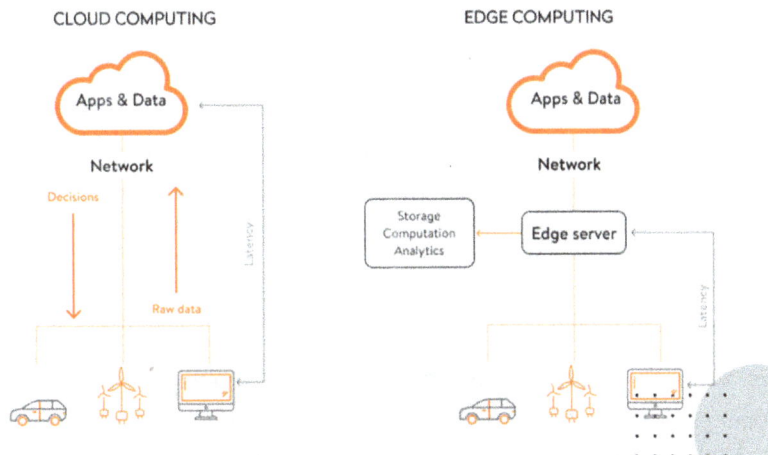

FIGURE 7.8 Traditional cloud computing and edge computing.

Instead of collecting the data streams into centralized (cloud) servers, edge computing brings data processing and computation closer to its source (Figure 7.8). With the explosive growth of the Internet of Things (IoT), the number of devices to be monitored, controlled, and analyzed has increased considerably. As a consequence, cloud computing is less preferable and edge computing is more preferable (Table 7.2).

Edge computing has some advantages:

1. Enabling real-time data processing: With the rapid expansion of IoT devices, the volume of data generated daily is unprecedented. Traditional cloud computing models require constant data transmission to centralized servers, which increases latency and consumes bandwidth. Edge computing solves this challenge by allowing local processing and analysis, reducing reliance on cloud infrastructure. This approach also conserves bandwidth and energy, making it an ideal solution for environments with limited connectivity.

2. Enhanced security: Unlike traditional cloud computing, where sensitive data must be transmitted over public networks, edge computing keeps data localized. This reduces security risks, minimizes exposure to cyber threats, and protects user privacy. For industries such as finance, healthcare, and government, where data confidentiality is paramount, edge computing offers a secure alternative to cloud-based processing.

3. Scalability and flexibility: Organizations can deploy edge computing infrastructure in various environments, from factories and hospitals to smart cities and retail spaces depending on the demands. Thus, more new applications and solutions emerge without the need to scale up a centralized computation.

TABLE 7.2 Edge vs. cloud computing.

Feature	Edge Computing	Cloud Computing
Latency	Extremely low	Higher due to data transmission
Bandwidth Usage	Reduced	High
Data Privacy	Stronger (local data processing)	Weaker (data sent to cloud)
Connectivity	Can operate offline	Requires constant internet
Best For	Real-time processing, IoT, AI, and industrial automation	Large-scale data storage, enterprise applications

The adoption of 5G networks is accelerating the shift toward edge computing. With faster data transfer rates and ultra-low latency, 5G enhances real-time data analysis and processing at the edge. This means less dependence on cloud services, leading to lower bandwidth costs, reduced energy consumption, and a smaller carbon footprint. Furthermore, the integration of 5G networks and recent GPUs technologies will provide even more powerful edge computation power so that near-instant data processing for applications such as smart cities and augmented reality can occur.

Centralized vs. Edge vs. Hybrid Architectures for IVA Systems

IVA requires not only sophisticated algorithms but also the thoughtful deployment of compute resources. Depending on the scale, latency needs, and network constraints of the environment, IVA systems are typically architected using three primary models: Centralized, Edge, or Hybrid.

Centralized Computing

In a centralized architecture, all video feeds are transmitted to a core data center, server room, or cloud platform where analytics processing occurs. This model simplifies infrastructure management by consolidating compute, storage, and analytics into a single location.

- **Advantages**
  - Easier centralized maintenance and model updates
  - Greater compute resources available (high-end GPUs, storage clusters)
  - Simplified integration with enterprise VMS and data platforms
- **Challenges**
  - High bandwidth consumption, especially for HD or 4K video streams
  - Latency concerns—critical alerts (e.g., intrusion detection) may suffer delays
  - Risk of centralized single-point failure unless High Availability (HA) is architected

Use Cases
  - Small-to-medium facilities (e.g., office campuses, smaller airports) where bandwidth is plentiful and response latency is not critical

Edge Computing

In edge computing architectures, video analytics processing occurs close to the source—either within smart cameras, edge servers, or local gateways.

- **Advantages**
  - Real-time processing with ultra-low latency (critical for safety and intrusion alerts)
  - Reduced upstream bandwidth since only metadata or event clips are transmitted
  - Better privacy compliance (sensitive video data remains on-premises)
- **Challenges**
  - Requires robust, sometimes ruggedized, edge hardware
  - Increased complexity in managing distributed analytics nodes
  - Higher upfront investment in local infrastructure

Use Cases
- Smart cities, transportation hubs, critical infrastructure, where latency and resiliency are paramount
- Industrial plants or remote facilities with limited WAN connectivity

Hybrid Architectures

Hybrid architectures blend the strengths of centralized and edge approaches. Lightweight analytics modules (such as motion detection, people counting, and zone crossing) operate at the edge, while deeper analysis (such as multi-camera re-identification, trajectory prediction, and behavior modeling) is conducted in a centralized system.

- **Advantages**
  - Balances real-time local responsiveness with centralized high-power analytics.
  - Optimizes bandwidth by sending only enriched, pre-processed event data upstream.
  - Enables modular scaling: add edge nodes or centralized nodes independently.
- **Challenges**
  - More complex orchestration and monitoring needed
  - Requires synchronization mechanisms between edge and cloud/core

Use Case Example: A Smart Airport

- Edge processing: Smart cameras count people in queues, detect abandoned luggage, blur faces for GDPR compliance—all locally at the gate.
- Centralized processing: Deeper behavior analysis correlates movements across multiple terminals to detect suspicious patterns, run predictive crowd management, or coordinate emergency evacuations.

INFRASTRUCTURE ORCHESTRATION, RESILIENCE, AND SECURITY IN EDGE-AI DEPLOYMENTS

As intelligent video analytics systems grow in complexity, especially in smart cities and industrial deployments, computing infrastructure must also support scalable deployment, resilient operations, and secure edge and cloud components interaction. This section explores practical considerations for orchestrating edge/cloud AI workloads, maintaining system uptime, and ensuring security at scale.

Virtualization and Containerization for Edge and Cloud Workloads

Modern video analytics systems often use container-based orchestration platforms, such as Docker and Kubernetes, to manage software modules on both edge and cloud infrastructure.

- Containers allow for the lightweight deployment of AI models, video ingestion pipelines, or analytics services across heterogeneous hardware (e.g., Jetson devices, industrial PCs, and cloud VMs). Containers can be used for decoupling analytics modules from hardware, enabling easier upgrades, fault isolation, and cross-site consistency. For example, Docker containers provide lightweight, isolated environments that package analytics applications (such as AI inference models using TensorFlow or OpenVINO, video processing pipelines, or supporting services) with all their dependencies. This ensures a consistent execution across diverse hardware and operating systems, abstracts away underlying infrastructure differences, promotes modular system design through microservices, and simplifies dependency management.
- Kubernetes (K8s) enables automatic scaling, load balancing, and self-healing in large-scale environments, including edge clusters using K3s or MicroK8s distributions. For example, Kubernetes manages containerized applications deployed across clusters of machines. They automate critical operational tasks essential for large-scale or distributed video analytics, including automatic scaling of services based on the load (e.g., varying the number of video streams), load balancing requests across available instances, and self-healing capabilities (automatic restarts or rescheduling of failed containers) to ensure high availability and resilience.
- CI/CD pipelines are increasingly used to roll out updates to analytics algorithms (e.g., TensorFlow or OpenVINO models) without manual intervention. The pipelines leverage containerization and orchestration to automate the build, testing, and deployment lifecycle of video analytics software. This allows for rapid, reliable, and frequent rollout of updates, such as improved algorithms or retrained AI models, with minimal manual intervention, accelerating innovation and maintaining system integrity.

Integration of VMS with Compute Infrastructure

A well-architected video analytics system relies on the seamless interaction between the Video Management System (VMS) and the underlying compute infrastructure. This integration is to connect systems and optimize data flow, minimize latency, and enable intelligent decision-making based on video insights.

In a typical deployment, the VMS is the central nervous system for video data. It directly interfaces with a diverse range of edge devices and cameras. For example, this could involve the following:

- IP cameras streaming video feeds using protocols like RTSP or ONVIF to the VMS for recording and live viewing. Think of hundreds of cameras across a manufacturing plant, each providing a real-time view of production lines and safety protocols.

- Smart cameras with onboard processing that might perform basic analytics like motion detection or line crossing and send metadata or triggered video snippets to the VMS. Imagine a smart parking lot camera that detects when a car enters a restricted zone and alerts the VMS with the timestamp and bounding box coordinates.
- IoT gateways acting as aggregators for video streams from simpler cameras or sensors, forwarding processed data or events to the VMS. Consider a scenario in a warehouse where multiple low-cost cameras feed into a gateway that summarizes activity in different sections before sending relevant information to the central VMS.

The VMS is responsible for managing these video streams, which includes the following tasks:

- Recording and archiving video data based on predefined schedules, retention policies, or triggered events. For instance, a retail store might configure its VMS to continuously record during business hours and only record on motion detection after closing.
- Providing live viewing capabilities for security personnel or operations teams to monitor activities in real-time. This could involve a security operator viewing multiple camera feeds in a control room or a remote manager checking on a specific location via a web interface.
- Triggering analytics. This is where the compute infrastructure becomes important. The VMS can initiate an analysis in two primary ways:
  - Native Analytics: Some VMS platforms offer built-in analytics modules for common tasks like motion detection, basic object counting, or tamper detection. For example, a VMS might natively detect if a camera has been physically moved or obstructed.
  - Calling Containerized Inference Services: More sophisticated analytics, such as facial recognition, object classification (e.g., distinguishing between people, vehicles, and animals), or anomaly detection, are often performed by specialized AI models deployed as containerized inference services (e.g., using Docker and Kubernetes). The VMS would then send video frames or clips to these services via APIs (like REST or gRPC) and receive the resulting metadata. Imagine a VMS triggering a containerized service that identifies individuals entering a secure area and compares them against an access control list.

The choice of where to run the VMS platform significantly impacts performance and integration:

- Virtualized environments (e.g., VMware, Hyper-V, cloud instances like AWS EC2, Azure VMs, and GCP Compute Engine): This offers flexibility, scalability, and easier management. For instance, a large enterprise with multiple locations might deploy its VMS in the cloud for centralized management and cost-effectiveness. However, this might introduce slight latency, which could be a concern for very real-time critical applications.

- Bare-metal servers: For applications demanding ultra-low latency and direct hardware access, such as real-time industrial control or high-frame-rate analytics in a sports broadcast, deploying the VMS on dedicated bare-metal servers might be necessary. This provides maximum performance but can be less flexible in terms of resource allocation.

The power of VMS integration can be best utilized when the compute infrastructure can interact with the VMS programmatically using APIs and SDKs. Consider these examples:

- Injecting metadata: A license plate recognition (LPR) system running on a separate server could use the Milestone MIP SDK to inject the recognized license plate number and associated timestamp as metadata directly into the Milestone VMS recordings. This allows security personnel to easily search and filter video footage based on license plates.
- Receiving events: An access control system could subscribe to events from the Genetec SDK. When a door is forced open (detected by an integrated camera and analyzed by a containerized service), the Genetec VMS could trigger an event that is received by the access control system, initiating an alarm and locking down other doors.
- Controlling recording logic: A building management system could use the VMS API to programmatically enable high-resolution recording on specific cameras when an unusual temperature fluctuation is detected by environmental sensors. This allows for targeted data capture only when necessary.

For optimal performance and scalability, especially in large deployments, the following best practices are highly recommended:

- Edge VMS instances for real-time coordination: Deploy smaller, localized VMS instances closer to the cameras at individual sites or within specific zones. These edge VMS instances can handle immediate real-time analytics, local recording, and trigger local alerts with minimal latency. For example, in a multi-story building, each floor could have its own edge VMS instance managing the cameras on that floor and triggering immediate security responses.
- Connecting to cloud VMS or central servers for fleet-wide visibility and analytics aggregation: These edge VMS instances then connect to a central cloud-based VMS or a powerful on-premise central server. This allows for a unified view of all video data across the entire deployment, enabling fleet-wide analytics (e.g., identifying trends across all retail locations), centralized reporting, and easier management of the entire video security infrastructure.

By carefully considering these integration aspects and leveraging the power of APIs and distributed architectures, we can build robust and intelligent video analytics solutions that provide valuable insights and enhance security and operational efficiency.

Resilience: Redundancy and Failover for Video Analytics

For critical video analytics like public safety or traffic management, system resilience is paramount.

- Compute node redundancy: Design with active-passive edge servers. For example, in a city surveillance system, if the primary server analyzing traffic flow at an important intersection fails, a standby server immediately takes over processing the video feeds and running the vehicle counting and anomaly detection algorithms, ensuring continuous traffic monitoring.

- Data redundancy: Implement RAID 5 or RAID 6 on recording servers to protect against hard drive failures. For cloud-based VMS, utilize replication services (e.g., AWS S3 Cross-Region Replication) to duplicate video archives in geographically separate locations. Consider distributed storage systems like Ceph for large-scale deployments, ensuring data availability even if multiple storage nodes fail.
- Workload distribution and failover: Employ load balancers to distribute incoming video streams and analytics requests across multiple compute nodes. If a node becomes overloaded or fails, the load balancer automatically redirects traffic to healthy nodes. Use message queues like Kafka to buffer analytics tasks. For instance, if an edge server processing pedestrian detection temporarily goes offline, the video frames waiting for analysis are queued and automatically processed when the server recovers or a backup takes over.
- Design rule examples:
  - Edge AI: For an edge device performing license plate recognition at a gate, include a secondary, simpler algorithm running locally that can still identify vehicle presence even if the primary LPR model fails due to a software issue.
  - Edge VMS: In a campus security deployment, ensure a secondary, lightweight VMS instance can temporarily record essential camera feeds if the primary VMS server experiences a hardware failure.
  - Cloud-reliant systems: For a cloud-based parking management system, design for Internet fallback. If the primary internet connection to a parking garage is lost, the local system should still be able to record entry and exit times, even if advanced cloud analytics are temporarily unavailable. Consider degraded offline functionality where basic analytics like vehicle counting continue to function locally.

Security Architecture for Edge-to-Cloud Video Analytics: Design Considerations

Securing edge-to-cloud video analytics, especially in exposed environments, requires a proactive, built-in approach.

- Network isolation: Design separate VLANs for camera networks and edge compute nodes. For instance, in a smart city deployment, cameras monitoring public parks should reside on a VLAN isolated from the city's administrative network, preventing lateral movement in case of a camera compromise.
- Secure boot and device authentication: Specify the use of hardware-based Trusted Platform Modules (TPM) in edge devices. During boot-up, the TPM verifies the digital signature of the firmware, ensuring only authorized software runs on devices like smart parking cameras, preventing the execution of malicious code.
- Firewall and VPN: Mandate that all video and metadata transmission between edge devices and the cloud VMS is encrypted using TLS 1.3. Design the network so that edge devices communicate with the cloud only through a secure VPN tunnel or a Zero Trust architecture, like using mutual TLS authentication for each device connecting to the cloud analytics platform.

- User Access Controls: Implement Role-Based Access Control (RBAC) within both the edge device management interface and the cloud VMS. For example, a "Security Operator" role might have permission to view live feeds and recorded video, while an "Analytics Engineer" role has access to configure analytics pipelines and view model performance metrics, adhering to the principle of least privilege.
- Audit logs and monitoring: Design the system to log all access attempts to edge devices (successful and failed), configuration changes, and model inference activities. For example, track every instance a user logs into a smart camera's Web interface or when a new object detection model is deployed to an edge server. Regularly review these logs for suspicious activity, such as repeated failed login attempts or unauthorized model deployments.

Master Slave Architecture for Edge Computer Vision

In edge-based computer vision systems, **master-slave inference architecture** enables efficient **distributed model serving**. The **master node** is typically a **GPU-powered edge server** that runs **heavy AI workloads**, while the **slave nodes** are resource-limited devices (e.g., IP cameras, IoT gateways, Jetson Nano boards) that only have **CPU** or **NPU** capabilities. Slave nodes handle **lightweight tasks** such as motion detection, image cropping, or feature extraction. The master node then performs **deep inference** like object detection, semantic segmentation, or anomaly detection. This separation optimizes **resource allocation** by keeping high-complexity models centralized while leveraging slaves for preprocessing.

The **orchestration layer** is what makes this architecture scalable and efficient. It decides when and what to send from slave nodes to the master and how the master distributes inference workloads across multiple slaves. For example, the system can dynamically schedule tasks so that NPUs in cameras perform early-stage detections and only **trigger relevant frames** to the master GPU when anomalies occur, reducing **bandwidth usage**. In multi-master setups, orchestration can also balance workloads between several GPU servers, prevent bottlenecks, and ensure **high availability**. This coordination is often handled via **edge inference frameworks** (e.g., NVIDIA Triton, OpenVINO Model Server, TensorRT on Jetson, or KubeEdge) combined with lightweight **messaging protocols** like MQTT, gRPC, or WebSocket streams. Essentially, orchestration ensures that the entire pipeline: camera, slave, master, storage, and cloud work together seamlessly.

This orchestrated master-slave inference architecture is widely deployed in **smart cities, manufacturing, logistics, and public safety**. In traffic analytics, NPUs in roadside cameras pre-detect congestion, while GPU masters run **multi-object tracking** and feed insights to the city's control center. In industrial quality control, slave IoT modules perform basic defect pre-screening, while masters handle **high-resolution inspection** and **predictive maintenance**. In security systems, orchestration allows multiple slave cameras to coordinate with a central master server for **real-time face recognition**, **threat detection**, and **incident replay**, all without overloading the network. This setup provides **low latency**, **scalability**, and **cost efficiency**, making it ideal for large-scale video analytics on the edge.

CASE STUDY AND FURTHER APPLICATION

Edge computing has become the most useful approach for deploying intelligent video analytics systems in the field. With real-time responsiveness, bandwidth efficiency, and increased control over data, edge AI opens up a wide array of applications across industries—from manufacturing and transportation to public safety. Let's consider several high-impact use cases that illustrate how edge computing is applied in real-world video analytics systems.

1. Industrial safety monitoring and predictive maintenance: In factory or plant environments, CCTV paired with edge AI can do more than just security; it can become a real-time safety supervisor. Video analytics can detect if workers are entering hazardous zones without protective gear, monitor for spills or fire risks, and flag machine anomalies like overheating or abnormal vibration. These insights, processed at the edge, allow teams to act immediately, preventing costly downtime and improving workplace safety.

2. Retail analytics and loss prevention: Retail stores are increasingly equipping edge-powered cameras to analyze customer behavior, queue lengths, and product engagement in real time. The same system can also detect unusual activity such as shoplifting gestures or after-hours movement. Running analytics locally ensures video never leaves the premises, keeping customer data private and reducing dependency on cloud storage.

3. Site perimeter and construction zone monitoring: Edge analytics enables automated perimeter protection and equipment monitoring without relying on high-bandwidth internet in construction sites or remote facilities (e.g., solar farms and oil rigs). Systems can detect intrusions, unauthorized vehicles, or if machinery is left running outside allowed hours. Alerts are sent instantly to supervisors even in low-connectivity environments, enhancing both security and compliance.

4. Smart city applications such as traffic and crowd management: In dense urban environments, edge-based video analytics enables real-time traffic optimization and crowd safety management. Whether monitoring intersections, crosswalks, stadiums, or event areas, edge devices detect anomalies (e.g., sudden gatherings and blocked roads) and feed actionable data to command centers, allowing quick interventions before incidents escalate.

Below is a case study for a real-time traffic monitoring system summarized from *Edge-Computing Video Analytics for Real-Time Traffic Monitoring in a Smart City* by Barthélemy et al. (2019; all figures after this description up to the concluding remarks of this chapter are obtained from *https://doi.org/10.3390/s19092048*).

Background and Goals

Smart cities require robust and real-time data collection and analysis for effective urban planning and management. Traditional traffic monitoring systems often rely on intrusive methods or centralized cloud-based processing, which can be costly, bandwidth-intensive, and raise privacy concerns. The Liverpool Smart Pedestrians Project aims to overcome these limitations by developing a multi-modal, privacy-compliant, scalable, and interoperable traffic monitoring system that utilizes edge computing.

Important Objectives

A multi-modal detection and tracking system must detect and track pedestrians, vehicles, and cyclists with personal data should be stored or exchanged to protect individual privacy. This is achieved through object classification and bounding box tracking, potentially enhanced by features extracted in a privacy-preserving manner. Crucially, the system must avoid storing or exchanging personally identifiable information (PII) by employing techniques like on-edge processing, anonymization (blurring, pixelation, and silhouettes), temporary identifiers, and secure data handling to ensure individual privacy is protected while still providing valuable analytics on object movement and behavior.

Utilizing Existing Infrastructure

Existing CCTV systems represent a significant prior investment that should be maximized when deploying advanced video analytics. Instead of a complete replacement, these legacy systems can often be retrofitted to collect richer data. This can involve integrating existing analog cameras through encoders that convert their signals into IP streams, allowing them to be managed by modern VMS platforms. For older IP cameras with limited processing power, edge devices or gateways can be introduced to offload analytics tasks, enabling them to contribute valuable video data to the overall system. By strategically retrofitting existing infrastructure, organizations can significantly reduce the initial deployment costs associated with video analytics. This approach allows for a phased implementation, where advanced analytics capabilities are layered onto the existing camera network. For instance, a retail chain with hundreds of existing CCTV cameras can start by adding edge analytics to a subset of high-value locations or camera feeds, proving the ROI before a wider rollout, thus maximizing the return on their initial investment.

Furthermore, a well-designed video analytics platform should be technology-agnostic, allowing for the seamless integration of new sensors alongside the existing CCTV infrastructure. This means that organizations are not locked into a single vendor or technology.

An Edge-Computing Device for Traffic Monitoring: Functionality and Hardware

The core of the system is an edge-computing device designed to perform real-time video analytics (Figure 7.8). The hardware components are as follows:

1. NVIDIA Jetson TX2: A high-performance, power-efficient ARM-based embedded computing device with specialized units for accelerating neural network computations. It runs Ubuntu 16.04 LTS.
2. CPU: ARM Cortex-A57 (quad-core) @ 2 GHz + NVIDIA Denver2 (dual-core) @ 2 GHz GPU: 256-core Pascal @ 1300 MHz
3. Memory: 8 GB 128-bit LPDDR4 @ 1866 Mhz
4. Pycom LoPy 4 Module: Handles LoRaWAN communications on the AS923 frequency plan (used in Australia, but capable of transmitting on every frequency plan supported by the LoRaWAN protocol).
5. CPU: Xtensa ® 32-bit (dual-core) LX6 microprocessor, up to 600 DMIPS
6. Memory: RAM: 520 KB + 4 MB, External flash: 8 MB
7. Wireless: Wifi 802.11b/g/n 16 Mbps, Bluetooth BLE, 868/915 MHz LoRa and Sigfox
8. IP Camera or USB Webcam: For frame acquisition

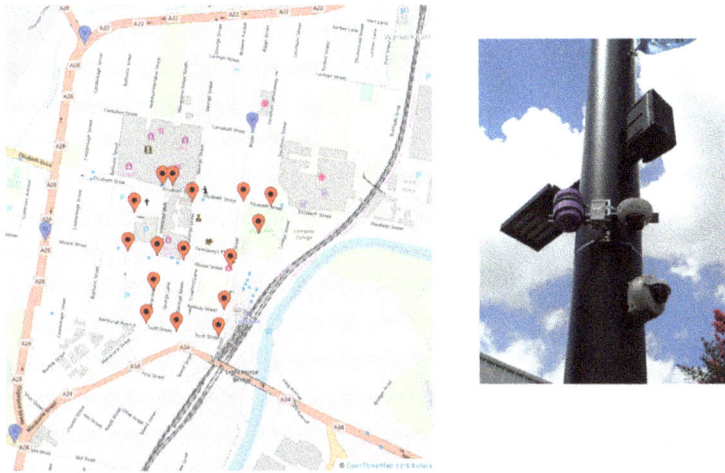

FIGURE 7.9 The location of the test and CCTV's placement.

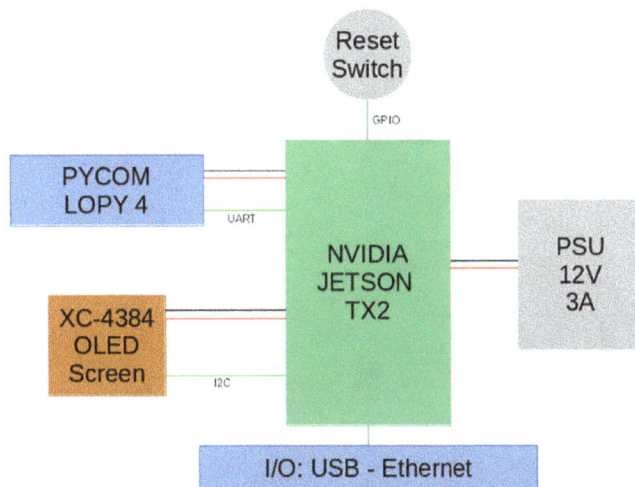

FIGURE 7.10 The proposed edge computing architecture for real-time traffic surveillance.

The functionalities (Figure 7.10) are as follows:

1. Frame acquisition: captures video frames from an IP camera or USB Webcam
2. Object detection: detects objects of interest (pedestrians, vehicles, and cyclists) in the frame using YOLO V3
3. Object tracking: tracks objects by matching detections with those in previous frames using SORT
4. Trajectory update: updates the trajectories of objects already stored in the device database or creates new records for newly detected objects
5. Data transmission: transmits metadata (object counts, trajectories) via LoRaWAN

The object detection and tracking algorithms:
YOLO V3 (You Only Look Once Version 3):

1. Used for object detection due to its speed and accuracy
2. Detects six object types: pedestrian, bicycle, car, motorbike, bus, and truck
3. Outputs:
    i. centroid coordinates (x, y)
    ii. width (w) and height (h) of the bounding box
    iii. object confidence score (O)
    iv. class probabilities for each object type

SORT (Simple Online and Realtime Tracking):

   i. used for tracking objects across frames
   ii. estimates the state of each object using a Kalman filter
   iii. assigns identities to objects based on their proximity and motion

Features used for tracking:

   i. centroid coordinates (x, y)
   ii. area (a) and aspect ratio (s) of the bounding box
   iii. velocity of the feature

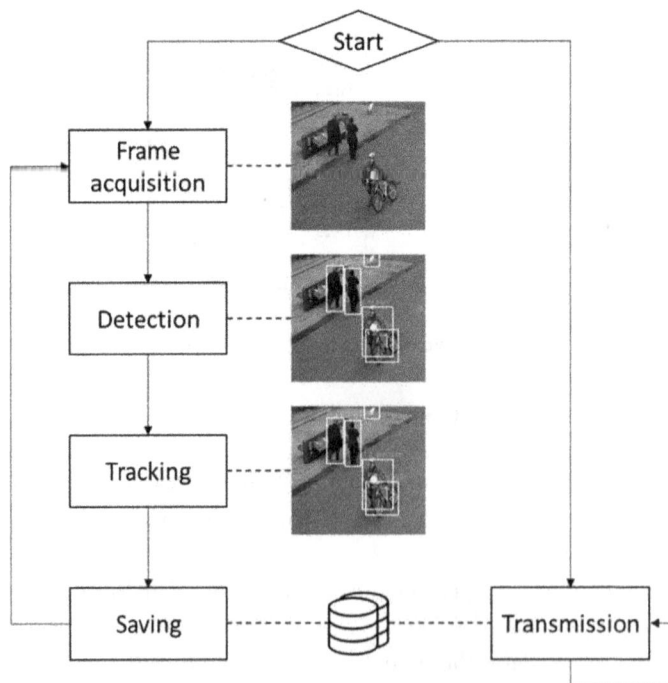

FIGURE 7.11 The object detection and tracking flow.

Sensors	Transport	IoT Core	Applications

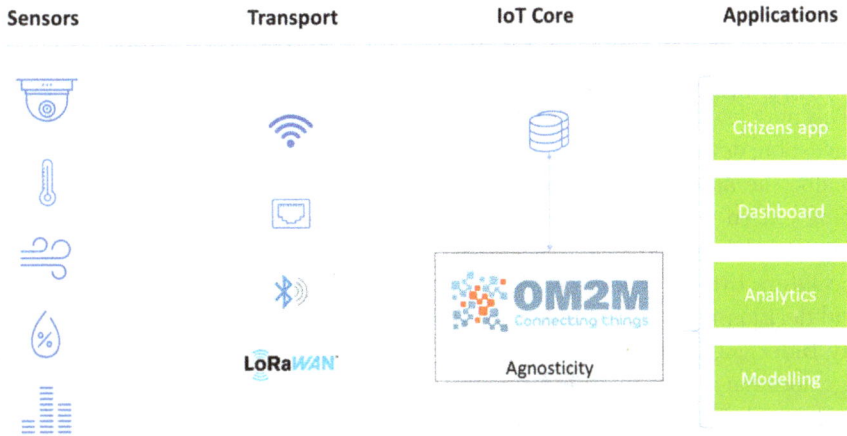

FIGURE 7.12 The general architecture of the project. The Agnosticity software stack relies on well-established open-source software. The data collection and access are ensured by the open-source implementation of the OM2M standard (Image courtesy of Agnosticity).

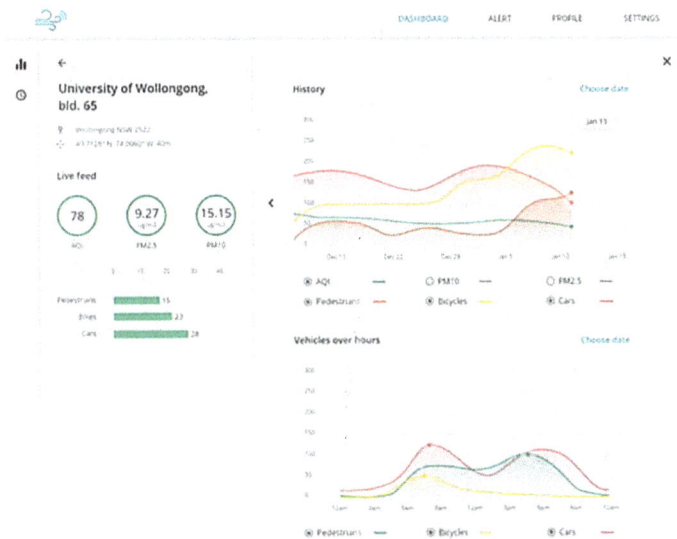

FIGURE 7.13 The Web-based interactive dashboard used to represent the collected data from the different sensors deployed for the Liverpool project. The interface is responsive and can be used both on desktop and mobile browsers.

Architecture and Dashboard of a Smart City IoT System

This smart city system integrates environmental and situational sensing with real-time data analytics using a modular Internet of Things (IoT) architecture (Figure 7.12). The smart city monitoring system is structured into three layers. At the *sensor layer*, various devices, including video cameras, temperature, humidity, air quality, wind, and noise sensors, are deployed throughout urban areas to capture environmental and situational data continuously.

The *transport layer* facilitates the transmission of this data using multiple communication protocols such as Wi-Fi, Ethernet, Bluetooth, and LoRaWAN, allowing for flexible and scalable connectivity. The IoT Core, built on the open-source OM2M platform, is at the heart of the system. This middleware provides a protocol-agnostic and device-agnostic infrastructure, managing data ingestion, device interoperability, and routing.

Finally, the *applications layer* leverages the processed data to support various services, including citizen-facing mobile applications, interactive dashboards, advanced analytics, and predictive modeling tools.

The interactive dashboard (Figure 7.13) functions as the central interface for city operators and decision-makers. It enables real-time monitoring by displaying live metrics such as Air Quality Index (AQI), PM2.5, PM10 levels, and counts of pedestrians, bicycles, and vehicles. With geolocation awareness, the dashboard maps sensor readings to specific urban locations or buildings, enhancing spatial context. Users can explore historical trends to analyze air quality and traffic volume over time, while behavioral pattern visualizations reveal vehicle flow dynamics across hours of the day, helping to identify peak usage or unusual conditions. This architecture and dashboard empower municipalities with data-driven insights to enhance sustainability, operational efficiency, and citizen engagement.

Validation Experiments: Accuracy, Performance, and System Utilization

The system's performance was evaluated through validation experiments focusing on accuracy, performance, and system utilization based.

Figure 7.14 illustrates the accuracy of the sensor compared to ground truth across 4,500 frames. The results show an inverse correlation: accuracy was higher when ground truth detections were low and decreased in denser crowds. This decline is likely due to occlusions in crowded environments, where one person may obscure another, leading to missed detections. Additionally, YOLO V3's non-maximum suppression algorithm, which filters overlapping bounding boxes, contributes to this effect.

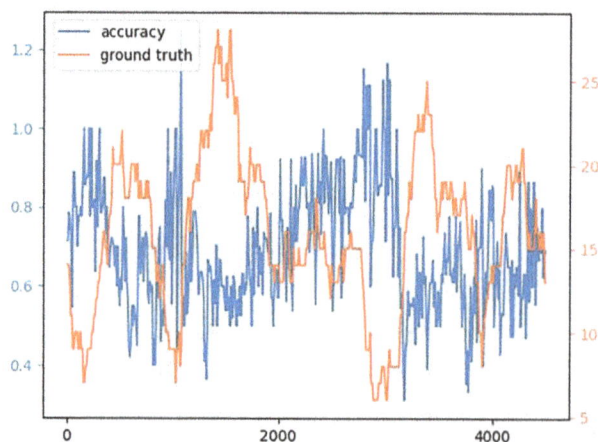

FIGURE 7.14 The evolution of the accuracy (blue lines, with an ideal value of 1.0) is shown alongside ground truth data (orange lines) over time. Accuracy is higher in smaller groups but declines in larger crowds.

Figure 7.15 shows the variation in CPU, GPU, memory, and disk usage, as well as average temperature and network utilization, measured every 2 seconds during a real-world sensor deployment. This 10-minute experiment connected the sensor to a CCTV system overseeing a building entrance and the surrounding street.

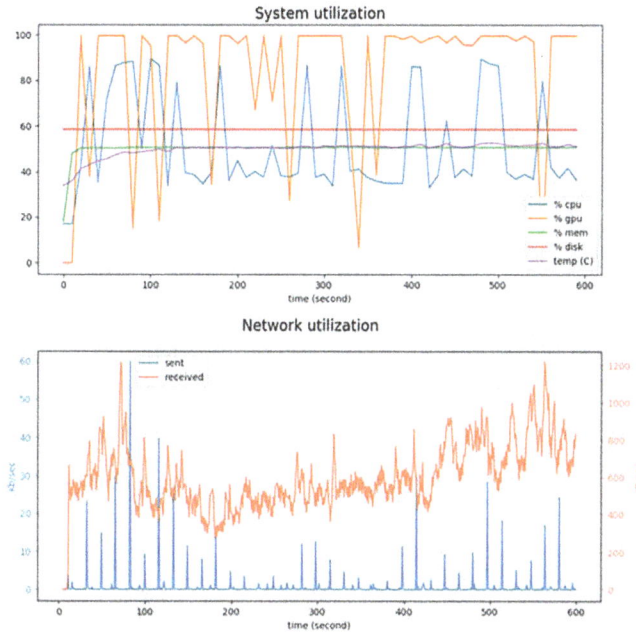

FIGURE 7.15 A 15-minute observation of CPU, GPU, memory, and disk usage, along with the average temperature (top) and network utilization (bottom), recorded during a real-world sensor deployment. Over this period, 280 unique objects were detected.

Enhancing Deployment Robustness in Real-World Video Analytics Systems

Deploying video analytics systems in operational environments, such as urban intersections, public spaces, transportation hubs, or industrial facilities, requires more than just implementing functional detection and tracking algorithms. While systems like the Liverpool Smart Pedestrians Project demonstrate the feasibility of edge-based video analytics, ensuring consistent performance, reliability, and compliance in real-world conditions demands a more comprehensive approach to system design.

This section introduces four essential design principles that enhance the robustness of edge-based video analytics deployments: latency, modularity, resilience, and privacy. Together, these principles form a foundation for building scalable, maintainable, and trusted analytics solutions that operate effectively even in constrained or sensitive environments.

Latency: Achieving Real-Time Responsiveness

Latency refers to the time it takes for the system to process an event, from capturing a frame to generating an actionable output. In many public and industrial applications, low latency is critical to enable timely responses, such as triggering alerts, updating traffic signals, or guiding security personnel. To reduce latency in production systems:

- Use optimized models: Replace heavier models (e.g., YOLOv3) with lightweight alternatives such as YOLOv8-Tiny, NanoDet, or other quantized neural networks that offer faster inference times.
- Deploy inference locally: Perform all critical processing and detection, tracking, and decision logic on the edge device to avoid delays caused by network transmission.
- Apply adaptive frame handling: Implement frame skipping or throttling mechanisms to balance real-time performance with system load during high-traffic periods.

A well-optimized edge system should aim for sub-second latency between input and output, particularly in safety-critical applications.

Modularity: Enabling Flexible, Maintainable Systems

Modularity ensures that a video analytics system can be easily maintained, extended, and adapted as requirements evolve. In monolithic implementations, updates to one component (e.g., detection logic) may require system-wide changes. In contrast, modular systems support each component's independent development, testing, and deployment. Best practices for modular system design include the following:

- Containerization: Use container technologies (e.g., Docker) to isolate and manage components such as image acquisition, detection, tracking, data transmission, and system monitoring.
- Defined interfaces: Use lightweight APIs or message queues (e.g., gRPC, MQTT, or NATS) to facilitate communication between modules.
- Plug-in architecture: Design systems so that components—such as object detectors or event filters—can be swapped or upgraded without downtime.

Modular systems are especially beneficial in large-scale deployments where different sites may require different analytics models, sensors, or integration rules.

Resilience: Sustaining Operation Under Failure Conditions

In operational environments, failures are inevitable. Devices may overheat, connections may drop, and compute loads may fluctuate. A *resilient* system continues to function, or degrades gracefully, in the presence of such disruptions. Important resilience strategies include the following:

- Health monitoring and recovery: Implement system watchdogs that detect stalled processes or system anomalies and automatically trigger recovery actions (e.g., restarting containers or rebooting devices).
- Offline fallback: Allow edge nodes to buffer and store data locally when disconnected from the network, and resume synchronization once connectivity is restored.
- Redundant coverage: In high-priority areas, deploy overlapping sensors or redundant nodes to maintain functionality during hardware failure.
- Load adaptation: Monitor system resources (CPU, GPU, memory, and thermal levels) and dynamically reduce analytic intensity to avoid crashes or performance drops.

Resilient design ensures high system availability, essential in use cases like traffic control, crowd monitoring, and critical infrastructure protection.

Privacy: Safeguarding Public Trust and Legal Compliance

Privacy is a central concern in video analytics, particularly in public and sensitive environments. The collection and processing of video data can raise ethical, legal, and regulatory challenges, especially when identifiable individuals are involved.

To strengthen privacy in system design:

- Perform analytics on the edge: Process video data locally and transmit only anonymized metadata (e.g., object counts, trajectories, and classifications) to central servers.
- Apply visual obfuscation: Implement techniques such as face or license plate blurring before storage or transmission.
- Use secure communication channels: Encrypt all data in transit using protocols such as TLS or VPN tunnelling to protect against interception.
- Implement access controls and audit trails: Enforce strict user roles and maintain logs of system access to ensure accountability and support compliance audits.
- Segment networks: Isolate video analytics devices using VLANs or Zero Trust architecture to minimize attack surfaces.

Privacy-aware design is not only a matter of compliance but also a means to build and maintain public trust, especially in smart city and surveillance applications.

THE EMERGENCE OF UAVS AS FLYING EDGE NODES

In modern surveillance ecosystems, drones (unmanned aerial vehicles, UAVs) are evolving into flying edge computing platforms, augmenting traditional ground-based CCTV networks with mobility, agility, and situational flexibility. Equipped with stabilized cameras (RGB, infrared, or thermal), edge compute modules such as NVIDIA Jetson Xavier/Orin or Qualcomm RB5, and multi-channel communication links (4G/5G, LTE mesh, or Wi-Fi), these drones can process computer vision workloads directly onboard. By running inference on-device, drones can autonomously detect anomalies, classify objects, and trigger alerts without relying on constant high-bandwidth streaming. This paradigm of edge inference in motion reduces latency, improves reliability in low-connectivity regions, and allows drones to act as independent nodes in the surveillance fabric.

IVA Workloads in the Sky

Drone-mounted IVA models unlock use cases not feasible with static CCTV. Examples include real-time crowd density estimation during public gatherings, traffic flow analysis from aerial vantage points, thermal anomaly detection in fire monitoring, and search-and-rescue operations where drones detect human presence in challenging terrain. Unlike fixed sensors, UAVs can be dynamically dispatched to hotspots, making them invaluable for perimeter patrols, infrastructure inspections, or disaster response. Recent advancements in frameworks like FlytBase highlight integrated capabilities such as autonomous flight scheduling, drone-in-a-box deployment, fleet orchestration, multi-camera streaming, and geofenced BVLOS (Beyond Visual Line of Sight) operations. These features position UAVs as scalable, automated layers of the video surveillance architecture rather than one-off pilot projects.

Integration with Command and Control

For drone surveillance to be operationally effective, it must integrate seamlessly with Video Management Systems (VMS) and Command & Control Centers (C4I/C4ISR). Modern setups allow drones to transmit metadata (detections, alerts, heatmaps) rather than raw video, conserving bandwidth while ensuring timely decision support. Mission orchestration software enables operators to trigger drone missions automatically in response to IVA events detected on fixed cameras—for instance, dispatching a drone when a perimeter breach is detected at night. Likewise, live drone feeds can be fused with ground cameras in a unified dashboard, giving operators multi-angle situational awareness. This orchestration transforms UAVs into first responders in security workflows, extending coverage beyond the static footprint of CCTV.

FIGURE 7.16 Warehouse Drone Security Surveillance.

Case Insight: IKN Nusantara and Drone Surveillance

In Indonesia's new capital, IKN Nusantara, drones already play a dual role, first in urban planning and mapping through aerial photogrammetry, and increasingly in operational surveillance. Given IKN's vast green and urban development zones, UAVs provide flexible oversight of construction areas, forest perimeters, and public gatherings. This reflects a broader global trend where drones are no longer experimental pilots but a core part of smart city surveillance strategy, bridging the limitations of fixed sensors with agile, autonomous aerial monitoring. As cities expand their reliance on intelligent video analytics, drones represent a natural extension of edge computing: *mobile, AI-powered, and integrated into the command fabric of urban safety systems.*

SUMMARY

The evolution of computing technologies has profoundly transformed video analytics, enabling real-time data processing, pattern recognition, and intelligent automation. While CPUs efficiently manage logic-driven and sequential tasks, GPUs excel in parallel computing, making them indispensable for AI-powered video analysis and deep learning.

The rise of edge computing has further revolutionized video analytics by addressing latency, security, and bandwidth constraints. By enabling real-time decision-making at the data source, edge computing enhances the performance and reliability of mission-critical applications in sectors such as security, healthcare, industrial monitoring, and smart city infrastructure.

The convergence of cloud and edge computing allows organizations to adopt hybrid architectures that combine the low-latency responsiveness of edge nodes with the scalability and long-term storage capabilities of cloud infrastructure. This hybrid model is especially valuable in large-scale deployments, where different analytic components must operate at different locations and time horizons.

As real-world deployments grow in complexity and scale, the focus must shift from merely achieving functional analytics to ensuring that systems are robust, adaptable, and sustainable. Four foundational principles—latency, modularity, resilience, and privacy—emerge as critical to designing production-ready systems:

- Latency ensures timely insights and rapid response in dynamic environments. Practitioners must leverage optimized models, local inference, and adaptive data handling to maintain sub-second responsiveness.
- Modularity enables flexible system integration and long-term maintainability. By decoupling system components through containerization and API-driven communication, analytics platforms can adapt to evolving requirements without disruptive overhauls.
- Resilience ensures continuity and fault tolerance in the face of real-world challenges, including device failures, network instability, and resource constraints. Systems should be designed to self-heal, buffer data, and recover "gracefully" during partial outages.
- Privacy safeguards user trust and ensures regulatory compliance. Edge analytics must prioritize local data processing, encrypted communications, and secure access control while minimizing data exposure.

Looking ahead, advancements in 5G connectivity, AI accelerators, and energy-efficient GPU architectures will drive the next generation of intelligent video analytics systems. These technologies will enable near-instantaneous processing, higher model precision, and broader sensor integration, all while reducing operational overhead.

To fully capitalize on these developments, organizations must adopt a strategic and architectural approach that integrates cloud, edge, CPU, and GPU capabilities within a framework that prioritizes latency control, system modularity, operational resilience, and strong data governance.

By doing so, they will be well-positioned to build and scale intelligent video analytics platforms that deliver real-time insights and meet the operational, ethical, and performance demands of today's increasingly data-driven world. Also, drones have evolved into mobile edge nodes that extend surveillance beyond fixed cameras, offering coverage in hard-to-reach areas and delivering real-time IVA inference from the air. Their ability to run models onboard, stream critical data over 4G/5G, and integrate with command centers makes them essential for modern security and emergency response. In IKN Nusantara, drones are already used not only for city planning but also for surveillance, proving their value as a core component of smart-city edge ecosystems. By combining mobility, intelligence, and seamless orchestration, drones highlight the future of surveillance—dynamic, distributed, and integrated across land and air.

CHAPTER 8

SECURITY, SAFETY, AND OPERATIONAL EFFICIENCY PRINCIPLES

The utilization of intelligent video analytics has profoundly reshaped the role of surveillance systems. No longer passive tools for recording events, modern video analytics platforms have evolved into dynamic, intelligent ecosystems capable of executing the full Sense-Understand-Action workflow, enabling organizations to act upon information in near real-time with precision and purpose. In the earlier chapters, we progressively built this foundation:

- Sensing: capturing data through networks of cameras and sensors (Chapters 1–4)
- Understanding: interpreting video content through AI-driven analysis, behavior recognition, and anomaly detection (Chapters 5–6)
- Infrastructure: enabling efficient real-time processing through edge and cloud computing strategies (Chapter 7)

These layers allow systems to capture data and evaluate the environment. Yet without the ability to act on these insights, they remain incomplete. *Action*, the critical third pillar, transforms video intelligence into operational outcomes that enhance security, ensure safety, and optimize efficiency. This chapter shows how video analytics moves beyond sensing and understanding into deciding and acting by translating intelligence into tangible operational decisions. In doing so, we also reframe and connect the core pillars of security, safety, and operational efficiency to the video analytics ecosystem, emphasizing how actionable insights directly support these strategic objectives.

This chapter also introduces a vital new concept, *decision and action workflow* (DAW), which ensures that the AI-driven understanding phase leads to structured, responsive, and auditable operational actions. The concept of DAW will be explored in detail, showing how it serves as a bridge between AI insight and operational execution through defined rules, logic paths, escalation handling, and integration with SOPs. We will explore how video analytics drives responses at both the building level (through control rooms) and the citywide scale (through integrated command and control centers), creating environments that are not only smarter but also safer, more secure, and operationally optimized.

INTRODUCTION

The growing reliance on intelligent video analytics has significantly transformed the landscape of security, safety, and operational efficiency across industries. Where traditional surveillance systems were largely passive methods of observation, modern AI-enabled video analytics platforms have evolved into dynamic, intelligent ecosystems capable of executing a full Sense-Understand-Action workflow. These systems are no longer limited to monitoring or recording events; they are designed to perceive, interpret, and most critically, respond in real time.

Earlier chapters in this book laid the technological foundations: sensing, understanding, and enabling infrastructure. However, sensing and understanding alone are insufficient. Action is the critical third pillar that transforms intelligent video analytics into an active agent of safety, security, and efficiency which have emerged as paramount concerns as societies become increasingly digital and interconnected. Organizations must not only detect potential risks, including cyberattacks, physical intrusions, and hazardous conditions, but also act swiftly and decisively to mitigate them. Safety, in particular, demands proactive protection of individuals across workplaces, public spaces, and residential environments. Workplace safety regulations, such as Occupational Safety and Health Administration (OSHA) standards, mandate that organizations maintain environments free of hazards to safeguard employee well-being. Video analytics supports these safety mandates by enabling automated monitoring of unsafe behaviors, early detection of incidents, and rapid deployment of corrective actions. Operational efficiency, where data-driven video insights optimize workflows, resource allocation, and overall system performance, is also becoming important in organizations.

Simultaneously, the rise of AI-driven surveillance introduces new ethical and regulatory challenges. Organizations must navigate concerns over privacy, data protection, and ethical AI deployment, ensuring that surveillance technologies comply with frameworks such as the General Data Protection Regulation (GDPR) and national privacy laws. Responsible implementation demands privacy-enhancing technologies, such as data anonymization, secure storage, and access controls, to prevent misuse of personal information.

Thus, integrating intelligent video analytics presents both opportunities in predictive analytics, automation, and improved responsiveness, and challenges in cybersecurity, ethics, and compliance.

REFRAMING SECURITY AND SAFETY WITH VIDEO ANALYTICS

In designing intelligent surveillance systems, it is crucial to differentiate between security and safety, even though they often overlap in practice.

- *Security* refers to the prevention of intentional threats, including unauthorized intrusions, theft, vandalism, sabotage, and terrorism. Its goal is to protect people, assets, and infrastructure from deliberate malicious actions that could cause harm or disruption.
- *Safety*, in contrast, focuses on protecting individuals from unintentional risks such as accidents, hazardous conditions, and emergencies.
  It emphasizes creating environments where individuals are shielded from harm due to negligence, environmental hazards, or unforeseen incidents.

While both security and safety aim to protect and preserve, they address different threat models and require tailored video analytics strategies to be effectively managed.

Table 8.1 illustrates how intelligent video analytics transforms traditional approaches in these domains:

TABLE 8.1 Traditional approach vs. IVA

Aspect	Traditional Approach	With Intelligent Video Analytics
Security	Surveillance cameras monitored by physical guards; perimeter fencing; manual access control.	Automated intrusion detection, perimeter breach alerts, weapon detection, behavioral anomaly analysis.
Safety	Workplace safety regulations (e.g., Occupational Health and Safety (OHSE) standards), manual inspections, reactive incident management.	Real-time fall detection, hazard zone monitoring, automated evacuation alerts, early detection of environmental risks.

Traditionally, organizations relied heavily on human vigilance, security guards manually monitoring camera feeds, safety officers conducting scheduled inspections, and response teams acting after incidents had already occurred. This model was inherently reactive, limited by human attention spans and response times.

By contrast, intelligent video analytics offers a paradigm shift:

• Enabling continuous 24/7 monitoring without fatigue
• Proactively detecting risks and threats before they escalate
• Triggering automated or semi-automated actions to contain or mitigate incidents in real time

Layers of Physical Security

Physical security is crucial in safeguarding assets, infrastructure, and personnel from unauthorized access and physical threats. Modern AI-powered video analytics significantly enhances traditional physical security measures by providing real-time monitoring, advanced threat detection, and automated alert generation.

The key components of an integrated physical security system include the following:

• Perimeter security: The first line of defense, consisting of fences, gates, barriers, and other physical measures designed to deter and delay unauthorized access. Video analytics enhances perimeter security by detecting and classifying potential breaches, such as individuals loitering near fences or vehicles approaching restricted areas.
• Surveillance systems: Traditionally reliant on human monitoring, surveillance systems today incorporate intelligent video analytics to automatically detect suspicious activities, abnormal behaviors, or potential threats. These systems not only record events for forensic analysis but also generate real-time alerts, enabling swift responses to emerging situations.
• Access control systems: Controlling who is allowed to enter specific zones within a facility is a core aspect of physical security. While traditional systems used keys or ID badges, AI-enhanced systems now leverage biometric authentication, face recognition, and behavioral analytics to verify identities dynamically and detect unauthorized access attempts.

• Intrusion detection systems: Motion detectors, door sensors, and glass break detectors form the backbone of intrusion detection.

Today, AI-powered video analytics supplements these systems by detecting more complex intrusion patterns such as individuals bypassing access points or moving against authorized flow paths and automatically escalating alerts for verification and response.

FIGURE 8.1 Examples of deterrence systems surrounding prisons.

Integrated Layers of Physical Security

A robust physical security framework is not composed of isolated components but of interdependent layers designed to deter, detect, delay, and respond to threats effectively.

FIGURE 8.2 Security guards on patrols.

These layers include the following:

- Physical barriers and deterrents: Tangible obstacles such as fences, walls, bollards, and gates create physical impedance. Visual deterrents like prominently placed security cameras and warning signage amplify psychological barriers against intrusion.
- Electronic security systems: A network of surveillance cameras, access control systems, intrusion sensors, and alarm networks that provide continuous monitoring and automated threat detection. Intelligent video analytics augments these systems by filtering noise, prioritizing genuine threats, and enabling fast, focused responses.
- Procedural controls: Policies and operational protocols govern how physical security is maintained, including visitor management, employee identification, incident escalation processes, and emergency response plans. Integration with AI-driven systems ensures that procedures are not only documented but also automatically enforced and audited.
- Environmental design (CPTED: Crime Prevention Through Environmental Design): The strategic design of physical spaces using natural surveillance lines, controlled access points, territorial reinforcement, and proper lighting reduces opportunities for criminal behavior. Intelligent video analytics enhances CPTED principles by dynamically monitoring these spaces, ensuring that environmental controls remain effective even as conditions change.

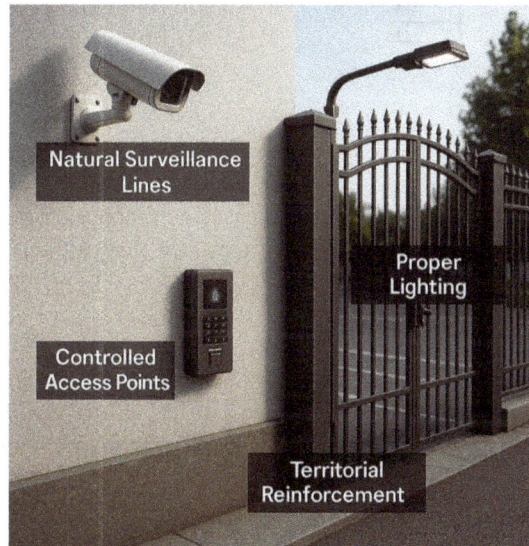

FIGURE 8.3 Example of CPTED.

Security for Electronic Devices

In addition to physical security measures, protecting electronic devices is crucial in today's digital landscape. Cyber-physical threats, such as hacking, unauthorized access, and malware attacks, pose significant risks to modern security infrastructures. AI-powered security measures can enhance the protection of electronic devices by utilizing the following:

- Encryption and secure authentication: ensuring sensitive data on devices is encrypted and only accessible by authorized personnel through multi-factor authentication (MFA)
- AI-Based Intrusion Detection Systems (IDS): monitoring network traffic for unusual patterns that may indicate a cyber threat
- Endpoint security solutions: AI-enhanced security software that detects malware, unauthorized access attempts, and other cyber threats in real-time
- Behavioral analysis for cybersecurity: AI algorithms analyze user behavior and detect anomalies that could signal a security breach, helping to prevent unauthorized access
- IoT device security: protecting interconnected security devices, such as smart cameras and biometric scanners, from cyber intrusions

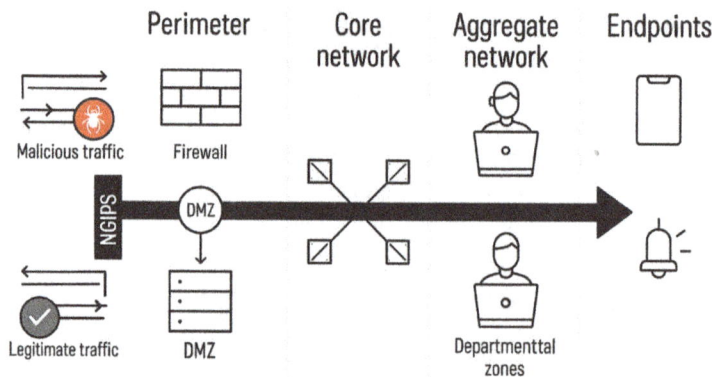

FIGURE 8.4 Example of a security architecture to block malicious network traffic.

By integrating AI-powered cybersecurity measures into physical security frameworks, organizations can establish a multi-layered security approach that protects both tangible and digital assets.

Threat Detection and Prevention Systems

AI-driven video analytics enhances security by providing real-time monitoring and instant alerts for potential threats. Modern surveillance systems utilize deep learning models to detect suspicious activities, identify unauthorized individuals, and predict security breaches before they occur.

Important components of AI-enhanced threat detection systems include the following:

- Facial recognition technology: AI-powered facial recognition systems identify individuals in restricted areas, alert security personnel to unauthorized access, and maintain a database of authorized individuals.
- Anomaly detection: Machine learning algorithms analyze behavioral patterns and flag unusual activities, such as loitering in restricted areas or unauthorized entry attempts.
- Automated perimeter security: AI-integrated surveillance cameras monitor perimeter boundaries and detect breaches in real time, significantly reducing response times.

- Weapon and object detection: AI-powered video analytics can detect concealed weapons, unattended packages, or suspicious objects in crowded areas, reducing potential security threats.
- AI-driven access logs and tracking: AI-based security systems track entry and exit points, ensuring that every movement is recorded and analyzed for suspicious behavior.

FIGURE 8.5 The guard is aware of human movement within the perimeter.

The adoption of AI-driven security solutions in high-risk environments, such as airports, banks, and government facilities, has proven effective in mitigating security risks and improving situational awareness.

FIGURE 8.6 Example of an automated gate with AI surveillance systems.

Integration of AI in Physical Access Control

Physical access control systems have evolved significantly with the integration of AI and biometric authentication technologies. Traditional access control measures, such as keycards and passwords, are vulnerable to unauthorized use and security breaches. AI-powered access control systems improve security with the following:

- Multi-factor authentication (MFA): AI-enabled access control systems incorporate multiple authentication methods, including facial recognition, fingerprint scanning, and RFID verification, to enhance security.
- Automated identity verification: AI-driven systems instantly verify personnel identity at entry points, reducing the risk of unauthorized access and identity fraud.
- Real-time access monitoring: AI-powered surveillance systems track access patterns and identify anomalies, such as tailgating or repeated failed access attempts.
- Adaptive security protocols: AI-based access control systems adjust security measures dynamically based on real-time risk assessments, restricting access to sensitive areas when potential threats are detected.
- Smart badge and RFID integration: AI-enhanced RFID badges automatically track personnel movement and grant access based on predefined security policies.

Industries such as healthcare, corporate environments, and critical infrastructure facilities benefit greatly from AI-enhanced access control systems, improving security while ensuring seamless and efficient access for authorized individuals.

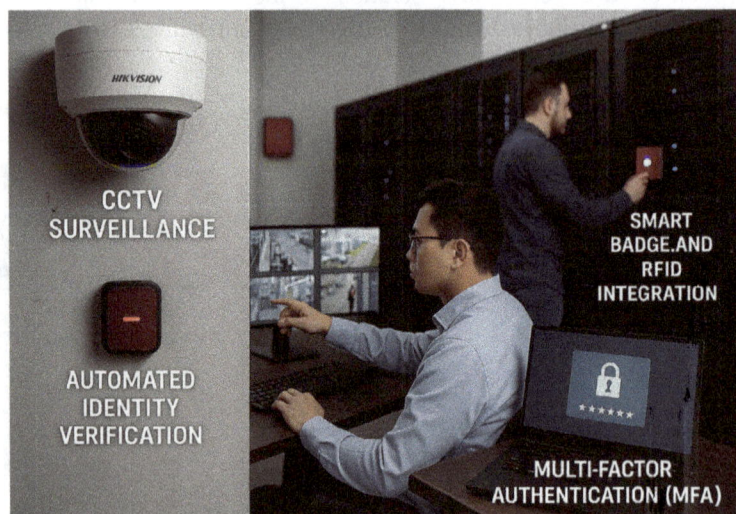

FIGURE 8.7 An IoT-enabled AI video surveillance system at a data center.

Real-World Examples of Advanced Surveillance Systems

Several industries have integrated AI-powered video analytics to enhance security, demonstrating its effectiveness in real-world applications. The following case studies highlight the impact of AI in physical security:

- Airports: AI-driven facial recognition expedites passenger verification, reducing boarding times and enhancing security screening procedures. AI-integrated baggage screening systems detect prohibited items with higher accuracy than traditional screening methods.
- Retail: AI-powered security cameras analyze customer behavior, detect theft attempts, and improve store layout planning by identifying high-traffic areas.
- Smart Cities: AI-enhanced CCTV networks monitor urban environments, detect violent incidents, track suspicious individuals, and manage emergency response operations in real time.

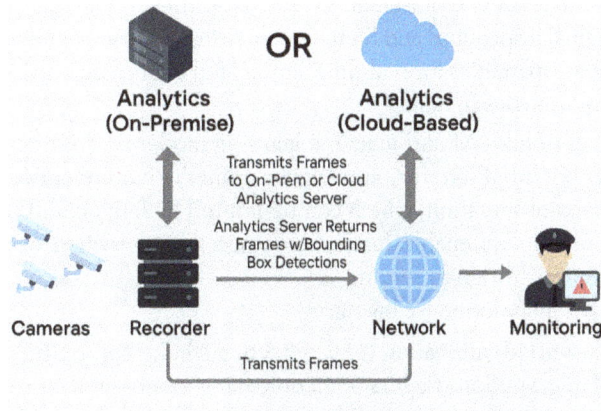

FIGURE 8.8 A flexible architecture cloud or edge computing can be used to obtain surveillance results from the camera.

- Banking and financial institutions: AI-powered security systems monitor ATM transactions, detect fraudulent activities, and prevent identity theft.
- Educational institutions: AI-based surveillance systems identify unauthorized individuals on campus, monitor emergency exits, and ensure compliance with institutional safety policies.

FIGURE 8.9 CCTV, AI, 4G/5G solutions, and third-party cameras combined into an integrated, advanced surveillance system.

Action Framework for Safety Using Video Analytics

1. Introduction to Safety

   Safety is a foundational objective in any operational environment, aimed at protecting individuals, property, and the community from harm caused by accidents, hazardous conditions, or emergencies. It involves proactive risk identification, mitigation strategies, regulatory compliance, and continuous vigilance to ensure hazard-free environments. Frameworks such as Occupational Safety and Health Administration (OSHA) standards guide these efforts by establishing formal safety requirements across industries. While safety traditionally depended heavily on manual inspections and human monitoring, the rise of intelligent video analytics has introduced new capabilities for real-time, automated safety assurance.

2. Role of Video Analytics in Safety

   Video Analytics utilizes AI and machine learning models to continuously monitor environments, detect potential hazards, and trigger immediate interventions. Rather than relying solely on human observation, which can be limited by fatigue and delayed reaction times, video analytics systems enable faster, more accurate detection of unsafe conditions and provide a seamless bridge to action.

   The advantages include the following:

   - Real-time hazard identification (e.g., detecting smoke before fire alarms activate)
   - Automated intervention triggers (e.g., unlocking emergency exits during evacuations)
   - Enhanced situational awareness for safety officers and emergency responders
   - Detailed incident documentation to support regulatory compliance and incident review

   Video analytics transforms traditional safety practices from a reactive process into a proactive, predictive system.

3. HSE (Health, Safety, and Environment) Overview

   The Health, Safety, and Environment (HSE) domain encompasses the following:

   - Health: protecting employees from occupational illnesses and injuries
   - Safety: preventing accidents and ensuring secure operational environments
   - Environment: safeguarding natural resources and minimizing environmental impacts

   Effective HSE programs integrate safety standards, employee training, incident management, and continuous monitoring of risks. By embedding video analytics into HSE frameworks, organizations can automate hazard detection, accelerate emergency responses, and enhance their overall HSE compliance posture.

4. Structure of the Action Framework for Safety

   The Action Framework for Safety using Video Analytics consists of three interlocking pillars:

   - Hazard Identification and Monitoring
     - Regular assessment of operational environments for safety risks
     - Continuous video-based monitoring to detect unsafe behaviors and conditions dynamically
     - Proactively identify potential hazards across health, safety, and environmental dimensions
     - Deploy intelligent video systems to monitor key risk zones, including high-traffic areas, hazardous machinery zones, and emergency exits

- Real-time Detection and Response
  - Immediate identification of hazards through AI-driven video analytics. Use real-time video analytics models to detect slip, trip, and fall incidents. Presence of smoke, fire, chemical spills, or unsafe equipment usage. Overcrowding and bottlenecks in evacuation routes.
  - Automated or semi-automated response actions triggered to prevent escalation. Trigger automatic responses such as dispatching first responders. Activating alarms and evacuation messages. Unlocking or rerouting emergency exits dynamically.
- Post-incident Review and Learning
  - Detailed analysis of incidents captured by video analytics
  - Identification of root causes and refinement of safety strategies through historical data insights
  - Analyze incident footage to determine causes, response effectiveness, and potential process/procedural (Standard Operation Procedure) gaps
  - Use historical video data trends to adjust preventive measures and optimize future system configurations

Over time, this feedback loop increases the predictive accuracy of hazard detection models, enhances response protocols, and reduces the frequency and severity of safety incidents.

This cycle is designed for continuous improvement, ensuring that safety practices evolve with operational complexity and new environmental risks.

TABLE 8.2 Hazard and action triggered by video analytics

Hazard Detected	Action Triggered
Slip, Trip, or Fall Incident	Dispatch on-site medical team; alert control room; log incident for OHSE compliance.
Smoke or Fire Detected	Trigger building-wide fire alarm; unlock emergency exits; alert fire response units.
Overcrowding in Evacuation Routes	Open alternative exits; broadcast evacuation guidance via public address systems; notify emergency coordination teams.

Through intelligent video analytics, these actions can be initiated within seconds, dramatically reducing reliance on delayed human reporting and enhancing the reliability of safety systems.

The Transformation: From Passive Observation to Intelligent Action

By integrating traditional security and safety frameworks with AI-driven video analytics, organizations make a profound shift, from passive observation to intelligent, responsive operations. Historically, physical security and safety systems depended heavily on human observation, periodic inspections, and post-incident reaction. Such methods, while foundational, were limited by response delays, inconsistency, and human error. Today, intelligent video analytics systems enable a more advanced, automated model that aligns perfectly with the Sense–Understand–Action paradigm:

- Sense: The system continuously captures real-time data from surveillance cameras, sensors, and IoT devices. This includes visual inputs (e.g., human activity, smoke, fire, and unauthorized access) and environmental signals (e.g., crowd density, lighting conditions, and motion trajectories).
- Understand: The system uses AI models to interpret and classify events and patterns, identifying anomalies, threats, or safety violations. This may include detecting suspicious behavior, recognizing a fall incident, identifying an unauthorized individual, or predicting the buildup of crowd pressure. The system also prioritizes threats based on context, severity, and historical patterns, ensuring that the most critical risks are surfaced for immediate attention.
- Action: Once a threat or hazard is recognized, the system automatically initiates predefined response protocols, which may include the following:
  - Alerting on-site security personnel or safety officers
  - Locking or unlocking specific access points
  - Triggering sirens, public address systems, or evacuation guidance
  - Dispatching emergency responders or notifying law enforcement
  - Logging the incident for audit, compliance, and post-event review

This intelligent closed-loop flow, from sensing to understanding to acting, results in significantly improved response times, greater situational accuracy, and operational consistency across the organization.

This evolution not only enhances incident detection and response; it aligns physical security and safety functions with broader strategic goals:

- Operational efficiency: Human resources can focus on high-value tasks by automating routine monitoring and first-line response actions, reducing cost and increasing responsiveness.
- Regulatory compliance: Systems support safety audits, OHSE documentation, and real-time policy enforcement, helping organizations meet legal and industry standards.
- Resilience and scalability: AI-driven systems adapt to complex environments, from a single building to a multi-site enterprise or an entire city, scaling protection and response as needs evolve.

In essence, video analytics systems become not just the "eyes" of the organization, but its "nervous system"—sensing risk, understanding its significance, and taking immediate action to protect lives, assets, and continuity.

This shift marks a critical milestone in building smarter, safer, and more resilient environments, where security, safety, and efficiency converge into a unified, intelligent operational model.

OPERATIONAL EFFICIENCY THROUGH VIDEO ANALYTICS

While security and safety are critical drivers for the deployment of intelligent video analytics, a growing number of organizations are leveraging these systems to improve operational efficiency.

In modern facilities, industrial campuses, transportation networks, and smart cities, the ability to sense, interpret, and act upon visual data in real time has unlocked opportunities to optimize workflows, reduce operational costs, enhance user experiences, and improve sustainability.

Rather than treating video as a passive source of historical evidence, organizations are now treating it as an active decision-making input, a source of dynamic, real-time intelligence used to automate, adapt, and optimize daily operations.

This approach aligns with the Sense–Understand–Action framework:

- Sense: Capture real-time visual and spatial data through a network of cameras and IoT sensors.
- Understand: Analyze this data using computer vision and pattern recognition to detect inefficiencies, anomalies, or trends.
- Action: Trigger workflows or adjustments automatically or semi-automatically to enhance performance, reduce waste, or improve experiences.

Below are key areas where operational efficiency is being transformed by video analytics.

Improving Customer Service

Operational Goal: Reduce customer waiting times, improve satisfaction, and allocate resources dynamically.

Video Analytics Role:

- Monitor queue lengths in retail stores, banks, airports, and ticketing counters
- Analyze customer dwell times in specific zones or counters
- Detect long idle times or uneven staff distribution

Example: At a busy banking branch, cameras monitor customer queues in real-time. When the queue exceeds five people or an average wait time of 4 minutes, the system will automatically trigger a notification to the branch manager, recommending additional tellers be deployed from the back office. In airports, if video analytics detect prolonged queues at immigration checkpoints, it can notify supervisors or even trigger digital signage to redirect passengers to less crowded lines.

Optimizing Traffic and Mobility

Operational Goal: Reduce congestion, improve traffic flow, and minimize wait times.
Video Analytics Role:

- Count vehicles at intersections and analyze congestion patterns
- Detect illegal parking, blocked lanes, or accidents in real time
- Predict high-traffic zones based on historical video data

Example: In a smart city intersection, video analytics detects a high buildup of vehicles approaching from the southbound direction. The system sends a signal to the traffic control platform to dynamically extend the green light phase by 30 seconds, reducing vehicle delay without manual intervention. In bus rapid transit systems, video analytics can monitor the punctuality of buses at designated lanes, detect illegal usage by non-bus vehicles, and trigger fines or alerts accordingly.

Enhancing Maintenance and Housekeeping Efficiency

Operational Goal: Enable responsive cleaning, maintenance, and repair operations based on actual conditions rather than fixed schedules.

Video Analytics Role:

- Detect trash accumulation in bins or around rest areas
- Identify malfunctioning escalators, elevators, or lighting systems via anomaly recognition
- Monitor restrooms or food courts for cleaning needs based on usage patterns

Example: In a shopping mall, video analytics detects overflowing bins in a high-traffic food court. Instead of relying on a fixed cleaning schedule, the system alerts the maintenance team to dispatch staff specifically to that zone, improving responsiveness and reducing customer complaints.

In industrial settings, thermal cameras can detect overheating equipment or leaks, automatically triggering maintenance dispatch or machine shutdowns to prevent downtime.

Improving Energy Efficiency

Operational Goal: Reduce energy consumption in lighting, HVAC, and other building systems through occupancy-based automation.

Video Analytics Role:

- Use people-counting and zone-based activity detection to adjust lighting or air conditioning
- Identify underutilized spaces to reconfigure resource allocation
- Support green building certifications by enabling usage-aware energy systems

Example: In a smart office, video analytics counts the number of people on each floor in real time. When the occupancy in certain zones drops below 10%, the system reduces lighting intensity and lowers HVAC cooling load automatically, without affecting comfort or requiring manual input.

In conference centers, when no motion or presence is detected in a reserved meeting room for more than 15 minutes, the system releases the room in the booking system and powers down unnecessary equipment.

TABLE 8.3 Operational goal and video analytics role

Operational Goal	Video Analytics Role	Action Triggered
Improve customer service	Queue length and dwell time monitoring	Dispatch staff, optimize counters, redirect customers
Optimize traffic flow	Vehicle counting, congestion and violation detection	Adjust signals, dispatch traffic control, trigger fines
Enhance maintenance	Trash, malfunction, cleanliness detection	Dispatch cleaning, repair, or maintenance crew
Improve energy efficiency	People counting, area utilization analysis	Adjust lighting/HVAC, release unused rooms, log usage patterns

Beyond Efficiency: Building Adaptive Operations

By embedding video analytics into operational workflows, organizations gain the ability to adapt in real time to changing conditions. This transition from rigid procedures to data-driven flexibility allows facilities to become more responsive, cost-efficient, and user-centric.

It also supports long-term objectives such as the following:

- Workforce optimization: reducing overstaffing while ensuring responsiveness
- Predictive operations: using patterns from video data to forecast needs and prevent delays
- Sustainability: lowering energy usage, emissions, and waste through smarter facility management

DECISION AND ACTION WORKFLOW (DAW)

In previous sections, we established the foundational framework of Sensing → Understanding → Action as the core of intelligent video analytics. While much has been written about sensing technologies and AI-based understanding (e.g., object detection, tracking, and anomaly detection), there remains a gap in how these insights translate into real-world impact. This section formalizes that missing link: the Decision and Action Workflow (DAW).

DAW is a structured, rule- and logic-based mechanism that governs a system's behavior after it "understands" an event or pattern. This layer defines the flow of activities, decisions, escalation paths, and execution methods, bridging AI perception with operational outcomes in security, safety, and efficiency contexts.

What is DAW?

Decision and Action Workflow (DAW) is a modular and extensible framework that captures the sequence of responses and operational actions triggered by machine or human understanding of video analytics results.

DAW's purpose is to convert raw AI outputs into organized, impactful actions within operational systems. It serves as the programmable layer that bridges AI's insights and their direct application in real-world system behavior.

While the detection component of AI frameworks is extensively discussed in academic literature and commonly integrated into commercial products, the subsequent stages, particularly the actions or responses driven by these detections, are often not adequately addressed However, in mission-critical environments, it is not the alert itself, but what follows the alert, that determines system success. DAW ensures

- Alerts lead to structured, traceable responses
- Multi-level escalations and acknowledgments are possible
- Integration with external systems (e.g., alarms, locks, and dispatch) is seamless
- Human-in-the-loop and automated responses can co-exist

DAW Workflow Components

- Trigger: an event understood by AI, such as an intrusion is detected, a person falls, or there is loitering in a restricted zone

- Decision Logic: IF/THEN conditions, thresholding, and timing constraints, such as if a person loiters > 60s + at night → escalate
- Response Channel: where the action is sent, such as the dashboard, WhatsApp, email, actuator, alarm system, or a guard post
- Escalation Rules: What happens if the first action fails or is ignored? For example, a guard does not respond → notify supervisor
- Action Logging and Feedback: recording the event, who responded, and timestamp. Feed the information into audit, retraining, or policy refinement.

DAW Design and Implementation Process

Before filling in and deploying DAW components, organizations should follow a structured preparatory process to ensure contextual relevance, operational clarity, and readiness for deployment. A well-implemented DAW does not begin with logic blocks; it begins with understanding the environment and anticipating scenarios.

1. Scenario Planning
   - Analyze past incidents and project potential threats or opportunities in terms of safety, security, and operational efficiency.
   - Develop realistic "what-if" situations to guide the DAW configuration.
2. Define DAW Components
   - For each scenario, define the trigger, logic, response channel, escalation, and logging.
   - Align these with SOPs and human roles.
3. Simulation and Testing
   - Simulate scenarios manually or with low-code automation tools to test the DAW flow.
   - Validate the logic paths, escalation timing, and integration points.
4. Deployment
   - Roll out the DAW logic using orchestration tools or platforms (e.g., Vantiq, IoT-Ticket, and Centaurops).
   - Monitor and iterate based on field feedback and system logs.

This phased approach ensures that DAW becomes not just an AI logic system, but an operational decision backbone for intelligent video analytics.

DAW and Organizational SOP Alignment

DAW is not meant to replace an organization's Standard Operating Procedures (SOPs); it is meant to enhance and automate their enforcement. Where SOPs define what should happen in response to a situation, DAW operationalizes how it happens in real-time using video intelligence.

In real-world deployments, DAW implementations are typically designed and executed by systems integrators, software developers, or deployed through Intelligent System Management platforms such as Vantiq, IoT-Ticket, or Centaurops. These platforms provide the orchestration layer and integration capabilities required to connect AI outputs with devices, human interfaces, and enterprise systems. By aligning DAW logic with SOP documents, the following is true:

- Trigger conditions mirror SOP criteria for incident classification.
- Decision logic enforces SOP-prescribed thresholds, zones, and timing.
- Escalation paths mirror the organizational chain of command.
- Response channels match the prescribed communication protocols (e.g., the security dispatch and plant operations team).
- Logging provides the required audit trail for regulatory and internal compliance.

In practice, DAW can be used to create AI-enforceable SOP templates that reduce ambiguity and improve response consistency. This integration enables organizations to not only react faster but to also evaluate and optimize their SOPs based on real-world data and system performance feedback.

Example DAW

Below are some examples of DAW for security, safety and operational efficiency use cases.

1. Security: Unauthorized Entry Detection
   - Trigger: Human-shaped object crosses restricted perimeter
   - Logic: If time = night + no prior schedule
   - Response: Sound siren, notify security guard via SMS
   - Escalation: No response in 15s → call supervisor
   - Log: Save 10-sec clip, mark as "Critical Security Event"
2. Safety: Worker Without Helmet
   - Trigger: Detected person without PPE
   - Logic: If zone = hazardous + entry time logged
   - Response: Display warning, notify safety officer
   - Escalation: Repeat violation → daily report
   - Log: Archive image + worker ID
3. Operational Efficiency: Conveyor Congestion
   - Trigger: Object buildup at line B3
   - Logic: More than 10 objects detected stationary for > 90s
   - Response: Alert control room, slow upstream line
   - Escalation: Persisting issue → notify maintenance
   - Log: Generate shift report

CASE STUDY: THE 2011 OSLO BOMBING – A COUNTERFACTUAL DAW ANALYSIS

The July 22, 2011, attacks in Norway involving a car bombing in Oslo and a mass shooting on Utøya island tragically exposed critical failures in the country's physical security infrastructure. Anders Behring Breivik's two-part attack resulted in 77 deaths and over 200 injuries. This section re-analyzes the attack using the Sense–Understand–Action framework and expands with a DAW (Decision and Action Workflow) model that illustrates how intelligent systems could have changed the outcome.

Background of the Attack

1. **Oslo Bombing (3:25 PM)** – A car bomb was detonated near the Prime Minister's office, killing eight and injuring over 200.
2. **Utøya Mass Shooting (5:21–6:35 PM)** – Disguised as a police officer, Breivik conducted a mass shooting at a youth camp, killing 69.

These attacks exposed vulnerabilities across all layers of physical security: deterrence, detection, delay, response, and asset protection.

How IVA Could Have Avoided the Incident

1. **Deterrence**: The post-incident security assessment revealed several critical vulnerabilities. Notably, the Prime Minister's office lacked anti-vehicle barriers, making it vulnerable to direct vehicular attacks. Additionally, the absence of visible patrols or deterrents likely created a perception of low security, potentially emboldening an attacker. While Norway values an open and accessible society, this cultural stance appeared to reduce visible defensive measures, creating exploitable gaps. Video analytics can help strengthen security without compromising openness. Strategically placed surveillance cameras can enhance perceived safety, even if passively monitored. These systems provide continuous visual input, which AI can analyze in real time to detect abnormal patterns, especially suspicious vehicle behavior near sensitive areas. For instance, a vehicle that remains parked unusually long in a restricted zone could be flagged by the system. This would trigger a chain of responses: loudspeaker warnings, real-time alerts to nearby security personnel, or visual deterrents like flashing lights, all without human initiation.

    Had such a system been in place during the 2011 Oslo bombing, Breivik's van parked for an extended period in a high-security area might have been identified as a threat. The system could have issued an automated warning, alerted guards, and possibly disrupted the plan, forcing him to abandon or relocate the vehicle.

    In this situation, DAW can be applied as follows:

    • Trigger: Vehicle parked >10 minutes in a red zone with unregistered plates
    • Logic: High-risk anomaly → escalate
    • Response: Automated public speaker warning + control center alert
    • Escalation: No manual response → dispatch on-site patrol
    • Logging: Time-stamped incident with captured image frame for review

2. **Detection**: The post-incident review exposed major failures in detection and access control. Breivik's vehicle, which carried a hidden bomb, passed through without any form of vehicle scanning or inspection. His disguise as a police officer allowed him to bypass scrutiny, exposing a dangerous oversight, there were no verification protocols for uniformed individuals. The absence of License Plate Recognition (LPR) systems and behavior analysis tools left the area highly vulnerable. Video analytics can close these gaps by establishing a layered surveillance infrastructure. Cameras placed at important checkpoints can monitor both vehicles and individuals entering secure zones. Using AI-driven analysis, the system

enters the "understand" phase, LPR can cross-reference vehicle plates against white- and blacklists, while person re-identification tracks movements across zones and flags inconsistencies, non-authorized individual. Here is the DAW application for this scenario:

- Trigger: LPR mismatch + no badge
- Logic: If an unknown car and an individual → verify
- Response: Alert checkpoint for manual verification.
- Escalation: Auto-notify senior guard and log for law enforcement.

3. **Delay**: The security investigation revealed a major failure. Breivik was able to park his van packed with explosives directly outside the Prime Minister's office without any resistance or alarm. This points to a complete lack of physical barriers or early detection mechanisms in the vicinity of a highly sensitive government facility, representing a critical vulnerability in passive perimeter defense. Video analytics offers a proactive and intelligent approach to address such gaps. In the "Sense" phase, strategically positioned cameras continuously monitor vehicle movement and parking behavior in sensitive areas. This constant visual feed provides the foundation for detection. In the "Understand" phase, AI algorithms analyze the footage to spot anomalies such as vehicles stopping in unauthorized locations or remaining stationary in restricted zones beyond a normal duration. These deviations from expected behavior are key indicators of a potential threat. The "Act" phase turns detection into response. If a suspicious vehicle is identified, the system can automatically trigger physical countermeasures—such as activating barriers, alerting on-site guards, or broadcasting deterrent messages—before the threat reaches its target. For instance, if video analytics had been integrated with access control systems outside the Prime Minister's office, any uncredentialed or erratic vehicle could have been intercepted early. Automated gates or spike strips could have blocked its entry, and immediate alerts could have prompted a manual inspection disrupting the attacker's plan before detonation was possible. DAW can be applied in this scenario as follows:

- Trigger: Unauthorized vehicle enters red zone.
- Logic: Time-of-day policy check + unauthorized plate → trigger lockdown
- Response: Activate bollards/barriers.
- Escalation: Alert perimeter team with map of approach.

4. **Response**: The emergency response assessment revealed serious shortcomings in both on-site security and the speed of external intervention. When the attack began, there were no armed personnel or immediate responders present to confront the threat. At Utøya, the SWAT team's arrival was delayed due to poor coordination and logistical hurdles, critically impacting the outcome. Video analytics can play a pivotal role in enhancing real-time situational awareness and speeding up emergency response. In the "Sense" phase, cameras actively monitor areas for signs of distress, such as people running, sudden crowd dispersal, or individuals collapsing. This constant feed becomes the system's early warning mechanism. During the "Understand" phase, AI algorithms analyze visual and audio data to detect patterns indicating violence. These may include gunfire signatures, erratic movement, or aggressive behaviors. The system classifies such events as high-risk and worthy of immediate attention. The "Action" phase ensures that these detections are translated into swift responses. The system can initiate safety protocols such as lockdowns, sound alarms, or issue instructions via public ad-

dress systems. At the same time, it alerts first responders with real-time updates, for example, "armed person detected near northeast camp zone", along with live visual feeds.

In the case of Utøya, a system with violence recognition and fall detection could have triggered alerts within seconds of the shooting starting. GPS-tagged video clips could have been shared with police and emergency services, helping guide rapid deployment by helicopter or drone. This real-time intelligence might have enabled a faster, more coordinated intervention—possibly reducing casualties and shortening the duration of the attack. DAW can be applied in this scenario as follows:

- Trigger: Sudden crowd dispersion + multiple falls detected
- Logic: Multiple persons fall + panic route deviation → classify as violence
- Response: Activate emergency protocol, alert police drone unit.
- Escalation: Share live video + GPS with responders

5. **Asset Protection**: The investigation exposed serious weaknesses in the physical infrastructure and emergency preparedness of the affected sites. Government buildings were not built with blast-resistant materials, leaving their occupants exposed to explosive threats. At the youth camp, there were no secure shelters or clearly defined evacuation procedures, increasing the risk during emergencies.

Video analytics, when integrated with building systems, can significantly strengthen preparedness and resilience. In the "Sense" phase, specialized cameras and sensors continuously monitor structural integrity and occupancy levels across zones. These tools provide critical real-time data on how the building is functioning and how people are moving inside it.

In the "Understand" phase, AI analyzes this data to detect potential dangers such as early signs of structural stress that could indicate collapse or overcrowding that could obstruct evacuation. This predictive insight allows proactive intervention before conditions escalate into crises.

The "Act" phase enables immediate safety measures. If anomalies are detected, like excessive stress on a structure or a zone exceeding safe occupancy limits, the system can automatically activate evacuation protocols. This includes sounding alarms, guiding people via dynamic signage and audio prompts, or initiating lockdowns where containment is required. For example, an AI-powered building management system integrated with video analytics could automatically lock vulnerable areas, redirect occupants along safer routes, and keep them informed with live instructions. These smart interventions help ensure faster, more orderly evacuations, enhancing safety and survival rates during critical incidents. DAW can be applied in this scenario as follows:

- Trigger: Overcrowding in unsecured zone
- Logic: If zone capacity > 150% + incident detected → activate evacuation plan
- Response: Trigger signage, lock unnecessary exits.
- Escalation: Guide to designated safety shelters.

This DAW-based counterfactual shows how combining AI video analytics with structured workflows could have disrupted Breivik's plan. It reinforces that "Understanding" must always be followed by structured "Action", and the DAW model provides the operational backbone to make such action feasible and immediate. The following case study demonstrates how DAW can be embedded within an operational environment to enhance security responsiveness and SOP compliance. By following a structured Decision and Action Workflow, organizations can achieve not only automated detection but also intelligent resolution paths.

SUMMARY

Chapter 8 has shown that the value of intelligent video analytics lies not just in seeing or understanding, but in acting quickly, accurately, and decisively. By embedding video analytics into security, safety, and operational systems, organizations can shift from reactive incident management to proactive decision-making and real-time control. We explored how traditional physical security layers (deterrence, detection, delay, response, and asset protection) are significantly strengthened when augmented by AI-driven systems. We examined how Health, Safety, and Environment (HSE) programs can benefit from automated hazard detection and incident response, and how operational workflows in smart buildings and cities can be optimized using video intelligence for energy efficiency, traffic management, queue reduction, and predictive maintenance.

The Sense–Understand–Action framework is the unifying idea throughout this chapter:

- Sense: Capturing real-time data from video and sensors.
- Understand: Extracting meaning and identifying patterns through analytics.
- Action: Motivating timely, context-aware decisions that enhance resilience, safety, and performance.

This chapter also introduced the Decision and Action Workflow (DAW) as a critical structure that enables the "Action" component to be implemented in a programmable, auditable, and automated manner. DAW ensures that AI insights lead to structured outcomes via defined triggers, decision logic, escalation paths, and aligned SOPs. It transforms video analytics from a detection tool into a proactive operational system. As we move into the next chapter on system design, architecture, and deployment (Chapters 9 and 10), we will focus on how to engineer video analytics systems end-to-end, connecting the insights and actions discussed here into scalable, secure, and interoperable technical solutions.

CHAPTER 9

DESIGNING END-TO-END VIDEO ANALYTICS SYSTEMS

End-to-end design is the cornerstone of successful intelligent video analytics deployments. It ensures that every component—from video capture at the edge to analytics processing, secure storage, and real-time decision outputs—functions as a cohesive, interoperable system. A robust design not only facilitates core objectives such as security, safety, and forensic capability, but also enables predictive maintenance, operational optimization, and automated responses in both smart city and industrial contexts.

This chapter integrates the diverse topics explored in earlier chapters, including CCTV hardware selection, camera optics and placement, networking fundamentals, image preprocessing, deep learning workflows, analytics pipelines, system architecture, and compute infrastructure into a coherent, production-grade deployment blueprint.

We move from modular understanding to system-level engineering: how to orchestrate these elements under performance constraints, cybersecurity frameworks, and operational realities. Practical trade-offs between cloud and edge, scalability, data privacy, fault tolerance, and regulatory compliance are addressed in detail, with deployment scenarios across urban surveillance, transportation, critical infrastructure, and industrial sites.

INTRODUCTION

The *Video Analytics Design Line* framework is a structured methodology for systematically designing video analytics solutions from start to finish. This chapter covers architectural principles, a step-by-step design process, technical best practices, a comparative analysis of design approaches, and a practical case study, providing a comprehensive reference for system designers.

ARCHITECTURAL PRINCIPLES AND OVERVIEW OF END-TO-END SYSTEMS

An effective video analytics system architecture can be conceptualized in four important layers: input, processing, storage, and output (Figure 9.1). Each layer plays a distinct role, and together they form the pipeline that turns camera footage into actionable intelligence.

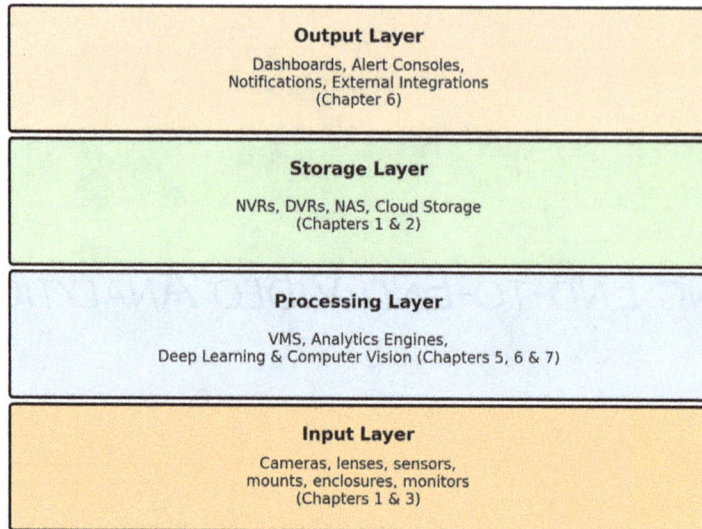

Output Layer

Dashboards, Alert Consoles,
Notifications, External Integrations
(Chapter 6)

Storage Layer

NVRs, DVRs, NAS, Cloud Storage
(Chapters 1 & 2)

Processing Layer

VMS, Analytics Engines,
Deep Learning & Computer Vision (Chapters 5, 6 & 7)

Input Layer

Cameras, lenses, sensors,
mounts, enclosures, monitors
(Chapters 1 & 3)

FIGURE 9.1 Video analytics system architecture.

Below is an outline of these layers and their roles (with cross-references to earlier chapters for more detail):

- **Input Layer:** This layer comprises the video capture devices such as CCTV or IP cameras (including their lenses and sensors), along with related equipment like camera mounts, enclosures, and monitors. This front-end was covered in Chapter 1 (Introduction to CCTV and its Devices) and Chapter 3 (Camera Types and Principles). The quality and configuration of the input layer (such as camera resolution, placement, and field of view) set the foundation for the entire system's performance. For instance, using appropriate camera types for the environment (see Chapter 3 for camera types and image sensors) and ensuring proper installation (angles, focus, and lighting considerations) will determinehow the system can "see" events.

- **Processing Layer:** This includes the video management system (VMS) and analytics engines that handle incoming video streams. This layer is responsible for recording, decoding, and analyzing video either in real time or in batches. As discussed in Chapter 6 (video analytics and content analysis concepts), the VMS connects to all cameras and provides functions like live viewing, video recording, event management, and often basic analytics (motion detection and tampering alerts). On top of the VMS, specialized analytics software (or built-in camera analytics) processes the video for intelligent analysis – detecting events, recognizing objects or faces, and generating metadata. This layer can be implemented on local servers, edge devices, or in the cloud, and we must consider the placement of analytics (edge versus cloud) as it impacts latency and bandwidth (see Chapter 7 for edge computing principles). A modern processing layer might involve edge AI devices for immediate analysis and cloud servers for heavier processing, orchestrated to work together.

- **Storage Layer:** This manages the retention and retrieval of video data and derived information. This includes on-premises recording devices like Network Video Recorders (NVRs) or DVRs, network-attached storage, or cloud storage services. Important considerations are capacity (how many days of video to keep, and at what quality), reliability (redundancy, backup, and retrieval speed). Chapter 1 introduced CCTV recording principles, and Chapter 2 covered storage and bandwidth considerations for video. In an end-to-end system, storage solutions must align with requirements: for example, a high-throughput local disk array for recent footage and possibly cloud archival for older footage. Data retention policies (how long footage is kept) often relate to regulatory requirements (see Chapter 2 for privacy and data retention regulations). The storage layer should be designed so that critical video is safely stored with minimal risk of loss, and relevant metadata (timestamps and object tags) is indexed for easy search during investigations.
- **Output:** This provides the end results to users and downstream systems. This includes user interfaces like surveillance dashboards, alert consoles, mobile notifications, or integrations with external systems (e.g., an access control or law enforcement database). The output layer turns analytics results into actionable information; for instance, displaying an alarm on an operator's screen when a threat is detected, or logging an event in a security incident management system. Many of the analytics outputs and use-cases described in Chapter 6 (such as dashboards for crowd density or alerts for perimeter breaches) manifest in this layer. The output layer could be as simple as a security guard viewing live cameras, or as advanced as an AI-powered alert management system triaging events. Ensuring the output layer is intuitive and provides the right information to the right people is essential for the system's effectiveness.

One core component that ties these layers together is the video management system (VMS). The VMS acts as the central hub: it connects to cameras (input), manages recordings (storage), interfaces with analytics modules (processing), and presents video streams and alerts to users (output). Many commercial VMS platforms (such as Milestone) provide an all-in-one solution for connecting cameras, recording video, and enabling some analytics and user interface capabilities. The architectural design must consider how the VMS and analytics components will interact – whether analytics are built into the VMS, added via plugins, or run on separate systems that feed results into the VMS.

Beyond the functional layers, several architectural *cross-cutting principles* influence an end-to-end design:

- **Network Topology and Bandwidth:** Video feeds require a substantial network bandwidth, especially as camera counts and resolutions increase. Chapter 2 discusses network design for surveillance, including the use of IP networks, PoE (Power over Ethernet) switches to power cameras, and considerations like VLANs. A well-designed architecture ensures the network can carry video streams reliably. Techniques such as video compression (e.g., H.265 encoding to reduce bit rates) and multicast streaming (to let multiple viewers watch a feed without duplicating streams) are often used to optimize bandwidth. For example, streaming video via RTSP in a multicast mode can significantly cut down network load when the feed is viewed by many clients. If the system relies on a cloud backend, the WAN or internet uplinks must be sized for the aggregate video traffic (or mitigated by doing more edge processing and sending only metadata communications links might employ adaptive bitrate streaming or quality-of-service controls to maintain performance. (Networking for CCTV is discussed in Chapter 2, including bandwidth calculation and compression standards).

- **Scalability:** The design should accommodate growth – adding more cameras or higher resolution streams in the future should not require a complete redesign. This means selecting scalable components (e.g., a VMS that supports clustering multiple recorders, or cloud services that can expand on demand) and modular architecture. For instance, a small system might start with one server, but the architecture could allow adding additional servers or edge processing nodes as the deployment scales up (see Chapter 7 for computing scalability strategies). Cloud-based components naturally offer scalability, but even on-premises, planning for extra capacity (CPU, GPU, storage, and network throughput) or using virtualization can help. A rule of thumb is to design for current needs plus a buffer (say 20–30% extra capacity or easy expansion headroom) so the system can grow without immediate overhaul.

- **Latency and Placement of Processing:** End-to-end latency (the delay from an event happening on camera to the time an alert or result is produced) is critical for real-time analytics use cases. To minimize latency, designers often move processing closer to the source (edge computing). For example, analytics performed on-camera or on a local gateway can generate instant alerts, whereas sending video to a cloud server might introduce network delay. Therefore, responsiveness is an important requirement (e.g., detecting and responding to a security breach within seconds), an edge or on-premises processing architecture is preferable (Chapter 7 introduced edge vs. cloud trade-offs). However, if the use case tolerates delay (like end-of-day reporting or forensic analysis), cloud-centric processing is acceptable and can leverage powerful centralized resources. Many systems adopt a *hybrid architecture*, where they perform critical low-latency analytics at the edge and send summary data or clips to the cloud for more intensive analysis or long-term aggregation. For example, an edge device might run object detection and only send metadata (object type, time, and location) upstream, where a cloud service aggregates data from many sites or runs deeper AI analysis. This hybrid edge-to-cloud pattern is illustrated in Figure 9.1, which shows cameras feeding video to local processors (running, say, NVIDIA DeepStream for object detection) and only alerts/metadata being transmitted to a cloud analytics platform for storage and further insight.

- **Reliability and Redundancy:** A video system is often part of a security infrastructure, so it must be resilient to failures. Critical points of failure include network links, servers, storage devices, and even the cameras themselves. To mitigate these, the architecture can incorporate redundancy at multiple levels. For instance, it should have redundant network paths or switches so that if one link fails, the video streams reroute through another path. The system should use failover servers or NVRs that can take over if the primary server goes down (some VMS solutions support automatic failover recording servers). The system should implement RAID storage or multiple recording devices so that a single disk failure does not result in lost footage. Backup power (UPS units or generators) for cameras, network gear, and servers is also crucial so that a power outage does not disable the surveillance. These principles align with general IT best practices and were mentioned in Chapter 2 (which discussed network and device reliability) and Chapter 7 (computing infrastructure best practices). A reliable design ensures continuous operation and data integrity, which is especially important for applications like security where downtime or data loss could be catastrophic.

- **Compliance and Security:** Video surveillance systems must adhere to privacy laws and cybersecurity best practices. Privacy considerations may dictate how cameras are used and how data is stored or shared (for example, GDPR in Europe requires careful handling of personal data like faces). The system architecture might need to include features like video anonymization (blurring faces or obscuring texts), configurable retention policies (automatically deleting or archiving footage after X days), or access controls to ensure only authorized personnel can view sensitive feeds (see Chapter 2 for an overview of data protection and compliance in CCTV deployments). Cybersecurity is equally important; cameras and VMS servers are network-connected devices that can be targets for a breach, which could lead to unauthorized viewing of cameras or tampering with recordings. Therefore, from an architectural standpoint, we isolate and harden the system: for example, placing cameras on a separate network segment (VLAN) with restricted access, using firewalls to control communication, and enforcing strong authentication for all system components. Chapter 7 discusses cybersecurity considerations for IoT and edge devices, and Chapter 2 provides fundamentals of securing network devices; those principles apply here to ensure the surveillance system is not the weak link in an organization's security posture.

In summary, the architecture of an end-to-end video analytics system must align with the deployment's size, use cases, and constraints. It should ensure that video feeds flow smoothly from cameras to analysis to storage, and that outputs are delivered to users with appropriate speed and reliability. By utilizing the foundational knowledge from earlier chapters – camera hardware (Chapter 3), networking (Chapter 2), imaging (Chapter 4), AI analytics (Chapter 5), VMS/analytics software (Chapter 6), and computing infrastructure (Chapter 7) – designers can create architectures that are robust, scalable, low-latency, and secure. A thoughtful architectural design sets the stage for the detailed system design process described in the next section.

THE "VIDEO ANALYTICS DESIGN LINE" SIGNATURE FRAMEWORK

Designing a complex video analytics system benefit from a structured methodology. The Video Analytics Design Line is a four-step framework that guides practitioners from the initial concept to a detailed system proposal. By following these steps (Figure 9.2) – Requirement Gathering, Requirement Analysis, System Design, and Proposal Documentation – designers ensure that the final architecture meets customer needs and incorporates industry best practices. We will discuss each step in detail, integrating insights from prior chapters where relevant.

- Site Layout
- Objectives

Gathering Customer Requirements

- VRD (Video Analytics Requirements Document)
- Feasibility Factors
- Constraints

Analyzing Customer Requirements

- Refined VRD

System Design

- System Architecture Blueprint

Proposal Documentation

VDD (Video Analytics Design Document)

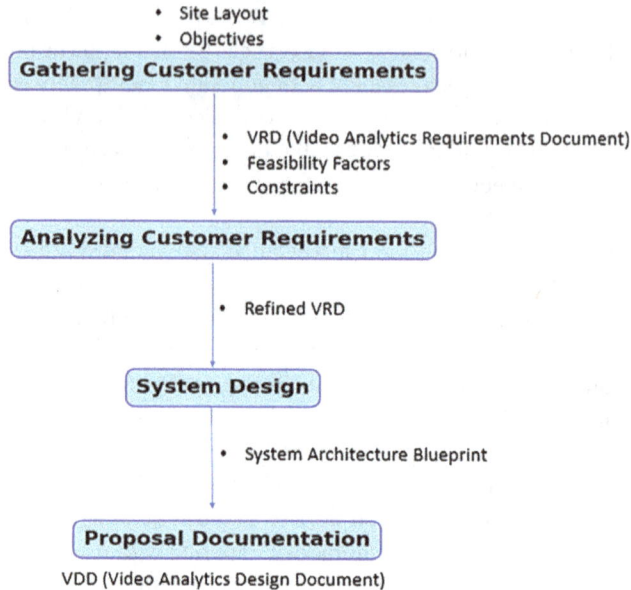

FIGURE 9.2 Video Analytics Design Line framework.

Step 1: Gathering Customer Requirements

Effective design starts with a deep understanding of the customer's surveillance objectives and constraints. In this first step, the design team engages with stakeholders to gather all relevant requirements. This involves asking detailed questions about the *surveillance area* and *context*, the *goals of the system*, and any *specific features* needed.

For example, determine the type of environment: Is it an indoor office building, a retail store, an outdoor parking lot, or a city intersection? The physical environment – lighting conditions, weather exposure, size of area – will influence camera selection and analytics performance (for instance, outdoor low-light areas might require cameras with infrared illumination or thermal imaging; see Chapter 3 for camera types and Chapter 4 for image sensor and optics principles related to lighting).

Obtain site layouts (floor plans or maps of the area) to understand where cameras could be placed and the coverage needed (as discussed in Chapter 3's section on camera placement and field of view).

Next, clarify the *primary goals* for video analytics. Different stakeholders may have varying specific needs, but common surveillance and analytics goals include: security and safety (e.g., detecting intruders and monitoring for fights or accidents), operational efficiency (e.g., optimizing traffic flow and queue management in a store), forensic investigation (being able to search video after an incident for evidence), and even business intelligence (e.g., analyzing customer behavior in a retail setting). It is important to identify which goals are most important.

To ensure the system meets not only analytical but also operational needs, requirements should be framed within the Decision and Action Workflow (DAW) model introduced in Chapter 8. DAW operationalizes AI insights by mapping them into a chain of real-time system behavior. For every requested analytic feature, designers should ask the following questions:

- What is the triggering event (e.g., intrusion and loitering)?
- What decision logic should apply (e.g., duration and time-of-day thresholds)?
- What response channels are needed (e.g., VMS alert, WhatsApp, and alarm system)?
- What escalation rules apply if the first response fails?
- How should the event be logged and audited?

Embedding DAW thinking into the early requirement phase not only clarifies what the system must detect, but how it must behave in response, ensuring traceability, accountability, and operational alignment from day one.

Many projects combine multiple use cases; for example, a transportation hub might equally value security (preventing incidents) and operational analytics (people counting, congestion detection). For each goal, there may be associated *analytics features*: for instance, if security is a goal, the customer might require face recognition to flag barred individuals, or license plate recognition for vehicle monitoring. If operational efficiency is a goal, perhaps people counting or queue length detection is needed. All requested analytics features should be noted and prioritized as "must-have" or "nice-to-have." (Chapter 6, which covers video content analytics concepts, can provide context on capabilities like intrusion detection, counting, and recognition algorithms that the customer might request.)

While gathering requirements, also identify all *user roles and stakeholders* who will interact with the system. A modern video analytics system might have security officers, IT administrators, and even non-security personnel (like a store's marketing team or a building manager) as end-users of certain analytics outputs. Each of these user roles might have different requirements for access and usage. For example, security staff may need real-time alerts and live video, IT staff will care about maintainability and integration with IT systems, and business analysts might need periodic reports or the ability to run specific searches on archived data. Understanding who will use the system and how ensures the design will accommodate their needs (user management and roles are topics that tie back to system security in Chapter 2 and possibly VMS features in Chapter 6).

Lastly, record any *constraints or preferences* expressed by the customer at this early stage. This can include budget constraints ("we have roughly $X to spend"), brand preferences ("we prefer cameras from Manufacturer Y"), or existing infrastructure ("we already have 50 cameras installed that need to be integrated"). It also includes operational details like hours of operation (e.g., the cameras should record 24/7 or only after hours or analytics should run only at night), retention time for video, and any privacy guidelines (like certain areas that should not be recorded or faces need to be anonymized for non-security viewing, aligning with privacy regulations mentioned in Chapter 2). All of this information forms the foundation that will guide the subsequent steps. A thorough requirement gathering phase is critical: It ensures the designers are solving the right problem and sets the expectations for what the system must accomplish.

To ensure these diverse needs are addressed systematically, it is essential to capture them in a structured format that guides the system's design and implementation. Therefore, the requirements outlined for each user role—ranging from real-time responsiveness to system maintainability and data accessibility—will be formally documented in a *Video Analytics Requirements Document (VRD)*. This VRD will serve as a foundational reference for both technical development and stakeholder alignment throughout the lifecycle of the video analytics system.

Step 2: Analyzing Customer Requirements

Once the raw requirements are collected, the next step is to analyze and validate the VRD. This involves reviewing the needs to ensure they are feasible and compliant with any external constraints such as laws or standards. It is often useful to have requirements review meeting with the stakeholders to "play back" what was captured: confirming the understanding of each requirement and clarifying any ambiguities. The output of this step is a refined set of requirements that are agreed-upon, feasible, and prioritized.

During analysis, the design team will consider various *feasibility factors and constraints*:

- **Technical Feasibility:** Evaluate whether the desired analytics can be achieved with current technology, given the context. For example, if the customer wants to detect very subtle behaviors (like loitering in a low-light corner of a parking lot), the team must assess if available computer vision algorithms (perhaps from Chapter 5 on deep learning and CV) can perform reliably under those conditions. This might involve quick tests or consulting with analytics experts. If a requirement is pushing the boundaries of what is possible (e.g., real-time identification of very small objects at long distance), the team might flag it as a risk or suggest a modified approach. Chapter 5's discussion on deep learning capabilities and limitations can help in gauging what is realistic. In some cases, requirements might need to be adjusted once these limitations are understood.

- **Budget and Scale Constraints:** It is critical to align the design aspirations with the budget. At this stage, one should categorize the project's scale (small, medium, or large) because scale often determines the cost. A small-scale deployment (5–10 cameras in a single site) will have a vastly different budget and design than a citywide system with hundreds of cameras. By now, the team should have a general idea if the project is, for example, under $100,000, or in the multi-million-dollar range, based on the number of sites and cameras discussed. If the customer's desired outcomes seem to outstrip the budget, this is identified early so either the budget is increased or the requirements are revised down. Additionally, scale and budget will influence choices like what network infrastructure is possible or how many servers are needed (as seen in Chapter 2, network devices and servers have costs that must fit the budget). In summary, ensure the scope is realistic for the budget; this sometimes means prioritizing must-haves and possibly deferring or cutting nice-to-haves if needed.

- **Regulatory and Compliance Check:** Cross-check the requirements against legal and regulatory requirements. Surveillance projects often have to abide by privacy laws, industry regulations, or organizational policies. For instance, data protection laws may affect how facial recognition can be used or mandate that video footage of public spaces be stored only for a certain duration. If a requirement conflicts with any such regulation, the design team must flag it and find a solution. For example, if continuous recording is required but privacy law says footage must be deleted after 30 days, the system design must include an automatic deletion mechanism to comply. If audio recording is desired, one must confirm it is legal in the jurisdiction. Chapter 2 discusses some of these concerns (like data retention policies and privacy considerations in networked video systems). Additionally, certain industries have specific guidelines (e.g., casinos have regulations on camera coverage and retention, and public institutions might need to follow open procurement rules). All these factors need to be considered to ensure the design will not have compliance issues. Part of this analysis might result in adding requirements as well (for compliance) – for example, "The system shall anonymize video feeds for public viewing monitors" could be added to satisfy a privacy mandate.

- **Infrastructure and Integration Constraints:** Assess what existing infrastructure the customer has and how the new system will integrate. Perhaps the site already has some legacy CCTV cameras or an access control system or a network infrastructure in place. The design might need to reuse or interface with those. For example, if analog cameras exist, the design could include video encoders rather than replacing all cameras outright. Or if the customer uses a specific cloud provider, the design might need to align with that for any cloud components. Also, check power and network availability where cameras need to be installed – if certain remote areas lack a network, wireless links or new cabling might be needed (linking back to Chapter 2's discussion on network planning). Understanding these baseline conditions ensures the system design will fit into the customer's environment.

By the end of Step 2, the design team will have a validated and refined requirements document (refined VRD). This document clearly states what the system must do (functional requirements) and outlines key constraints (non-functional requirements like performance benchmarks, compliance needs, and budget limits). Often, splitting requirements into functional vs. non-functional categories is helpful: for example, functional might include "detect motion in restricted area and trigger alarm," while non-functional includes "store video for 30 days" or "system uptime 99.9%." Both types are crucial. With requirements refined and feasible, the team is now ready to move into the creative phase of architecting the solution in Step 3.

Budget and networking considerations here relate to Chapter 2, which covers network planning and cost implications. Compliance issues are related to Chapter 2 as well, where data protection in CCTV was introduced. Technical feasibility of analytics relates to the capabilities from Chapter 5 on AI and CV algorithms.

Step 3: System Design

In this step, the design team translates the requirements in refined VRD into a real system architecture and specifications. *System design* is where all the pieces—cameras, network, processing hardware/software, and storage—are chosen and structured to meet the requirements. This step typically produces diagrams, equipment lists, and a narrative explaining how the system will work.

A good approach is to start by outlining the high-level architecture. Decide on the overall topology: will this be a centralized system, a distributed edge-based system, or a hybrid? For example, in a small single-site deployment (e.g., a small office with a handful of cameras), one might choose a simple centralized architecture where all cameras connect to a single network video recorder (NVR) or server that handles recording and analytics. For a medium-sized deployment (dozens of cameras, perhaps across multiple floors or a campus), the design might involve multiple switches (possibly dedicating a separate VLAN for video traffic as recommended in Chapter 2) and perhaps multiple recording servers or a scalable VMS to handle the load. Large-scale systems (hundreds of cameras or multi-site deployments) often require a hierarchical design: edge recording/processing at each site and a central management system to coordinate or aggregate data from sites. Chapter 7's principles of distributed computing and edge computing can guide how to structure such a system so that it remains manageable and performant as it grows. At this stage, designers will draw network diagrams showing how cameras connect through switches to servers, where the processing will happen, and how all components communicate.

Camera selection and placement are a crucial part of system design. Using the site survey information, the team decides exactly how many cameras are needed and of what types. Each camera location is determined based on coverage requirements (ensure there are no blind spots in critical areas) and the purpose of that camera (overview monitoring vs. capturing detail like faces or license plates). Referencing Chapter 3 is valuable here: for each position, choose a camera type that fits, e.g., a PTZ camera to cover a large parking lot with the ability to zoom in, or a fixed wide-angle dome camera for an office lobby. Determine the resolution needed. If an area needs facial recognition, a higher resolution or a camera positioned closer is needed to get enough pixels on the face (Chapter 3 discusses how resolution and distance affect identification).

Consider special features: low-light capability (if monitoring at night, maybe use a camera with a good low lux rating or infrared illumination, see Chapter 4 regarding imaging in low-light), Wide Dynamic Range (if the camera is facing a doorway with bright backlight, WDR is needed to see both inside and outside clearly), weatherproof housing for outdoor cameras, and possibly anti-vandal features for cameras within reach. Each planned camera should have a rationale tied to requirements (e.g., "Camera 5: 4K bullet camera covering main entrance, needed for face capture for recognition").

It is often helpful to overlay camera coverage on a floorplan to confirm placement logic. Additionally, this is a point to consider the use of specialized cameras if required—like a panoramic fisheye camera for 360-degree coverage in a lobby (with the trade-off of some distortion, as noted in Chapter 3), or thermal cameras for perimeter monitoring at night if standard cameras might not be effective.

Parallel to camera planning, the design team defines the network architecture in detail. This involves selecting network equipment and configurations to support the video traffic. Key questions include the following:

- How will the cameras be powered (likely via PoE switches to simplify installation)?
- How will the network traffic be segregated? (It is a best practice to isolate the surveillance network—perhaps using a dedicated physical network or at least a VLAN —so normal corporate data traffic does not interfere and for security isolation; see Chapter 2 on VLAN usage.)
- What is the bandwidth requirement, and does the proposed network (switches, routers) support it with headroom? For instance, dozens of high-resolution cameras can generate hundreds of Mbps of traffic; the backbone links and uplinks must be sized accordingly (10 Gbps fiber links might be needed in large buildings to aggregate all floor switches).

If the design includes wireless links (for cameras in hard-to-wire spots) or uses the corporate LAN/WAN, ensure quality-of-service and reliability measures are in place. Also, decide if remote monitoring or cloud connectivity is needed. If yes, ensure there is a secure gateway or VPN in the network design to allow video streams or events to securely leave the local network (Chapter 2's network security principles apply here).

In a multi-site design, consider the topology connecting sites, perhaps a hub-and-spoke with each site forwarding events to a central location or a completely decentralized design if each site is independent. By the end of this, the network diagram should show all switches, routers, and links, with an indication of which network segments are carrying video.

The next major decision area is processing and analytics deployment. Based on requirements for real-time versus batch analytics, and considering latency and bandwidth, decide where analytics will run. There are a few patterns to choose from (and these were introduced conceptually in Chapter 7 on computing infrastructure and Chapter 5 on analytics):

- **On-camera analytics:** Some modern cameras can run simple analytics on board (like motion detection, line crossing, and even basic AI person detection). This can be utilized for very distributed processing and low latency, but usually these on-camera algorithms are limited in complexity.

- **On-premise edge processing:** Using one or more local servers (or specialized AI edge devices) that receive the camera streams and run analytics (object detection, face recognition, etc.) in real time. This is common when real-time alerts are needed because it avoids the latency of cloud. If choosing this, specify the server hardware, e.g., a server with a strong CPU and possibly a GPU if deep learning analytics are needed (Chapter 5 and 7 provide guidance on hardware for AI – for example, using an NVIDIA GPU for deep neural network analytics or an AI accelerator device). The design should indicate how many analytics processes or camera streams each server can handle, to ensure the system can scale (for instance, "each server can handle up to 20 camera streams of 1080p analytics, so for 50 cameras we need 3 servers").

- **Cloud processing:** In some designs, especially if wide geographic coverage or if utilizing a cloud's scalability, video (or metadata) is sent to a cloud service for analysis. This introduces more latency and requires good internet connectivity but allows virtually unlimited compute. If the requirement is to consolidate data from many distributed sites or to apply heavy analytics (like large-scale cross-camera tracking or big data analytics on video archives), the cloud could be part of the design. If cloud is used, detail what data is sent (continuous video vs. only events metadata) and what cloud services are employed (e.g., using a cloud video analytics platform or custom cloud VMs running analytics software). A hybrid is very common: e.g., run immediate detection on-premises (edge) and use the cloud to do periodic, deeper analysis or long-term trend analysis. The design might say, for example, "Edge analytics devices at each site do people detection; counts are sent to the cloud, where a dashboard aggregates occupancy data over time."

At this stage, it is also important to design the storage strategy. Based on the requirements for video retention and retrieval, specify what kind of storage system will be used. If the requirement is, for example, 30 days retention of all footage at full resolution, calculate the total storage needed (Chapter 1 provides formulas for storage based on bitrate, and Chapter 2 discusses storage technologies). Decide between using large-capacity NVRs (appliances with built-in storage), general-purpose servers with attached storage (RAID arrays or NAS units), or cloud storage. Perhaps recent footage will be kept on fast local disks for quick access, while older footage is archived to cheaper cloud storage to save cost (this tiered storage approach can meet retention requirements cost-effectively). Also consider redundancy: Will there be RAID-6 arrays to tolerate disk failures? Will the video be replicated to a second server or location for backup? These choices are driven by how critical the footage is and the budget available. The design documents might include a table like "Storage Calculation: X cameras * Y bitrate * Z hours * N days = required TB; therefore, proposing 2x 100TB NAS devices to handle it with RAID redundancy."

Another design aspect is the selection of software platforms, namely the VMS and analytics software. Here, the team decides whether to use a commercial off-the-shelf VMS or an open-source solution (or even a custom solution). Each has pros and cons: A commercial VMS (e.g., Genetec Security Center, Milestone XProtect) usually offers robust features, support, and integration with many camera brands, which can greatly speed up deployment and ensure reliability, but it comes at a licensing cost and might lock the solution into a particular ecosystem.

An open-source or in-house solution (like using ZoneMinder, OpenCV-based custom analytics pipeline, or a combination of open video streaming tools) could reduce licensing costs and allow more customization, however, this requires more development effort and in-house expertise to maintain. In deciding this, refer back to the requirements and possibly Chapter 6 (which covers video analytics frameworks) as well as Chapter 7 (for how the computing platform could be managed). For instance, if the project demands a lot of custom AI analytics, a flexible open approach might be better; but if the project is standard (just needs reliable recording and basic analytics), a proven commercial VMS might be the safest choice.

Sometimes the decision also depends on the client's preference or existing systems (if they already use a certain VMS in another facility, they may want to stick with it). Document the choice and justification, e.g., "Milestone XProtect chosen for VMS due to its proven scalability to 100+ cameras and native analytics integration" or alternatively "Open-source VMS (ZoneMinder) chosen to avoid recurring license fees, given the client's IT team can support the software."

Throughout system design, it is important to incorporate best practices for performance and security. Some examples that should be reflected in the design are as follows: If we have high camera counts or high-resolution streams, we might plan to slightly throttle or downsample certain feeds for analytics (for example, the design might note that analytics will use sub-streams at lower resolution to save processing load, while full-resolution is still recorded, which is a common practice). Or we may specify that all deep learning models will be optimized (using libraries like NVIDIA TensorRT on GPUs or Intel OpenVINO on CPUs) to achieve real-time inference speeds. We also must plan for system management aspects, e.g., will there be a health monitoring system to alert if a camera goes offline or a disk is failing? Many enterprise VMS solutions include these features; if not, the design could include a separate monitoring tool. Crucially, we must integrate cybersecurity measures into the design: for instance, the design might state that the cameras will be on an isolated network with a firewall, all devices will use strong passwords and certificates, and remote access will be via VPN only (these points align with the best practices in Chapter 2 for securing networked devices).

By the end of Step 3, we will have a clear blueprint of the system's architecture. This typically includes one or more diagrams (a network diagram showing cameras, network gear, servers, and cloud connections) and a narrative or specification sheet detailing each component. It should be clear *which camera goes where, how each subsystem (camera, network, processing, and storage) is implemented, and how data flows.* Essentially, it answers the following questions: What hardware and software will be used? How will they interconnect to meet the requirements? This blueprint is what the stakeholders will review and, once approved, what the implementation team will follow. But before implementation, we formalize everything into a proposal in Step 4.

Camera selection here builds on Chapter 3's guidelines for matching cameras to scenarios. Network and topology choices draw from Chapter 2. Deciding on edge vs. cloud computing is informed by Chapter 7. Also recall Chapter 5's insight into what AI algorithms need in terms of compute because that influences hardware selection. Cybersecurity measures follow recommendations in Chapter 2. By referencing these, the design is grounded in the solid principles covered earlier in the book.

Step 4: Proposal Documentation

The final step of the Design Line framework is compiling all design decisions and plans into a comprehensive design proposal document which is called a VDD (Video Analytics Design Document). This document is both an internal blueprint and an external-facing description that the customer or stakeholders will review and approve. It should be written in clear language, including diagrams and tables, so that decision-makers (who may not be technical experts) can understand what is being proposed and why it will meet their needs.

A typical VDD includes the following elements:

- **Executive Summary:** This is a brief overview of the customer's requirements and the proposed solution. It should highlight key features (e.g., number of cameras, use of AI analytics, edge/cloud approach) and the main benefits (such as improved security and compliance with requirements). This is for readers who just want an overview.
- **Architecture Diagram(s):** This is a visual representation of the system architecture. At a minimum, a high-level diagram shows all major components: cameras, network infrastructure, servers, storage, cloud services, and how they connect. For example, one diagram might depict a building layout with camera locations marked, and another might show the network topology (switches connecting to a core switch, servers in the server room, and an internet link to cloud). These diagrams reinforce understanding, for example, one can quickly see "there are 50 cameras feeding into 6 switches, which connect to 2 servers and 1 cloud link." Diagrams should use icons or labels indicating camera types (referencing Chapter 3's camera categories) and network components (from Chapter 2's discussions on network layouts). If applicable, include a data flow diagram that highlights how video and data moves through the system (perhaps using arrows to show video streams going to storage and metadata going to the cloud).
- **Detailed Component Specifications:** This section itemizes the chosen hardware and software. It can be in text or a table format. It should list camera models (with important specifications like resolution, lens type, and indoor/outdoor), recording servers (with CPU, RAM, GPU specs if used, and operating system or VMS software specified), storage devices (NVR model or server storage specification, including capacity and redundancy), network equipment (such as switch models, router or firewall, indicating support for PoE, and bandwidth), and any other infrastructure (racks, UPS, and cables). For software, list the VMS platform (name and edition), analytics software or frameworks (e.g., "ABC Analytics Module for intrusion detection" or "Custom analytics using TensorFlow/TensorRT"), and database or cloud services, if any (e.g., "AWS S3 for long-term storage"). Each item might

include a reference or reasoning drawn from earlier chapters; for instance, "4MP dome cameras with WDR (as recommended in Chapter 3 for areas with challenging lighting) will cover the lobby, ensuring facial details can be captured even with backlight." Similarly, "an NVIDIA Jetson edge device is included at the gate for ALPR processing, leveraging edge computing concepts from Chapter 7 to minimize latency." Such references reassure that choices are grounded in best practices.

- **System Operation Description:** Explain in prose how the system will work once implemented. Explain a typical scenario. For example: "Cameras will continuously stream video to the VMS; the edge analytics device will analyze the gate camera feed for license plates and send plate numbers to the server; the server will run face recognition on lobby camera streams; all video will be recorded to the NVR with 30-day retention; and when an unauthorized person is detected, an alert will pop up in the security control room software and be sent to on-call staff's mobile app." This narrative helps stakeholders mentally simulate the system's behavior and confirm it meets their expectations. It also highlights the integration between components (for instance, integration between the face recognition system and the building access control database, if that is part of the design).

- **Compliance and Security Measures:** Summarize how the design addresses any regulatory or security requirements. For example, "To comply with privacy regulations, the system will blur faces on recordings from public areas when accessed by general users, with full unblurred video only accessible to approved security managers." Another example is "All network communication from cameras will be encrypted and the surveillance network is isolated as a VLAN with strict firewall rules (as per cybersecurity best practices from Chapter 2)." Listing these measures in the proposal is important for stakeholder confidence; it shows that the design is not just functional but also responsible and secure.

- **Implementation Plan:** Briefly outline how the system will be deployed. Will it be rolled out in phases (perhaps a pilot phase with a few cameras, then scaling up)? What is the timeline? Are there any downtime considerations for existing systems? This might include notes like "Initial deployment of 10 cameras at one entrance for a 2-week pilot, then gradual installation of remaining cameras per floor over 3 months." If using cloud or containerized deployment, mention how the software will be delivered (e.g., "analytics modules will run in Docker containers for easy deployment and updates").

- **Cost Breakdown:** A detailed breakdown of the expected costs, often in a tabular form. Categories typically include the following: cameras, servers/hardware, storage, networking equipment, software licenses, and installation/services. Each category should have quantity, unit price, and total (for example, list 40 cameras at $X each, 1 server at $Y, and software licenses (maybe broken down by type, e.g., 50-camera VMS license, 2 analytics licenses)). Do not forget installation labor or maintenance contracts, if applicable. This section is related to the budget constraint: It demonstrates that the design can be built within the budget (or if it is over, it provides justification for additional money). The proposal should highlight any trade-offs made to control cost, such as "using existing network cables saved $Z" or "opting for a hybrid cloud approach reduced the need for an additional server, saving cost while meeting performance needs" (see Chapter 7 for the benefits of hybrid approaches).

- **Justification of Key Decisions:** It is a good practice for the proposal to include rationale for major design choices, especially if the audience might question them. For instance, if the design recommends a hybrid edge/cloud solution, explain why: "A hybrid architecture is proposed to balance latency and scalability. Critical alerts are handled on-site (edge) for quick response, while less urgent analytics are done in the cloud, allowing future scalability" (this aligns with the edge vs. cloud design discussion in Chapter 7). Or, if an expensive high-end camera is chosen for a particular spot, justify it: "We chose a 4K PTZ camera for the parking lot to allow zooming in on license plates from long range, which a standard camera could not achieve (as needed for the LPR requirement; refer to Chapter 3 on camera zoom optics)." Such justifications show that each choice was made deliberately to satisfy a requirement or constraint, which increases the stakeholders' confidence in the design.

Once the proposal document includes all the above, it should be reviewed internally and then presented to the customer/stakeholders for approval. The proposal serves as a contract of sorts: It says, "this is what we will build and how." When approved, it will guide the implementation teams (such as installation technicians and IT integrators) in deploying the system as designed. It also provides a baseline against which any future changes can be measured (for example, if partway through deployment the customer wants a change, the proposal helps assess the impact). The thoroughness of the Design Line process ensures that by the time you reach this proposal, there is a very clear alignment between customer needs and the system being proposed, with traceability from requirements all the way to specific components in the design.

Technical Design Best Practices

Having established the framework and an example process for designing video analytics systems, we now compile a set of technical best practices and recommendations that engineers and architects should consider in any end-to-end design. These best practices derive from industry knowledge and the detailed discussions in previous chapters, and they serve as guidelines to optimize system performance, reliability, and maintainability. We will cover best practices across various domains: deployment architecture (edge vs. cloud), camera hardware selection, video management and networking, analytics performance optimization, installation considerations, and cybersecurity. Adhering to these will help ensure that the system not only meets initial requirements but also operates efficiently under real-world conditions.

Edge vs. Cloud vs. Hybrid Analytics Deployment

One fundamental design choice is where to perform the video analytics processing: at the edge (on cameras or on-site devices), in the cloud, or a combination of both. Each approach has advantages and trade-offs, and often the best solution is a hybrid that mixes them to get the best of both worlds.

- **Edge Analytics:** In edge-centric designs, video data is processed close to where it is captured, either directly on smart cameras or on a local gateway/edge server at the site. The benefit is minimal latency; decisions or alerts can be generated almost instantly since there is no need to send large video streams over a network. Edge processing also dramatically reduces bandwidth usage, because instead of sending all raw video to a central location, the device can send just the metadata or event results. For example, an edge device might detect a person or a license plate and send just the ID or cropped image, rather than streaming hours of video. This approach is ideal for real-time security use cases (e.g., an intruder alarm that needs to go off the moment someone crosses a line) or in environments with limited connectivity (remote locations, or where internet is slow/unreliable). However, the downside is that edge devices (including on-camera processors) have limited compute resources. A small AI chip on a camera or a mini-PC can run a few analytics algorithms but may struggle with very complex tasks (like running multiple deep neural networks simultaneously on many video feeds). There's also a cost factor: equipping every camera or site with powerful computing can be expensive initially. Edge analytics should be used for tasks that truly require immediacy or data reduction at source. Many modern systems use edge analytics as the first filter, e.g., do motion or object detection at the edge to decide which footage is important, then send that to the cloud for further analysis.

- **Cloud Analytics:** Cloud-centric designs send video data (or in some cases, processed streams) to data center servers (public cloud services or a central private cloud) where heavy-duty processing occurs. The cloud offers virtually unlimited scalability; if more processing is needed, one can add more cloud compute instances. It is very useful for compute-intensive analytics like training AI models, running large-scale facial recognition against big databases, or aggregating data from many locations. Cloud analytics also simplifies multi-site deployments; rather than having separate servers at each site, all data can come to one central platform. However, cloud approaches face challenges with latency and bandwidth. Streaming raw video from dozens or hundreds of cameras to the cloud can consume enormous bandwidth (often not feasible without high-speed links) and introduces delay (depending on internet latency). Even with good bandwidth, real-time responsiveness might suffer; an event has to be uploaded and processed before an alert comes back, which could be several seconds at best. Cloud is well-suited for scenarios where real-time reaction is not as critical, or as a second stage of analysis. It also makes sense when consolidating data: for example, citywide analytics where patterns are gleaned from many cameras might only be possible in a central cloud. Cost-wise, cloud shifts expense from upfront capital to ongoing operational costs (pay-as-you-go cloud services, which can accumulate over time). It provides great flexibility and ease of updates (you can deploy new analytics algorithms centrally without touching on-site devices), but one must architect carefully to handle the data transfer securely and efficiently. (Chapter 2's network considerations and Chapter 7's cloud computing discussions are relevant here.)

- **Hybrid Analytics:** In practice, many systems adopt a hybrid approach, combining edge and cloud to exploit the advantages of both. A common pattern is a two-tier analytics pipeline: initial processing at the edge to handle immediate needs and reduce data volume, followed by cloud processing for deeper or aggregated insights. For example, an edge device at a retail store detects people and counts them (real-time alert if a crowd forms), but then sends hourly counts to a cloud service that analyzes long-term shopping trends across all store locations. In security, an edge might detect motion and only upload video clips when something moves, so the cloud does not store endless hours of empty footage. Hybrid designs can also be split by function: simple rules and triggers on the edge, advanced AI in the cloud. It is important to design a communication workflow between the edge and the cloud, often using IoT messaging protocols or event queues so that the cloud only receives relevant events or compact summaries from the edge. This keeps bandwidth usage optimal while still utilizing the cloud's power when needed. Edge-cloud coordination is a critical design aspect if hybrid is chosen; one must ensure that data sent to cloud is secure (encrypted, which ties into cybersecurity best practices) and that if connectivity is lost, the edge can temporarily operate standalone. Many solutions (as noted in Chapter 7) now provide frameworks for managing such hybrid deployments, and Chapter 5's mention of federated analytics also aligns with this idea. In summary, hybrid is often the recommended approach for large, sophisticated deployments: it ensures low latency for critical tasks and scalability for heavy analytics. It also provides a form of redundancy: if cloud services fail, the edge can still provide basic functionality, and vice versa.

When choosing between these options, consider the use-case priorities. If instant response is paramount, edge might be the best option. If utilizing big data and cross-site insight are the goals, the cloud might be the best option. In many cases, use the edge for first-layer processing and cloud for second-layer processing. Designing an optimal mix requires carefully thinking through which tasks run where, something we did conceptually in Step 3 of the Design Line framework.

This topic relates back to Chapter 7, which discusses edge computing devices and cloud computing, and Chapter 2, in terms of what the network can support. Chapter 5 also implies that some AI models might be too heavy for edge without optimization. In practice, many vendors like NVIDIA have solutions (e.g., DeepStream) for exactly this edge-to-cloud pipeline.

Camera Hardware and Image Capture Best Practices

The quality of analytics outcomes is directly related to the quality of the video input. Thus, selecting the right cameras and configuring them properly is one of the most important design decisions. Here are the best practices regarding camera hardware, lenses, and image capture settings:

- **Match Camera to the Use Case:** Always start by considering what each camera's purpose is. If the goal is face recognition at an entrance, the camera should be positioned at roughly head height and capture frontal faces with sufficient resolution (generally, standards suggest at least 40–50 pixels between the eyes of a person for reliable face recognition). A high-resolution camera (1080p or above) with a narrow focus on the entry point might be appropriate, possibly a camera with a telephoto lens to get a close-up view. If the goal is general surveillance of a wide area (such as a parking lot or lobby), a wide-angle camera or a fisheye 360° camera might be better to cover more area. For license plate recognition (LPR), use specialized LPR cameras or regular cameras with settings optimized for capturing plates (often high shutter speed to avoid motion blur, IR illumination to see plates at night, and positioned at a proper angle and distance to the plate). If people counting in a hallway is needed, an overhead camera looking down can be effective. The most important idea is that *one size does not fit all*: Choose the camera type (fixed vs PTZ vs panoramic), resolution, lens, and features based on what each camera is meant to observe. we must also compare camera types like fisheye, PTZ, fixed in terms of strengths and limitations; for instance, PTZ cameras provide flexible views but require either manual control or intelligent auto-tracking to catch events, whereas fixed cameras continuously watch one spot (ideal for access control points).

- **Ensure Sufficient Resolution and Frame Rate:** Resolution determines the level of detail. A common guideline is the "pixels per foot" (or per meter) requirement for an application. For facial identification, one might need >100 pixels per foot of the target area; for license plates, similarly high detail at the license plate region (which might equate to a 4K camera if covering multiple lanes, or a 1080p camera zoomed on a single lane). If the camera's field of view is too wide, targets of interest may appear too small in the image for analytics to work accurately. It is often better to have more cameras covering an area with proper zoom than one camera trying to cover everything with insufficient detail. Frame rate (frames per second) is also a factor: For most analytics, 10-15 fps can be sufficient to capture motion, but fast actions (like vehicles speeding or people running) benefit from higher frame rates (25-30 fps or more) to avoid motion blur and not miss critical moments. However, higher frame rates and resolutions greatly increase data volume, so it is a balance. A best practice is to use the lowest frame rate and resolution that still meets the analytics requirement; this minimizes bandwidth and storage load.

  For example, you might record at 15 fps, but the analytics algorithm could sample at 5 fps internally if that is enough to detect what it needs (some VMS allow analytics on a lower sub-stream). Always test a camera's view by collecting sample footage and seeing if a human or the intended algorithm can identify the target (face, plate, or object) at the planned distance.

- **Optimize for Lighting Conditions:** Lighting can make or break video analytics. Many cameras boast day/night capability with infrared (IR) mode for darkness. Ensure cameras designated for low-light areas have good low-lux performance (some can see down to 0.01 lux in black and white mode) or come with IR illuminators (either built-in or external IR spotlights). In outdoor night scenes or indoor dark corners, IR is essential for standard cameras, but remember that IR only covers a certain range and field. Ensure the IR illuminator range matches the area of interest. If an area has highly variable lighting (like an entrance with bright daylight outside and a dark interior inside), use cameras with a Wide Dynamic Range (WDR) feature, which can handle high contrast and not blow out bright areas or lose detail in shadows. Also consider backlighting. If a camera faces a window or the sun at certain times, reposition it or use WDR/backlight compensation to avoid a silhouette effect where subjects appear dark. In some cases, additional lighting (such as motion-activated flood lights) might be added to improve video quality at night. As a last resort in extremely dark environments or where standard cameras fail (such as smoke, fog, or complete darkness), consider thermal cameras which detect heat signatures and are immune to lighting issues. Thermal cameras can detect people in total darkness or through certain obscurants, though they do not provide visible details like faces, so they might be used in tandem with regular cameras. Perform a lighting survey for day and night and choose cameras (and possibly auxiliary lighting) to ensure the scene is always adequately illuminated for the analytics to work reliably.

- **Lens Selection and Field of View (FOV):** The lens determines how wide or narrow a scene the camera sees and at what focus. A best practice is to use varifocal lenses or zoom lenses during installation so you can fine-tune the view. During design, one can use tools (like JVSG design software, as mentioned in some best practice guides) to simulate camera coverage and ensure the FOV meets requirements. A wide lens covers more area but with less detail per area; a narrow lens (telephoto) covers less area but with greater detail. Identify critical zones that need detail (e.g., entrances, cashier desks, and the license plate capture point) and use narrower FOV for those, while use wider FOV for general overview. Depth of field is another consideration; if you need both near and far objects in focus, ensure the lens (and camera sensor) combination can support that or pick a midpoint focus that is acceptable.

During installation, ensure cameras are focused and configured for the typical lighting (some cameras allow setting a focus position for day and night separately if needed). Another tip: if using any special lenses like the fisheye, the analytics software must support *dewarping* (correcting the distortion) or be able to analyze warped images properly.

Some advanced analytics can now work on fisheye views directly, but many require the normal view. If the design includes PTZ cameras with guard tours (automatically moving to cover different preset views), be aware that while the camera is moving or looking elsewhere, it may miss events – so critical areas should ideally be covered by fixed cameras even if a PTZ is used for flexibility (the PTZ can then be used to zoom in for detail upon an alert, either manually or via an automated response from the analytics system).

- **Compression and Bandwidth Settings:** Each camera will compress video (using codecs like H.264 and H.265) before sending it over the network. Use modern compression standards; for example, H.265 can save about 30-50% bandwidth compared to H.264 at the same quality. Many camera manufacturers have optimized codec implementations (and some have smart codecs that dynamically adjust encoding based on motion or regions of interest). Enable features like dynamic or adaptive bit rate (where the camera lowers the quality when there is no motion or when the network is congested) to conserve bandwidth. However, balance this with analytics needs; too low quality or too aggressive compression during motion can degrade analytics accuracy. A best practice is to tune the compression. Use constant quality mode, if possible, rather than constant bit rate mode, so that the video quality does not drop below a threshold.

  Also consider using secondary streams: Many IP cameras support dual or triple streaming at different resolutions. For example, a camera can stream 1080p at high quality for recording, and simultaneously a 360p low-bandwidth stream for live viewing on a mobile device or for certain analytics. Designing the system to take advantage of multiple streams can offload processing (the VMS can record the high-res stream but run motion detection on the low-res stream). This is mentioned in Chapter 6 and Chapter 7 discussions of VMS and computing efficiency. Use the highest compression that does not noticeably harm the important details. This often requires testing or manufacturer guidance. Do not forget to account for audio (if any). If cameras have microphones and audio analytics or recording is needed, the audio stream will add bandwidth (though minor compared to video). If audio is not needed, disable it to save resources (this is also sometimes required by privacy laws in certain places, as noted in earlier chapters).

- **Installation and Placement Considerations:** Beyond choosing camera specs, the physical installation matters. Mount cameras at an appropriate height: for facial recognition or identifying people, eye-level (5-6 feet off the ground) at entrances yields the best angle. For general surveillance, ceiling mounts (8-10 feet for indoor, or on poles/buildings for outdoor) give a wide view while still capturing enough detail on faces from above in many cases.

Avoid placing cameras where they can be easily tampered with or where obstructions can block their view. Use vandal-resistant housings in high-risk areas (like reachable by hand). Ensure the field of view is not partially obscured by infrastructure (e.g., a dome camera's view might be half blocked by a wall if not positioned correctly).

Overlapping coverage is a best practice. Important areas should ideally be covered by more than one camera from different angles so that if one view is obstructed or a camera fails, another camera can still see the area. This also helps analytics like tracking an individual from one camera to the next (Chapter 5 mentions multi-camera re-identification; overlapping views facilitate that). Plan cable routes and power. All cameras need reliable power (PoE usually) and a network. If a camera is far away (beyond 100 meters), plan to use midspan repeaters or fiber.

Environmental factors are important considerations. For outdoor cameras, use proper enclosures and mounts rated for wind, rain, and temperature. For indoor cameras, consider aesthetics, as well. For example, some clients prefer dome cameras in public-facing areas because they are less obtrusive, whereas box cameras might be preferred in back-room hallways.

In summary, treat camera deployment as its own sub-system design. Each camera should be optimally chosen and placed to ensure the video it provides is suitable for the analytics tasks at hand. A well-deployed camera network is the foundation; even the most advanced analytics can make up for poor image quality or coverage gaps. It is often worth spending more on a better camera or additional cameras to cover an area than to try to compensate later via software. This principle is to is get the basics right (camera and lighting) which will be critical to CCTV effectiveness.

These best practices are mentioned in Chapter 3 (camera types and specifications) and Chapter 4 (imaging and optics). The importance of lighting and WDR relates to Chapter 4's coverage of camera sensors. Installation considerations are addressed in Chapter 1, which is discussed in the section about CCTV deployment. The compression and dual-streaming aspect links to Chapter 2's networking and Chapter 6's note on VMS features. By following the best practices, one ensures the "garbage in, garbage out" pitfall is avoided, that is, we provide the analytics software with good quality video.

Video Management, Networking, and Infrastructure Best Practices

The next set of best practices concerns the supporting infrastructure such as the video management system, networks, and computing hardware that underlie the analytics solution. These ensure that once cameras capture video, it can flow through the system efficiently and be managed properly.

- **Video Management System (VMS) Architecture:** As the heart of the surveillance operation, the VMS's architecture should be chosen to fit the size and needs of the deployment. For small systems, a single server-based VMS (or even an NVR appliance that combines recording and management) may suffice. For larger systems, consider a distributed VMS, where multiple recording servers are organized in a hierarchy, with local recorders feeding information up to a central aggregation system. Chapter 6 and the user-files on VMS categorize typical VMS setups as server-based, edge-based, or cloud-based. The best practice is to ensure the VMS can scale to the number of cameras and retention needed. Check the throughput limits, as many VMS vendors specify how many Mbps or cameras a single server can handle. If those limits will be exceeded, plan to split the load (by area or camera function). If using a cloud VMS (where video is stored in the cloud, like Video Surveillance as a Service, VSaaS), ensure the bandwidth is available, and note that local viewing might be slower. Hybrid options do exist (such as with cloud management but local recording). Edge-based video management (where cameras themselves manage storage, each camera recording to an SD card or NAS) can work for very small or distributed systems, but they become difficult to manage at scale, so typically an overarching system is still used for coordination. In summary, choose a VMS architecture that can reliably handle the camera load with some headroom, and that provides the needed features (such as motion search, alarm management, and user permissions, as discussed in Chapter 6's content analysis context).

- **Open-Platform vs Proprietary Systems:** When selecting a VMS or analytics platform, consider integration needs. An open-platform VMS (one that supports cameras from many manufacturers and allows third-party analytics integration via standards) is usually desirable for flexibility. It allows mixing different camera brands and adding new analytics modules later (for instance, via ONVIF interface or SDK plugins). A proprietary end-to-end system (where cameras, recorders, and analytics are all from one vendor) might offer seamless operation and optimized performance but could limit adding components from other manufacturers. The best practice for most scenarios is to utilize open standards unless a single-vendor solution has a clear advantage and the client is comfortable with the decision. Chapter 6's overview of video analytics frameworks suggests the industry trend is towards interoperability, but there are still large companies that offer closed systems. If a proprietary VMS is chosen (like one requiring specific camera types), ensure it meets all requirements and the vendor's approach and specifications align with the client's future needs (for example, some older proprietary systems struggled to integrate AI analytics from other vendors).

- **Networking Best Practices:** The network can be thought of as a "highway" for all video data. The best practices for managing networks are as follows:
  - **Use Power over Ethernet (PoE) switches for camera connectivity**: This approach simplifies the power delivery (no separate power run needed) and allows for the use of a central UPS backup for cameras through the switch. Ensure the PoE budget of the switches is sufficient for all connected cameras (especially if using PTZ or IR cameras that draw more power).
  - **Network Segmentation:** Place cameras on an isolated network or VLAN to contain the broadcast traffic and enhance security (the camera VLAN can be routed to the VMS servers but not have direct access to other corporate resources).
  - **Adequate Bandwidth:** Calculate the worst-case bandwidth if all cameras are streaming at full resolution and frame rate. Design the switch uplinks and core network to handle that with at least 20-30% spare capacity for the future. For instance, if 100 cameras at 4 Mbps each feed into a building core, that is ~400 Mbps, so using at least a 1 Gbps uplink (preferably 10 Gbps for growth) is recommended. Avoid connecting too many high-bandwidth cameras to a single 1 Gbps switch if that approach can overwhelm it; load-balance across switches or use link aggregation, if needed.
  - **Multicast vs. Unicast:** If multiple clients will view streams (like a video wall or operator PCs), configure multicast streaming on the VMS/cameras so that the network

is not sending duplicate streams per viewer. This might involve enabling IGMP Snooping on switches and making sure cameras and VMS support multicast.

- **Quality of Service (QoS):** Tag video traffic with QoS to ensure it is not dropped or delayed if sharing the network with other data. QoS can prioritize critical video or control streams, especially if it is using a WAN.

- **Latency considerations:** If using wireless links or long WAN connections, be mindful of added latency; for PTZ control or real-time viewing, too much can be problematic. Keep the network path as short and high-performance as possible for live control scenarios (for example, a security guard controlling a PTZ remotely might find managing real-time scenarios challenging if there is a 1-second delay). In multi-site designs, sometimes a dedicated WAN or MPLS links is used for surveillance to guarantee the bandwidth, and it is separate from the general Internet. Also consider network monitoring; implement tools to monitor traffic loads, packet loss, and device status (some VMS have built-in health monitoring, or use standard network management systems). This helps to proactively catch any network issues affecting the video (for example, if a switch port starts dropping packets, you would see video artifacts and can investigate).

- **Computing Hardware and Acceleration:** For analytics servers, use the appropriate hardware.

  - Take advantage of hardware acceleration for video decoding and AI inference. Modern CPUs and GPUs have capabilities like Intel QuickSync or NVIDIA NVDEC to quickly decode multiple video streams; ensure the chosen software can utilize these. For AI, an NVIDIA GPU with Tensor cores can drastically speed up deep learning inference; if the budget allows, include GPUs for heavy analytics tasks (face recognition or object detection) rather than trying to do everything on the CPU. If the situation requires CPU-only, then choose high-core count servers and possibly use accelerators like Intel OpenVINO to optimize model execution. Also consider the form factor: For edge deployments, sometimes using an industrial GPU-enabled IoT device (like NVIDIA Jetson series) is more practical than using a full server. Those can handle a few cameras each and are small/power-efficient.

  - **Utilize Virtualization or Containerization for the Software:** Running VMS and analytics in virtual machines or Docker containers can improve deployment flexibility and fault isolation. It allows multiple services on one hardware to be separated and makes it easier to scale out (spin up new VMs for new components). Some advanced deployments even use Kubernetes to orchestrate analytics workloads across a cluster of servers. If the project is large, planning for such an orchestrated environment from the start can save significant manual effort later when updating models or adding new analytics streams.

- **Storage Strategies:** We briefly discussed storage in design, but here are some best practices related to it:

  - Use surveillance-grade hard drives in NVRs/servers (they are designed for continuous writing). Ensure there is redundancy (RAID) if data loss is unacceptable. For large storage pools, consider dividing storage into volumes per camera or per group for manageability. If using cloud or network storage, ensure latency to storage is low enough to not cause frame drops.

- Plan periodic maintenance. For example, what happens when a drive fails (Do you have hot spares?) or when storage fills up (the system should have an overwrite policy, typically FIFO deletion of oldest footage). If retention is critical, consider backup solutions (such as an offsite backup of the video, perhaps with lower frame rate copies, to protect against a local disaster). In some sensitive applications, video is even stored in two separate physical locations concurrently for high assurance. Those are high-end measures, but worth noting if designing critical infrastructure.

- **Failover and Redundancy:** Besides storage, other components can have failover. The best practices for larger systems are as follows:
  - A failover recorder server can be on standby and it can automatically take over if the main VMS server fails. Some VMS have this built-in (one license covers a hot standby).
  - Redundant power supplies on servers, network devices, and using UPS units for each critical component is recommended. Having a network diagram that shows redundant links (if any) helps in understanding single points of failure. If the system is guarding high-security premises, consider redundant cameras watching the same view (in case one is sabotaged, the other still works, such as having two cameras on opposite corners of a lobby). Build resilience in layers.

In essence, these infrastructure best practices aim for a system that can handle the heavy load of video data smoothly and survive failures or growth. The knowledge from Chapter 2 (networks), Chapter 7 (computing hardware, virtualization), and earlier CCTV design principles all feed into these recommendations. By following them, one avoids common pitfalls like network bottlenecks, under-powered servers, storage failures, or difficulty integrating new components down the line.

Analytics Performance Optimization and Model Management

Designing the system hardware is important but so is managing the software and analytics. With video analytics increasingly involving AI models, it is important to ensure they run efficiently and accurately. Here are best practices for optimizing analytics algorithms and managing them:

- **Optimize AI Models for Inference:** Use optimization toolkits if you are using deep learning models for tasks like object detection and face recognition. For NVIDIA GPUs, as noted, TensorRT can take a trained neural network and optimize it (by fusing layers and quantizing to a lower precision, like FP16/INT8) to run much faster on the GPU. For Intel CPUs or VPUs, OpenVINO is a useful toolkit that optimizes models from frameworks (such as TensorFlow or PyTorch) to run efficiently on the CPU (using vector instructions). These can often double or triple inference throughput without changing the model's outputs. It is a best practice to incorporate these into the deployment pipeline, for example, after training a model or choosing a pretrained model, generate an optimized runtime version for production. Also consider using smaller models if possible; for instance, if a huge ResNet-based detector is too slow, maybe a smaller MobileNet-based detector could achieve slightly lower accuracy but still meet requirements and run in real time. It is often practical to test a couple of model options to see which gives the best accuracy-speed trade-off on the target hardware (Chapter 5 discusses model architectures; those insights help in choosing a suitable one).

- **Use Multi-Threading and Parallel Processing:** Many analytics tasks (like processing multiple camera streams) can be parallelized. Ensure the software is configured to use all available CPU cores or GPU concurrency. If using a GPU, the batch processing of frames from multiple cameras together can improve efficiency (some VMS/analytics allow batching frames before sending to the AI, spreading overhead costs over time). On a CPU, using threads for each camera or each analytic task avoids idle cores. These are more implementation details, but as a designer, one might specify "the analytics software should run with X threads" or expect the vendor's system to handle it. Monitoring tools can help verify full resource utilization during testing.

- **Adjust Analytics Parameters to Reduce Load:** If certain analytics are too heavy, consider adjusting their parameters. For example, run analysis on every nth frame instead of every frame (if 15 fps is coming in, analyzing at 5 fps may still catch most events and reduce CPU usage by ~66%). You may also wish to restrict detection zones so the algorithm only looks at part of the image (some VMS let you define regions of interest for motion detection or analytics, so it ignores irrelevant areas like swaying trees in the background). Another idea is to use a cascading approach; for example, a lightweight motion detector or background subtractor runs first, and only if motion is present do you invoke the heavier AI model on that frame. That way, during periods of no activity, the AI model is not running. Many modern systems use such multi-tier analytics to conserve cycles.

- **Regularly Update and Maintain Models:** The field of AI changes quickly. A best practice, especially for long-term deployments, is to plan for model updates. New versions might be more accurate or faster. If using a vendor's analytics, get their updates, which often include improved algorithms. If custom models are used, retrain them periodically with new data (particularly for things like face recognition, where new people might need to be added, or for detection models if the environment changes, such as for when new types of objects or clothing become common). However, any change to models should be tested thoroughly to ensure it does not introduce new issues. Maintain a versioning system for models so you can roll back if needed.

- **Benchmark and Load Test the Analytics:** Before finalizing the design, it is a best practice to simulate the expected load. If the system is supposed to handle 100 camera streams with analytics, set up a test (using recorded video if not all cameras are installed yet) to see how the system performs. This can reveal if additional hardware is needed or if certain analytics need tweaking. Monitoring CPU/GPU usage, memory, and throughput during such tests will validate that the design meets performance requirements with some headroom. It is better to find bottlenecks in a staging environment than after deployment.

- **Leverage Edge AI Capabilities:** Some cameras come with AI chips (e.g., cameras with Ambarella or Huawei chips that can do person detection inside the camera). Offloading simple tasks to these cameras can save processing on the servers. A best practice is to use camera-side analytics for preliminary filtering when available (for example, a camera might output metadata of objects it sees, which can be consumed by the VMS). Standards like ONVIF have begun to include how cameras publish metadata/event streams. Ensure the chosen cameras and VMS support that if intending to use it. This is related to the hybrid approach, which is basically distributing the analytics.

- **Environment and False Alarm Tuning:** Many analytics (especially motion or rule-based ones) require tuning to the specific environment to minimize false alarms and missed detections. For instance, video motion detection sensitivity might need to be lower in an outdoor environment to avoid being triggered by small movements like those made by leaves. AI analytics software might require calibration. For example, in certain zones, the software may need to be calibrated to ignore reflections or masks to exclude areas with repetitive irrelevant motion. Allocate time in the project for this tuning phase. A best practice is to perform a site calibration after the initial installation: Adjust the camera settings and analytic parameters after observing a few days of operation. Some advanced systems can even self-tune (such as learning the background over time), but human oversight is usually needed.

By following these practices, the analytics component of the system will be more robust and efficient. Essentially, it is about making the software smarter and leaner to fully utilize the available hardware. This not only ensures current performance but also can reduce the need for expensive hardware upgrades in the future (which is related to the cost best practices).

Chapter 5's content on deep learning and the mention of frameworks/tools like TensorRT and OpenVINO in Chapter 7 are directly relevant here. The concept of model lifecycle management is related to how AI is an evolving field, something to consider in "future-proofing" which is mentioned in the conclusion.

Cybersecurity Best Practices

In any modern networked system, especially one that deals with sensitive video feeds (which might contain personal or critical security information), cybersecurity is a concern. A breach in a video analytics system could lead to malicious actors hijacking cameras, stealing footage, or disabling the system when it is needed most. Therefore, from design through deployment, strong security practices must be implemented. Here are the cybersecurity best practices for end-to-end video analytics systems:

- **Secure Device Access:** Change default credentials on all cameras and IoT devices. It is alarming how many deployments leave cameras with factory default usernames/passwords, which are well-known and easily exploitable. Upon installation, each camera and network device should be set with a strong, unique password. Use complex passwords or passphrases and wherever possible, use devices that support modern authentication (e.g., digest authentication for cameras or certificate-based authentication). Some systems allow integration with directory services (like LDAP/Active Directory) for centralized account management, which you should consider for larger systems to avoid "password sprawl", where users have too many different passwords to track and manage effectively.
- **Network Segmentation and Isolation:** Treat the entire video surveillance network as an untrusted zone that should be isolated from the rest of the IT network. As recommended earlier, putting cameras on a separate VLAN or physical network ensures that even if a camera is compromised, the attacker cannot easily breach corporate databases or other sensitive systems. The VMS servers can be positioned at the junction with dual network interfaces, one on the camera network and one on the corporate network for client access. This way, clients (user workstations) talk to the VMS, not directly to cameras. Implement firewall rules to block any direct traffic from camera LAN to other LANs. Only the necessary ports/protocols between cameras and VMS (and VMS to clients) should be allowed. This principle of least privilege at the network level can prevent some breaches.

- **Secure Network Hardware:** On switches that connect cameras, enable port security features. For example, lock each switch port to a specific camera's MAC address. This prevents someone from unplugging the camera and plugging in a rogue device to gain network access. The switch would shut down or ignore a device with an unauthorized MAC. Also disable any unused ports and place them in an isolated VLAN. Use management VLANs and secure SNMP configurations for network gear so that it is not easily tampered with.

- **Use Encryption for Data in Transit:** Where possible, use encrypted protocols for video streams and control. Many IP cameras now support HTTPS or SRTP (secure RTP) for video, rather than plain RTSP. If the cameras and VMS support it, turn on encryption so that even if someone breaches the network, they cannot view the feeds easily. If using a cloud connection, definitely use a VPN or secure tunnel for any data leaving the local network. Ensure the VPN is configured with strong ciphers. If remote viewing is needed (e.g., from a mobile app), prefer a solution where the connection is initiated from the secure side (to avoid opening inbound firewall ports) or use a well-secured relay service. In addition to encrypting video streams, also encrypt any sensitive control channels or databases at rest (for example, if face recognition data or personal info is stored, encrypt those databases). Chapter 2's fundamentals on network security and encryption apply here.

- **Role-Based Access Control:** Implement strict user permissions on the VMS and analytics software. Not every user should have access to all cameras or all functions. Follow the principle of least privilege for accounts. For instance, an operator who monitors lobby cameras does not need administrator's rights to change configurations. Create separate admin accounts for system maintenance versus monitoring accounts for daily use. Also, separate accounts that are used by systems vs. humans, such as the account the VMS uses to log into cameras should be a limited one that only has the ability to fetch the video stream, not to change camera settings (many cameras allow creating a viewer user vs. admin user). That way, even if the VMS credentials are compromised, the attacker cannot change camera configurations. Regularly audit user accounts and remove any defaults or old/unused accounts. Enable account lockout or alerting for suspicious login attempts, if possible.

- **Device Firmware Management:** Cameras and NVR appliances often have firmware that occasionally needs updates to patch vulnerabilities. Part of the design's operational plan should include regular firmware updates on all cameras, VMS appliances, and servers. Schedule updates during maintenance windows to avoid downtime. Use models from reputable manufacturers who have a track record of releasing security patches. There have been cases of backdoors or serious vulnerabilities in certain off-brand cameras, so choosing trusted vendors (as mentioned earlier) is a security decision as well. Some organizations even restrict use of equipment from certain manufacturers due to cybersecurity concerns or national security guidelines – be aware of any such restrictions in your context.

- **Monitoring and Alerting for Security Events:** Just as we monitor the video for security, monitor the system itself. Set up alerts for anomalies like a camera going offline unexpectedly (which could be a sign of tampering), a sudden increase in network traffic from a camera (which could indicate it has been hacked and is sending data out, or being used in a DDoS attack), multiple failed login attempts (which may be someone trying to use brute force to obtain access), or new devices connecting to the surveillance network. Modern VMS systems or network management systems can log these events. Even something like a camera rebooting frequently could indicate instability or an attack. Treat the security system's health with the same seriousness as any IT system containing sensitive info.

- **Physical Security of Equipment:** Do not forget the physical security of the cameras and servers. Lock server racks, use tamper-evident seals on equipment if needed (some attackers might try to physically insert a device in line with a camera if they have access, so prevent unauthorized access to wiring and hardware). Use secure enclosures for outdoor cameras to prevent direct access to their network connections. Ensure backups of configurations (such as network device configs or a VMS database) are kept securely. In case of a ransomware attack on the VMS, you might need clean backups to restore.

- **Cyber-Hygiene Training:** If the system is managed by an IT team or security team, ensure they follow good practices. For example, do not install random software on the VMS servers, do not use those servers or consoles for Web browsing or email which could introduce malware, and be cautious with USB devices around those systems. Segment admin workstations or use jump servers to access the surveillance system if necessary.

Following these cybersecurity practices is essential to prevent the surveillance system from itself becoming a point of vulnerability. A breach could undermine the safety that the system is meant to enhance. In a worst-case scenario, hackers could manipulate camera feeds or disable alarms during a heist (which has happened before). Thus, building a strong defense in depth (by using device hardening, network security, user access control, and monitoring) around the video analytics system ensures it remains trustworthy.

These recommendations align with Chapter 2's discussions on securing network devices, as well as Chapter 7's notes on edge device security. By implementing them, a designer ensures that the advanced video system does not inadvertently cause new security problems. Cybersecurity is an ongoing process, so these practices should be revisited periodically as new threats emerge.

With the above best practices across architecture, hardware, network, analytics optimization, and security, we create a video analytics system that is not only functional but engineered for high performance, reliability, and safety. The next section will compare different design approach choices and illustrate how these practices function in a real-world scenario.

CASE STUDY – DESIGNING A FIVE-STORY OFFICE BUILDING SYSTEM

To illustrate how all these pieces work together in practice, let's consider a case study. We will design an end-to-end video analytics system for a hypothetical five-story office building, incorporating features like face recognition for access management, license plate recognition (LPR) for parking control, and integration with a VMS for general surveillance. This scenario demonstrates how to apply the Design Line framework, use best practices, and make design choices based on requirements. We also reference earlier chapters to show how each component of the system draws on those fundamentals.

Scenario Description

The building is a mid-sized corporate office with five floors of office space, a main lobby entrance at the ground floor, a secondary back entrance for staff, and an attached parking garage.

The security goals are to control who enters the building (only authorized people and vehicles), monitor the premises for any incidents (theft, unauthorized access, and safety issues), and provide forensic capabilities (you must have the ability to investigate if an incident occurs by reviewing footage). The client specifically requests an automated vehicle entry system using license plate recognition at the garage, facial recognition in the lobby to supplement badge access control, and a modern VMS that allows security staff to monitor cameras in real-time and quickly search recordings. They also want at least 30 days of video storage for all cameras, and the system must integrate with their existing electronic door lock system (for unlocking doors when an authorized face is recognized or when someone badges in).

Let's first discuss the design components for this case: the cameras, network, analytics deployment, and overall system integration.

License Plate Recognition for Vehicle Access

At the parking garage entrance, we install a specialized Automatic License Plate Recognition (ALPR) camera (Figure 9.3). This camera is positioned at the gate such that it has a clear view of the front of each incoming vehicle at a choke point (where the vehicle stops).

FIGURE 9.3 Camera for Automatic License Plate Recognition (ALPR).

It is housed in an outdoor weatherproof enclosure and has built-in IR illumination to capture plates at night. We choose a camera model known for ALPR, which can provide a high shutter speed to freeze motion and possibly has onboard ALPR analytics. The license plate numbers will be read by an ALPR software module. To ensure low latency (so that the gate opens quickly as a car arrives), we opt to perform the plate recognition at the edge. An edge processor at the gate (this could be an industrial mini-PC or an AI-enabled camera) will run the OCR (Optical Character Recognition) to decode the plate. This way, the system does not need to stream the entire video to the server constantly; it can send just the plate text and a snapshot image when a plate is detected. The recognized plate is then checked against an authorized vehicles database (which is maintained by security and lists employee cars and frequent visitors). If it is a match, the gate control system (which is connected to the edge processor or the server) will automatically open the gate. If the plate is not recognized or is on a "watch list" (e.g., former employees or other flagged vehicles), it will alert a guard and the gate will remain closed. This setup streamlines vehicle entry for authorized users (they have no need for swipe cards or use an intercom, as the system is essentially the "credential") and enhances security by logging every vehicle.

From a design perspective, we integrate this as follows. The edge ALPR unit is part of the camera network and also communicates with the central server to report events. We ensure that the camera covering the license plate is high-resolution enough to capture plates clearly (typically 2MP is enough for a single lane if tightly focused). We also include an overview camera for the license plate recognition for vehicle access. At the parking garage entrance gate, we deploy an ALPR camera. As a vehicle approaches, this specialized camera captures a clear image of its license plate. An ALPR software module then reads the plate number and instantly checks it against the database of authorized vehicles (e.g. employees and registered visitors). If the plate is recognized, the system automatically triggers the gate to open; if not (or if the plate is on a blocklist), an alert is sent to security for review. To achieve real-time response, we implement this as an edge analytics solution: the plate reading (OCR) is done locally at the gate, on an edge processor, in real time.

The edge device then sends only the plate text (and perhaps a snapshot) to the central system, which logs the entry and handles the gate control. By processing at the edge, we preserve bandwidth (no need to stream full video continuously to the server) and minimize latency. The gate can open almost immediately as the car is recognized. This ALPR setup streamlines parking access (employees do not need to swipe badges for garage entry) and provides an automated log of all vehicle entries/exits for security auditing.

We also configure alert rules: if a watchlist plate (e.g. an ex-employee's car or an unknown vehicle) is detected, the security team is immediately notified and can view the live camera feed at the gate to take action. In addition to the ALPR camera (focused on plates), we include an overview camera covering the entrance lane and gate area. This second camera provides a broader context by capturing the vehicle's make/model and the scene, which is useful for security personnel (for example, to see if a vehicle tailgates another or if multiple occupants are present). Both cameras are integrated into the video management system, and the ALPR events (plate numbers with timestamps) are logged and linked to the video clips for easy retrieval (so one can search the system for a particular license plate and quickly retrieve the corresponding video).

Face Recognition for Security and Attendance:

At the main lobby entrance, we deploy a facial recognition camera aimed to capture the faces of people as they enter (Figure 9.4). The system compares each face against a database of authorized personnel (employees and perhaps frequent contractors or visitors).

FIGURE 9.4 Face recognition.

This serves two primary purposes.

1. **Security:** If an unknown person (not in the employee database) or a flagged individual (e.g., a terminated employee or someone on a security watchlist) enters, the system will immediately alert the front-desk or security staff. In essence, the camera acts as an automated guard, supplementing the normal badge-based access control system.

2. **Attendance tracking:** For convenience, the company can use the face recognition system to automatically log employees' entry times. Employees who consent and enroll their faces would no longer need to swipe an ID for clock-in; the system can record their presence when they walk in. We discussed privacy implications with the client. Since this is a workplace with voluntary participation, employees provide consent for their images to be used for access/attendance. The data is stored securely and used only for these purposes (aligning with corporate privacy policies and relevant regulations, see Chapter 2 on compliance).

The face recognition works in a hybrid processing manner: the camera (or a small edge device at the site) performs the initial face detection in each video frame (locating faces and possibly extracting an encoded representation of each face), then a central server performs the more computationally heavy face matching, which is comparing the face against the database of stored face profiles.

This design ensures fast local detection (so no face is missed due to latency) while leveraging the powerful GPU on the server for accurate recognition against potentially thousands of known faces. If a match is found and the person is authorized, the system can, if configured, automatically unlock the door or turnstile for that person, or simply log their entry. If there is no match, an alert is generated before they reach secured areas. The system is also configured to help detect *tailgating*, which can occur if two faces enter on one badge swipe (one employee badges in and someone else follows closely). The camera will "see" an extra face that is not associated with an access event and flag a possible tailgating incident.

In our case, a security officer in the control room would receive an instant alert with the person's image if someone not recognized (or known to be barred) walks in, enabling a quick response. On the positive side, authorized staff benefit from a seamless entry (the system effectively becomes a hands-free access credential), and attendance can be automatically recorded in the HR system.

We have integrated the face-recognition system with the building's existing access control and elevator systems. For example, when a face match confirms an employee, the lobby turnstile opens and the elevator can be called to their floor, streamlining the start of their day (such integrations are increasingly feasible with modern APIs in both access control and analytics platforms).

Applying the DAW Framework to Office Security

With the analytics features in place, it is critical to define how the system should respond to events in real time. This is where the Decision and Action Workflow (DAW) model introduced in Chapter 8 plays an important role. DAW transforms passive detections into structured, programmable operational behavior, ensuring the system does not just "see and understand," but also *performs* in a way that aligns with security objectives and standard operating procedures.

The office building's use cases map neatly to DAW workflows.

Example 1 – Vehicle Access via LPR

- **Trigger:** Unrecognized license plate detected at garage entrance.
- **Decision Logic:** If plate is not on whitelist + time = working hours → flag for guard verification
- **Response Channel:** Send alert to security dashboard with vehicle snapshot.
- **Escalation Rule:** No verification within 20 seconds → deny gate access
- **Action Logging:** Log the event with the plate, time, and guard response (approved/rejected).

Example 2 – Face Recognition at Lobby

- **Trigger:** Face is not matched to known personnel.
- **Decision Logic:** If access attempt at lobby entry + match confidence < threshold → require badge swipe fallback
- **Response Channel:** Notify access control system to prompt for manual credential.
- **Escalation Rule:** If second attempt fails → alert building security and lock entry
- **Action Logging:** Record the face snapshot, match score, and access result.

These examples demonstrate how DAW bridges the gap between AI insight and real-world decision-making. It ensures the system can not only automate first-level decisions but also escalate, log, and adapt to complex scenarios, such as a visitor arriving early, a known employee forgetting their badge, or a vehicle with expired access.

By embedding DAW logic into the system design early, stakeholders gain transparency, traceability, and operational control, turning an intelligent video analytics system into a smart, responsive security partner.

Network and System Design Considerations

The office building's cameras and processing devices connect over a robust internal network dedicated to surveillance. Each floor has a network closet containing a PoE switch that all local cameras plug into. These switches provide power to the PoE cameras and aggregate traffic from that floor. All floor switches uplink via high-throughput connections (gigabit or 10-gig fiber uplinks) to a core switch in the server room. The surveillance network is segmented on its own VLAN (or even a physically separate switch infrastructure) so that camera traffic is isolated, as recommended in our best practices. Even though the switches might be shared with corporate data in some cases, the VLAN ensures video traffic and corporate IT traffic are logically separated and security controls restrict any cross-access.

This means if someone were to plug into a camera port, they cannot reach the corporate LAN, and vice versa, containing any potential breaches. The server room hosts the central Video Management System server, which also runs the analytics services (such as the face recognition server software and ALPR central database). This server is a high-performance machine with a multi-core CPU and a suitable GPU to handle the face recognition tasks. It also runs the VMS software that manages recordings and user access. For redundancy and storage, we include a dedicated NVR appliance (or a server with large storage arrays) that stores all camera feeds for at least 30 days at full 1080p resolution. Important videos (like from lobby and gate cameras) could be stored at even higher resolution or backed up to cloud storage periodically, depending on retention policy.

CCTV Layouts and Placements Using CCTV Design Software (JVSG)

For precise and optimal camera placements within the five-story office building, a specialized CCTV design software like JVSG is utilized. JVSG provides an accurate graphical representation of camera fields of view (FOV), pixel density, blind spots, and potential overlaps, significantly enhancing the planning and implementation process.

The design team inputs the architectural floor plans of each level into JVSG, defining walls, entry points, windows, corridors, elevators, and other significant structural elements. Each camera—whether it is positioned for general surveillance, facial recognition at entry points, or license plate recognition at parking areas—is carefully positioned virtually first. The software immediately visualizes coverage areas, indicating if the resolution and viewing angles are sufficient for analytics tasks such as face identification or license plate capture.

This virtual modeling enables rapid adjustments without the expense of physically repositioning hardware, thus streamlining project timelines and budgets. It also allows stakeholders to easily visualize and validate the planned security coverage, improving decision-making and stakeholder buy-in. Moreover, JVSG's built-in features help ensure adherence to best practices discussed in Chapters 3 and 4, confirming camera resolution, lens focal length, and appropriate angles for optimal analytics performance.

In the context of our case study, utilizing JVSG for planning helped ensure each floor of the office building was comprehensively covered, with minimal camera count yet optimal overlap, redundancy, and clarity required for high-performance analytics.

CCTV Layouts and Placements Using CCTV Design Software

For precise and optimized camera placements within the five-story office building, specialized CCTV design software is utilized. Several software tools commonly used by professionals include JVSG, IP Video System Design Tool, CCTV Design Lens Calculator, and VideoCAD.

These software tools provide accurate graphical visualizations of camera fields of view (FOV), pixel density coverage, blind spots, and areas of overlap. This visualization significantly enhances planning accuracy, streamlining both the design and implementation processes.

In our case study, the design team imports architectural floor plans of each level into the chosen CCTV design software. Structural elements like walls, doors, windows, elevators, and corridors are clearly defined. Each proposed camera—whether for general surveillance, facial recognition at entry points, or license plate recognition at parking entrances—is virtually positioned, allowing immediate visualization of coverage, resolution adequacy, and analytics suitability.

By using these tools, designers can rapidly adjust camera positioning, lens focal lengths, and resolutions virtually, avoiding the significant costs and time associated with physical adjustments post-installation. Stakeholders can easily visualize and validate planned camera coverage, thus enhancing decision-making and project confidence.

Utilizing CCTV design software ensures adherence to best practices covered extensively in Chapters 3 and 4, verifying that each camera provides sufficient pixel density and suitable angles to support effective video analytics.

In our example office building scenario, employing such specialized CCTV design software guaranteed comprehensive coverage across all floors, delivering optimal analytics performance with the minimal necessary number of cameras.

We chose IP cameras with 4 MP (megapixel) resolution for most general surveillance areas; this provides a bit higher detail than standard 1080p, useful for digital zoom-in during investigations, and a few 4K ultra-HD cameras for critical detail areas (the lobby face camera and the ALPR camera in particular, to ensure maximum clarity for recognition).

All cameras are either dome or bullet type, depending on the location: Dome cameras are used indoors for their wide view and aesthetic low-profile (hallways, open office areas), and bullet cameras or weather-proof domes are used outdoors and in the parking garage for durability. We paid special attention to camera placement to achieve full coverage. Entrances and exits are covered from multiple angles (for example, the lobby has one camera facing incoming traffic for face recognition and another overview camera from above to cover the whole lobby), each elevator lobby is monitored, and long corridors have cameras at each end looking down the corridor. We ensured overlapping fields of view so that there are minimal blind spots. For instance, the end of one corridor camera's view is covered by the start of another camera's view, and stairwells or emergency exits (often forgotten) are also covered by nearby cameras. This overlap means if one camera fails or is obstructed, another can still see the area. All cameras inside are mounted at about 8–10 feet height on walls or ceilings, and outdoor cameras are mounted high enough to avoid vandalism (and are in vandal-resistant housings). We also included sufficient infrared lighting for cameras covering low-light areas (the parking garage at night, and the back entrance after hours) to ensure the video is usable 24/7. The end result is a well-planned camera network: ~40 cameras in total (this includes roughly 8 cameras per floor for offices and hallways, a few per entrance, and a handful in the parking area). These connect through 5 PoE switches (one per floor), feeding into the core network gear in the server room.

Analytics Workflow and Integration

All camera feeds are continuously recorded and managed by the VMS. The system architecture follows the hybrid edge/cloud model we described in previous: the ALPR at the gate is handled by an edge device which sends plate read events to the central server, and the facial recognition is partially edge (for detection) and central (for recognition). In practice, this works as follows: Each camera streams video to the VMS in real-time. The ALPR camera's video is processed by the local ALPR unit; whenever a plate is recognized that unit sends the plate number and a snapshot over the network to the central VMS/analytics server, which logs the event (and can store the snapshot and plate text in a database). The lobby face camera's feed is streamed to the server, where the face recognition module runs (with assistance from the camera's edge analytics for detection). Other cameras (e.g., hallway cameras) are using the VMS's built-in analytics for basic motion detection and tampering alarms; for example, if a camera is covered or moved, the VMS will alert security (a standard feature discussed in Chapter 6).

Security operators have a unified interface in the security control room: they can view live feeds from any camera, receive pop-up alerts from the analytics (e.g., "Unrecognized face in lobby at 9:02 AM" or "Blacklisted license plate at garage entrance"), and acknowledge or respond to those alerts. All analytics events are stored with timestamps and linked to the video; the VMS provides a forensic search function that utilizes these analytics.

For instance, if an incident occurred the day before, an operator could quickly filter video by motion events in a specific corridor during a specific time window, or search for all instances of people in red clothing in the lobby (if the system has object metadata indexing). These capabilities greatly speed up investigations; instead of manually reviewing hours of footage, the operator can pinpoint the relevant clips in minutes.

We integrated the video system with the building's access control system, as well. When an employee uses their badge to open a door, that event is tagged in the video timeline for the nearest camera. Later, one can click on a badge event in the access log and immediately see the video of that entry, verifying it was indeed the authorized person and no tailgater followed. Conversely, if the face recognition system identifies an employee, we could (with appropriate safeguards) signal the access control to unlock the door for them as a convenience. All such integrations are done via software APIs and were configured during system setup. The network is configured such that even if the connection to any external network is lost, the on-site system (such as the cameras, server, and gate controller) all continue to function autonomously, which was a design choice made for reliability.

Example Design Proposal and Cost Breakdown

In the proposal document to the client, we provided a detailed bill of materials and cost breakdown for this system. To summarize, the system includes roughly 40 IP cameras (a mix of indoor dome cameras and outdoor bullet cameras for the parking area and entrances), 1 central server with GPU for video management and analytics, 1 NVR appliance (with ~100 TB of usable storage, configured in RAID for redundancy) for 30-day video storage, and networking equipment (about 6 PoE switches for camera connectivity and one core switch, plus a firewall/router for secure remote access management). The ALPR camera and the special facial recognition camera were specified by model, noting their built-in analytics capabilities (the ALPR camera, for example, has an on-board inference chip optimized for OCR). On the software side, we included a VMS software license supporting 50 cameras (to allow some expansion) and analytics licenses for the ALPR module and face recognition module (these are often licensed per camera or per channel of analytics). The cost breakdown (Figure 9.5) was approximately

- **Cameras and Accessories:** ~30% of the total cost (this covers all 40 cameras, mounts, housings, and the ALPR special camera, which is more expensive than standard ones).
- **Server and Storage Hardware:** ~25% of the cost (the main server with the GPU, NVR storage system, racks, and UPS for power backup).
- **Software Licenses:** ~20% of the cost (VMS licenses, analytics licenses, and any database or middleware software needed).
- **Networking Equipment:** ~15% of the cost (such as the PoE switches, core switch, cabling, and firewall).
- **Installation & Services:** ~10% of the cost (such as the professional installation labor, configuration services, and training for the client's staff).

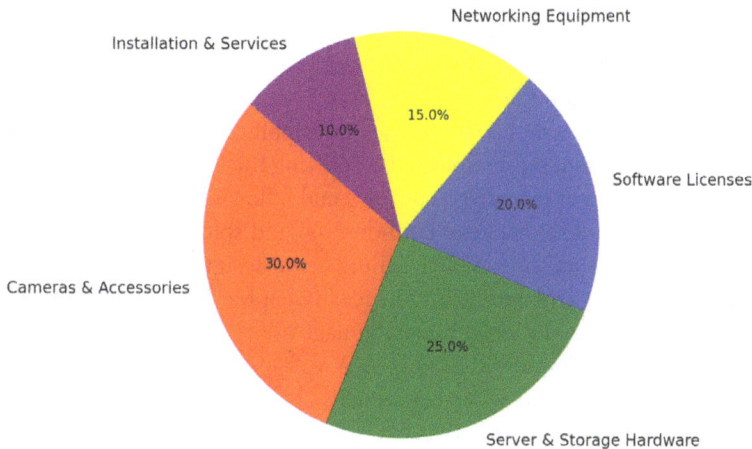

FIGURE 9.5 Budget allocation percentage for the video analytics project.

Each category was accompanied by its justification. For instance, we explained that choosing a hybrid edge/server approach for the analytics (ALPR and face recognition) slightly increased the hardware cost (due to the edge device and a GPU server) but was critical to meet the real-time requirements and to keep sensitive data on-site. License plates and faces are processed locally and only relevant metadata is stored centrally, aligning with the client's privacy preferences. We also justified the high-performance GPU server as necessary to achieve accurate face recognition: cheaper hardware might not handle the load or could introduce lag, whereas the chosen server ensures we can recognize faces in real time as people move through the lobby.

The proposal highlighted expected the ROI (Return on Investment): By automating vehicle entry, the company could reduce or reassign security personnel who used to manually manage the gate, and by enhancing monitoring with intelligent alerts, the system could help prevent or respond faster to incidents (potentially avoiding costly security breaches or business interruptions). The convenience to employees (such as through automated attendance and seamless entry) was also a "soft" benefit, contributing to productivity and workplace satisfaction. In sum, the case study design met the client's goals through a combination of carefully chosen technology and adherence to the design principles we have discussed.

This case study demonstrates how the Design Line framework is applied end-to-end, from understanding the requirements (such as the need for automated access and better security) to analyzing feasibility (ensuring face recognition and ALPR would work in the given environment and budget), then system design (putting together the right cameras, network, and analytics approach), and finally documenting the solution with clear rationale and cost estimates. The result for this office building is an integrated, intelligent video analytics system that controls access, provides situational awareness, and simplifies investigations, all while leveraging the foundational technologies from Chapters 1–7.

SUMMARY

In conclusion, designing end-to-end video analytics systems is about successfully creating a connection between hardware and software, between on-site edge computing and cloud services, and between automated analytics and human operators. This chapter discusses how to combine concepts from across the video analytics pipeline, from camera lenses to neural networks, into a cohesive design methodology. By applying the architectural principles (the layered approach from camera input to analytics output) and following the Video Analytics Design Line framework steps, system designers can confidently build solutions that are effective today and adaptable for tomorrow's advancements. An effective design draws on the fundamentals discussed in earlier chapters: robust CCTV devices (Chapter 1), reliable network infrastructure (Chapter 2), appropriate camera selection and image optimization (Chapters 3 and 4), advanced AI analytics capabilities (Chapter 5), intelligent VMS and content analysis techniques (Chapter 6), and efficient computing and security practices (Chapter 7). In fact, an important takeaway of this chapter is that successful video analytics deployments integrate multidisciplinary knowledge. The best camera or algorithm alone does not create a strong system. It is instead the thoughtful combination of all components working in concert (see Chapter 6 for how analytics depend on good data, or Chapter 2 for how network bandwidth can bottleneck an otherwise good system).

The Design Line framework provides a structured process: starting from clear requirements, validating feasibility, meticulous system design, and finally thorough documentation. This ensures no aspect is overlooked—from legal compliance to end-user training—and that the final proposal aligns with customer needs. By following this approach and incorporating the technical best practices (from camera placement to cybersecurity hardening), designers can avoid common pitfalls and deliver a system that meets performance goals from day one. The comparative analysis of design options (such as edge vs. cloud or open vs. proprietary) equips decision-makers with an understanding of trade-offs, enabling them to choose architectures that best fit their constraints and objectives.

It is important to consider future-proofing in system design. The field of intelligent video analytics is rapidly evolving: AI algorithms are becoming more accurate and more specialized (for example, new behavior analysis models might soon detect subtle suspicious behaviors automatically, not just objects). Computing trends also shift: What is done in the cloud today might be doable on tiny edge devices in a few years as processors become more powerful (or vice versa, organizations may choose cloud services to reduce on-prem maintenance). A design should therefore be modular and scalable, allowing upgrades or expansions as new technology emerges. For instance, if new deep learning models arise (as discussed in Chapter 5) that improve detection, the system should allow those to be deployed (perhaps via software updates or plugin modules) rather than being locked into outdated analytics. Privacy regulations are also tightening worldwide – future systems must be ready to incorporate privacy-by-design features, such as automatic blurring of faces for certain viewers, selective masking of video, or on-device data processing to minimize transmitting personal data (themes introduced in Chapter 2 on data protection). We anticipate that designs will increasingly need to account for ethical and legal considerations, making features like audit logs, consent management, and data encryption even more central. Furthermore, as cities and enterprises get "smarter," video analytics will integrate with other sensor networks (such as traffic sensors, access control, and incident management systems). Thus, building with open standards and interoperability in mind (as we emphasized with open-platform VMS) will be useful when integrating with IoT ecosystems or citywide platforms.

In summary, Chapter 9 has presented a comprehensive guide to designing end-to-end video analytics systems that not only utilizes current state-of-the-art technology but can also adapt to future trends. By carefully balancing the system components and following a methodical design process, practitioners can create intelligent surveillance solutions that are scalable, secure, and effective. Such systems will form the backbone of safer, smarter environments, whether it is an office building, a retail store, a city intersection, or a transportation hub, where video data is transformed into actionable intelligence and tangible benefits. Chapter 9 demonstrates how the theoretical concepts from previous chapters are applied in real-world Intelligent Video Analytics projects. The end-to-end perspective ensures that a weakness in one part (be it a blurry camera or an insecure network) does not undermine the whole: instead, each link in the chain is strong. Designing with this holistic mindset means the video analytics system delivered will not only meet its initial goals but remain reliable and relevant as technology advances and new challenges arise.

DEPLOYMENT, HANDOVER, AND OPERATIONALIZATION OF VIDEO ANALYTICS SYSTEMS

After designing a comprehensive end-to-end video analytics system in Chapter 9, the next step is bringing that system into real-world operation. Even the best-designed solution can falter without a solid deployment strategy and effective operational practices. This chapter discusses how to transition from design to deployment, ensure a smooth handover to the customer, and maintain the system over its life through operational best practices and MLOps (Machine Learning Operations). We will discuss the practical aspects of installation and rollout, division of responsibilities in ongoing support (including managed services), and strategies for maintaining AI models in production. Special attention is given to edge deployment considerations (extending principles from Chapter 7) and to delivering custom analytics models under service level agreements (SLAs) as a competitive advantage. By the end of this chapter, professionals will have a structured understanding of how to deploy, handover, and operationalize video analytics systems in real-world projects, ensuring the solutions designed in earlier chapters deliver value consistently and sustainably.

INTRODUCTION

This section outlines the phases following the design of an intelligent video analytics system (building upon the architectural foundation established in Chapter 9), encompassing the practical aspects of deployment and installation, and the smooth handover to the customer through comprehensive deliverables and training. We also discuss the ongoing operationalization with defined service level agreements and support structures, including remote and on-site assistance, even in locations like large cities. We will also cover the specific considerations of MLOps for managing the lifecycle of AI models in production, the potential for custom AI model development with machine learning-focused SLAs, and finally, a summary of key lessons and best practices for ensuring successful and sustainable system operation. A structured and phased approach is essential to transition a video analytics solution from design to real-world operation.

Chapter 10 is built around a three-stage framework that captures the lifecycle of post-design activities: Deployment and Installation, Handover to Customer, and Operationalization and Managed Services.

Each stage plays a role in ensuring that the system not only functions technically but also delivers value consistently, is adopted by the users, and is maintained effectively over time. These stages are interlinked, as the output of one becomes the input of the next, and together they represent the backbone of a successful video analytics project delivery. The image in Figure 10.1 provides a visual summary of this end-to-end framework, outlining the subcomponents within each phase, the main deliverables, and the transitions between stages. Readers are encouraged to use this framework as a reference point throughout the chapter to contextualize the best practices and technical implementations.

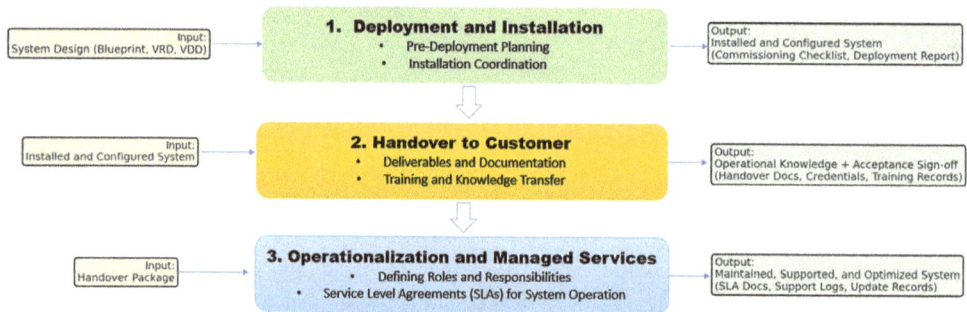

FIGURE 10.1 Three-stage lifecycle for deploying, handing over, and operationalizing intelligent video analytics systems.

DEPLOYMENT AND INSTALLATION

Deploying a video analytics system in the field requires meticulous planning and coordination. Unlike the design phase (Chapter 9), which is done off-site on paper or in staging area, deployment brings real-world constraints like site conditions, installation logistics, and live network environments. This section outlines how to prepare for deployment, execute the installation, and set up the backend systems to turn the design into a working reality. A successful deployment emphasizes ease of installation and efficient configuration, which are important factors for reducing risk and downtime during roll-out.

Pre-Deployment Planning

Proper planning before going to the installation site is essential. Pre-deployment planning bridges the gap between the design documents and the actual on-site work. Important planning steps include the following:

- **Site Readiness Check:** Verify that the installation site is prepared for new equipment. This may involve ensuring mounting points for cameras are in place, server rooms or data center space is allocated, adequate power supply and network cabling are available (drawing on the network design principles from Chapter 2), and environmental conditions (such as temperature and ventilation for hardware) meet the specifications for the equipment. If civil works(all the physical, non-electrical/non-software construction tasks required to get the infrastructure ready for the camera system to be installed and powered) or mounting poles are needed (as per the design), those should be completed or scheduled prior to device installation.

- **Staging and Pre-Configuration:** Whenever possible, pre-configure systems before going on-site. This can dramatically reduce the installation time and troubleshooting in the field. For example, servers or edge devices can be set up in the lab with the required operating system, security updates, video management software, and analytics applications installed. Storage drives can be formatted and tested, and software licenses activated, *before* deployment to the site. By staging the core system in a controlled environment, integrators can catch and resolve configuration issues in advance. As a best practice, many integrators will assemble the entire software stack (VMS, analytics engine, and databases) in the office, load initial configuration (such as camera lists and basic analytics settings), and even simulate a few camera feeds to verify everything works. This pre-installation testing ensures that once on location, the team's focus is on physical installation and final tuning, rather than software debugging. (For example, ensuring the video analytics server is fully patched and that all licenses from the vendor are valid will prevent delays on-site.)
- **Logistics and Scheduling:** Coordinate the deployment schedule with all stakeholders. Installation may require downtime or at least access to critical areas (for instance, mounting cameras in a busy facility might require off-hours work). The plan should minimize disruption to the customer's operations. If this system replaces an existing one, a cut-over plan is needed to transition from old to new with minimal surveillance gaps, which may mean sometimes running systems in parallel for a brief period as a safety net. Ensure that all equipment has arrived on-site or is readily available when technicians need it. This includes not only cameras and servers but cables, network switches, mounting brackets, tools, and spare components. A checklist of all components helps avoid missing pieces that could stall the install. Additionally, confirm that any required permits or security clearances for working on-site are obtained (some facilities require work permits or escorts for contractors).
- **Team briefing:** Before deployment day, conduct a kickoff meeting or briefing with the installation team. Review the design documents the installation steps, and safety considerations. Everyone (installers, network engineers, and system integrators) should understand their roles and the sequence of tasks. For complex projects, it is useful to assign a deployment project manager to coordinate between these groups and the customer's facility managers or IT department.
- **Back-out and Contingency Plans:** Prepare for the unexpected. Despite planning, issues such as bad weather, hardware failures, or unanticipated site problems can occur. Have contingency plans like rescheduling options, spare hardware available for critical components, and a clear communication plan to inform the customer of any changes. For example, if a particular camera location is found to be unsuitable (it may have an obstructed view or it is unsafe to mount), the team should have authority (or a predefined process) to choose an alternative location in consultation with the design team or customer, adjusting the design if necessary (documenting any such deviation for the final as-built documentation).

By thoroughly preparing in these ways, the actual installation will be more predictable and efficient. For simplicity, the reader can download the *Deployment Readiness Checklist* from *www.intelligentxhub.com* which consolidates the critical preparatory tasks into a clear, actionable format suitable for use by system integrators, project managers, or field technicians.

Installation Coordination

Installation involves mounting cameras, setting up computing devices, and making all necessary connections as laid out in the system design. Effective coordination during installation ensures that each component is installed correctly and in the right order.

- **Physical Installation of Devices:** The deployment team will mount cameras and sensors at the specified locations. Proper installation techniques must be followed; for example, the mounting height and angle must match the designed field of view, and weather-proofing must be applied for outdoor cameras. It is crucial not to compromise on these during installation: a mis-positioned or unstable camera can significantly degrade analytics performance (e.g., a slight shift could miss a critical zone or produce false detections). Technicians should also ensure camera lenses are focused and calibrated. Any edge computing units should be installed in their designated locations, such as equipment racks or enclosures. Ensure adequate ventilation and cooling for these devices as specified.
- **Network and Power Connections:** Connect each camera to the network and power sources as per the network topology.. This step often involves working closely with the customer's IT or networking team to plug into the existing infrastructure or setting up dedicated network equipment for the surveillance system. All network switches, routers, and firewalls that were planned should be installed and configured with the correct settings (such as the IP address schemes for cameras, quality of service if required, and firewall rules to permit video streams to reach the analytics server). If the system uses wireless links (for example, in a large campus or a citywide deployment, some cameras might connect via wireless bridges), those links must be aligned and tested.

! TIP

Test the connectivity for each camera as it is installed. For instance, use a laptop or mobile app to verify the camera comes online and streams video so issues can be caught immediately rather than after all devices are up. This incremental testing accelerates troubleshooting by isolating any problem to the most recently added device.

- **Backend System Setup On-Site:** With cameras going up, parallel efforts can focus on the backend. If a central Video Management System (VMS) or analytics server is on-premises, the hardware (server chassis or appliance) is placed in the server room and connected to the network. Any backend storage systems (NAS/SAN or local disks) should also be connected and configured as per the storage design. On installation day, the team might install the server hardware (if not pre-staged) and then load the pre-configured software or adjust settings for the site (like setting the IP addresses and hostname, if those couldn't be finalized until connecting to the site network). For cloud or hybrid deployments, installation involves setting up network routes or VPNs so that the video streams can reach the cloud platform securely (for instance, ensuring the Internet connection and firewall at the site are ready as planned). Coordination with the customer's IT for firewall opening or NAT configurations is often necessary.

- **System Integration and Configuration:** Once devices are physically installed and networked, the next step is integrating them into the system. The team will add all cameras into the VMS software, ensuring each feed is live and correctly named/associated with its location. This is where automatic discovery (e.g., via ONVIF or vendor-specific discovery protocols) can help find devices on the network. The installer should verify each camera's video stream quality and orientation (and make adjustments, if needed). After basic video feeds are confirmed, configure the analytics functions for each camera as designed: for example, set up detection zones, calibration parameters, or analytic rules (such as the tripwire lines, intrusion regions, and counting lines, as discussed for various analytics in Chapter 6). If certain cameras are designated for specific analytics (such as for license plate recognition or face recognition), ensure those analytics modules are properly deployed on the correct video channels and that any necessary calibration (like focusing specifically on a gate area for license plates) is done. This configuration often requires close attention to detail to match the design: misconfiguring an analytic rule (e.g., drawing a detection zone incorrectly) could lead to missed detections or false alarms.

- **Coordination and Communication:** Throughout installation, communication within the team and with the client is important. One effective practice is to give the client periodic updates on progress; for example, one update might be, "By noon we have mounted and connected 50 of 100 cameras, the server is online, and we're starting configuration." This practice ensures the customer is informed and confident in the progress. This is much like good project management: people prefer to understand how the installation is progressing. If the deployment spans multiple days, daily briefings on what was accomplished and what is next can help manage customer expectations. It also helps to quickly surface any issues that might need the customer's input (for instance, if an unexpected obstacle is found at a camera location and a decision is needed).

- **Initial Testing and Tuning:** After the installation is complete, the team should perform the initial system tests. This includes verifying that every camera feed is recording and that analytics events are triggering as expected. It can be useful to create test scenarios on-site; for example, have someone walk through a zone that should trigger an alert (such as a simulated intrusion or a test object for object detection) and verify the system captures it. Adjust the sensitivity or zones on the spot if the results are not satisfactory. Additionally, test system functions like live viewing from client workstations, playback of recorded video, and the functionality of any integrated systems (for example, if the video system is integrated with an alarm panel or access control, trigger those events and ensure the video system responds appropriately). Any performance issues noticed during this phase (such as a camera with lagging video or an analytics module consuming excessive CPU) should be addressed now, possibly by fine-tuning settings or verifying the hardware resources match the load (if needed, recalling the hardware sizing guidelines from Chapter 7 to make adjustments).

- **Backend Reliability Setup:** Finally, set up the operational parameters on the backend: configure user accounts and permissions (ensuring the right staff have access as planned in the design's user policy), set up system backup routines (like database backups or configuration backups), and configure failover if the design includes redundancy. For instance, if a failover server is part of the system , test that it takes over when the primary is shut down. Also, implement cybersecurity hardening in this stage: change default passwords on devices, apply any final encryption or firewall settings, and make sure remote access for support is secure. These steps ensure the system is not only working now but is also maintainable and secure going forward.

HANDOVER TO CUSTOMER

Once the system is installed and tested, the focus shifts to handing over the system to the customer. Handover is a critical milestone. It is the point at which the project transitions from implementation to the operational phase, often with the customer's team taking over day-to-day responsibility. A smooth handover ensures the customer has everything they need to operate and maintain the video analytics solution successfully. This section covers the deliverables that should be provided, the importance of documentation (including any source code, if custom development was involved), and the training and knowledge transfer necessary for the customer's team.

Deliverables and Documentation

A professional handover includes a package of deliverables that encapsulate the entire project's outcomes. This "handover package" typically contains the following:

- **As-Built Documentation:** All design documents updated to reflect the final installed system. While Chapter 9 dealt with the design proposal (which was a plan), the *as-built* documents record what was actually implemented, including any changes made during deployment. This includes the final network diagrams, camera layout maps (with any relocation noted), server and software configuration details, and an updated Bill of Materials listing all equipment with model numbers and serial numbers actually deployed. Essentially, it is the blueprint of the delivered system. For example, if the design originally called for 90 cameras but two extra were added during implementation, the as-built documents should list 92 cameras and their details. These documents are invaluable for future maintenance and any troubleshooting. They tell the customer (and any future integrator or engineer) exactly what is in place.
- **Configuration Settings and Credentials:** A record of all important configuration settings should be handed over. This includes network configurations (such as the IP addresses of the cameras, servers, and gateways, as well as the VLAN IDs used), storage settings (retention period and storage volume allocations), and, very importantly, passwords and login credentials for all system components. The customer must have administrator access to their system. Often, integrators will provide a secure document listing the admin username/password for the VMS, the Windows/Linux admin account on servers, the camera admin credentials, and any database or cloud service keys used. It is critical not to overlook this because without the passwords for the devices in the system, the customer cannot fully own the system. (During the handover meetings, a best practice is to demonstrate how to log in with those credentials to ensure they work and the customer knows how to use them.) If the system was put online to a cloud account, ensure the customer either has access to that account or it is transferred to them as per the agreement.

- **Original Proposal and Change Log:** It can be helpful to include the original project proposal or scope of work document and a log of changes made during the project. This provides context to the customer about how the project evolved. For instance, if certain features were added or removed through change orders, having that recorded prevents confusion later about what was agreed upon. This might be more of an internal project document but sharing at least a summary of changes is transparent and useful to the customer's management or technical teams who will reference the scope later (especially when evaluating future expansions or comparing the delivered system to initial goals).
- **Source Code and Custom Components (if applicable):** If part of the video analytics system involved custom software (for example, a tailor-made AI model, a custom integration module, or scripts to connect the VMS to another system) the question arises: Does the customer receive the source code? This depends on the contract and intellectual property agreements. In many cases, if the work was a bespoke development for the client and they have rights to it, the source code (and documentation for it) should be delivered.

  This might include trained AI model files, code for any dashboards or user interface customizations, and any API documentation. If the vendor is providing these as a product with the proprietary code, they might instead provide executables and retain the source, but even in those cases, detailed user guides or API guides must be handed over so the customer can use and maintain the custom components.

  For example, if a custom "wild animal detection" analytics plugin was developed, the deliverable could include the model file, the configuration file for that analytic, and instructions on how to retrain or update it, even if the underlying source code is not shared. It is important that the customer is not left with a "black box" they don't understand; they should have at least the means to support the security system or the understanding for how they will get support for it.
- **Testing and Commissioning Report:** Typically, after installation, a commissioning or acceptance test is performed (often jointly with the customer or their representative). A report documenting the results of this test should be part of handover. It will state that each camera was tested, analytics alerts were verified under certain scenarios, and any outstanding punch-list items (minor fixes or adjustments) are noted with a timeline for resolution. Having this formal sign-off document ensures both parties agree the system is operational to specifications. It also marks the start of warranty or support agreements.
- **User Manuals and Guides:** While most products (such as cameras and VMS software) come with their own manuals, it is helpful to curate a set of relevant manuals and quick-start guides for the customer. For instance, compile the user manual for the VMS, the administrator manual for the analytics system, any cheat sheets for common tasks (such as how to export footage and how to acknowledge an alarm). If these were provided earlier (during training, for example), ensure they are included in the final documentation package as well. Many integrators will also create a custom "System Handbook" that summarizes how this specific system is configured and how to operate it. This handbook should be tailored to the customer's environment, referencing their camera names and their floor plans to make it easy to understand.

All documentation should be organized neatly (nowadays often delivered digitally, e.g., on a secure cloud folder or a USB drive). Provide a hard copy of critical information such as network schematics or contact lists, as these can be handy in a crisis when you might not have immediate digital access.

<hr>

NOTE *If you would like to download a complete handover checklist template (including editable formats for system diagrams, configuration records, and sign-off sheets), please visit www. intelligentxhub.com.*

Training and Knowledge Transfer

Even the most advanced video analytics system is only as effective as the people using it. Training the end-users and administrators is therefore an important part of the handover process. The goal is to empower the customer's team to confidently operate the system, respond to its alerts, and perform first-line maintenance or troubleshooting.

Important aspects of training include the following:

- **Operational Training:** This is training for the day-to-day users, for example, security personnel who will monitor cameras and respond to analytics alerts, or operations staff who will use analytics dashboards for business insights. The training should cover how to use the VMS software (such as live view, playback, and exporting video), how to interpret and handle analytics events (e.g., if a "intrusion detected" alarm pops up, what steps the guard should take within the system and procedurally), and how to use any user-facing features like search (for example, searching recorded video for a particular object or person, if the analytics support forensic search). Often, scenario-based training helps simulate an incident and guide the users through acknowledging the alarm, investigating it, and determining useful evidence, which makes the training more engaging and practical.
- **Administrative/Technical Training:** This is for the customer's IT or technical staff who will maintain the system. They need to know how to manage user accounts, how to check system health status (such as the disk health, CPU usage on servers and camera connection status), how to replace a camera or add a new one (if the system is expected to expand), and how to adjust analytics settings if needed (or at least how to contact support for complex changes). They should also learn how to apply firmware updates or software patches, unless the system will be completely vendor-managed. If custom AI models are part of the solution, the customer's team might need training on how to label new data or how to trigger a model update, depending on how much of that workflow they will handle versus the vendor (to be detailed under MLOps).
- **Training Materials and Formats:** The training can be delivered in various formats: in-person workshops, remote webinars, or even self-paced e-learning modules. In many cases, the integrator/vendor will conduct an in-person training session at the customer site right after installation, using the actual system. It is a great opportunity to use the newly installed system for training. Trainees can practice on the real interface they will use, and even utilize real footage from their cameras. Providing reference materials is important. Slides, handouts, or recordings of the training (if done via Webinar) can be used so that new employees of the customer can be trained later or current ones can refresh their knowledge.

Some vendors offer certification programs (for example, an "operator certification" course). If such a program exists, the integrator can point the customer to those resources for more in-depth learning at the user's own pace.

- **Emphasize Engagement:** The ultimate aim of training is not only to prevent misuse or underuse of the system but to drive user engagement. When users understand the system's capabilities, they are more likely to take full advantage of them, uncovering more value. For instance, after thorough training, the security team might start using the system not just for reactive monitoring but also for proactive tasks (like using people-count data to adjust staffing, as one case in Chapter 6 illustrated). In one real-world example, SpaceX deployed a video system initially for security, but once hundreds of staff members from various departments were trained, they found creative uses for the system, from monitoring engineering tests to creating time-lapse videos for marketing. This kind of engagement only happens when users are comfortable and knowledgeable, which underscores how good training can turn a video analytics system into a widely utilized tool rather than a niche application.

- **Handover Meeting and Q&A:** Typically, there is a formal handover meeting where the integrator walks the client through the delivered system and documentation. This meeting is a useful time to also address any remaining questions. Encourage the customer's team to ask questions or even operate the system in front of the integrator to confirm they are confident. It is better to confirm the customer understands the system now than to have confusion later when the integrator's team has left the site. If time permits, some integrators can schedule a follow-up training or Q&A session a few weeks after handover. By then, the users have real experience and may have new questions or need fine-tuning of their workflow.

In summary, the handover phase is about transferring knowledge, ownership, and confidence to the customer. By delivering comprehensive documentation and training, the vendor ensures the customer understands their new system after the installers leave. The customer's team should feel that the system is *theirs* to run, with the vendor as a supportive partner rather than a necessary operator. A successful handover assists with the system's long-term success and is often formalized by an acceptance sign-off, after which we move into the operational phase under support agreements.

OPERATIONALIZATION AND MANAGED SERVICES

After deployment and handover, the video analytics system enters the operational phase. This is the phase in which the system runs 24/7, delivering the intended analytics and alarms, and must be maintained over months and years. *Operationalization* refers to the processes and practices that keep the system running effectively in real-world conditions. This includes monitoring the system's health, performing routine maintenance, managing updates, and responding to any issues or incidents with the system. Many customers opt for managed services or support contracts with the vendor or integrator to assist in these tasks, rather than handling everything with their in-house team. In this section, we examine how responsibilities can be divided between on-site and remote support, the nature of service level agreements (SLAs) that govern system performance and support response, and special considerations for supporting systems in remote or critical locations.

Defining Roles and Responsibilities

The first step in effective operationalization is clearly defining who is responsible for what once the system is live. Typically, the responsibilities are shared between the customer's internal team (on-site) and the vendor/integrator's team (often providing remote support and expertise). The exact split can vary based on the customer's capabilities and the support contract, but a common division is as follows:

- **On-site Customer Responsibilities:** These are tasks that require physical presence or immediate hands-on action. For example,
    - **Routine Hardware Maintenance:** This includes cleaning camera enclosures (important for outdoor cameras that might get dirty or obscured), checking that camera housings, mounts, and connections remain secure (especially after storms or accidents), and replacing failed hardware components. If a camera or a network switch fails, the customer's facilities or IT team might handle the physical replacement (possibly with spare units provided as part of the project).
    - **First-level Troubleshooting:** The customer's trained IT/security staff can handle basic troubleshooting like rebooting a hung camera or server, checking cable connections if a device goes offline, or verifying power status. They might also handle simple software restarts (e.g., restarting the VMS service) if something becomes unresponsive. Chapter 2's content on network devices and Chapter 7's on computing hardware provide background knowledge that the customer's technical team can use in these efforts (for instance, using network monitoring tools to determine if a camera's IP is reachable).
    - **Monitoring Day-to-Day Operations:** While the system can have automated health monitoring, often the on-site team will be the first to notice an issue simply in the course of usage, e.g., a camera feed that is black or an analytic alert that is not triggering when it should. The on-site staff should report these anomalies (either address them if minor or escalate to the vendor if needed).
    - **Security and Access Control:** The customer usually manages who has access to the system on their end. This means creating or removing user accounts in the VMS as staff changes (with guidance from admin training provided at handover, referencing Chapter 6's notes on user privilege considerations in video systems). It also means ensuring that the system's client software is only installed on authorized workstations and keeping those workstations secure.
- **Vendor/Integrator Responsibilities (Often Remote):** These are typically specialized or higher-level tasks that the customer uses the vendor's expertise for, often done remotely:
    - **System Health Monitoring:** The vendor can employ remote monitoring tools to keep an eye on the system's status. For example, the integrator might receive automated alerts if a camera goes offline, if a server's CPU is consistently overloaded, or if disk usage is nearing capacity. Many modern VMS or analytics platforms have built-in health dashboards that can be securely accessed by the support provider. The vendor's operations center can then proactively inform the customer (for example, "Camera 12 at Gate 3 has been offline for 10 minutes. Please check if it has power or if there's an obstruction"). Sometimes the customer might not even notice an issue until notified by the remote team.

- **Software Updates and Patches:** Over time, the various software components (camera firmware, VMS software, and analytics algorithms) will have updates to fix bugs or improve features. As part of a managed service, the vendor will test and apply these updates. Typically, they will schedule a maintenance window with the customer (often after-hours) to remotely deploy updates. For example, updating camera firmware might be done in batches so as not to take all cameras down at once. The vendor's knowledge from Chapter 2 about network security and from Chapter 7 about system reliability informs best practices here, e.g., ensuring firmware updates do not disrupt network settings, or verifying system compatibility (a test environment at the vendor's lab might mirror the client system to test updates before applying). This continuous updating keeps the system secure (patching vulnerabilities) and optimal.
- **Advanced Troubleshooting and Repairs:** If something goes wrong that is beyond a simple reboot, perhaps the analytics engine is consistently underperforming or there are database errors, the vendor's technical team will assist. They can remotely collect logs, diagnose problems, and fix software configurations. If a serious hardware failure occurs (like a server crash), the vendor might coordinate sending a replacement part or dispatching a technician if the support agreement covers on-site repair. Essentially, anything that requires expertise (which the customer's general IT might not possess in the specialized realm of video analytics) would be considered part of the vendor's support.
- **Analytics Performance Monitoring:** In addition to system uptime, the vendor might also monitor the performance of the analytics itself. For example, tracking if the frequency of certain alerts has unexpectedly dropped to zero (which could indicate the analytics program is not functioning or the conditions have changed). If the contract includes an SLA for analytics accuracy (discussed later in this section and in the next section on ML SLAs), the vendor will need to actively check that the analytics are meeting the agreed benchmarks, and take corrective action (like model recalibration or retraining) if not.
- **Joint Responsibilities:** Some aspects of operation are collaborative.
  - **Incident Response:** If the analytics generates a security alert (such as a perimeter breach detection), the customer's security team responds on the ground. If it is a false alarm or missed detection, they might work with the vendor to fine-tune the system (e.g., adjust the sensitivity or add an excluded zone to avoid false triggers). This interplay means the customer provides feedback from operational experience and the vendor adjusts the system accordingly.
  - **Scaling and Expansion:** Over the operational life, the customer might want to add more cameras or new analytics features. Planning these expansions involves both parties; the customer defines new requirements, and the vendor analyzes whether the current system can handle them or if an upgrade is needed (which is related to the design principles in Chapter 9). They would jointly plan any new deployment phases.
  - **Service Reviews:** If an SLA is in place, regular meetings (monthly or quarterly) between the customer and vendor to review performance metrics are common. Both sides discuss any issues, uptime statistics, incident reports, and plan improvements. This keeps the operation aligned with business goals and maintains accountability as per the support agreement.

To download a fully customizable RACI (Responsible, Accountable, Consulted, Informed) **NOTE** _template for video analytics operations, including pre-filled examples for deployment, monitoring, maintenance, and incident handling, visit www.intellligentxhub.com._

Service Level Agreements (SLAs) for System Operation

When a video analytics system becomes mission-critical, customers will often require guarantees on its performance and availability. This is where _Service Level Agreements (SLAs)_ becomes important. An SLA is a formal commitment by the service provider (the vendor or integrator managing the system) to meet certain performance and support benchmarks. It serves as both a target for the provider and a reassurance for the customer and usually includes remedies (like penalties or free services) if the SLA is not met.

For video analytics systems, typical SLA elements might include the following:

- **Uptime and Availability:** A guarantee that the system (or specific components like the VMS server) will be operational a certain percentage of time. For example, a common SLA is 99% uptime per month for critical servers, which allows for only about 7 hours of downtime in a month (including both planned maintenance and unplanned outages). High-availability setups (see Chapter 7 on failover mechanisms) can help in meeting stringent uptime targets by reducing single points of failure. If the system is down beyond the allowed downtime, the SLA might stipulate service credits or other compensation.

- **Response Time to Issues:** SLAs often categorize issues by severity and assign response and resolution times. For instance, a critical issue (system-wide outage) might require immediate acknowledgment within 15 minutes and a restoration or workaround within four hours. A minor issue (non-urgent bug or a single camera failure) might have a next-business-day response. These timelines ensure the customer that if something goes wrong, the vendor's support will react swiftly. The vendor in turn must have support processes in place (like a 24/7 helpdesk or on-call engineers) to meet these promises.

- **Performance Metrics of the System:** Some SLAs go beyond just uptime to specify performance metrics. For example, if the system is supposed to process video at real-time, the SLA might guarantee that analytics alerts are generated within 2 seconds of the event 95% of the time or that recorded video will be available for playback within a certain network latency. In specialized cases, they might even guarantee analytic accuracy levels Performance SLAs can be challenging because many factors can affect them (such as network congestion and environmental changes); thus, they are often defined in a controlled way (e.g., under normal operating conditions and with the recommended hardware, the system will perform at a certain level).

- **Maintenance Windows:** The SLA should clarify how routine maintenance is handled. Typically, the provider will reserve certain hours (like Sunday 2 AM – 4 AM) as a maintenance window where the system might be intermittently unavailable for updates, and this does not count against uptime SLA. This sets expectations with the customer so they are aware of when maintenance can occur. In critical environments that truly run 24/7 (e.g., a casino or a city surveillance network), maintenance windows might be very tight or require coordination to not disrupt operations; sometimes redundant architectures allow rolling updates without downtime in those cases.

- **Support Scope and Exclusions:** The SLA must define what is covered and what is not. For example, the vendor might guarantee the software and system availability but if the customer's network goes down (outside the surveillance VLAN perhaps) and causes a loss of video, that may be outside the SLA scope. Damage due to vandalism or disasters might be excluded or handled separately. The terms of the service must be clearly written down to prevent disputes later. The agreement may also cover who is responsible for what type of fixes, e.g., "on-site support for hardware replacement is included" vs. "customer will return failed units for depot repair."
- **Field Support in Remote Areas:** For systems deployed in remote or hard-to-reach areas the SLA should address how support will be provided. If the area lacks quick access to technicians, the vendor might establish a local presence or train local personnel as part of the contract. For instance, the SLA might say any critical failure will have a technician on-site within 48 hours, knowing that immediate 4-hour response is physically impossible in certain regions. Alternatively, it might incorporate the use of remote management tools extensively to solve as much as possible without site visits. In critical infrastructures (like a border security surveillance in a forest), the SLA might even include provisions for satellite phones or backup communication methods to manage the system if primary networks fail. This ensures that even in remote operations, there is a clear plan to uphold system functionality.
- **Reporting and Reviews:** The SLA will usually commit the provider to providing regular reports on service performance, such as a monthly report detailing uptime percentage, incidents occurred, and the mean time to repair. For a video analytics system, reports might also include usage stats (how many analytics alarms were handled and the system load statistics) which can be valuable for the customer to see the value they're getting. Regular review meetings are often part of the SLA to discuss these reports and any action items.

A well-crafted SLA not only holds the service provider accountable but also fosters trust. It shows the customer that the vendor is confident enough in their solution and processes to make binding commitments. In competitive bids, offering a strong SLA can be a differentiator (e.g., a vendor that offers 99.9% uptime guarantee vs one that offers 95% will be seen as more reliable; of course, the costs might differ accordingly).

In practice, managed services for video analytics might be offered in tiers. For example, a basic tier with 8x5 support and best-effort response versus a premium tier with 24x7 support and strict SLAs, perhaps even including on-site personnel, would have different costs. Customers can choose based on how critical the system is to their operations and their budget.

To ensure SLA commitments are met, the vendor may employ various tools and techniques:

- Automated monitoring systems (sometimes integrated into the VMS) can send heartbeat signals and even create trouble tickets automatically.
- Keeping spare parts and spare pre-configured servers ready for rapid dispatch is useful.
- Having local partners or subcontractors in various regions act quickly (particularly important for remote areas, where partnering with a local service company there for quick response can be part of the strategy).
- Training the customer's staff to handle certain scenarios to allow enough time for the vendor to intervene (e.g., instructing them on how to do a safe reboot of the system if needed, or how to switch to a backup network link if the primary fails).

In summary, operationalization of a video analytics system is a collaborative effort to maintain excellence in performance. The customer and vendor should function almost as one extended team. Clear delineation of responsibilities and strong support agreements (SLAs) ensure that when issues arise, and inevitably some will, they are resolved quickly and the system continues to deliver on its intended purpose, whether that's security, safety, or business intelligence.

NOTE *To download an SLA Target template, visit 10.4 MLOps and AI Model Lifecycle Management*

A distinctive aspect of intelligent video analytics systems (compared to traditional CCTV) is the utilization of AI models for tasks like object detection, facial recognition, and behavior analysis. Unlike static software, these models have a lifecycle: They are trained on data, deployed to production, and over time, they might need to be updated or retrained as conditions change. *Machine Learning Operations* (MLOps) is the practice of applying DevOps-like principles to manage the lifecycle of machine learning models in production. In the context of video analytics, especially at the edge, MLOps ensures that the AI models continue to perform well over time and that updates can be rolled out in a controlled, reliable manner. This section covers how to monitor for model drift, how to manage retraining and deployment of models (using tools like MLflow for experiment tracking, and CI/CD pipelines for continuous integration/deployment), and how to allocate responsibilities between the vendor and the customer for these AI-related tasks.

The Need for MLOps in Video Analytics

In earlier chapters, we discussed how AI models are developed and integrated into video systems. Once those models are deployed (the inference phase, as noted in Chapter 6), one might be tempted to consider the project finished. However, model performance can change over time or may need improvement as new data becomes available. Several factors drive the need for ongoing model management:

- **Model Drift:** The environment that the model operates in can change. For example, an analytics model detecting vehicles might have been trained on mostly daytime data. If the cameras now also monitor at night under new lighting (for example, the site installed new LED lamps that flicker in the camera's view), the model's accuracy might drop because the visual input changed distribution. Similarly, if the system is in a retail store and suddenly a seasonal change in store layout occurs (with different decorations, etc.), the people-tracking model might get confused. *Drift* refers to this change in input data characteristics (data drift) or in the relationship between input and output (concept drift). MLOps involves continuously monitoring the model's performance to detect drift early. This could mean tracking metrics like the rate of detections or false alarms over time and looking for significant deviations from the baseline. For instance, if historically a camera detected an average of 50 people entering a day and now it is consistently 20 (with no known external reason like a lockdown), the model might be missing entries, which is a red flag to investigate.
- **Emergence of New Scenarios:** Over time, new scenarios or object types might need to be recognized. Perhaps the video system was installed in a parking lot to detect cars and now electric scooters have become common. The existing model might flag them as unknown objects or ignore them. To adapt, the model needs to be extended to new classes.

This is part of the lifecycle that initial training could not cover if the scenario was not known at design time.

- **Continuous Improvement:** Even without drift, there is often a desire to improve accuracy or reduce false alarms based on real-world experience. The first deployed model may function properly, but after collecting a few months of real footage and examples of its mistakes, one can retrain the model to perform better. MLOps provides the pipeline to do this in a repeatable way, rather than a one-off ad hoc retraining.

Given these factors, a video analytics deployment should be treated as not static but rather as an evolving system. Incorporating MLOps means planning for regular updates to the AI, just as one plans for software patches.

Principles and Tools for MLOps

MLOps extends the principles of DevOps (continuous integration, continuous delivery, and collaboration between development and operations teams) to the machine learning domain. For edge-based video analytics, we often use the term *Edge MLOps* to emphasize that the deployment environment includes edge devices (cameras or on-site servers) in addition to possibly cloud or central servers.

Key principles of (Edge) MLOps include version control, automation, and governance:

- **Version Control for Models and Data:** Just as we use Git or other version control for source code, we need to version our datasets, model training code, and the trained model binaries. This ensures traceability. If a new model is deployed and performs worse, we can roll back to a previous version quickly. Tools like MLflow or proprietary model management systems allow data scientists to log experiments with tags (including code version, data used, and resulting model accuracy) and promote certain models to a "production" registry. For example, MLflow can store Model v1.0 that was trained on the original dataset, and later Model v1.1 trained on additional data. Each is packaged and can be reproduced or compared. Chapter 5 introduces the idea of training and testing ML models; here, we extend it by ensuring each iteration is tracked. For data versioning (since videos are large), solutions may involve storing just incremental new data or using specialized data versioning tools (like DVC, Data Version Control) to keep track of what data was used in each training run.
- **Automation of the Pipeline:** Automation is at the center of MLOps. This means reducing manual steps in collecting new data, retraining models, testing them, and deploying them. For instance,
  - Set up a data collection pipeline where new video footage that had interesting events (false alarms or missed detections as identified by operators) is automatically archived to a training dataset. Perhaps the system flags video clips where an operator manually intervened or corrected something (like marking an object that was missed); these clips can go to a "retraining" folder.
  - Use scheduled or triggered *retraining jobs*. For example, once a month, a job runs to train a fresh model on all accumulated data. This can be automated using scripts or ML platforms. The training might happen on a cloud GPU instance or a powerful server offline from the production system.

- Implement CI/CD for models: Similar to software CI/CD (Continuous Integration/Continuous Deployment), where each code change triggers tests and potentially deployment, a model CI/CD would trigger when a new model is available. Before deploying automatically, it should go through a validation process: evaluate the new model on a hold-out test set or even shadow test it on the live system (running in parallel to the current model to compare outputs) to ensure it is truly better or at least not regressive.

- If tests pass, then automatically deploy the model to production (Continuous Delivery). In edge contexts, this might mean pushing the model file to the edge devices. Containerization can be very helpful here: if the analytics algorithm is packaged in a Docker container, deploying a new model could be as simple as deploying a new container image version. Technologies like Kubernetes (even at the edge or in hybrid cloud) or lightweight orchestrators can manage these updates rolling out to all edge nodes. Automation ensures these updates happen consistently and with minimal downtime. For example, a rolling update that updates one edge device at a time so the entire system isn't offline.

- **Monitoring and Governance:** After deployment, automated monitoring should be in place to track model performance (as discussed: monitoring output rates, perhaps using statistical process control to detect drift). If performance drops or certain thresholds are met (like false alarm rate > X% for a week), that could automatically trigger the pipeline to retrain or to alert an engineer. *Governance* refers to maintaining compliance and ethical standards: ensure that any new data collected is handled according to privacy laws (Chapter 2 mentioned data privacy considerations, which remain important here), and that models are checked for biases or issues (especially if expanding to new classes, ensure no unintended bias is introduced). Governance might also involve documenting each model version's intended purpose and limitations, so the operations team knows what to expect (e.g., "Model v2.0 was trained to detect orangutans and elephants, but will not detect smaller animals like monkeys. Avoid misusing it for that purpose.").

To implement the above, a variety of tools and frameworks can be used:

- **MLflow**: This can be used for experiment tracking and model registry. Data scientists can log parameters and metrics of training runs and register a model as "Production" stage when ready. The operations pipeline can query MLflow for the latest prod model to deploy.

- **Continuous Integration servers** (like Jenkins and GitLab CI): These can be used to orchestrate the tasks. For example, a Jenkins pipeline might trigger on new code or model and then run steps to test and deploy.

- **Containerization**: Packaging the analytics code and model together, so that the runtime environment is consistent between training and inference. This helps avoid "it worked on my machine" problems by encapsulating dependencies.

- **Edge-specific MLOps platforms**: There are emerging platforms (some open source, some commercial) aimed at edge AI management. These provide features like remote model deployment, health monitoring of edge devices, and even on-device training capabilities. One example mentioned in industry discussions is the use of edge impulse, which allows versioning and deploying models to IoT devices, though it is often geared towards smaller edge ML use-cases. For large video analytics, one might integrate something like NVIDIA's Fleet Command (for orchestrating AI on NVIDIA edge devices) or Azure IoT Edge with Azure ML for edge deployments, etc. The principle is the same: centrally manage and update distributed intelligent devices.

Vendor vs. Customer Roles in MLOps

Managing AI models is a specialized task. Typically, the vendor or solution provider (who likely has data scientists or ML engineers) will take the lead on MLOps tasks, rather than the average end customer. However, the customer's involvement and consent are important, especially when it comes to data.

Here is a possible approach to role distribution:

- **Vendor's Role in MLOps:** The vendor will usually perform the following:
  - Define the MLOps process and set up the pipeline. They might host the retraining infrastructure on their cloud or servers, or use a cloud service.
  - Be responsible for developing improvements to the models (since they have the expertise). They will handle data preprocessing, choosing model architectures (as covered in Chapter 5), and validating model performance.
  - Deploy the model updates as part of the managed service. Essentially, the vendor treats the machine learning model similar to a component of the software that they must support. They might include model updates in the SLA ("We will update the AI models quarterly to ensure at least X% accuracy on the defined tasks").
  - Monitor the performance remotely. The vendor might also get anonymized telemetry or samples from the system to judge how the model is doing. For example, the system could be configured to send a thumbnail image every time it triggers an alert (assuming privacy rules allow that). The vendor's team can review a random sample of these to verify if the alerts are valid or if there are many false alarms slipping through.
- **Customer's Role in MLOps:** The customer can support the MLOps process by doing the following:
  - Providing feedback and domain knowledge. They are the ones on the ground seeing the system in action. If they report, "the system often misses people wearing a certain uniform" or "the animal detector is confusing wild boars with dogs," that information is gold for the vendor to decide how to retrain. In some cases, the customer might even help by labeling data. For instance, security personnel might tag some recorded video events as "true incident" or "false alarm." This labeled data can flow into the training set (essentially the customer becomes part of the data annotation pipeline).
  - Data sharing agreements: The customer needs to permit the use of their video data for improving the model. Often, surveillance data is sensitive, so the contract should spell out that recorded footage or images will be used solely for improving the system, and perhaps require anonymization (the faces blurred, unless the model is about faces) or limiting data access. Some customers may have policies that the footage never leaves the premises. In such cases, the vendor might need to perform model retraining on equipment on-site at the customer's location rather than taking data back to their lab.
  - In cases where the customer has their own data science team (maybe large government or corporate clients do), they might take on part of the MLOps workload themselves. For example, they could use the provided model and continue training it with their

team. In such scenarios, the vendor should ensure the customer has the necessary tools: e.g., provide the training scripts, documentation, and perhaps a sandbox environment. The vendor might then play more of a support or consulting role, stepping in when issues arise or when a major model version upgrade is needed.

It is worth noting that not all video analytics deployments will have an active MLOps process. Some simpler systems might run with a fixed algorithm for years if it continues to meet needs. But as AI becomes more prevalent and customers demand higher accuracy or new features, vendors offering MLOps as part of their service will have an edge. It essentially means the product (the analytics system) gets better over time instead of stagnating.

One approach is for vendors to offer an *Analytics Assurance Program* (or Analytics Warranty) where, for a subscription fee, they handle all these MLOps details: continuous monitoring of the analytics, periodic model updates, and even periodic reports to the customer on accuracy and improvements. This can be related to the SLA. An SLA might explicitly cover analytic performance, which forces the vendor to use MLOps to uphold that performance.

Edge MLOps Considerations

Given many video analytics systems involve edge devices (such as cameras with AI chips and on-premise edge servers), we should highlight some special considerations for MLOps at the edge (Figure 10.2):

- **Resource Constraints:** Edge devices have limited compute/storage compared to cloud. MLOps must account for that. For example, a new model may be larger and more accurate, but if it cannot fit or run efficiently on the edge device (such as a smart camera), the pipeline needs a step to optimize the model (quantize or prune it) before deployment. In other words, part of the MLOps pipeline might include *model optimization* for the edge, which involves converting a model to a format like OpenVINO or TensorRT for faster edge inference, and validating that it still behaves correctly after optimization.
- **Connectivity:** Edge devices may have intermittent or low-bandwidth connectivity to the central system. The MLOps process should be tolerant to that. For instance, a model update might need to be packaged in a relatively small size or delivered via a mechanism that can resume if interrupted. If the edge is completely offline (not typical for central-managed systems, but possible for extremely isolated ones), then MLOps might involve a person manually updating devices with a USB drive – a very old-school approach, but sometimes necessary (in which case the "pipeline" might output a firmware file that a technician can apply). In a remote forest area, for example, if cameras on towers have AI, one might physically go around with a laptop every few months to update them if network is not reliable. This situation is hopefully rare, but planning for such scenarios is part of edge MLOps thinking.
- **Edge Data Collection:** Getting data off edge devices for retraining can be challenging if bandwidth is limited. Strategies include doing more at the edge: perhaps running a lightweight process on the device that summarizes data or even does partial training. An emerging concept is *federated learning*, where models are partially trained on the device with local data, and only the learned parameters are sent back to aggregate into a global model. While cutting-edge, federated learning could be an approach if privacy or bandwidth makes raw

data transfer impractical. For our current scope, a simpler approach is: have edge devices periodically send back small clips or even just metadata about detections. If bandwidth is an issue, one could store a lot of data locally and then when a technician visits, they offload the stored data for retraining purposes.

• **System Updates and CI/CD on the Edge:** Edge MLOps do not happen in isolation. They often coincide with general system updates. A coordinated CI/CD pipeline can ensure that a new model is compatible with the edge software. For example, if a new model requires an updated runtime library (like a newer version of TensorRT), the deployment package should update that too. This can be complex, requiring an orchestrated update of multiple components. Containerization helps here by encapsulating model and runtime together, so that deploying the new container inherently updates the runtime for that model without affecting other system parts.

In summary, MLOps in video analytics ensures that the AI implemented with CCTV continues to learn and adapt. By setting up a robust model lifecycle management practice, vendors and customers can move from a one-off project mindset to a *continuous improvement mindset*. The video analytics system essentially becomes a living system that grows more capable over time, rather than degrading or becoming obsolete. This not only maintains performance as changes occur, but can also incorporate innovation (for instance, if a new, better algorithm emerges in the research community, the vendor's MLOps pipeline could integrate that into the product, and seamlessly deploy it to existing installations as an upgrade, giving customers the benefit of the latest technology without a forklift replacement).

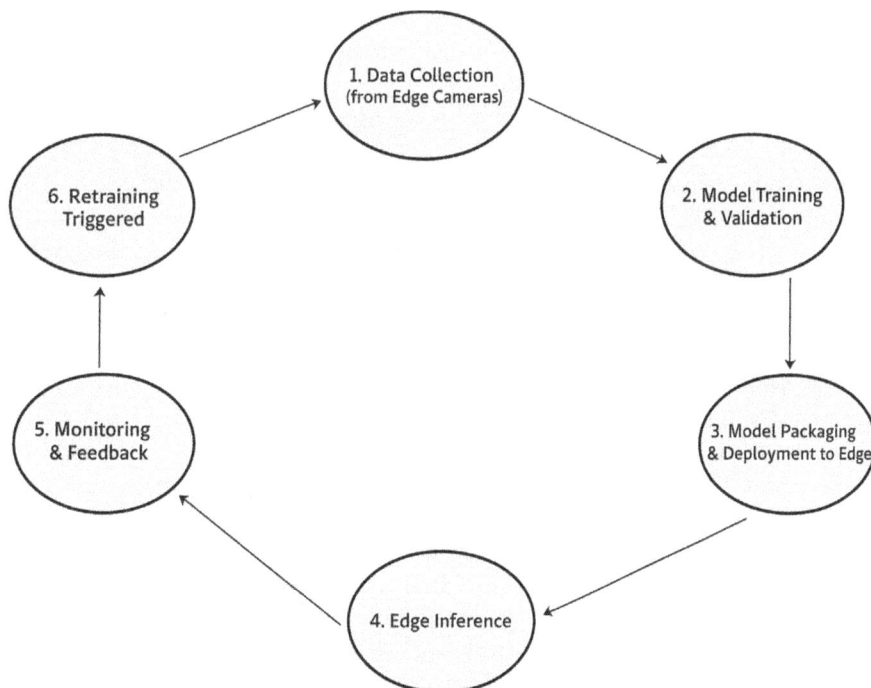

FIGURE 10.2 MLOps for an edge video analytics system.

Custom AI Models and ML SLAs

One of the strengths of intelligent video analytics is the ability to tailor AI models to very specific use cases. In some deployments, the out-of-the-box analytics provided by a vendor might not cover a specialized need, so the vendor (or a third-party AI team) develops a custom AI model to fulfill the customer's requirements. We mentioned the source code handover for such custom components in the "handover" section. Here, we dive deeper into how vendors can deliver and operationalize custom models and how they can formalize their performance commitments through Machine Learning SLAs (ML SLAs). We use the following example of a custom wildlife detection model for a heavily forested area to illustrate these concepts.

Delivering Custom Video Analytics Models

In many real-world projects, especially large or innovative ones (like a new smart city deployment in a heavily forested area), customers have needs that go beyond standard analytics (like basic motion detection or license plate recognition). For instance, consider a scenario where the city developers want an early warning system for wild animals encroaching on construction zones or highways to prevent accidents and also protect endangered wildlife. There may be no off-the-shelf product that detects specific animals on a construction site. A vendor bidding for this project could win by offering a custom AI model trained to detect the specific animals of concern in that region.

Here are the steps and considerations for developing and deploying such a custom model:

- **Requirement Scoping:** Clearly define what the model needs to detect or do. In our example, which animal species need to be monitored? At what distance or image quality? Does the customer require real-time alerts or just recorded occurrences? The environment (tropical forest edges) might have certain lighting or background motion (trees) that the model needs to handle. This scoping should be done during the design phase (Chapter 9's requirement gathering would capture this), but it becomes more realistic when planning the model development.

- **Data Collection for Model Training:** The crucial first step is gathering a dataset of the target classes (wild animals) in conditions similar to the deployment environment. This might involve sourcing footage of those animals. If it is a known use case, some datasets might exist in research (for example, researchers or parks might have camera trap footage of their wildlife). Otherwise, the vendor might need to create a dataset by installing a few cameras in known wildlife areas for a few weeks to collect sample videos of animals or augmenting with synthetic data (rendering animal models into video frames) to have enough training examples. Data should also include *negative examples* (scenes without animals, or common moving objects like construction machinery, so the model learns the difference). This data collection could be made in collaboration with local authorities or the customer.

- **Model Development:** Using the techniques from Chapter 5 (deep learning), the vendor's AI team trains a model (likely a deep neural network for object detection) on the collected data. They might start with a pre-trained model (e.g., something pre-trained on COCO or ImageNet that knows about generic animals) and fine-tune it to these specific animals. This saves time and typically yields better results given limited data. They will experiment with different model architectures to balance accuracy with speed (especially if it must run on edge hardware from Chapter 7's selection). The outcome is a trained model that, in lab tests, can detect the target animals with the required accuracy.

- **Integration and Testing in System:** A custom model is only useful if it works within the overall system. The vendor integrates this model into the video analytics software pipeline. If the system has an AI module that normally loads models, they add this one. Or, if it is a bespoke software package, they might run it as a separate service that feeds alerts into the VMS. Then they test end-to-end: feed in sample video (maybe recorded from the forested sites) to verify the model correctly identifies animals and triggers the right alerts, and that false positives are within acceptable limits. It is likely to be an iterative process: you test, find that the model confuses a construction worker wearing brown clothes for an animal, and then refine the model to fix that problem. You may need to add more training examples or adjust thresholds.

- **Deployment (Edge vs. Cloud):** Decide where this custom model will run. Perhaps each camera feed goes to an edge server on site where the model runs (ensuring low latency for alerts). Or if network allows, video could be sent to a central cloud where a beefy server runs the model. For remote areas with uncertain connectivity, edge deployment is safer (the system can alert local personnel even if the internet is down). The vendor must ensure the model is deployed on hardware that can handle the inference, possibly using GPUs or AI accelerators in the field. If power is an issue, the model may need to run on efficient hardware like an NVIDIA Jetson device at each camera site.

- **Handover and Documentation:** When delivering this custom model, besides the usual documentation, the vendor should provide specifics such as what accuracy was achieved in testing, what the known limitations are (e.g., "the model is not guaranteed to detect juveniles if they are under 50 cm tall" or "heavy rain may reduce accuracy"), and how to interpret its output. They should also provide guidelines for maintenance. For instance, if a new animal species becomes an issue, how that would be handled (perhaps requiring additional data and retraining). Essentially, treat the custom model as a component with its own mini user-guide.

- **Ethical and Legal Considerations:** Particularly with surveillance involving animals (or people), ensure that the deployment complies with any wildlife protection regulations. In this example, detecting animals is likely beneficial for conservation as it may prevent vehicle-animal collisions, but one must ensure it is not used to harm the animals (which is a policy issue and not really a technical issue). Also, if cameras might inadvertently also watch people (e.g., rangers or trespassers), data privacy laws may require informing people or avoiding certain areas.

Operationalizing Custom Models

Once a custom model like our wild animal detector is deployed, its operationalization follows the MLOps principles from the previous section, but with some additional considerations:

- **Performance Monitoring Specific to the Model:** If part of the service, the vendor might guarantee certain detection rates. It is important to gather ground truth to verify performance. How do you know if an animal passed but the system missed it? One way is periodic manual review: maybe once a week, a human reviews an hour of footage from a known active time to see if any animals were present that the system did not trigger an alert on. Alternatively, corroborate with other sensors if available (maybe park rangers report sightings and you check if the camera system caught them). This is challenging, but necessary if the service is safety-critical. False positives (false alarms) are easier to monitor. The system log will show if it is frequently alerting when nothing is there, and then one can investigate what it is seeing (such as wind in the trees or a stray dog) and adjust the model or system settings to filter those out.

- **Maintenance and Updates:** If the environment changes or new animals appear, the vendor will need to update the model. For example, if in a few years, a previously rare animal starts appearing in the area, the model would not recognize that animal. This loops back to collecting new data and retraining. With a custom model, it is even more likely that the vendor is fully responsible for these updates since the customer certainly will not have the expertise. The vendor should plan an update schedule or criteria (maybe an annual re-evaluation of the model, or sooner if issues are found). This becomes part of the ongoing service.

- **Scalability:** If this custom model proves useful, the customer might want to deploy it on more cameras or more sites. The vendor should design the solution such that scaling up is straightforward (e.g., not hard-coding it to only one camera feed). Using containerized microservices or a scalable cloud function can allow the same model to serve multiple video streams. The architecture should consider whether multiple instances of the model run independently per camera or if a centralized engine can handle many feeds. In a remote forested region, probably each site might have its own processing, due to network constraints between sites.

- **Integration with Operations:** Ensure the outputs of the custom model integrate with the customer's operational workflows. For example, if an elephant is detected near a road, what happens? Does the system send an SMS to drivers or alert a security team to respond? The vendor must integrate the alerting mechanism (perhaps connecting it to an existing safety notification system). Testing this end-to-end (model detects -> sends alert to right people -> those people take action) is part of operationalizing the solution.

ML SLAs – Service Level Agreements for AI Performance

Traditional SLAs include the uptime and response times, but *ML SLAs* include the performance of the machine learning aspects specifically. This is a relatively new concept, as many service providers prefer to avoid guaranteeing AI accuracy as it can be influenced by factors out of their control. However, offering ML SLAs can be a competitive differentiator, showing confidence in the solution's intelligence.

What might an ML SLA include? Here, we use wild animal detection as an example:

- **Detection Accuracy Guarantee:** The vendor might commit that the system will detect 95% of adult elephants and 90% of orangutans (Figure 10.3) that come within the camera's view under defined conditions (such as daytime, and within 50 m of the camera; specifying the conditions is important so the guarantee is realistic). If the system fails to meet that (determined perhaps by periodic field tests or known incidents), the SLA could state that the vendor will take corrective action such as providing additional equipment (maybe adding more cameras or thermal sensors to help) or improving the model at no extra cost. In extreme cases, an SLA could even include penalties, but more often for AI, the remedy is to fix it rather than provide financial compensation, because the latter does not directly address the customer's need.

- **False Alarm Rate:** Similarly, this is a guarantee that false alarms will be below a certain threshold (e.g., fewer than two per week per camera). This is very important because if false alarms are too frequent, the customer might start ignoring alerts. The SLA could say if false alarms exceed the threshold, the vendor will retrain the model or adjust the system within one month to bring it back in line.

- **Retraining Frequency:** The SLA might indicate that the vendor will retrain and update the model periodically (e.g., every six months) even if performance is good, in order to incorporate the latest data. This assures the customer that the model will not become outdated. It could be phrased as "as needed," and be related to performance triggers ("if accuracy drops by more than 5%, a new model will be developed within X weeks").

- **Data Management and Feedback Loop:** An ML SLA could outline how new data will be used. For instance, "All alert incidents will be logged and a selection of camera footage will be reviewed by our AI team monthly to look for any missed detections; any such misses will be fed into the next training cycle." This demonstrates a proactive stance. While not a numerical guarantee, it is a process guarantee that gives confidence the system will improve or at least maintain performance.

- **Scope of Analytics SLA:** Clearly define what is covered. If the SLA is specifically about animal detection, it will not cover other analytics in the system. If an analytics SLA is given for a face recognition system, it might specify the lighting conditions or camera placement needed for that accuracy, aligning expectations.

Offering an ML SLA requires the vendor to have a robust internal process (MLOps) to measure and uphold those metrics. It also requires honest communication with the client. An AI's performance can be probabilistic. Both sides need to agree on how to measure "accuracy" and have a realistic baseline. Often, an initial baseline test is done: deploy the system in a pilot phase, measure accuracy (e.g., 90% detection achieved), and then set the SLA slightly below that or at that level, with the agreement that conditions remain similar.

From a competitive standpoint, vendors that are confident can use ML SLAs as a selling point: "We don't just give you a model and walk away; we stand by its performance. If it fails to perform, we are obligated (and motivated) to fix it promptly." This alleviates a concern for customers adopting AI, which is the fear that it might not work as expected and they would not have a satisfactory solution to their monitoring issues. Instead, the risk is shared or taken on by the vendor.

In our forested region example, a vendor might say, "We guarantee that our system will detect 9 out of 10 large animals (defined as >50 kg) that enter the monitored zone, and we will maintain that performance over time. As part of our service, we will update the AI model as new environmental data becomes available, ensuring the system remains effective even as seasons and animal behaviors change." This kind of commitment could be the difference in winning a customer, especially for a public safety project, as it shows accountability.

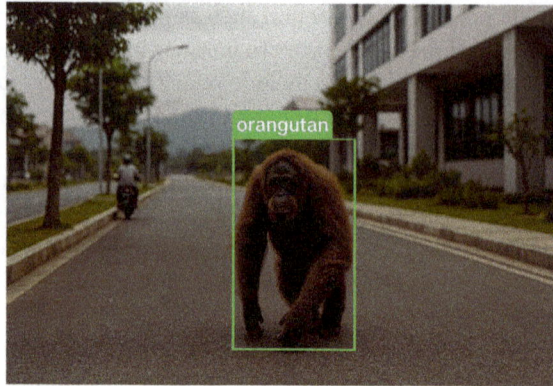

FIGURE 10.3 A camera view with an orangutan detected.

Finally, ML SLAs also have an internal benefit: They force the vendor's team to keep learning and improving. Knowing that you have a contractual obligation to maintain accuracy means the AI team must continually pay attention to the deployed systems, not just build and forget. It creates a continuous improvement cycle (which is what MLOps is all about).

In conclusion, custom AI models allow video analytics systems to address unique challenges, and when combined with ML-focused SLAs, they create a powerful value proposition. They show that the system is not a static product but a continuously supported solution tailored to the customer's needs. In domains like smart cities, defense, wildlife conservation, or specialized industry applications, this ability to customize and guarantee AI performance is often what elevates a solution from a generic surveillance tool to a mission-critical intelligent system.

SUMMARY

Chapter 10 guided readers through the complete lifecycle of an intelligent video analytics system, transitioning from final design to deployment, handover, and operationalization. While earlier chapters focused on planning and system architecture, this chapter emphasized that even the most advanced designs will fail to deliver value without precise execution, user readiness, and long-term operational commitment. Deployment and operations are not the final steps in the journey, they are where the system truly proves its worth.

Successful implementation begins with thorough pre-deployment planning. This includes infrastructure readiness checks, equipment staging, and coordination across teams to ensure smooth execution. A well-prepared deployment reduces risk, minimizes downtime, and lowers the total cost of installation.

Once on site, effective installation practices are essential. Installation teams must balance adherence to the design with flexibility to accommodate on-the-ground realities, such as lighting conditions or network constraints, without compromising performance. System testing should occur in real-time, camera-by-camera, as devices are installed, not left until the end.

A comprehensive and structured handover ensures that the end users are not only equipped with documentation but also trained to confidently operate and manage the system. A strong handover fosters trust and sets the stage for effective utilization, system longevity, and the discovery of new use cases.

Following installation, robust operational processes are critical for long-term success. Clear role definitions, proactive monitoring, scheduled maintenance, and incident response protocols ensure the system remains healthy and secure. Importantly, these processes must also embed cybersecurity best practices, such as password rotation, firmware updates, and network isolation, to mitigate evolving digital threats.

To formalize expectations, Service Level Agreements (SLAs) provide a transparent framework for ongoing support and performance metrics. When tailored to local realities and supported by the necessary logistics, SLAs build customer confidence and clarify responsibilities between service providers and clients.

Modern video analytics systems also incorporate machine learning components that evolve over time. The inclusion of MLOps practices, such as performance monitoring, data collection, and model retraining pipelines, ensures that AI accuracy remains high and adapts to real-world changes. This is particularly important when models are deployed at the edge, where conditions and data characteristics may shift over time.

As many video analytics systems depend on edge devices, deployment planning must account for edge-specific challenges, including resource constraints, offline operation, and the need for remote updates. Implementing remote management, graceful degradation mechanisms, and hardware health monitoring strengthens system reliability.

In more advanced implementations, custom AI solutions tailored to specific business needs can provide high strategic value. These must be treated with the same discipline as productized features: rigorous testing, performance tracking, documentation, and clear expectations aligned with ML-specific SLAs.

Finally, continuous communication and customer engagement remain central throughout the lifecycle. Regular check-ins, status reports, and review meetings allow integrators to detect emerging issues early, identify new use cases, and strengthen the relationship with the client. This open channel of dialogue helps transform reactive support into proactive partnership.

To consolidate these principles, the chapter concluded with a practical best practice checklist, offering readers a step-by-step operational guide that spans pre-deployment, system installation, customer handover, operational setup, model maintenance, edge readiness, and long-term system improvement.

By following these guidelines, practitioners will be equipped to deliver video analytics solutions that not only succeed at launch but continue to perform reliably, adapt to new challenges, and generate long-term value. In the field of intelligent video analytics, deployment and operations are not merely technical exercises. They are a way to have a sustainable impact.

This chapter reinforces a critical truth: design is only the beginning. Real value emerges through disciplined deployment, structured handover, and sustained operational excellence. Those who treat the operational phase with the same rigor as design and development will ensure their systems evolve from promising prototypes into transformative solutions that redefine how organizations utilize video data across industries and use cases.

CHAPTER 11

THE FUTURE OF INTELLIGENT VIDEO ANALYTICS

Thank you for reading about the frameworks, methodologies, and best practices outlined in *Intelligent Video Analytics*. Throughout this book, we have presented comprehensive and practical frameworks for designing, implementing, and operationalizing video analytics systems. Importantly, these are not merely theoretical constructs; their efficacy has been rigorously validated through real-world application. This validation comes from dual perspectives: the author's direct experience as a provider implementing these solutions, and equally importantly, through the successful adoption and positive outcomes reported by users: the systems integrators, consultants, and end-users who have put these principles into practice.

A strength of the outlined approach lies in its inherent flexibility and scalability, making it compatible with, and adaptable to, a diverse range of environments across the globe. This includes complex settings such as Smart City initiatives, large-scale public venues like stadiums and arenas, critical transportation hubs such as airports and train stations, retail environments seeking customer insights and loss prevention, industrial sites monitoring safety and processes, and public spaces requiring enhanced security surveillance. Essentially, the framework is suited for any location benefiting from advanced video analytics and smart surveillance capabilities to enhance safety, security, and operational efficiency.

This comprehensive approach is built upon the author's extensive, firsthand experience and research. Having meticulously studied and analyzed diverse surveillance system architectures, technologies, and operational strategies in various international contexts, including major cities and infrastructure projects across Europe, the United States, Singapore, Indonesia, and China, the author brings a rich, global perspective. This deep understanding of different technological landscapes, regulatory environments, and practical challenges has been instrumental in shaping the robust, adaptable frameworks presented. Our overarching goal remains to equip you, the practitioner—whether you are a systems integrator, AI consultant, solution architect, security professional, or technology enthusiast—with the practical tools, validated insights, and adaptable strategies necessary for achieving success in your intelligent video analytics endeavors.

A BRIGHT FUTURE FOR VIDEO ANALYTICS

The future of intelligent video analytics is exceptionally promising. Several technological trends and innovations are accelerating this transformation:

- Enhanced AI Capabilities: Breakthroughs in computer vision, deep learning, and AI-driven analytics will continue to enhance detection accuracy, object tracking, anomaly detection, behavior prediction, and facial and license plate recognition capabilities.
- Edge Intelligence: Increasingly sophisticated edge devices equipped with powerful neural processors will perform more complex analytics directly at camera endpoints, drastically reducing latency and bandwidth usage.
- Cloud-Edge Hybrid Architectures: Seamless integration of edge devices with scalable cloud infrastructure will enable optimized, cost-effective analytics solutions with flexible storage and processing capabilities.
- Integration with IoT and Smart City Platforms: Intelligent video analytics systems will deeply integrate with broader IoT ecosystems, enhancing urban safety, traffic management, environmental monitoring, and emergency response efficiency.
- Explainability and Ethical AI: Advances in transparent, explainable AI models and robust ethical guidelines will build trust and facilitate broader adoption, addressing concerns around privacy, bias, and responsible usage.
- Agentic and Autonomous Operations: The next generation of systems will incorporate autonomous operations enabled by Large Language Models (LLMs) and agent-based orchestration, significantly reducing manual intervention and operational overhead. Example of such system is CentaurOps (*www.centaurops.com*).
- Agentic Systems Design: An intelligent software agent that designed to autonomously process complex inputs such as goals, constraints, layouts, and budgets, and generate actionable, optimized outputs. These agents don't just follow pre-set instructions; they reason, adapt, and make decisions much like a human expert would, enabling faster, context-aware, and scalable design or operational solutions. In practical use, such as in **CentaurOps IVA Designer**, this means the system can take in site layouts, security objectives, and infrastructure limitations, then automatically recommend camera placements, AI model configurations, and deployment architectures. The system evaluates trade-offs, offers alternatives, and continuously improves its recommendations based on feedback—creating a truly intelligent and dynamic design assistant.
- Following the rise of **agentic and autonomous operations**, as seen in systems like CentaurOps, where intelligent agents can autonomously design, configure, and optimize IVA deployments, this paradigm naturally extends into **aerial surveillance through drones**. If agentic systems can reason about layouts, goals, and constraints on the ground, then UAVs become the mobile edge extensions of this orchestration layer, acting as autonomous nodes that dynamically adapt to mission requirements.
- In this trajectory, we move from fixed cameras and static deployments toward **adaptive, sky-based surveillance networks**, where drones operate as part of an orchestrated ecosystem. Equipped with onboard GPU/NPU accelerators, these drones can execute IVA models in real time, collaborate with ground sensors, and communicate with command

centers through high-bandwidth 5G or resilient mesh links. This convergence sets the stage for **autonomous drone swarms** that are not just remotely piloted assets but fully **agentic fleets**, capable of negotiating responsibilities, reallocating resources, and learning collectively via federated model

SUMMARY

The transformative impact of intelligent video analytics is clear and accelerating rapidly, reshaping industries from smart cities and public safety to industrial automation and beyond. As video data grows exponentially, the demand for intelligent analytics that deliver real-time insights and actionable intelligence has never been greater.

By equipping yourself with robust frameworks, you can effectively turn video streams into valuable strategic assets.

Our extensive resources, expert-driven content, and dynamic learning environment empower you to build smarter, safer, and more efficient video analytics solutions that truly transform your organization and community.

Thank you for choosing *Intelligent Video Analytics* as your trusted partner and guide. We are excited about your continued progress and look forward to celebrating your future successes together.

Take your next steps today by visiting us at *www.intelligentxhub.com*. Your journey towards innovation and excellence begins here!